# The Global Edwards

Australian College of Theology Monograph Series

SERIES EDITOR GRAEME R. CHATFIELD

The ACT Monograph Series, generously supported by the Board of Directors of the Australian College of Theology, provides a forum for publishing quality research theses and studies by its graduates and affiliated college staff in the broad fields of Biblical Studies, Christian Thought and History, and Practical Theology with Wipf and Stock Publishers of Eugene, Oregon. The ACT selects the best of its doctoral and research masters theses as well as monographs that offer the academic community, scholars, church leaders and the wider community uniquely Australian and New Zealand perspectives on significant research topics and topics of current debate. The ACT also provides opportunity for contributors beyond its graduates and affiliated college staff to publish monographs which support the mission and values of the ACT.

Rev Dr Graeme Chatfield
Series Editor and Associate Dean

# The Global Edwards

Papers from the Jonathan Edwards Congress
held in Melbourne, August 2015

Edited by
RHYS S. BEZZANT

Foreword by
KENNETH P. MINKEMA

WIPF & STOCK · Eugene, Oregon

THE GLOBAL EDWARDS
Papers from the Jonathan Edwards Congress held in Melbourne, August 2015

Copyright © 2017 Wipf and Stock Publishers. All rights reserved. Except for brief quotations in critical publications or reviews, no part of this book may be reproduced in any manner without prior written permission from the publisher. Write: Permissions, Wipf and Stock Publishers, 199 W. 8th Ave., Suite 3, Eugene, OR 97401.

Wipf & Stock
An Imprint of Wipf and Stock Publishers
199 W. 8th Ave., Suite 3
Eugene, OR 97401

www.wipfandstock.com

PAPERBACK ISBN: 978-1-5326-3595-3
HARDCOVER ISBN: 978-1-5326-3597-7
EBOOK ISBN: 978-1-5326-3596-0

Manufactured in the U.S.A.

Chapter 5 of this volume, "Jonathan Edwards, Christian Zionist" by Gerald R. McDermott, was taken and adapted from *The New Christian Zionism*, IVP, edited by Gerald R. McDermott. Copyright (c) 2016 by Gerald R. McDermott. Used by permission of InterVarsity Press, P.O. Box 1400, Downers Grove, IL 60515, USA.

With thanks for the camaraderie among
Edwards scholars worldwide

# Contents

*Contributors* | ix
*Foreword by Kenneth P. Minkema* | xiii
*Preface* | xv
*Abbreviations* | xviii

**Part I: Global Vision**

1. The Legacy of Jonathan Edwards in Britain | 1
   —DAVID BEBBINGTON

2. Jonathan Edwards and Terra Australis: His Perception of Us and Our Reception of Him | 22
   —STUART PIGGIN

3. Jonathan Edwards and Chinese Millennial Movements | 43
   —VICTOR ZHU

4. The Reception of Edwards's *A History of the Work of Redemption* in Nineteenth-century Basutoland | 59
   —ADRIAAN NEELE

5. Jonathan Edwards, Christian Zionist | 82
   —GERALD MCDERMOTT

6. Revivals in Eighteenth-Century Poland: Jonathan Edwards and the Conversion of Polish Jews | 103
   —JOEL BURNELL

**Part II: Global Conversation**

7. The Tension between Jonathan Edwards's *"Controversies"* Notebook and *Freedom of the Will* on Whether Reality Is Open and Contingent | 121
   —PHILIP FISK

8   "An Holy and Beautiful Soul": Jonathan Edwards
    on the Humanity of Christ | 136
    —Corné Blaauw

9   Being Seen and Being Known: Jonathan Edwards's
    Theological Anthropology | 158
    —Kyle Strobel

10  Learning from Jonathan Edwards: Toward a Trinitarian Theology
    of Contemplation and Action | 179
    —Seng Kong Tan

11  Faith and Feeling in the Theology of Jonathan Edwards | 203
    —Willem van Vlastuin

12  A Re-Formed Understanding of Imputation in
    Jonathan Edwards's *Original Sin* | 223
    —Heber Campos, Jr.

## Part III: Global Practice

13  "A Good and Sensible Man": John Wesley's Reading and
    Use Of Jonathan Edwards | 247
    —Glen O'Brien

14  Training Ministers of "Light and Heat": Jonathan Edwards's
    Home-Based Educational Approach and Its Legacy | 261
    —Andrew Schuman

15  Hero or Herald? Agency and Authority in *The Life of Brainerd* | 277
    —Rhys Bezzant

16  The Abolitionism of Samuel Hopkins: An Application of
    Edwards's Doctrine of True Virtue | 296
    —Richard Hall

17  Preach and Print: The Role of Printed Sermons in the Ministries of
    George Whitefield, John Wesley and Jonathan Edwards | 314
    —Ian Maddock

18  Visibility, Vitriol, and Vision: The Drama of Jonathan Edwards's
    Refusal to Plant a Second Church in Northampton | 330
    —Nick Coombs

19  Is God Really Angry at Sinners? A Stylometric Study of
    Jonathan Edwards's Representations of God | 349
    —Michał Choiński and Jan Rybicki

# Contributors

**David Bebbington** is Professor of History at the University of Stirling. His publications include *Evangelicalism in Modern Britain*, *The Dominance of Evangelicalism*, *Victorian Religious Revivals* and (as co-editor) *Evangelicalism and Fundamentalism in the United Kingdom during the Twentieth Century*.

**Rhys Bezzant** is Dean of Missional Leadership and Lecturer in Church History at Ridley College, Melbourne. He is the Director of the Jonathan Edwards Center Australia, and is Visiting Fellow at the Yale Divinity School. He has published *Jonathan Edwards and the Church*, and *Standing on their Shoulders*, and is presently writing a book on the mentoring ministry of Edwards.

**Corné Blaauw** is part-time Lecturer of Philosophy at The Bible Institute of South Africa in Cape Town. He is currently a PhD student at the University of Groningen and has written several academic papers for the *Jonathan Edwards Studies* journal.

**Joel Burnell** teaches Dogmatics and Moral Theology at the Evangelical School of Theology (EST) in Wrocław, Poland. He is a member of the board of the Dietrich Bonhoeffer Society, and Director of the Jonathan Edwards Center in Poland.

**Heber Campos Jr.** is Associate Professor of Historical Theology at Centro Presbiteriano de Pós-Graduação Andrew Jumper, in São Paulo, Brazil, and Director of the Jonathan Edwards Center for Brazil.

**Michał Choiński** is Assistant Professor in the Institute of English Studies at the Jagiellonian University, Kraków. His publications include *The Rhetoric of the Revival: the Language of the Great Awakening Preachers*. He has also translated *The Jonathan Edwards Reader* into Polish.

**Nick Coombs** is Lead Pastor of City on a Hill: Melbourne East, Australia. Nick holds a Master of Divinity from Ridley College, Melbourne.

**Philip Fisk** is Senior Researcher in Historical Theology at the Jonathan Edwards Center Benelux, within the Evangelische Theologische Faculteit, Leuven, Belgium. His publications include *Jonathan Edwards's Turn from the Classic-Reformed Tradition of Freedom of the Will*, and he is a contributor to the *Synopsis Purioris Theologiae / Synopsis of a Purer Theology*.

**Richard Hall** is Professor of Philosophy at Fayetteville State University, a constituent institution of the University of North Carolina. His publications include two books, *The Ethical Foundations of Criminal Justice* and *The Neglected Northampton Texts of Jonathan Edwards: Edwards on Society and Politics*, and chapters in *The Contribution of Jonathan Edwards to American Culture and Society*, *Josiah Royce for the Twenty-First Century*, and *Middlebrow Wodehouse*.

**Gerald McDermott** is Anglican Chair of Divinity at Beeson Divinity School in Birmingham, Alabama. His six books on Edwards include *The Theology of Jonathan Edwards*, co-written with Michael McClymond. His most recent books are *Famous Stutterers*, *Israel Matters*, and *The New Christian Zionism*.

**Ian Maddock** serves as Senior Lecturer in Theology at Sydney Missionary and Bible College. He received his PhD from the University of Aberdeen and is author of *Men of One Book: A Comparison of Two Methodist Preachers, John Wesley and George Whitefield*.

**Adriaan Neele** is Consulting and Digital editor and Director of the Works of Jonathan Edwards and the Jonathan Edwards Center at Yale University, and Director of the doctoral program and Professor of Historical Theology at Puritan Reformed Theological Seminary in Grand Rapids, Michigan. His forthcoming publication is called *Before Edwards: Sources of New England Theology*.

**Glen O'Brien** is Head of Theology, Booth College, and Associate Professor of Church History, at the Sydney College of Divinity. He has published widely on Wesleyan and Methodist studies, including contributing to, and co-editing with Hilary Carey, *Methodism in Australia: A History*.

**Stuart Piggin** is Conjoint Associate Professor of History, Macquarie University in Sydney, Australia. His publications include *Making Evangelical Missionaries*, *Evangelical Christianity in Australia*, *Shaping the Good Society in Australia*, and a number of articles and books chapters on Jonathan Edwards.

**Jan Rybicki** is Assistant/Associate Professor of English Studies at the Jagiellonian University in Kraków, Poland. He has published on stylometry in literature and translations (including *The Great Mystery of the (Almost) Invisible Translator: Stylometry in Translation*), and he has translated into Polish such authors as Golding, Fitzgerald, and le Carré.

**Andrew Schuman** is a recent graduate of Yale Divinity School and Yale School of Management, where he earned his MAR and MBA degrees and wrote an integrated thesis on Jonathan Edwards and education. He now serves as the Director of Veritas Labs, a higher education innovation lab at The Veritas Forum.

**Kyle Strobel** is Associate Professor of Spiritual Theology and Formation, Talbot School of Theology, Biola University, Los Angeles. His publications include *Jonathan Edwards's Theology: A Reinterpretation*, and *Jonathan Edwards: An Introduction to his Thought* (co-written with Oliver Crisp).

**Seng-Kong Tan** is Lecturer in Systematic and Spiritual Theology at the Biblical Graduate School of Theology, Singapore. His most recent publications on Edwards include *Fullness Received and Returned* and a chapter in *Idealism and Christian Theology*.

**Willem van Vlastuin** is Professor of Theology and Spirituality of Reformed Protestantism at the Vrije Universiteit in Amsterdam, Dean of the Hersteld Hervormd Seminary, and Co-Director of the Jonathan Edwards Center, Benelux. His most recent book is *Be Renewed: A Theology of Personal Renewal*.

**Victor Zhu** is PhD candidate at the University of Edinburgh.

# Foreword

IN THE WINTER OF 2015, nearly a hundred delegates assembled at Ridley College in Melbourne, Australia, for the first Jonathan Edwards Congress (JEDCON, to satisfy our modern infatuation with acronyms). There, for the space of a week, we heard papers, shared meals, and gathered for formal and informal discussions related to Jonathan Edwards, the eighteenth-century theologian, philosopher, revivalist, missionary, and educator.

Why meet in Melbourne—with its very name, its streets, parks, and architecture so evocative of the Victorian era—to hold a conference about Edwards, who lived halfway around the world and in another century? Because Edwards, widely regarded as colonial America's greatest religious figure, belongs to the world—a circumstance reflected in the conference's theme, "The Global Edwards." That theme was embodied in the attendees, who were from more than a dozen countries and from every continent except Antarctica. And as the contents of this volume indicate, the topics of the papers and sessions were as diverse and as rewarding as the constituents.

Picturesque and intimate, Ridley College is the location of one of a series of Jonathan Edwards Centers. Currently, there are such centers in ten countries. These affiliates of the parent Edwards Center, at Yale University in the United States, were founded over the past decade to foster, on a multinational scale, research, dialogue, education, and publication dedicated to the study and application of religious thought and history through Edwards and related figures and topics, serving both academia and the church. This network of international partners cooperates in a number of activities, including faculty and student exchanges, onsite and online classes, thesis and dissertation consultations, pastors' workshops, lecture series, monographs, reprints, and translations--and of course conferences, such as the Melbourne event.

Readership of Edwards over the past generation has become truly global, which is what makes the work of the authors in this collection so relevant an index of current work in the field and a guide to future directions. Indeed, graduate work on Edwards outside of the United States now outweighs work on him done within the United States. This globalization and democratization of Edwards has been made possible, first, because his legacy and his contributions to the history of Christian thought, revivalism, and missions have had a far-flung influence. That influence has recently become the focus of attention in a number of places and circles because of the breadth of scholarship on and appropriation of Edwards and his tradition. The free online availability of his complete writings, via the website of Yale's Edwards Center (edwards.yale.edu), exists to encourage this process.

What has resulted is an incredibly rich and growing community of scholars, religious leaders, and others from different backgrounds, from different places on the planet, who see in Edwards and in issues and figures related to him a valuable resource for answering their questions about God, humanity, history, and faith. The volume you hold in your hands is a distillation of that collective, ongoing search. To all who join the fellowship, welcome.

Kenneth P. Minkema
Jonathan Edwards Center, Yale University

# Preface

EVERY THREE OR FOUR years, the Jonathan Edwards Center at Yale, with its satellites, organizes a conference for scholars and pastors to come together for the enjoyment and promotion of Edwards's writings. These gatherings are a wonderful opportunity to discover how Edwards is being appropriated in other parts of the world, and to build esprit de corps among his fans. In August 2015, Ridley College in Melbourne, Australia, was privileged to host the most recent of these.

While traditionally the study of Edwards, and his place in the evangelical tradition more generally, has been concentrated in North America, this Congress is evidence that the Jonathan Edwards Center at Yale has been successful in diversifying its base and extending its reach. The study of evangelical history is taking new turns. For example, the rise of Pentecostalism in traditionally Roman Catholic South America has provoked questions concerning the contours of Christian spiritual experience, which Edwards helps to answer. The fall of apartheid in South Africa has called into question a very powerful Reformed tradition that actively supported racist government policies, so Edwards has provided new space to rethink conservative Protestantism in the modern world. In Poland, Edwards's revivalist preaching gives access to the development of rhetoric in the English language, while in China millennial movements can learn from Edwards's own eschatological reflections, especially his musings on the place of America in the divine plans. Here in Australia, where postmodernity and globalization have fragmented culture, Edwards gives us pause to remember what an integrated worldview can offer, and not incidentally a point of reference in learning about religion in settler societies. The following papers from JEDCON wonderfully represent this diverse world of Edwards scholarship.

In a world where pollsters have recently failed to predict political events, and where the local appears to trump the global, many universities again report a turn to history to explain and to guide. It is in this context that Edwards scholarship worldwide is making a significant contribution to our understanding of the role of the church in society and the importance of theological ideas in the formation of personal or national identity. This volume includes theological reflection on debates that have great contemporary resonance in both the academy and the pastorate. We are pleased to offer contributions on trinitarian views of anthropology, the connection between evangelical faith and the rationale for the state of Israel, missiology that acknowledges the value of networks, the development of church-planting movements both in the West and in the majority world, and the pedagogy of the revivals. Edwards helps us to understand spirituality, missiology, politics, and ecclesiology, among other concerns.

To further these disparate topics of debate, we wanted to include new conversation partners in our program who represented a variety of people of different ages, nations, and interests, and who had not been able to attend previous conferences. As the convener, I was therefore thrilled to welcome delegates from every continent (except Antarctica!), and from each state of Australia. In our country, where Jonathan Edwards is not well known, this was the first conference ever held that was devoted to his texts and teachings, and it was happily Ridley's first international conference. With colleagues from Brazil, China, Singapore, Indonesia, Poland, the Netherlands, Britain, South Africa, the US, and Australia, we enjoyed a stimulating academic conference with great opportunities to encourage each other's service in the church, the academy, or the world. Young scholars mixed with seasoned performers, and many different denominational affiliations were also celebrated. I was so heartened by what we experienced together.

To group the material thematically, the book is divided into three sections, each of which highlights the global dimensions of Edwards's legacy. The papers in the first part, *Global Vision*, discuss distinctive applications of Edwards to a variety of global regions. Edwards's teachings provide resources to integrate concerns of the worldwide church. *Global Conversation*, the second part of the book, brings together papers that highlight Edwards's contributions to global theological conversations, for no single church, agency, or region can hope to defend the last word on a topic of systematic interest. Papers in the final section, *Global Practice*, present more pastoral concerns, in which Edwards's voice is profitably heard. He spent his life preaching, praying and pastoring in several different contexts after all, and was passionately committed to the life of the local church.

I want to acknowledge here two other papers by keynotes not included in this volume. Ken Minkema, the patron saint of Edwards scholars, set before us a visual feast, documenting the material cultures of Edwards's world with photographic support, giving us a three-dimensional appreciation of

Edwards's working conditions and family life. Doug Sweeney, whose work on the exegetical Edwards knows no rival, presented a paper based on his recent book *Edwards the Exegete*.

I want to thank the Leon and Mildred Morris Foundation for their financial support of JEDCON, and also my colleagues at Ridley who were so forbearing for a number of years before the event. Gina Denholm is an extraordinary editor who has patiently worked through contributions that, while written in English, were in many instances conceived in the minds of presenters for whom English was not their heart language. And for those who traveled from the far-flung corners of the world to join us, a special word of gratitude. This volume ably attests the ancient tradition of *fides quaerens intellectum*, or faith seeking understanding, in which the work of the academy underwrites pastoral labors. Indeed, the space in the conference program for praying the Daily Office was an opportunity for delegates to celebrate this ancient quest. This volume also gives clear evidence of the vitality of the worldwide study of Edwards today, and the positive contribution that can be made by the evangelical tradition to the pursuit of theological inquiry more generally. As Stuart Piggin reminds us here, Edwards looked forward to a day when books of divinity would be written in the Antipodes. Perhaps he would be more surprised to discover that they have been written about him!

Rhys Bezzant
Ridley College, Melbourne

# Abbreviations

WJE    Edwards, Jonathan. *The Works of Jonathan Edwards.*
       Vols 1–26. New Haven: Yale University Press, 1977–2009.

WJEO   Edwards, Jonathan. *The Works of Jonathan Edwards* Online.
       Vols 27–73. Jonathan Edwards Center at Yale University,
       accessed 2017.

*Part I*

Global Vision

# I

# The Legacy of Jonathan Edwards in Britain

## David Bebbington

THE NAME OF JONATHAN Edwards does not loom large in histories of theology in Britain. The American is usually ignored, as in Bernard Reardon's study of *Religious Thought in the Victorian Age*, or relegated to a single allusion, as in Tudur Jones's *Congregationalism in England, 1662-1962*.[1] By contrast, accounts of parallel developments in the United States give Edwards pride of place. That is true of general overviews such as Mark A. Noll's *America's God* and E. Brooks Holifield's *Theology in America* as well as more specialist works such as Allen C. Guelzo's *Edwards on the Will: A Century of American Theological Debate* and Joseph A. Conforti's *Jonathan Edwards, Religious Tradition and American Culture*, both of which examine the subsequent reputation of the theologian.[2]

It is not surprising that American authors should lay stress on a homegrown product, but it is more culpable that writers about Britain should neglect him. The lacuna may be laid at the door of multiple presuppositions. One is a certain insularity, the silent assumption that Britain was self-contained in its doctrinal concerns, or, if affected at all, then swayed almost exclusively by influences emanating from Germany. Another is that the Church of England led the way in Christian intellectual affairs to the

---

1. Reardon, *Religious Thought in the Victorian Age*; Jones, *Congregationalism in England*, 170.

2. Noll, *America's God*; Holifield, *Theology in America*; Guelzo, *Edwards on the Will*; Conforti, *Edwards, Religious Tradition and American Culture*.

extent that patterns of thinking in other denominations were of little or no importance. And a third is that what mattered in Anglican thought in the nineteenth century was the emergence of the Oxford Movement and of liberal theology because they shaped the developments of the twentieth century—a belief that has discouraged the scrutiny of Evangelical thought at the time. All these notions may be detected in Reardon's lucid book on Victorian theology, the standard work of the last generation.

Yet in reality British readers frequently absorbed American texts, which after all were written in their own language. Many of these readers were outside the Church of England, for at mid-century nearly half the population at worship in England and Wales was Nonconformist and Scotland was overwhelmingly Presbyterian. And Evangelicalism, though it was to be eclipsed during the twentieth century, was in the ascendant in British society at large during much of the nineteenth century. Hence at that period, an American who was a non-Anglican Evangelical was likely to enjoy a wide influence. Despite the general neglect of Jonathan Edwards in the literature, his legacy to subsequent generations in Britain is amply worth exploring.

The near silence about Edwards in nineteenth-century Britain contrasts starkly with contemporary opinion. The two Congregationalists who edited the first collection of Edwards's works, which appeared in 1806–11 in Britain rather than in America, could assert that the theologian "ranks with the brightest luminaries of the christian church, not excluding any country, or any age since the apostolic."[3] If that bold claim might be considered the partisan appraisal of co-religionists, we can point to the judgment of Henry Rogers, the editor of the more popular selection from Edwards's works issued in 1834, that the American was "held in profound veneration by thinking men of all parties."[4] This selection reached a twelfth edition by 1879, demonstrating the wide circulation of the texts composed by Edwards. Rogers's verdict is further confirmed by the publications of the Religious Tract Society (RTS), a pan-Evangelical agency that printed much of the popular Christian literature of the time. The Society put into print a range of titles by Jonathan Edwards. It published *Sinners in the Hands of an Angry God* by 1831; *The History of Redemption* appeared in that year, followed two years later by *Select Sermons of President Edwards*; the *Exchange of Christ* and the *Life of David Brainerd* came out around the same time; and at about mid-century the Society went so far as to publish the *Treatise concerning Religious Affections* in 500 pages, an exceptionally long book for it to put on

---

3. Williams and Parsons, *Works of President Edwards*, volume 1, iv.
4. Rogers, "Essay," i. Again, however, Rogers was a Congregationalist.

its list.[5] As late as the 1880s the Society issued *Pardon for the Greatest Sinners* and a life of Edwards in its "New Biographical Series."[6] There was clearly a demand for the writings of the theologian, and even an interest in his own story down to around 1890. By comparison, the American Tract Society, the equivalent of the RTS in the United States, removed Edwards from its publication lists in 1892.[7] We can therefore conclude that British attention to the American lasted virtually as long as in his own country.

Edwards appealed to the British public not just because he was a profound explorer of Christian doctrine. As the titles printed by the RTS suggest, he was valued as a stirring preacher who could challenge unbelievers. His life of Brainerd, the pioneer evangelist among the Native Americans, exercised a fascination over a missionary-minded public. And his warm encouragement of spiritual experience, as in the *Treatise concerning Religious Affections*, acted as an aid to devotion. This book was, according to Rogers, "one of the most valuable works on practical and experimental piety ever published."[8] Yet it was as an authority shaping theological discourse that his influence was greatest. The Edwardsean paradigm was the framework within which a great deal of nineteenth-century theology was conceived. The doctrinal inheritance of Calvinist teaching remained powerful within most of the non-Anglican denominations, whether in England, Scotland, or Wales. For the ministers in the Calvinist traditions of the Baptists, Independents, and Presbyterians, the great task was to adapt their received body of doctrine to the currents of thought associated with the Enlightenment. The fresh ideas associated with light, liberty, and progress needed to be accommodated if the message of the gospel was to receive a hearing. Edwards taught that new light dawned in revival, that liberty was compatible with necessity, and that the Almighty willed the progress of the gospel for the welfare of humanity. So Edwards defended Calvinism in a way that was intellectually acceptable to the age.

British preachers appreciated the writings of others associated with Edwards for the same reason. In particular, Joseph Bellamy's *True Religion Delineated* (1750), with its teaching of a governmental theory of the atonement, gained widespread endorsement. "Were I forced to part with all mere human compositions but three," wrote John Ryland, later president of Bristol Baptist Academy, in 1790, "Edwards's 'Life of Brainerd,' his 'Treatise on Religious Affections,' and Bellamy's 'True Religion Delineated,' . . . would

5. Johnson, *Printed Works*, xi, 26, 91, 106, 96, 59, 43.
6. Jonathan Edwards, *Pardon for the Greatest Sinners*; Thomson, *Jonathan Edwards*.
7. Conforti, *Edwards, Religious Tradition and American Culture*, 143.
8. Rogers, "Essay," xlvii.

be the last I should let go."⁹ So it might be more accurate to speak of an Edwardsean legacy rather than simply the legacy of Edwards. But it is plain that this mode of thinking provided the way in which Evangelical Calvinists in Britain conceptualized their ideas.

The British reception of Edwards began during the eighteenth century. He first came to attention as a spokesman of revival. His *Faithful Narrative* (1737) was initially published in London, not America, and by 1750 ran to as many as seven British editions. John Wesley, though a stern foe of Calvinism, enthusiastically abridged Edwards's books relating to religious revival, including several of them in the Christian Library he commended to his Methodist followers. A circle of Scottish Presbyterian ministers identified with revival became Edwards's enthusiastic correspondents and one of them, John Erskine, minister of Old Greyfriars, Edinburgh, turned into his chief promoter globally, sending his writings to the Netherlands and Germany as well as England. It was Erskine who worked up a set of Edwards's sermons into the *History of the Work of Redemption*, first published in Edinburgh in 1774.¹⁰ Erskine also drew the attention of the Particular Baptists of the English East Midlands to Edwards's writings. John Ryland was at the heart of a group of ministers in the Northamptonshire Baptist Association who were fired by the American's vision. In 1784 they issued an English edition of Edwards's *Humble Attempt* and, in accordance with its principles, recommended monthly prayer meetings for the advance of the gospel throughout the world. It was from this circle that William Carey emerged to found in 1792 the Baptist Missionary Society, the first of the Anglo-American missions.¹¹ Through this British initiative, the modern missionary movement can claim Jonathan Edwards as its spiritual progenitor.

Edwards's theological influence, however, was much more widespread. A survey of its dimensions from the later eighteenth century onwards can usefully begin with the Baptists. During their early years in the seventeenth century, the Particular Baptists had found no difficulty in reconciling their Reformed beliefs with evangelistic practice, but in the following century many of their ministers, especially in London, adopted a higher form of Calvinism. The sovereignty of God, they believed, entailed the belief that the Almighty would unquestionably bring about his purpose of gathering the elect into his church. Human intervention seemed unnecessary, even impious. Free offers of the gospel from the pulpit seemed subversive of their confidence in divine providence. Yet preachers wanted to lead their hearers

---

9. John Ryland to Joseph Kinghorn in Wilkin, *Joseph Kinghorn of Norwich*, 183.
10. Yeager, *Enlightened Evangelicalism*, 171–72.
11. Stanley, *History of the Baptist Missionary Society*, 4–6.

to salvation. How could they proclaim the need for repentance and faith without infringing their Calvinist convictions? Jonathan Edwards provided a solution to their dilemma through the distinction between natural and moral inability in his *Freedom of the Will*. Human beings, according to Edwards, possessed the natural ability to believe the gospel. If they had suffered from natural inability, they would have been made by an arbitrary Creator with no opportunity for salvation, a charge often mounted by opponents of Calvinism. Instead, Edwards argued, some people showed a moral inability to embrace the gospel. Their refusal to repent and embrace the salvation offered them was the result of their own persistence in sin and so their eventual perdition was their own responsibility. Everybody was summoned to believe and so preachers could call on their hearers to respond. The message was one of "duty faith." Ministers, therefore, need have no inhibitions about making every effort to spread the gospel. Not only could they make free offers from the pulpit; they could also undertake fresh measures like the missionary society. The Reformed faith was rendered consistent with vigorous evangelism.

The most significant disseminator of the resulting Evangelical Calvinism among the Baptists was Andrew Fuller. As a leading member of the Northamptonshire Baptist Association, Fuller participated in the excitement of discovering Edwards's ideas during the 1770s. In 1785 he published *The Gospel Worthy of all Acceptation*, which was built on the contrast between natural and moral inability. The distinction, Fuller explained, was "calculated to disburden the Calvinistic system of a number of calumnies with which its opponents have loaded it."[12] He argued that all hearers of the gospel were under an obligation to believe and so all preachers should make free offers of salvation. This was the theology of the Baptist Missionary Society, of which Fuller became secretary. He went further than Edwards in modifying his Calvinist inheritance. In debate after the publication of *The Gospel Worthy*, Fuller went on to accept that in one sense the atonement was universal in scope. The work of Christ, he held, was sufficient for all. Yet he did not move from the traditional Calvinist belief that only the elect would be saved, for the application of the atonement depended on "the sovereign pleasure of God."[13] Thus, although Fuller's position was not identical with Edwards's, he was still defending a form of Calvinism. Moreover, he retained his admiration for the American until the end of his life. In his last letter to John Ryland before his own death in 1815, Fuller wrote that if critics of Edwards's theology "preached Christ half as much as Jonathan Edwards did . . .

---

12. Fuller, *Gospel Worthy of All Acceptation*, 133.
13. Fuller, "Three Conversations," 520.

their usefulness would be double what it is."[14] Although exercising freedom as a theologian, Fuller was loyal to the Edwardsean paradigm.

Other men played a similar part to Fuller. During the eighteenth-century tendency towards a higher type of Calvinism, Bristol Baptist Academy, the only denominational seminary in the country, had preserved a more moderate form that did nothing to discourage evangelism. Already in 1772 its president, Caleb Evans, was teaching the difference between natural and moral inability on the basis of Edwards's *Freedom of the Will*.[15] Evans's successor as president, John Ryland, was a particularly zealous advocate of the Edwardsean standpoint. In 1780 he published the theologian's sermon on "The Excellency of Christ" at the low price of four pence each, or "3 shillings per Dozen to those who give them away."[16] He even called his sons "David Brainerd Ryland" and "Jonathan Edwards Ryland."[17] The students who passed through the academy in preparation for Baptist ministry—roughly two hundred in the period of Ryland's presidency from 1793 to 1825—were imbued with the theology of Edwards.

Ryland's assistant in his last seven years and subsequently his successor, Thomas Crisp, adopted exactly the same point of view. So did two of the products of the academy who went on to be founding presidents of the next two Baptist academies to be established. William Steadman built up Horton Academy near Bradford to be a power-house of evangelism in the north of England between 1805 and 1835; and William Newman did the same for Stepney Academy between 1810 and 1826, making it a center for the diffusion of moderate Calvinism in London and its vicinity. These men did not offer varied theological standpoints, wanting students to evaluate their relative merits with a critical eye. On the contrary, they taught dogmatically and required acquiescence. Crisp, for example, according to the memories of one of his students, when conducting examinations "looked rather for an exact repetition of what he had said than for our own impressions."[18] College-trained Baptist ministers of the early nineteenth century were uniformly shaped in an Edwardsean mold.

The transition from a high Calvinism to the moderate version represented by Edwards was sharply contested in Wales. The first Baptist academy to be set up in Wales, at Abergavenny in 1807, had another Bristol

---

14. Andrew Fuller to John Ryland, 28 April 1815, in Ryland, *Life and Death of the Rev. Andrew Fuller*, 332–33.

15. Hayden, "Evangelical Calvinism," 217.

16. Johnson, *Printed Works*, 95.

17. Conforti, *Edwards, Religious Tradition and American Culture*, 69n.

18. Trestrail, *Reminiscences*, 22.

graduate trained by John Ryland, Micah Thomas, as its president. Thomas was a keen advocate of the Edwardsean approach to theology as embodied in Fuller's writings. As a result he was charged by the high Calvinists of south Wales as veering towards Arminianism. In 1811 he published a sermon called *Salvation of Sovereign Grace* in order, as he put it, to "refute groundless insinuations."[19] The rumors of his defection from sound doctrine, however, continued to circulate, and in 1834 critics were given ammunition by five disaffected students. They complained that at worship he used John Wesley's notes on Scripture, claiming that they were superior to the comments of John Gill, the doughty eighteenth-century champion of high Calvinist orthodoxy among the Baptists. The affair was complicated by petty attacks on Thomas for refusing permission for students to attend the local Welsh society and requiring residents to be in their rooms by 8 o'clock in the evening. The resulting controversy brought down the academy. The local Baptist association refused further financial support, a rival institution was planned, Thomas resigned, the academy closed, and a new institution had to be created elsewhere, at Pontypool. There, under a president trained at Stepney and a tutor from Bristol Academy, the position of Edwards, Fuller and the newer Calvinism was reinstated.[20] This episode reveals clearly that contemporaries recognized the sharp difference between the model of theology of Gill and the type associated with Edwards. Micah Thomas contrasted the two. The point of view embodied in Gill's thought was "that stringent and exclusive system" which was designed "to guarantee the orthodoxy of the preacher," differing from "the universally benign atmosphere of that blessed economy, which is . . . 'good tidings of great joy to all people.'"[21] In the end this warm-hearted Edwardseanism triumphed.

The newer pattern was enduring among the Baptists. It is true that the older style of Calvinism remained strong in areas other than Wales. In East Anglia, for example, a body of Strict and Particular Baptists separated from the associations that endorsed Fullerism, denouncing duty faith unsparingly.[22] It is also true that a newer form of anti-confessional teaching began to outflank Edwards's moderate brand of Calvinism. Some began to propose that the Bible only was a sufficient grounding for a preachable theology. At Regent's Park College, the new president inducted in 1844, Benjamin Davies, a biblical scholar, refused to teach systematic theology, preferring

---

19. Himbury, *South Wales Baptist College*, 22.
20. Ibid., 31–43.
21. Ibid., 36.
22. Grass, "*There My Friends and Kindred Dwell.*"

to approach doctrine only through biblical exegesis.[23] At Horton Academy, James Acworth, president from 1836 to 1863, who was described as "impatient of system and formulas," urged his students to make "your own system" based on study of the word of God.[24] Yet the prevailing mode of theological instruction remained indebted to Edwards. Joseph Angus, president of Regent's Park from 1849, reverted to having first- and second-year students read two of Fuller's works.[25] Angus was still endorsing the views of Edwards and Bellamy on the tests of regeneration as late as 1895.[26] When Charles Spurgeon, the great preacher at what from 1861 became the Charles Spurgeon Metropolitan Tabernacle, took up the task of ministerial training six years earlier, he insisted that Calvinistic teaching should be given in his college. Despite Spurgeon's love of seventeenth-century Puritan writings, the type of Calvinism inculcated was that of Edwards. The principal of Spurgeon's institution from 1881 to 1893, David Gracey, recommended Edwards rather than Charles Hodge, the American Presbyterian exponent of a higher Calvinism, on the subject of the imputation of sin. Gracey quoted Edwards with approval and praised the American's theological method.[27] Many of the Baptists remained attached to the outlook of Edwards down to the end of the nineteenth century and beyond.

The same is true of the Congregationalists. The figure among them equivalent to Andrew Fuller among the Baptists was Edward Williams, president of Oswestry Academy from 1781 to 1791 and of Rotherham Independent College from 1795 down to his death in 1813. It was Williams who, with Edward Parsons, produced the first collected edition of Jonathan Edwards's works. The notes, signed "W," were from Williams's pen, recasting Edwards's often-ungainly prose into a more assimilable form. "There is," Williams remarks at one point in a note to a sentence by Edwards, "a little intricacy in this mode of expression," before going on to give a concrete illustration of the point.[28] Readers were undoubtedly helped in their understanding. "I esteem EDWARDS'S works," wrote a correspondent from Wales, "a far more valuable possession, on account of your notes."[29] Williams

---

23. Cooper, *From Stepney to St Giles'*, 52. *Report of the Committee of the Baptist College at Stepney*, 8.

24. Medley, *Centenary Memorial of Rawdon Baptist College*, 26.

25. *Report of the Committee of the Baptist College at Stepney*, 9.

26. Angus, *Six Lectures on Regeneration*, 68.

27. Gracey, *Sin and the Unfolding of Salvation*, 109, 118, 128.

28. *Works of President Edwards*, volume 1, 187n.

29. John Roberts to Edward Williams, 20 July 2008, in Gilbert, *Edward Williams*, 440.

concentrated particularly on passages in *Freedom of the Will*, explaining the nub issue of the relationship between liberty and necessity. Arminians, he points out at one point, wrongly supposed that "to allow *any* kind of necessity, is the same as to allow an infallible *decree*."[30] Edwards, however, showed that events need not be decreed even though they are caused. Human beings could be at once necessitated by causes and free in their actions. This principle, Williams explained in his *Essay on the Equity of the Divine Government* (1809), was the kernel of the defense of Calvinism against its detractors. He was faithfully reproducing Edwards's central contention. The point is repeated in his other weighty book, *A Defence of Modern Calvinism* (1812). Reading Williams was said to have reclaimed whole churches in England from a higher Calvinism.[31] Just as Fuller persuaded many Baptists to adopt Edwards's version of the faith, so Williams convinced a large number of Congregationalists.

Because Williams was Welsh, his writings made a particular impact in the principality. One of Williams's former students, John Roberts of Llanbrynmair, Montgomeryshire, spread his tutor's views in the Welsh language. In 1807 Roberts published a *Friendly Address* to Arminians, arguing that they mistook the claims of Calvinists such as himself. They did not contend that the Almighty was the author of perdition, but that human beings were themselves responsible for their everlasting loss.[32] The principle reflected Edwards's teaching on natural and moral inability. Two years later Roberts showed the source of his views by issuing extracts from Edwards's *Religious Affections*.[33] His next publication, called a *Humble Attempt*, again drew, even in its title, from Edwards. His central case this time, in the manner of Fuller, was that the benefits of the atonement are universal.[34] Roberts was advocating a moderate Calvinist body of theology, differing on the one hand from the Arminianism of the Wesleyan Methodists and the high Calvinism that prevailed in Wales. He identified it as identical with Edward Williams's position, reporting to his former tutor that hundreds of "our poor Welsh pious people" approved his views.[35] This "New System," as it was called, grew in favor quickly and gave the impetus to the rapid expansion of the Congregationalists in northern Wales. In the south of the

---

30. *Works of President Edwards*, volume 1, 241n.
31. Gilbert, *Edward Williams*, 467.
32. Evans, *Welsh Theology*, 126.
33. Roberts, *Cyfarwyddiadau acAnogaethau i Gredinwyr* . . . . I am grateful to Professor Densil Morgan of Lampeter for this reference.
34. Evans, *Welsh Theology*, 131–32.
35. Gilbert, *Edward Williams*, 442.

principality David Davies, tutor at the college in Carmarthen from 1835 to 1855, did much to propagate the views of Williams.[36] The high standing of Edwards in the estimation of the school of Edward Williams gave rise to a demand for the publication of Edwards's works in Welsh. A succession of titles appeared: the *History of Redemption* in 1829, the *Religious Affections* in 1833, the *Freedom of the Will* in 1865, the *Two Dissertations* at about the same time, and *Original Sin* in 1870.[37] Each was translated by a Congregational minister. Virtually the whole Welsh denomination became committed to the standpoint of Jonathan Edwards.

The most distinguished student of Edward Williams was John Pye Smith, tutor at the Congregationalists' Homerton Academy in London from 1800 onwards and president from 1806 to 1850. Pye Smith was most celebrated for his book *The Scripture Testimony to the Messiah* (1818–21), a powerful refutation of Unitarian belief, but was a remarkable polymath, publishing on geology and the Bible in 1839 and mounting a reasoned defense of pacifism before it became respectable.[38] He thought nothing of delivering a lecture at the opening of a series on the divine decrees in 1832 with an elaborate statement about the gradual communication of revelation. His diary records that on that occasion he gave an "Account of the theory of Spinoza, Simon, Beck, De Wette, Vater, Gesenius, Gramberg, & Hartman, concerning the O. T."[39] Pye Smith continued Williams's enterprise of propagating Edwards's views. The London tutor's regular lectures on systematic theology made frequent reference to Edwards's collected works but also to other writings: the *Miscellaneous Observations* (1793), and the *Remarks on Important Theological Controversies* (1796). Pye Smith endeavored to explain Edwards's terminology in language more comprehensible to his students, for example by turning the American's definition of virtue as "love for being in general" into "voluntary obedience to the known will of God." In his zeal to communicate the substance of Edwards's teaching, he went so far as to criticize Edward Williams's notes. His admiration for Edwards shines through the lectures. On natural depravity he comments, "President Edwards has so established and elucidated the subject as, in my humble opinion, to leave no just ground for doubt." Since Pye Smith also valued the piety of the New Englander, he also recommended his students to read Edwards's resolutions for life "*frequently*, and with *self-application*."[40]

36. *Dictionary of Welsh Biography*, 114.
37. Johnson, *Printed Works*, 90, 43, 71, 82, 76.
38. Nuttall, *New College*, 10.
39. Pye Smith, "Diary."
40. Pye Smith, *First Principles*, 354, 155, 389, 5.

Because of his role in teaching students for half a century, the influence of Pye Smith was pervasive in his denomination. Two of the first three tutors at the Lancashire Independent College, founded in 1843 to strengthen Congregational witness in the northwest of England, were Pye Smith's trainees.[41] In the next decade Pye Smith's bust was placed in the new library of Spring Hill College, Birmingham.[42] When one of his former students went out with the London Missionary Society to India, a portrait of Pye Smith was the most conspicuous object in the drawing room of the missionary's home in Bangalore.[43] This highly influential figure cast his weight behind the intellectual synthesis provided by Edwards.

It is true that the sway of Edwards was not uniform across Congregationalism. Thus, when F. J. Falding was inaugurated as president of its Rotherham College in 1853, he declared "his decided preference for the older English theology."[44] By that he meant Owen and Howe, Bunyan and Baxter, the Puritan divines of the age before Edwards. Others such as the prominent publicist John Campbell shared a taste for the Puritans.[45] Again, in the 1860s candidates for Airedale College were expected to show some knowledge of A. A. Hodge's *Outlines of Theology*, which inculcated a much sterner form of Calvinism than that of the New England school stemming from Edwards.[46] Yet the predominant debt of Congregational theologians for much of the century was to the Edwardsean approach. David Bogue, president of Gosport Academy in Hampshire, referred to Edwards more than to any other author in his lectures and, as the chief trainer of candidates for the London Missionary society in the first quarter of the century, laid stress on the life of Brainerd as an exemplar.[47] George Payne, tutor of the Western Academy in Exeter and then Plymouth from 1829 to 1848, was deeply swayed by Edward Williams, with whom he corresponded before 1812, and owed much directly to Edwards. Payne's *Lectures on Divine Sovereignty, Election, the Atonement, Justification and Regeneration*, published in 1836, the year he held the chair of the Congregational Union, transmitted the same outlook to others.[48] Ralph Wardlaw, who taught at the Glasgow

41. Powicke, *David Worthington Simon*, 77.
42. Kaye, *Mansfield College*, 20.
43. Rice, *Benjamin Rice*, 20.
44. *British Banner*, 681.
45. Ferguson and Brown, *John Campbell*, 404.
46. Fraser, *Daniel Fraser*, 71.
47. Bogue, "Lectures on Theology." I am grateful to Dr. Cullen Clark for this reference.
48. Kaye, *Mansfield College* , 17.

Congregational Academy from 1811, produced the nearest approximation to an Edwardsean body of divinity for Congregationalism in his *Systematic Theology* (1856–57), and his three-volume treatise was used at both Airedale and Lancashire Independent Colleges shortly after publication.[49] But perhaps the greatest Congregational advocate of Edwards was Henry Rogers, an erudite man with an attractive personality who briefly in the 1830s held the chair of English Language and Literature at the new University College, London, before going on to the Congregational Spring Hill College, Birmingham, (1840) and Lancashire Independent College (1858), where he served as president. Unusually for a Dissenter, Rogers was accepted as a man of letters in society at large.[50] Consequently his edition of Edwards's works, the standard Victorian version, containing a discriminating introductory essay, was a respected monument to the American theologian. It confirmed the importance of Edwards to the British branches of the denomination to which he had belonged.

In Scottish Presbyterianism the reputation of Edwards had been established by John Erskine during the eighteenth century, but it was Thomas Chalmers, the leader of the Evangelical party within the Church of Scotland in the early nineteenth century, who did most to disseminate the perspective of the American. As a student at St Andrews University, Chalmers grappled with the *Freedom of the Will*—a text valued by his professor of divinity, George Hill, who, though not an Evangelical, saw Edwards as a capable champion of Reformed doctrine, especially on original sin.[51] After Chalmers's subsequent embracing of Evangelical faith, Edwards came alive for him. "The American divine," Chalmers wrote in 1821, "affords, perhaps, the most wondrous example, in modern times, of one who stood richly gifted both in natural and in spiritual discernment." Edwards combined "deep philosophy" with a "humble and child-like piety," showing that Evangelicals could deploy an acute intelligence in the service of the gospel.[52] Like so many of his contemporaries, Chalmers found in Edwards the solution to the resolution of the debate between freedom and necessity and so a vindication of moderate Calvinism.[53] There was no book he recommended more strenuously, he avowed, than Edwards's *Freedom of the*

---

49. Wardlaw, *Systematic Theology*; Kaye, *Mansfield College*, 108; *Lancashire Independent College . . . Report . . . 1859*, 10.

50. *Congregationalist*, 6 (1877), 654–64.

51. Hill, *Lectures in Divinity*, volume 2, 372; volume 3, 101.

52. Chalmers, *Civic Economy*, volume 1, 318.

53. Chalmers, "Edwards' Inquiry," 252–53.

*Will.*⁵⁴ As professor of divinity at Edinburgh from 1828 to 1843, and afterwards as the undisputed leader of the Free Church of Scotland, Chalmers set the doctrinal tone of Scottish Presbyterianism. His influence extended more widely too. Chalmers's *Prelections*, in which he argued for Edwards against his own former professor Hill, was used at the Congregationalists' New College in 1854.⁵⁵ Joseph Angus, who was to lead Regent's Park College for the Baptists and take a favorable view of Edwards, attended Chalmers's lectures in Edinburgh.⁵⁶ Lewis Edwards, a theologian who came to exercise unparalleled sway over the Calvinistic Methodists of Wales, also studied at Edinburgh and made Chalmers his hero.⁵⁷ Chalmers reinforced the sway of Jonathan Edwards over theological minds throughout Britain.

The Presbyterians of Scotland showed an enduring appreciation of Edwards. Two extra volumes of the theologian's works were published in Edinburgh to add to the Edward Williams edition in 1847 and they were reissued in 1875.⁵⁸ The practical and devotional works also appeared in fresh editions from the Scottish press. The *Life of Brainerd*, which stimulated the Scottish minister Robert Murray McCheyne to throw himself into missionary work, was republished in five new Scottish editions between 1824 and 1851.⁵⁹ Edwards's *Religious Affections* was widely valued by the Presbyterians of the middle years of the century.⁶⁰ The Evangelical Calvinism of Edwards, as transmitted through Chalmers, continued to exercise its sway. William Cunningham, Chalmers's successor as principal of the Free Church College in Edinburgh, praised Edwards's "great work on Original Sin."⁶¹ In resisting the critique of Calvinism by Sir William Hamilton, the leading Scottish philosopher of his day, Cunningham denied on Edwardsean grounds that necessity implied fatalism. Yet, he surmised, the doctrine of necessity did seem likely, because the argument of Edwards against the self-determining power of the will had not been answered.⁶² Cunningham's colleague in the Free Church College, John Duncan, expressed his admiration that "Jonathan Edwards and the New-Englanders" managed to combine the elements of law and ethics that other theologians prized apart. Edwards, he believed,

54. Conforti, *Edwards, Religious Tradition and American Culture*, 52.
55. Chalmers, *Prelections*, 131. New College, London . . . Report . . . 1854, 8.
56. Randall, *"Conscientious Conviction,"* 2.
57. *Dictionary of Welsh Biography*, 191.
58. Johnson, *Printed Works*, 112.
59. Bonar, *Robert Murray M'Cheyne*, 19; Johnson, *Printed Works*, 54–58.
60. *Congregationalist and Christian World*, 3 October 1903, 467.
61. Cunningham, *Historical Theology*, volume 1, 339.
62. Cunningham, *Theology of the Reformation*, 471, 512.

contained elements of pantheism, a view that, because of early sympathies for that position, Duncan appreciated.[63]

Nineteenth-century Presbyterians respected Edwards for a variety of reasons, but there is no doubt that he continued to occupy a firm place in their affections.

The Church of England had a less vigorous tradition of Reformed theology. Despite the firm attachment of its Reformers and many subsequent seventeenth-century divines to Calvinist doctrine, in the eighteenth century the principles of Calvin were associated with the Puritans who had killed King Charles I. Consequently the early Evangelicals who adopted a Calvinist position commonly played down their allegiance, preferring to stress their loyalty to Bible teaching. Jonathan Edwards also seemed too much of a metaphysician for many of them. John Newton, the former slave ship captain who became one of the most influential Evangelical clergy, at first enthused over Edwards, but subsequently regretted recommending his *Freedom of the Will* because the American school was too addicted to "Scheme, System, & Notion."[64] Thomas Scott, known as a biblical commentator but also a writer on doctrine, explained the distinction between natural and moral inability in a way clearly indebted to Edwards, and yet avoided mentioning the American.[65] One of the Evangelical Anglicans most attached to Edwards was Isaac Taylor, a *littérateur* of interdenominational sympathies, who in 1831 issued an edition of the *Freedom of the Will* that compared the American's "athletic force of intellect" to that of Aristotle. He went further. "We claim Edwards as an *Englishman*," he wrote: "he was such in every respect but the accident of birth in a distant province of the empire."[66] Taylor praised Edwards for redeeming Calvinistic doctrines from scorn, yet was wary of the abstract metaphysics so prominent in the New Englander's pages. The controversy over freewill, Taylor claimed, did not affect common life. Nor had Edwards settled the debate with the Arminians. Instead pious Calvinists and pious Arminians, Taylor predicted, would meet on the common ground of the Bible.[67] Taylor held similar views to those of Charles Simeon, the Cambridge don who set the course of mainstream Anglican evangelicals in the first half of the nineteenth century. Simeon repudiated the theoretical structure of Calvinism for the sake of insisting on the teaching of Scripture alone. "Be

---

63. Brown, *John Duncan*, 69.
64. Hindmarsh, *John Newton*, 167, 154.
65. Scott, *Remarks*, 94.
66. Taylor, "Introductory Essay," xx, xxi n.
67. Ibid., xxv, xxvi, xlii, lii.

Bible Christians," he urged, "not system Christians."[68] For most Evangelicals in the Church of England, Edwards did not erect the theological framework of their thinking that was so powerful among non-Anglicans.

Yet the relative weakness of Edwards's doctrinal influence does not mean that Anglicans failed to value him. The *Life of Brainerd* was the inspiration for the quixotic journey of Henry Martyn as a pioneer missionary to Iran.[69] Through Martyn's example, Brainerd became the model for many another Anglican missionary of the nineteenth century. Josiah Pratt, secretary of the Church Missionary Society from 1802 to 1824, abridged Edwards's *Life of Brainerd* for publication and his successor as secretary, Edward Bickersteth, issued a fresh edition in 1834.[70] The other text by Edwards to achieve wide popularity among Anglicans was the *Religious Affections*. In 1802 William Wilberforce found it an "excellent book." It used "simple and clear" reasoning to make "close scrutiny of the heart, and accurate observations of its workings."[71] Charles Bradley, shortly to become incumbent at St John's, Clapham, through Wilberforce's patronage, published an edition of *Religious Affections* in 1827, claiming it as the most valuable of Edwards's works. "Indeed," he wrote, "there is not a work in the English language, in which a greater knowledge of the human heart is manifested."[72] Nor did esteem for the *Religious Affections* fade away in the second half of the century. J. C. Ryle, Bishop of Liverpool from 1880 to 1900, also highly estimated its worth.[73] Thus Edwards was respected among Anglican evangelicals more for his encouragement of Christian activism and devotion than for his divinity. They aligned with the Methodists, who, as Arminians, maintained a principled objection to Edwards's doctrinal position while appreciating his practical works. The standard nineteenth-century edition of the *Life of Brainerd* was an adaptation of John Wesley's drastic abridgement.[74] Edwards formed the piety of Evangelicals even when he did not mold their theology.

Edwards, however, did not go unscathed by criticism. Because of his wide influence, opponents of Calvinism sometimes singled him out for censure. In 1827 Edward Grinfield, a traditional High Churchman associated with the Society for the Propagation of the Gospel, condemned Edwards's *History of Redemption*, which he described as "one of the most popular

68. Brown, *Recollections*, 269.
69. Conforti, *Edwards, Religious Tradition and American Culture*, 69n.
70. Pratt, *David Brainerd*, vii.
71. Wilberforce and Wilberforce, *William Wilberforce*, volume 3, 66.
72. Jonathan Edwards, *Religious Affections*, vii.
73. Ryle, *Holiness*, vi.
74. Conforti, *Edwards, Religious Tradition and American Culture*, 69.

manuals of Calvinistic Theology," for showing narrowness in restricting salvation to the elect.[75] Later in the century the eminent theologian F. D. Maurice, the most significant inspirer of the Broad Church tradition in the Church of England, offered strong praise for the *Freedom of the Will*. This philosophical formulation of Old Calvinism, Maurice wrote in 1862, "still remains its most original and in some respects its most important product." Yet Maurice went on to offer trenchant criticism of its capitulation to eighteenth-century modes of thought by depicting the Almighty as a "happy Being" with no participation in the miseries of his creatures. The incarnation of the "Man of sorrows," the express image of his Father, revealed on the contrary, according to Maurice, that God feels intense sympathy for suffering humanity.[76] Maurice heralded a revolution in theology, a shift from a cross-centered perspective associated with Evangelicals to a more liberal way of thinking focused on the incarnation. Two of the other leading figures in the transformation, both Scots, developed their ideas by critiquing Edwards. Thomas Erskine, who wrote *The Doctrine of Election* (1837) as a lay Episcopalian, praised Edwards as "a good and holy man" but argued that *Freedom of the Will* mistakenly appealed to logic rather than conscience. It therefore limited the love of God to a few, whereas the coming of Jesus to earth showed that his Father was "the common Father of men, prodigals and all." Hence Edwards's book was "directly opposed to the gospel of Jesus Christ."[77] Erskine's friend John McLeod Campbell, deposed from the ministry of the Church of Scotland and subsequently a Congregationalist, undertook a sophisticated analysis of Calvinist teaching in his book *The Nature of the Atonement* (1856). McLeod Campbell found Edwards more satisfactory than later writers of the same school such as Pye Smith and Chalmers, but ultimately condemned him for describing the work of Christ in the language of the law rather than the family.[78] Both critics were attacking the whole Calvinist tradition, but recognized that Edwards was among its most powerful advocates. Edwards remained a representative figure even for those who broke from the school that he defended.

The Edwardsean paradigm was gradually supplanted on both sides of the Atlantic in the later years of the nineteenth century. In his classic study of the process in America, Frank H. Foster dated the crucial shift to the years 1880–95. At the start of that period the New England theology stemming from Edwards reigned in the seminaries of the Congregationalists; by

---

75. Grinfield, *Christian Dispensation*, 427–28, quoted at 427.
76. Maurice, *Modern Philosophy*, 469, 470–71.
77. Erskine, *Doctrine of Election*, 347, 348 (quoted).
78. Campbell, *Atonement*, 50–51, 72, 101.

the end, it had vanished.⁷⁹ The last vigorous exponent of the New England scheme, Edwards A. Park, retired as president of Andover Seminary in 1868 and as professor of theology there in 1881, and within five years it was rocked by a controversy over the liberal position upheld by those in command of the institution.⁸⁰ In Britain there was a parallel process. Thomas Crisp retired as president of Bristol Baptist Academy in 1868 and Henry Rogers as president of Lancashire Independent College in 1869. Both were exponents of Edwards's general standpoint. The Leicester Conference controversy of 1877–78 over the possibility of defining the bounds of Christian fellowship by religious experience rather than doctrine, a position inimical to Edwards's point of view, showed the emergence of a significant school of theological liberals within Congregationalism by that date. In 1880 R. W. Dale, emerging as the denomination's leading theologian, pronounced Calvinism dead.⁸¹

Nevertheless, what requires stress is the enduring influence of the moderate Calvinism stemming from Edwards. At some of the colleges it was still dominant until late in the century. It was being taught by Robert Thomas at the Congregationalists' Bala College down to his retirement in 1880 and by Joseph Angus at the Baptists' Regent's Park College down to 1892.⁸² Those trained at these and similar institutions would have ministries that extended long afterwards. Although a number of them would no doubt modify the views they had imbibed at college, others would not. Some would certainly have preached essentially Edwardsean theology until well into the twentieth century.

The virtual silence of the secondary literature about the legacy of Jonathan Edwards in Britain is unjustified. Commentators during the nineteenth century were well aware of the stature of the American theologian and his works were in wide demand. Edwards and his successors in the tradition of New England theology enabled ministers to adapt their inherited Calvinism to the enlightened spirit of the age. Edwards was warmly received by several groups in the eighteenth century, including the Baptists who launched the modern missionary movement. In particular, his distinction between natural and moral inability provided a way of reconciling the divine sovereignty of Calvinism with the imperative to preach the gospel. Andrew Fuller and the tutors of the Baptist colleges adopted his moderate Calvinist standpoint, though there was resistance, especially in south

79. Foster, *New England Theology*.
80. Williams, *Andover Liberals*.
81. Hopkins, *Nonconformity's Romantic Generation*, 53.
82. *Dictionary of Welsh Biography*, 963; Cooper, *From Stepney to St Giles'*, 71.

Wales. The Congregationalists were led in the same direction by Edward Williams, whose views scored a notable triumph in Wales. John Pye Smith propagated Edwards's position, as did other tutors within the Congregational denomination. Thomas Chalmers was primarily responsible for a vogue for Edwards in Scotland, where his writings were widely appreciated. In the Church of England there was less enthusiasm for the theological core of Edwards's teaching, but Anglican Evangelicals, like Methodists, valued his missionary and devotional texts. Critics of Calvinism naturally turned their fire on Edwards because he was seen as its champion. As a more liberal theology came into fashion, Edwardseanism faded in Britain, just as it did in the United States, but some trained in that moderate Calvinist tradition would have retained their principles into the twentieth century. Later in that century there was to be a revival of interest in Jonathan Edwards through the work of Martyn Lloyd-Jones and the Banner of Truth Trust. Edwards once more became a favored theologian.[83] At an earlier period, however, and over a long time, Edwards provided the foundations for the normative scheme of Evangelical Calvinist theology. Jonathan Edwards exerted a profound effect on Britain.

## Bibliography

Angus, Joseph. *Six Lectures on Regeneration*. London: Alexander and Shepheard, 1897.
Atherstone, Andrew, and David Ceri Jones, eds. *Engaging with Martyn Lloyd-Jones: The Life and Legacy of "the Doctor."* Nottingham: Apollos, 2011.
Bogue, David. "Lectures on Theology." London: Congregational Library, L14/3.
Bonar, Andrew A. *Memoir and Remains of the Rev. Robert Murray M'Cheyne*. Dundee: William Middleton, 1844.
Brown, Abner W. *Recollections of the Conversation Parties of the Rev. Charles Simeon, M. A.* London: Hamilton, Adams & Co., 1863.
Brown, David. *Life of the Late John Duncan, LL.D.* Edinburgh: Edmonston and Douglas, 1872.
Campbell, John McLeod. *The Nature of the Atonement*. With a new introduction by Edgar P. Dickie. London: James Clarke and Co., 1959.
Chalmers, Thomas. *The Christian and Civic Economy of Large Towns*, 3 vols in 1. Glasgow: For William Collins, n. d.
———. "Edwards' Inquiry, with Introductory Essay." *Presbyterian Review* 2 (1831).
———. *Prelections on Butler's Analogy, Paley's Evidences of Christianity and Hill's Lectures in Divinity*. Edinburgh: Sutherland and Knox, 1849.
Conforti, Joseph A. *Jonathan Edwards, Religious Tradition and American Culture*. Chapel Hill: University of North Carolina Press, 1995.
Cooper, Robert E. *From Stepney to St Giles': The Story of Regent's Park College, 1810–1960*. London: Carey Kingsgate, 1960.

---

83. Atherstone and Jones, *Engaging with Martyn Lloyd-Jones*.

Cunningham, William. *Historical Theology.* 2 vols. Edinburgh: T. & T. Clark, 1870.
———. *The Reformers and the Theology of the Reformation.* Edinburgh: T. & T. Clark, 1862.
Edwards, Jonathan. *A Treatise Concerning the Religious Affections in Three Parts.* Edited by Charles Bradley. London: for L. B. Seeley and Son, 1827.
———. *Pardon for the Greatest Sinners.* London: Religious Tract Society, 1882.
Erskine, Thomas. *The Doctrine of Election.* 2nd ed. Edinburgh: David Douglas, 1878.
Evans, William. *An Outline of the History of Welsh Theology.* London: James Nisbet & Co., 1900.
Ferguson, Robert, and A. Morton Brown. *Life and Labours of John Campbell.* London: Richard Bentley, 1867.
Foster, Frank H. *A Genetic History of the New England Theology.* Chicago: Chicago University Press, 1907.
Fraser, Lucy A. *Memoirs of Daniel Fraser, M.A., LL.D. (Glasgow).* London: Percy Lund, Humphries & Co., 1905.
Fuller, Andrew. "The Gospel Worthy of All Acceptation." In *A Sourcebook for Baptist Heritage,* compiled and edited by H. Leon McBeth, 133-35. Nashville, TN: Broadman, 1990.
———. "Three Conversations." In *The Complete Works of the Rev. Andrew Fuller* 1:651-64: London: Holdsworth and Ball, 1833.
Gilbert, Joseph. *Memoir of the Life and Writings of the Late Edward Williams, D.D.* London: Francis Westley, 1825.
Gracey, David. *Sin and the Unfolding of Salvation.* London: Passmore and Alabaster, 1894.
Grass, Tim. *"There My Friends and Kindred Dwell": The Strict Baptist Chapels of Suffolk and Norfolk.* Ramsey, Isle of Man: Thornhill Media, 2012.
Grinfield, Edward W. *The Nature and Extent of the Christian Dispensation with Reference to the Salvability of the Heathen.* London: C&J Rivington, 1827.
Guelzo, Allen C. *Edwards on the Will: A Century of American Theological Debate.* Middletown, CT: Wesleyan University Press, 1989.
Hayden, Roger. "Evangelical Calvinism among Eighteenth-Century British Baptists with Particular Reference to Bernard Foskett, Hugh and Caleb Evans and the Bristol Baptist Academy, 1690-1791." PhD diss., Keele University, 1992.
Hill, George. *Lectures in Divinity.* 3 vols. Edinburgh: Waugh and Innes, 1821.
Himbury, D. Mervyn. *The South Wales Baptist College (1807-1957).* Cardiff: South Wales Baptist College, 1957.
Hindmarsh, Bruce. *John Newton and the English Evangelical Tradition: Between the Conversions of Wesley and Wilberforce.* Oxford: Clarendon, 1996.
Holifield, E. Brooks. *Theology in America: Christian Thought from the Age of the Puritans to the Civil War.* New Haven, CT: Yale University Press, 2003.
Hopkins, Mark. *Nonconformity's Romantic Generation: Evangelical and Liberal Theologies in Victorian England.* Carlisle: Paternoster, 2004.
Johnson, Thomas H. *The Printed Works of Jonathan Edwards, 1703-1758: A Bibliography.* Princeton: Princeton University Press, 1940.
Jones, R. Tudur. *Congregationalism in England, 1662-1962.* London: Independent, 1962.
Kaye, Elaine. *Mansfield College, Oxford: Its Origin, History and Significance.* Oxford: Oxford University Press, 1995.

*Lancashire Independent College . . . Report . . . 1859*. Manchester: Septimus Fletcher, 1860.
Maurice, Frederick D. *Modern Philosophy*. London: Griffin, Bohn and Co., 1862.
Medley, William. *Centenary Memorial of Rawdon Baptist College*. London: Kingsgate, 1904.
*New College, London . . . Report . . . 1854*. N.p.,: no pub., 1854.
Noll, Mark A. *America's God: From Jonathan Edwards to Abraham Lincoln*. New York: Oxford University Press, 2002.
Nuttall, Geoffrey F. *New College, London, and its Library*. London: Dr. Williams's Trust, 1977.
Powicke, Frederick J. *David Worthington Simon*. London: Hodder & Stoughton, 1912.
Pratt, Josiah. *The Life of the Rev. David Brainerd*. London: R. B. Seeley and W. Burnside, 1834.
Pye Smith, John. Diary of *John Pye Smith*. London: Congregational Library, L/18/23.
———. *First Principles of Christian Theology*. Edited by William Farrer. London: Jackson and Walford, 1854.
Randall, Ian. *"Conscientious Conviction": Joseph Angus (1816–1902) and Nineteenth-Century Baptist Life*. Oxford: Regent's Park College, 2010.
Reardon, Bernard M. G. *Religious Thought in the Victorian Age: A Survey from Coleridge to Gore*. London: Longman, 1980.
*Report of the Committee of the Baptist College at Stepney for MDCCCXLIV*. London: H. Teape and Son, 1844.
*Report of the Committee of the Baptist College at Stepney for MDCCCLIV*. London: H. Teape and Son, 1854.
Rice, Edward P. *Benjamin Rice, or, Fifty Years in the Master's Service*. London: Religious Tract Society, 1888.
Roberts, John. *Cyfarwyddiadau acAnogaethau i Gredinwyr . . . a Gasglwyd yn Benauf Allan o Waith Jonathan Edwards*. Bala: R. Sanderson, 1809.
Rogers, Henry. "An Essay on the Genius and Writings of Jonathan Edwards." In *The Works of Jonathan Edwards, A.M.* by Jonathan Edwards, 2 vols, revised and edited by Edward Hickman. 12th ed. London: William Tegg & Co., 1879.
Ryland, John. *Life and Death of the Rev. Andrew Fuller*. Charlestown, MA: Samuel Etheridge, 1818.
Ryle, John C. *Holiness*. 3rd ed. London: William Hunt and Co., 1887.
Scott, Thomas. *Remarks on the Doctrines of Original Sin, Grace, Free-Will, Justification by Faith, Election and Reprobation, and the Final Perseverance of the Saints*. 2nd ed. London: A. Macintosh, 1817.
Stanley, Brian. *The History of the Baptist Missionary Society, 1792–1992*. Edinburgh: T. & T. Clark, 1992.
Taylor, Isaac. "Introductory Essay." In *An Inquiry into the Modern Prevailing Notions respecting the Freedom of the Will*, by Jonathan Edwards, xx–xxi. London: James Duncan, 1831.
*The Dictionary of Welsh Biography down to 1940*. Oxford: Blackwell, 1959.
Thomson, J. Radford. *Jonathan Edwards*. London: Religious Tract Society, 1889.
Trestrail, Frederick. *Reminiscences of College Life in Bristol*. London: E. Marlboro and Co., 1879.
Wardlaw, Ralph. *Systematic Theology*. 3 vols. Edinburgh: A. and C. Black, 1857.

Wilberforce, Robert I., and Samuel Wilberforce, *The Life of William Wilberforce*. 5 vols. London: John Murray, 1839.

Wilkin, Martin H. *Joseph Kinghorn of Norwich*. Norwich: Fletcher and Alexander, 1855.

Williams, Daniel D. *Andover Liberals: A Study in American Theology*. New York: King's Crown, 1941.

Williams, Edward, and Edward Parsons. *The Works of President Edwards, in Eight Volumes*. London: James Black and Son, 1817.

Yeager, Jonathan. *Enlightened Evangelicalism: The Life and Thought of John Erskine*. New York: Oxford University Press, 2011.

# 2

# Jonathan Edwards and Terra Australis

## *His Perception of Us and Our Reception of Him*

STUART PIGGIN

## Introduction

IN 1724, JUST SHORT of his twenty-first birthday, reflecting on Isaiah 42.4, "And the isles shall wait for his law," Jonathan Edwards wrote on the fulfillment of this prophecy come the millennium:

> And what is peculiarly glorious in it, is the gospelizing the new and before unknown world, that which is so remote, so unknown, where the devil had reigned quietly from the beginning of the world, which is larger—taking in America, Terra Australis Incognita, Hollandia Nova, and all those yet undiscovered tracts of land—is far greater than the old world. I say, that this new world should all worship the God of Israel, whose worship was then confined to so narrow a land, is wonderful and glorious![1]

Like everything that Edwards wrote, this passage repays careful exegesis. It is crammed with his major concerns, which became life-long consuming interests and were to become constitutive of evangelical Christianity in general: the propagation of the gospel through the whole world

1. Edwards, "Notes on the Apocalypse," *WJE* 5:142.

(the conviction foundational to the later Anglophone missionary movement); a philosophy of history, with its post-millennial time frame; the status and conversion of the indigenous peoples of recently discovered and yet to be discovered regions of the earth. Here is a young man absorbed not only by divinity and moral and natural philosophy—the staple diet of the eighteenth-century minister of the Reformed faith—but also by history, geography, and ethnography.

The exuberance with which Edwards devoured these disciplines may be accounted for partly by adolescent religious enthusiasm. He had just finished his first pastorate in New York. There, his custom was to stroll along the banks of the Hudson with his soul mate, John Smith, with whose mother he boarded. Missions and the millennium fascinated them: "Our conversation used much to turn on the advancement of Christ's kingdom in the world, and the glorious things that God would accomplish for his church in the latter days." These topics fuelled his interest in geography and contemporary history: "If I heard the least hint of any thing that happened in any part of the world, that appeared to me, in some respect or other, to have a favorable aspect on the interest of Christ's kingdom, my soul eagerly catched at it; and it would much animate and refresh me."[2]

From all the references to Terra Australis in his writings, we can conclude that Edwards's interest in where Australia fitted into the History of God's Work of Redemption was life long. Given that Edwards was in the grave 13 years before Captain Cook chartered the east coast of Australia for the first time, his attention to Terra Australis is remarkable to say the least.

What might he have read about Australia that he "eagerly catched at"?

## What Might Edwards Have Read and Learned about Terra Australis?

Western speculation on the Great South Land may be traced back at least as far as the Alexandrine cartographer, Ptolemy, in AD 150. Terra Australis was commonly reputed to be of enormous size and fabulous wealth, but the sixteenth-century voyages of the Spanish and the seventeenth-century voyages of the Dutch had found little to support this belief.

Portuguese-born Spaniard Pedro de Quiros arrived at the New Hebrides in 1606 convinced that he had reached Terra Australis. He attempted to settle the island on which he had arrived and named it "Austrialia del Espiritu Santo," but after five weeks he gave up trying to quell the unrest of the Melanesians and he departed, leaving a legend which was not disproved

2. Marsden, *Jonathan Edwards: A Life*, 48.

for 150 years, and which has become the starting point for all twenty-first century civic Protestants of a conservative stripe who want to see de Quiros beatified for naming Australia what it should be (even if it is isn't).

Between 1642 and 1644, in two voyages, the Dutchman, Abel Tasman, mapped much of the Australian west coast and the southern part of Tasmania. He was not impressed with what he found: New Holland was barren and its people backward. There was little inducement to explore further.[3]

But, now, at the very end of the seventeenth century, shortly before Edwards's birth, Terra Australis was again an item of interest, thanks to William Dampier, the first Englishman to explore the seas around Australia. He, too, visited the west coast of New Holland in 1688, and again in 1699. Dampier's *A New Voyage Around the World* was an account so vivid that it inspired Daniel Defoe and Jonathan Swift, and S. T. Coleridge marveled at "old Dampier, a rough sailor, but a man of exquisite mind."[4] By 1717 it had gone through six editions. It gave a very unflattering picture of Australian Aboriginal peoples, "the miserablest People in the World," which was to become the standard European view.[5] On the other hand, explained Dampier to the First Lord of the Admiralty in London, the southern continent was the part of the world most meriting attention, adding that the "East Side of Hollandia Nova" abounded in "Gold and Silver Mines."[6] This was pure fantasy: no European had a clue where the east side of Hollandia Nova was before 1770.

The cartographer who sailed with Dampier, Herman Moll, published his comprehensive understanding of the whole region. He "divided *Terra Australis Incognita* into New Holland, Carpentaria, Terra Austral del Spiritu Santo, and Solomon's Islands to the north, and Diemen's Land and New Zealand to the south."[7] He then reverted to the traditional understanding that the whole land mass was "as large as *Europe, Asia*, and *Africa* combined,"

---

3. Williams and Frost, *Terra Australis*, 19. Peter Heylyn, in *Cosmographie* (1657), unaware of Tasman's voyages, mocked the whole enterprise. He undertook to try his fortune and search this *Terra Australis* for regions that "must be found either here or no where" and that went by the names of 1. *Mundus alter & idem* [the other and the same world], 2. *Utopia*, 3. *New Atlantis*, 4. *Fairy Land*, 5. *The Painters Wives Iland*, 6. *The Lands of Chivalry*, And, 7. *The New World in the Moon* (Williams and Frost, *Terra Australis*, 22).

4. As quoted in ""Edwards, "Editor's Introduction," *WJE* 26:41; Edwards, "The Hampshire Association of Ministers' Library," *WJE* 26:358.

5. Williams and Frost, *Terra Australis*, 122; quote from 124.

6. Ibid., 23.

7. Ibid.

so as to leave the earth "equally poiz'd."[8] This alluring combination of new perceptions and old fancies Moll presented in five volumes, known as *Atlas geographus: Or, a compleat system of geography, ancient and modern* (London, 1711–17).

The *Atlas Maritimus & Commercialis* (1728) included John Senex's "Map of the World" (1725).[9] This is remarkable for its critical assessment of our beloved country: the soil is barren and desart (sic); the rivers are only salt water; there are rats as big as cats (probably possums), and "vast numbers of troublesome flies."[10] This seems to have been based on William Dampier's unflattering account.[11]

In 1744, Moll's *Atlas* was revised by Emanuel Bowen in a two-volume work. It has the modest title *A complete system of geography. Being a description of all the countries, islands, cities, chief towns, harbours, lakes, and rivers, mountains, mines, &c. of the known world. Shewing the situation, extent and boundaries of the several empires . . . Comprehending the history of the universe both ancient and modern; and the most material revolutions and changes that have happen'd in it . . . To which is prefixed, an introduction to geography as a science.*

In the small print on his "A Complete Map of the Southern Continent," Bowen explains that nothing appears there that has not already been discovered, and that the white spaces between New Guinea and New Holland and between New Zealand and New Holland represent the unknown.

Did Jonathan Edwards know of these works? He had probably read all of them and more. During his first pastorate in New York in 1722, he began to keep a "Catalogue" of Reading.[12] It is probably a more faithful guide to what he wanted to read than to what he actually read.[13] But it is indicative of his intellectual aspirations and of how he intended to find out what God was doing in the world. Among the early entries in the "Catalogue," made at exactly the time of his first two known references to Terra Australis— namely in 1723 and 1724—he listed ten areas of study for which he intended to acquire and read the best books. The first of the ten is "the best Geography," and he notes that Cotton Mather recommends Moll's *Atlas*.[14] It is

---

8. Ibid.
9. Ibid., 25.
10. Ibid.
11. Ibid., 124.
12. Edwards, "'Catalogue' of Reading," *WJE* 26:117–318.
13. Edwards, "Editor's Introduction," *WJE* 26:13, 24–25.
14. Edwards, "'Catalogue' of Reading," *WJE* 26:164–66.

listed three times in Edwards's "Catalogue."¹⁵ Edwards is also known to have made a contribution of £20, an enormous sum for one as poor as he, to the Hampshire Association of Ministers' Library. It acquired, in 1741, William Dampier's *A New Voyage around the World*, but he had almost certainly read it before then. The works of Senex (probably) and Bowen (certainly) are also listed in Edwards's "Catalogue."

Other works on geography in Edwards's "Catalogue" include Edmund Bohun's *Geographical Dictionary* (1688);¹⁶ Jeremy Collier's *The Great historical, geographical, genealogical and poetical dictionary* (1694), a Catholic work, which Cotton Mather advised Edwards "should for all its Faults be in your Library"¹⁷; Edward Wells, *A treatise of ancient and present geography* (1701); Isaac Watts, *The first principles of astronomy and geography* (1726); John Fransham (friend of Daniel Defoe), *The world in miniature; or, The entertaining traveller* (1740), and other gazetteers and dictionaries.¹⁸

What understanding of Terra Australis would Edwards have gleaned from all such reading? He would have been aware of the coastline of more than half of Hollandia Nova; he would have been aware that some cartographers identified Hollandia Nova with Terra Australis while others thought they were two different land masses; the east coast of Hollandia Nova was yet uncharted; it was not known if there was a great land mass to the east of New Zealand which would lay a better claim to become known as Terra Australis; it was not known if Van Diemen's Land (Tasmania) was an island separated by a strait from the mainland of New Holland, it was not known if New Guinea was continuous with the mainland of New Holland, and it was not known if the New Hebrides (de Quiros's 1606 discovery of *Austrialia del Espiritu Santo*) was part of the east coast of Terra Australis or separate; and it was not known if Terra Australis Incognita—when no longer incognita—would be found to be bigger than all of the Americas, Asia, Africa, and Europe put together, as some enthusiasts had believed for centuries. All those unknowns were made known by Cook in his voyages of 1770 and 1774, with the exception of the question of whether or not Tasmania was a discrete island. That was not settled definitively until Bass and Flinders circumnavigated Tasmania in 1798. So, when Edwards wrote of "all those yet undiscovered tracts of land," he knew what he didn't know.

15. Ibid., 145, 153, 168.
16. Ibid., 177, 286.
17. Ibid., 178, 253.
18. Ibid., 205, 206, 275, 297; Edwards, "Books Recommended to Sir William Pepperrell," *WJE* 26:362.

Was he intrigued by all the unknowns, by the large claims of de Quiros, by the extravagant hopes of many who wanted to promote exploration of the south seas, and by the striking negativity of Tasman and Dampier? Was his prophetic imagination stirred by such opinions, hopes and fears, myths and fantasies about the Great South Land?

I do not know whether Edwards was in the habit of allowing his imagination to be stirred by myths. He inclined to discrediting the imagination as a path to knowledge, but he was prepared to sift myths for their grains of truth, for what he perceived to be their derivation from Scriptural truth. For example, in his "Notes on Scripture," entry 401 has the running head "Fables applied to Bacchus of Sacred Extract." Here, commenting on Genesis 10:8, he observes that "Many of those things that the heathen said of Bacchus were taken from Nimrod."[19] Edwards had no reason to suppose that what he found in the atlases and gazetteers about Terra Australis before Cook were myths or fables, but even if he had he would have brought all such data into submission to his overarching concerns. So, what did he have to say about Australia?

## What Did Edwards Have to Say about Australia?

### "Miscellany" 26

In June 1723, when 19-year-old Edwards was at home in East Windsor, Connecticut, between his time in New York and his taking up a pastorate at Bolton, Connecticut, he wrote:

> Millennium. How happy will that state be, when ... divine [and] human learning shall be ... diffused all over the world ... when we shall from time to time have the most excellent books and wonderful performances brought from one end of the earth and another to surprise us—sometimes new and wondrous discoveries from Terra Australis Incognita, the most divine and angelic strains from among the Hottentots, and the press shall groan in wild Tartary—when we shall have the great advantage of the sentiments of men of the most distant nations, different circumstances, customs and tempers; [when] learning shall be restrained [by] the particular humour of a nation or their singular way of treating of things; when the distant extremes of the world shall shake hands together and all nations shall be acquainted, and they shall all join the forces of their minds in

---

19. Edwards, "401. Genesis 10:8," *WJE* 15:400.

> exploring the glories of the Creator, their hearts in loving and adoring him, their hands in serving him, and their voices making the world to ring with his praise.
>
> ... There will continually be something new and surprising discovered in one part of the world and another [because of] the vast number of explorers, their different circumstances, their different paths to come at the truth. How many instructive and enlightening remains of antiquity will be discovered, here and there now buried amongst ignorant nations![20]

Edwards's early, almost Utopian, vision for the millennial Australia, then, was that it would make its own unique, but welcome, contribution to the diversity of human giftedness in the world. The beauty of God, Edwards believed, was represented by the harmony of this diversity. It was a sign that God's redeemed world would be multicultural.

Here, too, is the seed of the conviction, which was to become fundamental to the evangelical missionary movement, that all the peoples of the earth, including the indigenous peoples of Terra Australis, have equal value to their one Creator and are of equal potential through the grace of the gospel. In a sermon he preached shortly afterwards (December 1723) at Bolton, where he served a brief second pastorate, he expressed this conviction robustly. An Edwards sermon normally begins with one or more doctrinal propositions. Here is the first proposition:

> The gospel spirit is a catholic spirit, a noble and unconfined benevolence, like unto that of our Creator, not confined to any particular part of mankind exclusive of others; but the Christian's good will is general to all the seed of Adam.[21]

Did the later evangelical missionary work with the conviction that Australian Aboriginal peoples were "the seed of Adam"? Too many Australian European settlers did not share that view. But it was fundamental to the evangelical missionary movement.

An Edwards sermon concludes with applications, often many of them. One of the applications in this sermon affirms that:

> We are all made of the same blood. We are all descendants of the same heavenly Father who has made us all, and all from the same earthly father and mother; so that we are all brethren,

---

20. Edwards, "'Misc.' .26," *WJE* 13:212.
21. Edwards, "Living Peaceably One With Another," *WJE* 14:121.

of whatever nation, religion or opinion. Acts 17:26, "And hath made of one blood all nations of men."[22]

Such theology really mattered in practice. In 1823, William Horton, Wesleyan minister in Hobart, confessed that he would classify the Tasmanians as "amongst the inferior species of irrational animals" were it not for his theology:

> But as it is a revealed truth, that God has made of one blood all the nations of men that dwell upon the earth, however they may differ from each other in complexion, in features, in language and in manners, even the poor Aborigines of this island are partakers of the same nature with ourselves, offspring of the same God and objects of his redeeming love.[23]

With ample warrant, then, historian John Harris entitled his study of the Aboriginal encounter with Christianity, *One Blood*, for which he was awarded a Lambeth DD by Archbishop Rowan Williams.

## *Apocalypse Series*

Edwards also speculated on the geography of the millennium. His next series of references to Terra Australis, dated September/October 1723—about the time of his twentieth birthday, when he was at Windsor before assuming the tutorship at Yale—is found in what has been labeled the "Apocalypse Series."[24] There are, Edwards observed, three continents of the earth: the old continent comprising Europe, Asia, and Africa, the new continent, America, and the unknown or third continent, Terra Australis. At the very center of the old and principal continent is the land of Canaan, "most advantageously" created to be the place from where, come the millennium, the truth would "shine forth" and "spread around into all parts of the world." Because it lies at the end of the Mediterranean, a direct sea route opens from there to America. And because the Red Sea and the Persian Gulf also touch its borders just as much as the Mediterranean, a direct sea route connects it, via the Indian Ocean and the "great South Sea," with Terra Australis. To take the gospel to Australia you don't have to go right "round the Cape of Good Hope, or through the Straits of Magellan."

---

22. Ibid., 129.
23. Horton to the WMMS, 2 June 1823, in Horton, Letters.
24. Edwards, "Notes on the Apocalypse," *WJE* 5:133.

Although this God-given situation had not yet been fully exploited for the sake of the gospel's propagation, Edwards was confident that, come the millennium, the most glorious part of the church, from which the strongest rays of gospel light would emanate, would be Canaan. True, after the Great Awakening of 1740–42, he wondered if it might be that God intended America to be the center of gospel light on the grounds that the old continent had persecuted true believers and it might not be proper for it to have the honor of being the chief center of gospel light.[25] By the same argument, which Edwards calls an "analogy," one could argue that the third continent might have that singular honor.

Surely, you must be thinking, such gospel geography is from another planet. But it illuminates evangelical thinking in two major respects. First, it is consistent with the evangelical conviction that the light of the gospel must be taken to the whole world. And Australia, at the time of the first settlement, was understood by such evangelical leaders as Newton and the elder Venn as the base from which the light of the gospel would be shed abroad in the southern world and the Pacific. Second, Edwards again cited Acts 17:26 as partial justification for his gospel geography, "And God hath made of one blood all nations of men for to dwell on all the face of the earth, and hath determined the times before appointed, and the bounds of their habitation." But here he stressed not the "one blood," but God's determination of the time and place for all the nations. Such thinking would come to undermine any claim that Australia was terra nullius. Far from being unoccupied, Australia was the God-appointed habitation of the Aboriginal people. In 2009, with the history wars still raging, Peter Adam, Principal of Ridley College in Melbourne, preaching on Acts 17:26, contended:

> We have committed a great crime. We have not only failed to acknowledge that God allotted nations times and boundaries in this land. In order to commit these sins, we have committed the even greater sin of failing to acknowledge that we all come from one ancestor, that we are "one blood," that we are brothers and sisters of the indigenous peoples of this land. The doctrine of *terra nullius* treated people as if their existence had no meaning. But we must not treat people that way. For, as Calvin preached, the duty to love our neighbour extends to all.[26]

Adam sensationally argued not only for the fullest compensation for past wrongs, but that, since God had given the continent not to whites but to

---

25. Edwards, "Some Thoughts Concerning the Revival," *WJE* 4:355.
26. Adam, "Australia—whose land?"

blacks, the invaders should leave Australia unless permitted to remain by the Aboriginal owners.

## *Humble Attempt*

In the middle years of Edwards's ministry, the only reference to Terra Australis was in the work which, more than any other apart from Brainerd's *Diary*, influenced modern missions: *An Humble Attempt to promote explicit agreement and visible union of God's people in extraordinary prayer for the revival of religion and the advancement of Christ's kingdom on earth* (1747).

It is found in a section where Edwards is discussing the image of the growing river streaming from the temple in Jerusalem (Ezek 47:1–12). In his writings he referred to this passage often. And here in the *Humble Attempt* he wrote that in Ezekiel "the progress of religion is represented by the *gradual* increase of the waters spreading out to purify all the oceans of the world, resulting in the conversion of the peoples of Africa, Asia, America and [said Edwards 41 years before the first fleet] Terra Australis."[27] Missions would be the means by which this millennial glory would come. But while the millennium must come, it would not come easily or quickly. It would come "gradually." He warned that "vast and innumerable obstacles" were in the way: "It was a wonderful thing, when the Christian religion after Christ's ascension, so prevailed, as to get the ascendant in the Roman Empire in about 300 years; but that was nothing to this."[28] Thus Edwards encouraged Christian workers to expect success on a global scale, but only after patience, calculation and suffering. Here is the fundamental explanation for the indomitable perseverance of the Protestant missionary movement of the following century.

## *Original Sin*

Edwards's last known reference to Terra Australis was in his apologetic tome, *Original Sin*, which he began in 1756 and finished in 1757. It was published in 1758 a couple of months after his death at Princeton on 22 March 1758. It was a defense of Calvinism, specifically against the assault by one John

---

27. "And then in the next whole century, the whole heathen world should be enlightened and converted to the Christian faith, throughout all parts of Africa, Asia, America and Terra Australis . . . I have thus distinguished what belongs to a bringing of the world from its present state, to the happy state of the millennium . . . " Edwards, "An Humble Attempt," *WJE* 5:411.

28. Ibid., 412.

Taylor on the doctrine of the corruption of human nature as derived from Adam and the imputation of his first sin to all. Taylor was a Presbyterian divine from Norwich in England who joined English Presbyterianism in its "veritable landslide" into Unitarianism.[29]

Taylor contended that all people had an innate capacity for virtue as could be seen in the character of those who had never been touched by the gospel. Taylor claimed to be working from Scripture and reason. But Edwards could trump that.[30] He could work from Scripture, reason and experience, the last consisting of his acquaintance with American Indians. Before the arrival of the Europeans, what progress did they make towards obedience to the will of God? Had they moved away to "any degree from the grossest ignorance, delusions, and most stupid paganism"?[31] If there were any truth in Taylor's claim, argued Edwards, then all the "heathen," including every Indian, and "every inhabitant of the unknown parts of Africa and Terra Australis" would have made some progress beyond such a hopeless state. But they patently have not.

Overwhelmingly, evangelical missionaries in the ensuing century believed that their responsibility to the heathen, whether they be in North America, Africa, Asia, or Australia, was to convert them from "stupid paganism" and deliver them from the "grossest ignorance" and "delusions." Did that understanding of their responsibility come from Edwards? If it did, then they have ultimately, if understandably, misunderstood him. Insofar as that was their aim, they were not aiming at the real problem the heathen had. The real problem was their sin, which they inherited, not from their culture, but from Adam. The responsibility of the evangelical missionary is to address the problem of sin. That is to evangelize. Addressing "stupid paganism" and gross ignorance is to civilize and moralize. Too many missionaries identified that as their responsibility.

But, if they failed to understand Edwards in particular and evangelical Christianity in general on the implications of the teaching that all are sinners, then they did not fail to see the significance of another point that Edwards made in this debate. Taylor, Edwards alleged, had equated the cultivated niceties of cultivated European gentlemen with virtue. Unless they responded to the gospel, they too were still mired in gross immorality. Indeed, by comparison with them, the heathen who had not heard the gospel were babes.[32] This, too, was to be a commonplace argument of evangelical

---

29. Edwards, "Editor's Introduction," *WJE* 3:17n3.
30. McDermott, *Edwards Confronts the Gods*, 194.
31. Edwards, *Original Sin*, *WJE* 3:151.
32. Ibid., 183; McDermott, *Edwards Confronts the Gods*, 202.

missionaries in the ensuing century. Europeans who had heard the gospel had greater responsibility than those who had not had that advantage, and their culpability for rejecting the gospel was greater than that of the heathen. In the Australian colonies, too, missionaries repeatedly complained, unconverted Europeans were the greatest obstacles to the propagation of the gospel among the Indigenous peoples.

What Edwards tells us about Terra Australis, then, adds up to a powerful prophetic vision. Negatively, Terra Australis was the domain of the devil until the gospel arrived. Its people were in the grip of paganism, ignorance, and delusion. But, positively, they are of one blood with all other people. They are equal with all other people in that they are the sons and daughters of the one Creator. Their potential is the same as all other people through the grace of Christ. Their chief problem is identical to that of all other people, namely, that they are sinners. But they are also a unique people. New and wonderful discoveries will be made by them for the benefit of all humankind, and what they have already created will be revealed and revered. The differences between them and others will be treasured, and the harmony of that diversity will exhibit the beauty of God. It is their land. God determined that this land would be their habitation. If they choose to share it with us, we are to be grateful, and we owe them and all the other peoples of the earth "unconfined benevolence." This island continent would also be an honored base for the diffusion of gospel light. Australians will take their part in proclaiming this gospel and extending this kingdom to all the nations that the Lord will most certainly have for his inheritance in a new multicultural world. But that millennial glory will be accomplished gradually and by much hard work and sacrifice.

## What Has Been the Reception of Edwards in Australia?

Evangelical Christianity has been massively constitutive of Australian history since 1788. That is not a claim you will hear very often. I have called it "Australia's Missing Story" in my forthcoming study of the history of evangelical Christianity in Australia. Edwards was among the most influential shapers of that movement, and therefore his indirect influence has been considerable. The specific influence of Edwards is Australia's even-more missing story. He had an influence on the establishment of evangelical Christianity in Australia, on missions, and on Australian revivals.

## Edwards's Influence on Australia's Founding Leaders

The two best-known of Australia's evangelical pioneers—Samuel Marsden and John Dunmore Lang—owed a debt to Edwards. Lang, Australia's first Presbyterian minister, on a trip to America, visited the burial ground of the Presbyterian Church at Princeton, "to muse for a moment over the grave of Jonathan Edwards . . . the great philosopher and divine . . . It is a peculiarly interesting spot, from the hallowed associations which it calls up."[33]

Samuel Marsden read Brainerd's Diary on the voyage to NSW in 1793. Marsden recorded that he had been "reading of Mr Brainerd's success among the Indians," and he resolved that the "same power can also effect a change upon those hardened ungodly sinners to whom I am about to carry the words of eternal life."[34] Marsden is here comparing Indians to convicts, not Australian Aboriginal peoples, but missionaries to Australia longed for the conversion and even occasional revival of Aboriginal peoples, not only for their benefit, but as evidence that the proto-millennial power of God was at work here, too.[35] In April 1844, John Smithies, a Wesleyan missionary in Western Australia, began his report on an extensive and deep revival among his charges with the words:

> 21st Sabbath. The morning service was attended with divine unction. Several under the word were found weeping which led us to thank God and take courage . . . O to have seen these Australians bathed in tears, broken in heart, crying Jesus save me. O Lord save me; come and save now would have astounded infidels and gladdened the hearts of our English friends as it has done ours.[36]

It is probable that reading Brainerd's Diary on his work among the American Indians with the Australian Aboriginal peoples in mind would suggest many instructive parallels. There was the feeling that too little had been done towards the conversion of the Indians,[37] that the settlers had debauched them with strong drink rather than saved them with the water of life,[38] that the issue of land ownership was a guilt-induced concern,[39] that the uncivi-

---

33. Lang, *Religion and Education in America*, 294.

34. Marsden, *Life and Labours of the Rev. Samuel Marsden*, 5, 8; Grigg, *Lives of Brainerd*, 169.

35. Grigg, *Lives of Brainerd*, 145; McDermott, *Edwards Confronts the Gods*, 198.

36. Smithies, Letters; Roy, *Reappraisal*, 20.

37. Grigg, *Lives of Brainerd*, 144.

38. Ibid., 145.

39. Ibid.

lized state of the Indian heathen was an argument for, rather than against, missions,[40] and that any violent resistance from the heathen was more often the result of the vices of nominal Christian settlers than of inherent ferocity.[41] The exercise of comparing the Australian Aboriginal person with the American Indian could well begin with Gerald McDermott's chapter on the American Indians in his *Jonathan Edwards Confronts the Gods*.

## Edwards's influence on Australian revivals

As for revivals, Australia has seen far more of them than our historians have noticed—another dimension of Australia's missing story. Nineteenth-century Australian revivals were mainly local and mainly Wesleyan. Presbyterians had trouble with revivalism: altar calls, they felt, were not a great idea in small communities as everybody knew everybody else and, of all congregations, Presbyterians were the least mercurial.[42] Mercurialness apparently predisposes to revival. But Methodism was that part of the evangelical family that was growing more rapidly than any other. So Presbyterians had to take their practices seriously. In coming to terms with the possibility and desirability of revivals, Jonathan Edwards helped. The Reverend Archibald Mackray, Presbyterian minister of Ashfield in Sydney, gave a substantial, well-researched lecture on revival to an Association of Presbyterian Sunday School Teachers.[43] Mackray said that he agreed with Jonathan Edwards in viewing revivals as "those great periodical Religious movements which form the chief landmarks of history."[44] He likened them to revolutions, which shape history: "Does not the doctrine of Crisis hold an imperial place in the philosophy of history?"[45]

Mackray quoted at length the most famous passage in Edwards's classic account of revival in Northampton in 1734/5, *A Faithful Narrative of the Surprising Work of God in the Conversion of many hundred Souls in*

---

40. Ibid., 166.
41. Ibid.
42. Presbyterian Assembly of NSW, Blue Book, 1885, 48.
43. Mackray, *Revivals of Religion*. Mackray cites studies of revival by Gillies, *Historical Collections*; Froggatt, *Work of God in Every Age*; Edwards; D'Aubigné; Paton, Sprague; Burns; Prime; Edgar; Gibson; Reid; Carson; Bonar; Weir; Turner; Huntington; and numerous denominational reports and revival magazines. On church history he has read Neander.
44. Mackray, *Revivals*, 30.
45. Ibid., 31.

*Northampton* (1736), "furnished to Dr. Watts and Dr. Guise,"[46] as the normative, defining description of revival. The passage begins with the words "A great and earnest concern about the great things of religion and the eternal world became *universal* in all parts of the town, and among persons of all degrees and all ages . . ."[47] Mackray adds:

> The "Thoughts on the Present Revival," which this great theologian published at the time, and his later treatise on "the Religious Affections" ought to be carefully studied by everyone who is praying and working for a revival of the Lord's work in his own community.[48]

Addressing the three chief agencies in promoting awakenings—prayer, diffusion of revival intelligence, and the use of lay evangelists—Mackray tells us that "the revival in New England, which arose under President Edwards, is to be traced to the meeting for prayer of a few devoted Christians, maintained throughout the whole night. Barrenness and death is the righteous penalty for prayerlessness."[49]

John Auld, who took over the Presbyterian work in Ashfield from Mackray, retained Mackray's hope for revival. He was able to report an awakening move of the Spirit among his people first in 1876 and again in 1881. The latter accompanied a two-week long mission and followed a season of "unceasing prayer" for revival.[50] In 1885, Presbyterian missioner, David Allan, preaching through the Bathurst region west of Sydney, drew upon the work of Jonathan Edwards, "a great authority on the subject" to explain his success, quoting him to the effect that "A revival of religion is nothing but the immediate result of an uncommon attention."[51]

In the twentieth century, the Australian Anglican whose name is most often associated with revival is Geoffrey Bingham (1919–2009). Revival broke out in numerous of his missions both in Australia and overseas. He was profoundly influenced by Edwards.

In December 1999, Bingham documented the effects of Edwards on his life and ministry.[52] It is a revealing document. A criticism I had about

---

46. Ibid., 10.
47. Ibid.
48. Ibid.
49. Ibid., 28.
50. *Report of the Presbyterian Church, Ashfield*, 1938.
51. Blue Book, 1885, 48.
52. Geoffrey Bingham, "The Effects of Jonathan Edwards on my Life and Ministry," unpublished typescript, 9 December 1999.

Moore Theological College in Sydney, as it stood a couple of decades ago, was that, though it prided itself on being an evangelical college, it never taught the history of evangelicalism. It got stuck on the Reformers and the Puritans. Not any more. Edwards is now accorded a place in the curriculum. But, if Bingham is right, Moore College had not always neglected the founders of the evangelical movement. He claims that from the age of 20 he was familiar with Edwards. He writes: "I was in Moore Theological College in 1930 and his name was well known. . . . I returned to Moore College in 1952. There Edwards's name and fame was linked with others such as James Denney, Peter Forsyth, J. C. Ryle and R. W. Dale. We all thought of Edwards as being among the "greats.""

I was surprised to learn this and I can only surmise that after the departure of Marcus Loane as Principal of Moore in 1958, the spirituality associated with those names was lost in the rush to discard Keswick-style piety. Many babies were thrown out with that bath water.

Like John Wesley and the afore-mentioned Mackray, Bingham was influenced towards seeking revival in his ministry through reading Edwards's classic description of evangelical revival, *A Faithful Narrative* (1736). "I know it fired me forever," he wrote, adding: "That such happenings could arise from strong biblical preaching confirmed my belief that all that was required of the minister of the church was to preach sincerely the Scriptures and the Spirit of God would move in power."

Edwards appears to have been not only a critical, foundational influence on Bingham, but a constant companion. "There have been times," he wrote, "when I could turn to no other man but this one: no one has ever spoken quite like this one. I feel wonderfully at home with him. I have read innumerable books on revival, both histories of revivals, and revival theories. I have seen the futility of some of these theories, and have resonated to others of them because they comport with Edwards and the Scriptures." After mentioning Edwards's account of his weeping aloud over the beauty and sweetness of God in Christ, Bingham said: "I have not heard other writers talk quite this way. If I say I talk this way then it is not a matter of emulation or imitation, but that I know my experience is authentic when it is in parallel with his." Or, in another example where he compares himself with Edwards, he wrote:

> Edwards has been called "the theologian of the heart." In my case I was always this—if not on the level of Edwards—but he gave me heart to believe I was on the right track. I do not believe that the reading of Edwards necessarily induces "heart religion," but I believe it confirms and encourages those whose heart lies

in this direction. At the same time it rebukes an emotionalism which does not raise "holy affections" but those mainly born of the flesh.

In a recent biography, *A Quiet Revival: Geoffrey Bingham in Life and Ministry*, Martin Bleby reports that as Bingham's end drew near, he "continued to read, and found a kindred spirit particularly in the American puritan theologian Jonathan Edwards (1703–58), whose biography and writings he kept close to his bedside."[53] Bingham is Australia's Jonathan Edwards.

But we are in the land down under, so let me end, not on a high note, but with a rare discovery: a critic of Edwards.

### Edwards and "ideographic prophecy"

One of the fascinating differences between eighteenth- and nineteenth-century evangelicalism is the apparently rapid contraction in the latter of typology, of which Edwards was the master. But if it evaporated from evangelical theology, it reappeared in arguably the finest of Australia's literary classics, Joseph Furphy's *Such is Life* (1903).

Born in 1843, Furphy wrote the first of his juvenilia in 1858. Its author he identified as Josephus Australianicus, B. D. By B. D. he meant bullock driver—this, some fifteen years before he became one. Furphy was a bullock driver in the western plains of the Riverina from 1873 until 1884, when he began to write *Such is Life*. It was eventually published in 1903 under the pseudonym of Tom Collins, at that time a synonym in pub culture for idle rumor.[54] Collins's world is enchanted, at least potentially. For him, the flat landscape

> bespeaks an unconfirmed, ungauged potentiality of resource; it unveils an ideographic prophecy, painted by nature in her impressionistic mood, to be deciphered aright only by those willing to discern through the crudeness of dawn a promise of majestic day . . . Faithfully and lovingly interpreted, what is the latent meaning of it all?[55]

"Ideographic prophecy"—is that not another aspect of the "eternal language" that Edwards and Coleridge sought to learn from history and nature

---

53. Bleby, *A Quiet Revival*, 339.

54. It was purely by coincidence that in World War I, "furphy" became a synonym for the same thing, when those who drove the furphies or water wagons engaged in idle gossip and rumor.

55. Collins, *Such is Life*, 181.

as well as the Bible?[56] One evening, he—that is, Tom Collins—was reflecting on the intricacies of theology with the help of Jonathan Edwards when he spied the very Australian type of pilgrim, a swagman. But let Tom tell us about that in his own inimitable style:

> The refined leisure of the day had been devoted chiefly to the study of my current swapping-book—*Edwards on Redemption*—and now, half-stifled by the laborious blasphemy of the work, I was seeking deliverance from the sin of reading it by watching the multitudes of white cockatoos through my binoculars, and piously speculating as to their intended use.[57]

Edwards's *History of the Work of Redemption* was published posthumously in 1774. It was the equivalent of Augustine's *City of God* in that it presented his philosophy of history. It was about the divine plan worked out in heaven, earth, and hell. It is stifling and laborious. But it did not meander like *Such is Life*. It was focused and unrelentingly doctrinal. Furphy did not like doctrine, and he especially did not like Edwards's doctrine of predestination, which is the most likely reason that he described the book as "blasphemy." Significantly, Furphy was then a member of the Churches of Christ in Shepparton, in northern Victoria. It was, in 1884, a small player with only 2673 members in the Colony of Victoria, but its appeal to Furphy was that it was opposed to dogma—especially predestination—and sectarianism, and espoused free will and unity among Christians.

But Edwards's high seriousness was having the same effect on Furphy as it has on many who read him: it was making him think about the purpose of everything, even cockatoos. Edwards was a radical typologist who saw types of the glory of God and the work of redemption in every creature and every event, that is, in nature and history as well as in the Bible. So it is not all that surprising that, under the influence of Edwards, Furphy was speculating on the use of cockatoos, even if he felt the disingenuous Australian need to downplay that speculation as pious. It was then no sort of a leap to think of the pilgrim who came into the sights of his binoculars, namely the swagman, as a type of Christ:

> Heaven help him! That nameless flotsam of humanity . . . Few and feeble are his friends on earth; and the One who like him, was wearied with his journey, and, like him, had not where to lay his head, is gone, according to His own parable, into a far country. The swagman [unlike the earthly Jesus] we have always

---

56. Piggin and Cook, "Keeping alive the heart in the head," 383–414.
57. Collins, *Such is Life*, 105.

> with us—And . . . the Light of the world, the God-in-Man, the only God we can ever know, is by His own authority represented for all time by the poorest of the poor. Yet whosoever fails to recognise in the marred visage of any social derelict the image of Him who was despised and rejected of men . . . can have no place among the Architect's workmen, being already employed on the ageless Babel-contract.[58]

Furphy's Socialism is this-worldly and consistently opposed to respectable, institutionalized denominationalism, but it is a world replete with types, where bullock drivers and swagmen are the truest pilgrims precisely because Christ is happiest to identify with them in their poverty and need. Strong on morality and conscience, Furphy saw no reason for preserving Christian dogmas of heaven, hell, and judgment as of any relevance to their maintenance. On Furphy's departure from orthodoxy, and also his tone, historian Alan Atkinson observes with uncharacteristic impatience:

> Furphy was a man of simple life—bullock driver, husband, father, friend. He worked from habit and affection, and from his own inner spring. He might have been less cocky if he had had to decide on the fate of nations.[59]

But I think that what made him so cocky was that, with Jonathan Edwards's help, he reflected on the typological purpose of cockatoos. That is a joke, an expression of "the particular humour of the [Australian] nation," which, far from enduring beyond the onset of the millennium, will evaporate imminently if I trespass any further on your time.

## Bibliography

Adam, Peter. "Australia—Whose Land?" The Second Annual John Saunders Lecture, Monday 10 August 2009, http://www.tear.org.au/resources/australia-whose-land/ accessed 22 May 2015.

Atkinson, Alan. *The Europeans in Australia. Vol. 3: Nation*. Sydney: UNSW Press, 2014.

Bingham, Geoffrey. "The Effects of Jonathan Edwards on my Life and Ministry." Unpublished typescript, 9 December 1999.

Bleby, Martin. *A Quiet Revival: Geoffrey Bingham in Life and Ministry*. New Creation Publications Inc, Blackwood, SA, 2012.

Collins, Tom. *Such is Life*. Sydney: Angus and Robertson, 1980.

Edwards, Jonathan. "Books Recommended to Sir William Pepperrell." In *Catalogues of Books*, edited by Peter J. Thuesen, The Works of Jonathan Edwards 26:361–62. New Haven: Yale University Press, 2008.

---

58. Ibid., 107.

59. Atkinson, *Europeans in Australia*, 270.

———. "'Catalogue' of Reading." In *Catalogues of Books*, edited by Peter J. Thuesen, The Works of Jonathan Edwards 26:117–318. New Haven: Yale University Press, 2008.

———. "Genesis 10:8." In *Notes on Scripture*, edited by Stephen J. Stein. The Works of Jonathan Edwards 15:400–405. New Haven: Yale University Press, 1998.

———. "The Hampshire Association of Ministers' Library." In *Catalogues of Books*, edited by Peter J. Thuesen, The Works of Jonathan Edwards 26:357–60. New Haven: Yale University Press, 2008.

———. "An Humble Attempt to Promote Explicit Agreement and Visible Union of God's People in Extraordinary Prayer for the Revival of Religion and the Advancement of Christ's Kingdom on Earth, Pursuant to Scripture-Promises and Prophecies Concerning the Last Time." In *Apocalyptic Writings*, edited by Stephen J. Stein, The Works of Jonathan Edwards 5:307–436. New Haven: Yale University Press, 1977.

———. "Living Peaceably One with Another." In *Sermons and Discourses, 1723-1729*, edited by Kenneth P. Minkema, The Works of Jonathan Edwards 14:116–33. New Haven: Yale University Press, 1997.

———. "'Misc.' 26." In *The "Miscellanies" (Entry Nos. a-z, aa-zz, 1-500)*, edited by Thomas A. Schafer, The Works of Jonathan Edwards 13:212–13. New Haven: Yale University Press, 1994.

———. "'Notes on the Apocalypse.'" In *Apocalyptic Writings*, edited by Stephen J. Stein. The Works of Jonathan Edwards 5:95–305. New Haven: Yale University Press, 1977.

———. *Original Sin*. Edited by Clyde A Holbrook. The Works of Jonathan Edwards 3. New Haven: Yale University Press, 1970.

———. "Some Thoughts concerning the Revival." In *The Great Awakening*, edited by Clarence C. Goen, The Works of Jonathan Edwards 4:289–530. New Haven: Yale University Press, 1972.

Grigg, John A. *The Lives of David Brainerd: The Making of An American Evangelical Icon*. New York: Oxford University Press, 2009.

Holbrook, Clyde. A. "Editor's Introduction." In *Original Sin*, edited by Clyde A. Holbrook, The Works of Jonathan Edwards 3:1–101. New Haven: Yale University Press, 1970.

Horton, William. Letters. Box 52. Bonwick Transcripts, Mitchell Library, Sydney.

Lang, John Dunmore. *Religion and Education in America: With Notices of the State and Prospects of American Unitarianism, Popery, and African Colonization* (London: T. Ward and co, 1840), 294f.

Mackray, Archibald N. *Revivals of Religion: Their Place and Power in the Christian Church*. Sydney: John L. Sherriff, 1870.

Marsden, George M. *Jonathan Edwards: A Life*. New Haven: Yale University Press, 2003.

Marsden, J. B. *Memoirs of the Life and Labours of the Rev. Samuel Marsden, of Paramatta, Senior Chaplain of New South Wales*. London: Religious Tract Society, 1858.

McDermott, Gerald. *Jonathan Edwards Confronts the Gods: Christian Theology, Enlightenment Religion, and Non-Christian Faiths*. New York: Oxford University Press, 2000.

Piggin, Stuart, and Dianne Cook, "Keeping Alive the Heart in the Head: The Significance of 'Eternal Language' in the Aesthetics of Jonathan Edwards and S. T. Coleridge." *Literature and Theology* 18.4 (2004) 383–414.

Blue Book, Presbyterian Assembly of NSW, 1885.

Report of the Presbyterian Church. Ashfield, 1938.

Roy, Richard B. "A Reappraisal of Wesleyan Methodist Mission in the First Half of the Nineteenth Century, as Viewed Through the Ministry of Rev John Smithies (1802–1872)." PhD diss., Edith Cowan University, 2006.

Smithies, John. Letters, 1840–1871: WMMS, Australian correspondence, boxes 516–19. School of Oriental and African Studies, University of London.

Thuesen, Peter J. "Editor's Introduction." In *Catalogues of Books*, edited by Peter J. Thuesen, The Works of Jonathan Edwards 26:1–113. New Haven and London: Yale University Press, 2008.

Williams, Glyndwr, and Alan Frost, *Terra Australis to Australia*. Melbourne: Oxford University Press in association with the Australian Academy of the Humanities, 1988.

# 3

# Jonathan Edwards and Chinese Millennial Movements

## Victor Zhu

## Introduction

THE MILLENNIUM, IF DEFINED along the lines of non-Anglo-European religious traditions, is a "paradisiacal age" that will arrive in the near future. Chinese civilization is enriched by numerous apocalyptic, messianic, and millenarian traditions. The long history of Chinese indigenous millenarian beliefs, beginning in the Eastern Han dynasty (25–220 CE), gave birth to multiple millennial movements in China.[1]

Chinese millenarian traditions frequently and successfully absorb, incorporate and modify foreign millenarian beliefs. Instead of being replaced by Christian forms of millennial teachings from Anglo-European traditions, it seems that Chinese traditions reshape the imported ideologies by incorporating these into their own, in order to "create new forms of indigenous millennialism."[2] Since Christianity was brought into China in the seventh century CE, Chinese millenarian traditions are repeatedly found in Christian clothing but nourished by the teachings of Daoism, Buddhism, and Chinese folk religion. According to Chinese traditional belief, the afterlife and anything beyond this world is considered to be too mysterious

---

1. Lowe, "Chinese Millennial Movements," 309, 322.
2. Ibid.

to be understood.³ Therefore, the essential task of these Chinese millennial movements is to establish a Sinocentric, human-inaugurated heavenly kingdom *on earth*.

The Taiping Rebellion (1836–64) is a prominent example of a Sinocentric, human-inaugurated earthly kingdom. As it flourished in the nineteenth century, the key leader Hong Xiuquan was inspired by evangelical Protestant eschatology, but translated it into his own ambitious vision of establishing a Heavenly Kingdom of Great Peace.⁴ Having established a political base in Nanjing (Nanking), Hong and his followers ("God-worshippers") began acting as if they were emperors and princes, believing that they had fulfilled God's mission to establish the millennial kingdom. Therefore, unlike most of the farmers' rebellions in Chinese history, they had no intention of attacking Beijing, and no aim to overthrow the Qing dynasty.⁵

Furthermore, various elements from Daoism and Chinese folk religion can be traced in the ideological framework of Hong and his followers. First, the notion of an era of "Taiping" (Great Peace) is originally found in the Daoist classic the *Zhuangzi (Chuang tzu)*.⁶ Hong's dream of creating a heavenly realm of great peace was a mixed product of Christian millenarian and Daoist utopian hopes. Secondly, Hong claimed that he was raptured into heaven and his internal organs were completely replaced. Most notably, he asserted that in this rapture he was elected by God to be Jesus' younger brother. In Chinese history, it is common for a person to claim extraordinary experiences in order to gain a legitimate right for a royal position.⁷ Thus, it is not surprising to see Hong, an ordinary schoolteacher and a failed scholar, doing so. For the same reason, other key leaders of the Taiping Rebellion aligned themselves with local spirit-possession traditions and stated that they were possessed and empowered by all kinds of spirits that are either recorded in the biblical Scriptures or simply known among Chinese legends.⁸ These examples clearly indicate that Hong and his followers, so-called the God-worshippers, had forged a new Christianity and turned the Taiping Rebellion into a highly Sinicized millennial movement

---

3. Gernet, *China and the Christian Impact*, 197.

4. Weller, *Resistance, Chaos, and Control*, 50–68. See also Lowe, 310.

5. Lowe, 310.

6. Ibid., 309.

7. For instance, Liu Bang (247–195 BC), the first emperor of *Han* dynasty, declared in the early stage of his rebellion that he was conceived after his mother had sexual intercourse with a dragon, in order to be recognized as *longzi*, the Son of Dragon and *tianzi*, the Son of Heaven. For the details, see *Shiji*, vol. 8, no. 8, accessed August 13, 2015, http://ctext.org/shiji/gao-zu-ben-ji.

8. Weller, 69–80. See also Lowe, 315.

that included various ingredients drawn from biblical revelation, Daoism, and Chinese folk religion.

*Dongfang Shandian* ("Eastern Lighting") can be viewed as an alternative version of the Taiping Rebellion in contemporary China. It developed into a popular movement in the last two decades and is currently regarded as a "a highly Sinicized, aggressively evangelistic millennial group that has been recruiting forcefully and deceptively in northeastern China since 1989."[9] The leader of Eastern Lighting, a Chinese lady in Henan province (central China), has made similar claims to Hong, professing that she is the incarnate God and the returned Christ. She proclaimed that her "divine mission" is to destroy the PRC, which she teaches is the Red Dragon from the book of Revelation,[10] and to take her followers up to heaven.[11] Similar to the Taiping Rebellion, the ideological blueprint of Eastern Lighting is a blend of Christian millenarian beliefs, Daoist messianism, and Chinese folk religion.

In the light of these historical examples of problematic developments in Chinese eschatology, it may be helpful to explore alternative and robust Christian views of the millennium that might be more resistant to such socially destructive syntheses. Here I would like to offer the view of Jonathan Edwards, arguably the greatest American Reformed theologian, whose millennial consciousness is often legendarily misinterpreted as an overly optimistic and Americo-centric postmillennialism. In what follows I will offer both a new interpretation of Edwards's eschatology and demonstrate its suitability as a viable Christian alternative millennial view for a Chinese context.

## Edwards's Distinctive Millennial Awareness

### Edwards's Understanding of the Millennium

Edwards's millennial expectation is deeply rooted in and nourished by his study of biblical texts. For instance, from his reading of apocalyptic writings, Edwards asserted in *A History of the Work of Redemption* (hereafter abbreviated as *HWR*) that the millennium would be "a state of peace and prosperity" for the church.[12] He depicted it as "the principal time of the kingdom of heaven," as "great peace and love" and "excellent order in the

---

9. Lowe, 322.
10. Rev 12:3–18.
11. Lowe, 322.
12. Edwards, *History of the Work of Redemption*, WJE 9:479.

church of Christ."¹³ This period would see "the principal fulfillment of all the prophecies of the Old Testament" and "the church of God shall then be beautiful and glorious on these accounts."¹⁴ The Christian religion will "in every respect be uppermost in the world" and all nations will enjoy the benefits of the gospel.¹⁵ In short, it was the complete realization on earth of God's end in creation and redemption, being characterized by glorious harmony and everlasting blessings.¹⁶

There are two points concerning Edwards's millennial vision on which scholars have generally reached agreement. First, Edwards's chiliastic viewpoint departs from the basic Reformed position. For example, John Calvin did not accept any chiliastic notion and always treated the word "millennium" in a spiritualized sense. However, Edwards clearly believed that it would be an actual space-time reality on earth. Second, Edwards believed that during the millennium Christ would reign on earth through his Spirit, while his body remained in heaven.¹⁷ Apart from these two points however, there are a number of issues that have caused either controversies or misinterpretations among the Edwardsean commentators. Below I will discuss two such instances and offer a new, critical evaluation and interpretation.

### *The Imminent Millennium?*

There is a long-standing misinterpretation asserted that Edwards was as optimistic as some of his Puritan predecessors and contemporaries, such as John Cotton (1585–1652), Samuel Willard (1640–1707), Increase Mather (1639–1723) and Cotton Mather (1663–1728), in hoping for an imminent millennium.¹⁸ This misunderstanding was started by Perry Miller and C. C. Goen, and accepted by many, including Alan Heimert, Ernest Lee Tuveson, John Wilson, Harry Stout and others.¹⁹ This misleading interpretation, as McDermott points out, was caused by some scholars' misreading of Edwards's wording of his phrase "glorious work of God." A careful analysis

---

13. Ibid., 479–84.
14. Ibid., 479, 484.
15. Ibid., 484–85.
16. Gibson, "Integrative Biblical Philosophy," 158.
17. Edwards, "'Misc.' 827," *WJE* 18:537–38. See also McClymond and McDermott, *Theology of Jonathan Edwards*, 576; Goen, "Jonathan Edwards," 37.
18. For example, see Beeke and Jones, *Puritan Theology*, 784.
19. See Miller, *Jonathan Edwards*, 318; Goen, "Jonathan Edwards," 25–40; Wilson, "History, Redemption, and the Millennium," 134.
For Goen's other followers, see Rogers, "A Missional Eschatology," 26n8, 31.

shows that Edwards used this phrase to refer to "a long period of intermittent revival that would lead up to the millennium," rather than addressing the millennium itself.[20]

Nevertheless, several issues have not been pointed out previously. The first one is that Edwards believed that before the millennium there must be a continuous and progressive advancement of God's work of redemption. Therefore, Edwards employed three central images in his *HWR*: a building, a river, and light. The first two images illustrate the long and gradual progress of the work of redemption in which Christ's victory over his enemies is witnessed by humanity, while the third image stands for God's revelation and glory that are gradually unfolded and unveiled throughout all the ages.

Secondly, some commentators have neglected Edwards's description of the great and final revival that he believes will occur before the arrival of the millennium. At that time the Holy Spirit "shall be gloriously poured out for the wonderful revival and propagation of religion."[21] This revival will bring about two significant events. First, a great "work of conversion" that will "go on in a wonderful manner," and secondly, the overthrow of Satan's kingdom. Therefore, even though Edwards saw and admitted God's mighty work in the revivals, he did not regard any of them, including the "little revival" of 1734–35 and the Great Awakening starting in 1739, as the final and international revival that would usher in the millennium.[22] Actually, in contrast to the declaration that Edwards was optimistically hoping for the "*soon* coming" of Christ's kingdom,[23] Edwards confessed in *HWR* that he was "far from pretending to determine the time when the reign of Antichrist began," let alone to predict when the millennium would start.[24]

Thirdly, it is Edwards's consistent belief that a long and progressive advance was required to reach the millennium and the final consummation. In his early years, Edwards was quite conservative and cautious with predictions of the advent of the millennium. After 1738, Edwards re-evaluated his earlier conservative views of the Apocalypse and thought that he was at the

---

20. McDermott, *One Holy and Happy Society*, 51. McDermott's view has been affirmed by many other scholars. See Stephen, "Evangelical Eschatology," 138; Zakai, *Edwards's Philosophy of History*, 299–301; McClymond and McDermott, *Theology of Jonathan Edwards*, 573–74; Rogers, "Missional Eschatology," 31–33; Withrow, "Future of Hope," 76–77, 93–94.

21. Edwards, *History of the Work of Redemption*, WJE 9:460. See also Rogers, "Missional Eschatology," 30; Withrow, "Future of Hope," 87.

22. Rogers, "Missional Eschatology," 31.

23. Goen, "Jonathan Edwards," 33.

24. Edwards, *History of the Work of Redemption*, WJE 9:412.

era of the sixth, instead of the third, vial.[25] Even so, he still believed that "Satan's kingdom in the world will not be totally overthrown, his ruin will not receive its finishing stroke till the year two thousand."[26] This is why in his *HWR* Edwards described a time-consuming progressive process of Christ's triumph over Satan. This is also the reason why, in a letter to William McCulloch (1691–1771) on March 5, 1744, Edwards firmly refuted the rumor of his "imminent millennium" viewpoint: "It has been *slanderously reported and printed* concerning me, that I have often said that the millennium was already begun, and that it began at Northampton . . ."[27]

Finally, Edwards's belief of a gradual and progressive realization of the millennium is also informed by his full awareness of the complexity of the continual warfare between Christ and his enemies. In *HWR*, Edwards employed a notion from mechanical philosophy to describe the complicated process of history: it works like a giant machine that comprises numerous interlocking cogs, gears, and rotating wheels, moving forward in a complex, mysterious way.[28] The complexity of this "machine" and the mysterious occurrence of the historical events are caused by the constant conflict between Christ and Satan. As many scholars have noticed, Edwards followed a claim from the Reformed tradition that the Roman Catholic Church was apostate, a "standard Protestant belief" in his day.[29] Nevertheless, the Roman Catholic Church and the papacy are only *one* of the kingdoms of Satan mentioned by Edwards. Another is the "Mohammedan kingdom." If only one of Satan's kingdoms fell, there would still be a long process in overthrowing another.[30] Furthermore, Edwards pointed out, "Satan's visible kingdom" also includes corrupt opinions and Jewish infidelity. All of these forces of Satan will be united to fight against Christ and his church, before the millennium, as "the last and greatest effort of Satan."[31] As a result, it will be a long time and

---

25. Stein, "Editor's Introduction," *WJE* 5:36–37.

26. Edwards, "Notes on the Apocalypse," *WJE* 5:129. See also Stein, "Editor's Introduction," *WJE* 5:18, 29.

27. Edwards, "To William McCulloch," *WJE* 4:560, emphasis added.

28. Edwards's machine metaphor probably comes from his observation of clocks and elementary machines. See Zakai, *Edwards's Philosophy of History*, 213–14; Wilson, "Editor's Introduction," *WJE* 9:50. See also Hewitson, "As ordered and governed by divine providence," 6–20. Hewitson thinks Edwards uses the machine as his master metaphor to explain divine history, especially the complicated relationship between historical events and God's providence.

29. Goen, "Jonathan Edwards," 26. See also Withrow, "Future of Hope," 81.

30. Edwards, *History of the Work of Redemption*, *WJE* 9:410–11.

31. Ibid., 410, 415–16, 462–63; Edwards, "Notes on the Apocalypse," *WJE* 5:129, 410. See also Withrow, "Future of Hope," 96.

"great difficulties" will have to be overcome before Satan's visible kingdom on earth is completely destroyed.[32] Therefore, rather than being a triumphalist, Edwards in his *HWR* cited numerable cases to demonstrate that Christ's triumph over his enemies is not without pains, failures, or frustrations, but frequently arises out of his or his church's "defeat."[33]

In sum, contrary to the interpretation held by Goen and other recent scholars, Edwards's post-millennium position, in comparison with the view of an imminent millennium held by most of his Puritan predecessors and contemporaries, is less optimistic and more biblical. Because of his in-depth study of the Scriptures and his multifaceted theological framework, Edwards took a number of issues into consideration, including God's wisdom and his plan in the work of redemption, the complexity of warfare between Christ and his enemies, and the essential role played by revivals in the advancement of the work of redemption. As a result, he concluded that in line with the progressive development of the work of redemption, the millennium would arrive around year 2000. This viewpoint may seem highly optimistic for modern (and postmodern) readers today, but from Edwards's perspective we can see that it is quite conservative.

## An America-Oriented Millennium?

The geographical location of the millennium is another issue that divides commentators. As mentioned above, in his earlier years Goen states that Edwards believed in the imminence of the millennium that would "*begin in America.*"[34] Goen restates this notion later on, insisting that Edwards reinforced "America's persistent self-image as a 'redeemer nation'" and related this idea of a "redeemer nation" to "biblical prophecies of the millennium."[35] Goen's argument is followed by some scholars who claim that Edwards was no different from other Puritans who considered New England to be the "promised land" and "a city on a hill" that was "called to be God's light to the nations." [36] While it may sound reasonable, this model

---

32. Edwards, *History of the Work of Redemption*, WJE 9:454, 466.

33. In addition to his description of Christ's atonement that is evidently a story about glory that comes out of suffering, Edwards listed plenty of cases where Christ turns failures of his Church into advancement of the Work of Redemption, among them, the captivity of Jews. See ibid., 251–59.

34. Goen, "Jonathan Edwards," 29, emphasis added.

35. Goen, "Editor's Introduction," *WJE* 4:71–72.

36. Beeke and Jones, *Puritan Theology*, 779.

of Edwards's participation in the "America-oriented millennium" cannot be supported by the evidence.

Based on his studies of the Scriptures, Edwards clearly stated that the center of the coming kingdom would be Canaan, and not any other nation. Geographically speaking, Edwards's millennial vision is quite evidently not America- or New England-centered, but Canaan-centered. Some scholars, such as Nathan Hatch, claimed that due to spiritual decline in New England, Edwards could not find "signs of the coming Millennium exclusively in America" and had to shift the location of his millennial expectations to a wider world.[37] This is simply not true. It is Edwards's consistent belief that the millennium should be centered in Israel. In his early narratives, such as "Note of Apocalypse," Edwards addressed the geographical advantage of Israel in comparison with other nations (including America!) and believed that Israel would again be a distinctive nation to spread its spiritual influence to other parts of the world:

> That God did take care of the situation of his people Israel, upon their account, for the advantage of spreading the truth and diffusing the influences of religion, I think is evident from Deuteronomy 32:8–9, and from Acts 17:26–27 and from Habakkuk 3:6. *Now the world has never enjoyed the advantages of this situation as yet. What advantage has it been to America,* that the Mediterranean Sea opens from them to us; or what advantage has Hollandia Nova or Terra Australis Incognita from the Indian Ocean's reaching from them even to this land? Wherefore, *we do believe that the most glorious part of the church will hereafter be there, at the center of the kingdom of Christ, communicating influences to all other parts.*[38]

When the revivals each reached their climax, there was a very short period that Edwards seemed to assume that New England might be "the possible seat of God's new heavens and new earth" at the end of the world.[39] But it turned out to be nothing but "a passing speculation," as Stout correctly observes.[40] Therefore, in contrast to the misinterpretation that he always believed the millennium would start in America, in his mention of America made in 1747, Edwards describes it at length as a nation undergoing a thorough spiritual bankruptcy:

37. Hatch, *Sacred Cause of Liberty*, 32–33. See also "Missional Eschatology," 33.

38. Edwards, "Notes on the Apocalypse," *WJE* 5:134, emphasis added. See also Stein, "Editor's Introduction," *WJE* 5:18–19.

39. Stout, "Preface to the Period," *WJE* 22:38.

40. Ibid.

> And how lamentable is the moral and religious state of these American colonies? Of New England in particular? How much is that kind of religion, that was professed and much experienced and practiced, in the first, and apparently the best times of New England, grown and growing out of credit? What fierce and violent contentions have been of late among ministers and people, about things of a religious nature? How much is the gospel ministry grown into contempt, and the work of the ministry, in many respects, laid under uncommon difficulties, and even in danger of sinking amongst us? How many of our congregations and churches rending in pieces? Church discipline weakened, and ordinances less and less regarded? . . . .[41]

Furthermore, according to Edwards, the interaction between heaven, hell, and earth that extends throughout the history of fallen humankind is frequently "likened to a journey or progress."[42] In the artistic manner of Dante, Bunyan, and Milton, and by applying Ezekiel's vision of the wheels, Edwards displayed a cosmic redemptive-historical scheme. This scheme transcends both time and space, covering pre-historical, historical and post-historical dimensions, "beginning form eternity" and ending at "consummation of all things."[43] And it demonstrates the interaction among "all three worlds, heaven, earth, and hell,"[44] "telling the simultaneous stories of three realms."[45] In his grand structure of this redemption drama, not only is New England too small as the theatre, but also earth itself will not be big enough. Therefore, in Edwards's vision of the millennium, a larger cosmos, including the visible and invisible world, is included.[46] In his *HWR*, Edwards already clearly illustrated this scheme. First, with the arrival of the millennium, the whole earth will be impacted. The "visible kingdom of Satan" will be universally overthrown and "the kingdom of Christ set up on the ruins of it *everywhere, throughout the whole habitable globe*."[47] Secondly, this impact will reach the heavenly realm: "praise shall not fill the earth but also heaven," because the "church on earth and the church in heaven shall both gloriously

---

41. Edwards, "An Humble Attempt," *WJE* 5:358. See also McClymond and McDermott, *Theology of Jonathan Edwards*, 575–76.

42. Stout, "Preface to the Period," *WJE* 22:18–19.

43. Edwards, "To the Trustees of the College of New Jersey," *WJE* 16:728. See also Stout, "Preface to the Period," *WJE* 22:9.

44. Edwards, "To the Trustees of the College of New Jersey," *WJE* 16:728.

45. Stout, "Preface to the Period," *WJE* 22:9.

46. Ibid., 14–23.

47. Edwards, *History of the Work of Redemption, WJE* 9:472–73, emphasis added.

rejoice and praise God as with one heart on that occasion."[48] Thirdly, hell will be influenced. "The prince of hell," Satan, will see the era of the millennium "like Christ's coming to judgment in that it so puts an end to the former state of the world." [49] Satan will be greatly afflicted and threatened by God's wrath and Christ's reign during this dispensation, and will be more feared at the final judgment afterwards: "if Satan . . . trembles at the thought of it thousands of years beforehand, how much more will he tremble as proud and as stubborn as he is when he comes to stand at Christ's bar."[50] Here Edwards significantly departed from his Puritan predecessors, including Samuel Willard and John Winthrop (1588–1649), who fixed their eyes on New England, believing their eschatological vision could be realized in this nation and hoping to establish it as the example to the rest of world.[51]

In short, Edwards closely followed the Scriptures and noticed both the geographical and theological significance of Israel in divine redemptive history. We can see clearly that his millennial expectation is Canaan-centric rather than Americo-centric. Moreover, his theological vision is multi-angled, viewing the arrival of millennium in the light of heaven, earth, and hell. In this sense, contrary to what is declared by some commentators, Edwards's conception of the millennium is more biblical and comprehensive than most of his contemporaries.

## Edwards Speaks to Contemporary Chinese Millennial Movements

What contribution can Edwards's cosmic redemptive-historical vision make to Chinese Christian eschatology? What benefit does Edwards's millennial consciousness provide for contemporary Chinese millennial movements? There are at least two points to be addressed.

First and foremost, Edwards's rejection of an imminent millennium directly challenges claims made by contemporary Chinese millennial movements. The tendency of transplanting certain elements of indigenous Chinese millennial traditions into Christian belief is not limited to the heterodox movements that include the Taiping Rebellion and Eastern Lighting. Interestingly enough, while many Chinese Christians *do* think Christianity is not ultimately compatible with Daoism, Buddhism, or Chinese folk religion,

48. Ibid., 477.
49. Ibid., 478.
50. Ibid., 500.
51. For Winthrop's and other Puritans' millennial expectations on New England, see Beeke and Jones, *Puritan Theology*, 771–840.

they still incorporate various Chinese cultural elements, by design or by accident, into their Christian belief.[52] The intention may be to render Christianity more acceptable to Chinese people. Nevertheless, it undermines or even distorts Christian doctrine at the same time. For instance, Watchman Nee (*Ni Tuosheng*, 1903–72), the founder and leader of Christian Assembly (*Xiaoqun*, also called the Little Flock), held an imminent millenarian vision. As a dispensational pre-millennialist, Nee's teaching indicates that Jesus Christ would soon return and inaugurate a millennial reign. But he stressed that only the "Overcomer" Christians would be secretly raptured and then return to reign with Christ in the millennial kingdom.[53] Nee's imminent millennial kingdom was highly attractive to many Chinese Christians living in the turbulent period between the 1930s and 1940s. However, his key phrase—"today's spiritual condition determines the reign in the future"— may imply that God's redemptive work can be achieved by a Christian's good works, though he did not believe salvation is meritorious.[54]

This saying may also be misinterpreted and thus introduce the merit doctrine often found in Buddhism and Chinese folk legends into a Christian eschatological hope.[55] Even now, overemphasis on a Christian's good deeds is commonly accepted among Chinese Christians and advocated by many influential church leaders. Nevertheless, Nee was not Pelagian, though his soteriology was greatly informed by Keswick thinkers. His view, at least in relation to sanctification, is more like the synergism found in Eastern Orthodox theology, believing "salvation is complete when the will of a person is united with the will of God."[56] Again, this will be easily misunderstood as synergistic soteriology similar to what is found in Chinese religions and philosophies, i.e., "Heaven and Human in Unity/Harmony" (*Tian Ren Heyi*). As a result, in order to become *qualified* to reign with Christ in the millennium, Chinese Christians might be encouraged to become a self-made righteous man (*Shuling Junzi*), a profound man and super-sanctified Christian, through mystical union with God.[57]

---

52. Lin Yutang may be an exceptional example that finds many similarities between Christianity and Daoism. As a result, he affirms that Chinese should be aware of both Chinese philosophy and Chinese folk legends. See He, "Dialogue between Christianity and Taoism," 132–36.

53. Lian. *Redeemed by Fire*, 163–70. See also Cliff, "Life and Theology of Watchman Nee," 264, 271.

54. Chow, *Theosis*, 52–53.

55. Cliff, "Life and Theology of Watchman Nee," 263.

56. Chow, *Theosis*, 54.

57. Ibid.

In this case, Chinese Christians, by closely examining Edwards's perspective on the millennium, may prevent the transplantation of either Pelagianism or synergism into Christian faith. Edwards's rejection of the view of an imminent millennium popular among some of his Puritan colleagues, and more importantly his consistent quest for biblical truth, may serve as a good reminder for contemporary Chinese Christians to draw their final conclusions regarding the millennium from Scripture rather than culture. One may rightly argue that Edwards's interpretation of apocalyptic texts was far from perfect and that Edwards often took historical events into consideration to predict the advent of the millennium. Nevertheless, unlike many leaders of Chinese millennial movements, Edwards did not allow his cultural context to blind his reading of biblical revelation. Instead, he continued to realign his eschatological view with the Scriptures and proclaimed a more biblical vision of the millennium. Chinese Christians, when attempting to include Chinese cultural traditions in their Christian faith, either to secure their national and ethnic identities or to make Christianity more desirable to their Chinese fellows, should be aware of the danger of subverting Christian doctrines and thus turning Christianity into another religion altogether.

Furthermore, Edwards's rejection of an America-centric millennium directly challenges the claims of Sinocentric millennial movements. As with the Taiping Rebellion and Eastern Lighting, Chinese people traditionally and habitually tend to take China as the center of the world. In Chinese millenarian traditions, China is frequently regarded as the ideal location of a millennial kingdom. If not, at least it acts as the most essential factor in the realization of this kingdom. This "Sinocentric syndrome" may be found even in many Chinese missionary movements. The Back to Jerusalem Movement (BTJM) is a clear example. While it is a thrilling indigenous Christian missionary movement orchestrated predominantly by Chinese church networks, and may open a new page in the history of missiology, it is endangered by this Sinocentric syndrome. As Timothy Tennent observes, the BTJM believes that it is the Chinese churches' destiny to take the last step of the global missionary circuit in order to bring the gospel back to Jerusalem.[58] It seems that Tennent agrees with this claim and takes the BTJM as a suitable example in which to explore the relationship between eschatology and missions from four aspects of Edwards's

---

58. Tennent, *Theology in the Context of World Christianity*, 222–23. To the best of my knowledge, Tennent is the only one who examines the BTJM in the light of Edwards's millennial consciousness. See the ninth chapter of his book: "Eschatology: Jonathan Edwards and Chinese Back to Jerusalem Movement," 221–48. See also Hattaway, *Back to Jerusalem*, 4; Hattaway, *Heavenly Man*, 284.

millennial awareness: the pre-millennial advance of gospel, the eschatological conversion of Muslims and Jews, the possible massive persecution in the latter days, and the effectiveness of prayer.[59] While Tennent's exploration is both innovative and insightful, he failed to points out that the BTJM's Sinocentric belief does not have any reliable biblical references. No matter how much the Chinese may impact this world, there is no convincing evidence in Scripture that China is specifically chosen by God to complete the Great Commission before Christ's second return. In fact, beneath this claim there is nothing but "a salvation-historical self-understanding of China as God's appointed means for ushering in the millennium," as James Park rightly argues.[60] This Sinocentric self-understanding easily leads to ethnocentrism and territorialism.[61]

Therefore, both Tennent and the BTJM need to reflect on something more important in Edwards's eschatology. Particularly, Edwards was keenly aware of the unique position of Israel in God's millennial framework, informed by his extensive and complex cosmic redemptive-historical vision. The BTJM and Chinese Christians must agree with Edwards that the whole universe is the stage of God's redemptive work. God is the only one who is unfolding his grand design of redemption. In this sense, no nation can claim a special status or central force in the realization of *God's* millennial kingdom. If the BTJM is willing to take Edwards's cosmic redemptive-historical scheme and his Christocentric eschatology as remedy to its Sinocentric syndrome, it may yet be able to avoid the mistake repeatedly made by various millenarian groups in Chinese history, that is, realizing the "China Dream" in the name of Christian millennial movements.

## Conclusion

By situating Edwards in his historical context and taking his overall theological framework into consideration, we have found that Edwards held an optimistic chiliastic view that can be identified as a postmillennial position in the modern sense. While he assumed that the arrival of the millennium would be around the year 2000, his standpoint was still more conservative and biblical than most of his Puritan predecessors and contemporaries. Contrary to what has been claimed in some misinterpretations of Edwards that have been widely accepted, he did not expect either the imminent millennium or an Americo-centric one. Various elements of his time, including

---

59. Tennent, *Theology in the Context of World Christianity*, 221–48.
60. Park, "Chosen to Fulfill," 164.
61. Ibid., 171.

his own pastoral experience and his interaction with theological and intellectual debates, contributed to the formulation of his postmillennialism.

As a theologian who sought to deflate some of the excesses of immanent millennial thinking and expectations in the seventeenth and eighteenth centuries, Edwards's interpretation of the millennium will provide a corrective reading to a Chinese anticipation of a Sinocentric and human-inaugurated millennial kingdom that is deeply rooted in Buddhism, Daoism, and Chinese folk religion. In addition, it can also be of great help in avoiding ethnocentrism, territorialism, and the overt optimism found in contemporary Chinese millennial movements informed by dispensational theology and the eschatologies of the Little Flock churches and the Back to Jerusalem Movement.

## Bibliography

Beeke, Joel R. and Mark Jones. *A Puritan Theology: Doctrine for Life*. Grand Rapids, MI: Reformation Heritage Books, 2012.

Cao, Tian Yu et al., eds. *Culture and Social Transformations in Reform Era China*. Boston: Brill, 2010.

Chow, Alexander. *Theosis, Sino-Christian Theology and the Second Chinese Enlightenment: Heaven and Humanity in Unity*. New York: Palgrave Macmillan, 2013.

Cliff, Norman Howard. "The Life and Theology of Watchman Nee, Including a Study of the Little Flock Movement Which He founded." MA. Phil. Diss., Open University, 1983.

Edwards, Jonathan. *A History of the Work of Redemption*. The Works of Jonathan Edwards 9. New Haven: Yale University Press, 1989.

———. "An Humble Attempt to Promote Explicit Agreement and Visible Union of God's People in Extraordinary Prayer for the Revival of Religion and the Advancement of Christ's Kingdom on Earth, Pursuant to Scripture-Promises and Prophecies Concerning the Last Time." In *Apocalyptic Writings*, edited by Stephen J. Stein, The Works of Jonathan Edwards 5:307–436. New Haven: Yale University Press, 1977.

———. "'Misc.' 827." In *The "Miscellanies" (Entry Nos. 501–832)*, edited by Ava Chamberlain, The Works of Jonathan Edwards 18:537–38. New Haven: Yale University Press, 2000.

———. "'Notes on the Apocalypse.'" In *Apocalyptic Writings*, edited by Stephen J. Stein, The Works of Jonathan Edwards 5:95–305. New Haven: Yale University Press, 1977.

———. "To the Trustees of the College of New Jersey, October 19, 1757." In *Letters and Personal Writings*, edited by George S. Claghorn, The Works of Jonathan Edwards 16:725–30. New Haven: Yale University Press, 1998.

———. "To William McCulloch." In *The Great Awakening*, edited by Clarence C. Goen, The Works of Jonathan Edwards 4:558–60. New Haven: Yale University Press, 1972.

Gernet, Jacques. *China and the Christian Impact: A Conflict of Cultures*. Cambridge: Cambridge University Press, 1985.
Goen, Clarence Curtis. "Editor's Introduction." In *The Great Awakening*, edited by Clarence C. Goen. The Works of Jonathan Edwards 4:1–95. New Haven: Yale University Press, 1972.
———. "Jonathan Edwards: A New Departure in Eschatology." *Church History* 28 (1959) 25–40.
Hatch, Nathan O. *Sacred Cause of Liberty: Republican thought and the Millennium in revolutionary New England*. New Haven: Yale University Press, 1977.
Hattaway, Paul. *Back to Jerusalem: Three Chinese House Church Leaders Share Their Vision to Complete the Great Commission*. Downers Grove, IL: InterVarsity, 2003.
Hattaway. *The Heavenly Man: The Remarkable True Story of Chinese Christian Brother Yun*. London: Monarch Books, 2011.
He, Jianming. "Dialogue between Christianity and Taoism." In *Christianity and Chinese Culture*, edited by Paulos Huang Miikka Ruokanen, 124–44. Cambridge: Eerdmans, 2010.
Hewitson, James. "'As ordered and governed by divine providence': Jonathan Edwards' use of the Machine as Master Metaphor." *Interdisciplinary Humanities* 24 (2007) 6–20.
Holdsworth, Christopher B. "The Eschatology of Jonathan Edwards." *Reformation and Revival* 5/3 (1996) 118–47.
Lian, Xi. *Redeemed by Fire: The Rise of Popular Christianity in Modern China*. New Haven: Yale University Press, 2010.
Lowe, Scott. "Chinese Millennial Movements." In *The Oxford Handbook of Millennialism. [Electronic Resource]*, edited by Catherine Wessinger, 307–65: Oxford: Oxford University Press, 2011.
McClymond, Michael J. and Gerald R. McDermott. *The Theology of Jonathan Edwards*. New York: Oxford University Press, 2012.
McDermott, Gerald R. *One Holy and Happy Society: The Public Theology of Jonathan Edwards*. University Park, PA: Pennsylvania State University Press, 1992.
Miller, Perry. *Jonathan Edwards*. New York: William Sloane Associates, Inc., 1949.
Orchard, Stephen. "Evangelical Eschatology and the Missionary Awakening." *Journal of Religious History* 22 (1998) 132–51.
Park, James Sung-Hwan. "Chosen to Fulfill the Great Commission? Biblical and Theological Reflections on the Back to Jerusalem Vision of Chinese Churches." *Missiology: An International Review* 43/2 (2015) 163–74.
Reule, Tracy Dean. *The Changing Character of New England Puritan Eschatology: 1682-1758*. PhD diss., The Florida State University, 1994.
Rogers, Mark C. "A Missional Eschatology: Jonathan Edwards, Future Prophecy, and the Spread of the Gospel." *Fides et historia* 41 (2009) 23–46.
Spence, Jonathan D. *The Taiping Vision of a Christian China, 1836-1864*. Edited by University Baylor. Waco: Markham Press Fund, Baylor University Press, 1998.
Stein, Stephen J. "Editor's Introduction." In *Apocalyptic Writings*, edited by Stephen J. Stein, The Works of Jonathan Edwards 5:1–93. New Haven: Yale University Press, 1977.
Stout, Harry S. "Preface to the Period." In *Sermons and Discourses, 1739-1742*, edited by Harry S. Stout et al., The Works of Jonathan Edwards 22:3–47. New Haven: Yale University Press, 2003.

Tennent, Timothy C. *Theology in the Context of World Christianity: How the Global Church Is Influencing the Way We Think About and Discuss Theology.* Grand Rapids: Zondervan, 2007.

Weller, Robert P. *Resistance, Chaos, and Control in China: Taiping Rebels, Taiwanese Ghosts, and Tiananmen.* Seattle: University of Washington Press, 1994.

Wilson, John F. "Editor's Introduction." In *A History of the Work of Redemption*, Edited by John F. Wilson, The Works of Jonathan Edwards 9:1–109. New Haven: Yale University Press, 1989.

———. "History, Redemption, and the Millennium." In *Jonathan Edwards and the American Experience,* edited by Nathan O. Hatch and Harry S. Stout, 131–41. New York, Oxford: Oxford University Press, 1988.

Withrow, Brandon G. "A Future of Hope: Jonathan Edwards and Millennial Expectations." *Trinity Journal* 22 (2001) 75–98.

Zakai, Avihu. *Jonathan Edwards's Philosophy of History: The Reenchantment of the World in the Age of Enlightenment.* Princeton: Princeton University Press, 2003.

# 4

## The Reception of Edwards's *A History of the Work of Redemption* in Nineteenth-century Basutoland

ADRIAAN C. NEELE

"VOYEZ LE PRÉSIDENT EDWARDS: Nous le suivons presque entièrement dans cette recherché." Thus wrote French missionary to Basutoland, Adolphe Mabille (1836–94), in his *Dogmatique*—a recently discovered manuscript in the Morija Archives, Lesotho.[1] The reference to Jonathan Edwards in a systematic theology by a missionary of the Société des Missions Evangéliques chez les peuples non-chrétiens á Paris (Paris Evangelical Missionary Society, and hereafter PEMS) is puzzling, but offers also an intriguing prospect.

The appraisal of Edwards in relation to missiology has gained increasing interest since the late 1980s.[2] This interest, however, has largely concentrated on the American and British world,[3] and on English-speaking missionaries and missionary societies, such as the London Missionary Society (LMS) and Baptist Missionary Society,[4] giving primary attention

---

1. Mabille, *Dogmatique*, 147: "See president Edwards: [Who] we [will] follow almost entirely in this study."

2. Minkema, "Edwards in the Twentieth Century," 661, 662, 665, 666.

3. Rooy, *Theology of Missions*; Marsden, "Edwards, the Missionary"; Berg, *Constrained by Jesus' Love*, 83, 91–93; Manor, "Britain's Age of Empire," 38–54; Davies, *Edwards and His Influence*.

4. See for the Baptist missionary movement, for example, Payne, *Prayer Call*, 4–11.

to Edwards's *Humble Attempt* and *The Life of David Brainerd*.[5] There is negligible attention to the reception of Edwards's *A History of the Work of Redemption* (hereafter, *HWR*), however, in the history of missions in general, and the reception of Edwards's works in the history of French missionary movement of the nineteenth-century in particular.[6] Mabille's reference to Edwards, then, not only necessitates a reassessment of Edwards's reception in the history of mission, but may also contribute to a more comprehensive understanding of the appropriation and transmission of Edwards's thought in mission history.

Mabille's work in Basutoland, nowadays Lesotho, illustrates the use of Edwards's work in an education and mission context. In regard to the former, the reference to Edwards in Mabille's systematic theology contributed to writing a catechism in the Sesotho language modeled after Edwards's work. As to the latter, Mabille's training and teaching contributed to the transmission of Edwards's thought in a mission context.

## Edwards's *HWR* and Nineteenth-Century Missions

Edwards's discourse on redemptive history was preached as a series of thirty sermons at Northampton between March and August 1739.[7] This sermon series was a part of Edwards's strenuous remedial effort to address the spiritual backsliding of the congregation following the Connecticut Valley awakening of 1734–35. This awakening was not only a defining but also a disruptive moment in Edwards's theological reflections. The revival resulted in the carefully constructed narrative, *A Faithful Narrative of the Surprising Work of God*, published in London in 1736 and in Boston a year later. Although the publication propelled the preacher on the outskirts of the New World into a transatlantic world of revival-minded evangelicals, however, the reputation of the Northampton congregation declined in its pastor's eyes.[8]

---

5. See Edwards, *United Prayer* and *United and Extraordinary Prayer*. For *The Life of David Brainerd*, see Johnson and Lesser, *Printed Writings*, 68–89. The Methodist missionaries were instrumental for the distribution of several editions of *An Extract of the Life of the Late Rev. Mr. David Brainerd by John Wesley, M. A.*

6. Exceptions are Davies, "'Prepare Ye'"; Edwards, *History of the Work of Redemption*, 27; Bebbington, "Remembered Around the World," 186; Piggin, "Expanding Knowledge of God," 279.

7. For the historical setting and composition of the sermons see, Edwards, *A History of the Work of Redemption*, edited by Wilson.

8. Edwards, "A City on a Hill," *WJE* 19:547–48. On the Connecticut Valley awakening, see Goen, "Editor's Introduction," *WJE* 4:19–25.

The Redemption Discourse and other theological reflections on revival, on the other hand, defined Edwards's ministry in the years to come.[9] It resulted in his abandonment of the idea of writing "A Rational Account of the Main Doctrines of the Christian Religion Attempted," an outline of systematic theology that would include topics such as:

> The being and nature of God; Of created minds, free will, etc.; Of excellency; Trinity, and God's attributes; God's decrees; necessity, contingency, etc.; Creation: the ends of it; Things made in analogy to spiritual things; Treat the fall of the angels after the fall of man; Faith, or a right believing divine truths; Faith in Christ; Free grace, [and] Justification.[10]

The thought of writing a system of theology, however, never left him,[11] and resurfaced roughly twenty years later in his letter to the Board of Trustees of the College of New Jersey:

> I have had on my mind and heart (which I long ago began, not with any view to publication) a great work, which I call *A History of the Work of Redemption*, a body of divinity in an entire new method, being thrown into the form of an history, considering the affair of Christian theology.[12]

Writing from Stockbridge on October 19, 1757, as a missionary to the Housatonnuck Indians, Edwards envisioned an "entire" new method of writing Christian theology: a "body of divinity," in "the form of an history." For Edwards, redemptive history was interwoven with the "parts of divinity."[13] This promising *summa theologica* or "body of divinity" was to have been grounded on the Redemption Discourse of 1739. This is also how Jonathan Edwards Jr. (1745–1801) and John Erskine (1721–1803), its first editors, understood and entitled the discourse in the posthumous publication of 1774, *A History Of the Work of Redemption containing the Outlines*

---

9. Following the publication *A Faithful Narrative*, Edwards continued to reflect on revival in sermons, such as "On the Parable of Wise and Foolish Virgins," as well as *The Distinguishing Marks of a Work of the Spirit of God*; *Some Thoughts concerning the Present Revival of Religion in New-England*; and *A Treatise concerning Religious Affections*.

10. Edwards, "Outline of a "Rational Account,"" *WJE* 6:396–99.

11. See for example, a sermon on Hebrews 5:12 (1739), in which he defined the prolegomena and practice of theology, and *"Misc."* no. 832, which may have been written in 1740, is entitled "Preface to the Rational Account." Chamberlain, "Editor's Introduction," *WJE* 18:24–29; Edwards, "'Misc.' 832," *WJE* 18:546–47.

12. Edwards, "To the Trustees of the College of New Jersey," *WJE* 16:727.

13. Ibid., 728.

of a Body of Divinity, in a Method entirely new. Finding its way to the Dutch Republic via Erskine's network of enlightened evangelicals, the treatise was translated into Dutch in 1776 and published at Utrecht.[14] The Edinburgh and Boston publication and the Dutch translation of the *HWR* were followed by many other reprints and translations.[15]

It is important to note that nineteenth-century evangelical and mission-minded organizations were major disseminators of Edwards's *HWR*. The British-based *Religious Tract Society* (1799), for example, reprinted the *HWR* with the title *History of the work of redemption, comprising a summary of the history of the Jews up to the destruction of Jerusalem* in 1831, 1835, 1837, 1838, and several times in 1841.[16] The publication by the *Religious Tract Society* enjoyed a positive reception, though the review in *The Imperial Magazine* was more tempered:

> But when he [Edwards] enters on "the completion of the work of redemption" in a future state, the ground on which he stands appears less secure. Entering a region that is veiled by the clouds and shadows of futurity, the light by which he is guided becomes, on many subordinate particulars, somewhat dim and indistinct.[17]

The organizers of this tract society belonged to the same group of evangelicals who founded the LMS in 1795. The latter provided book allowances to their overseas missionaries, such as the catechist George Gogerly. Gogerly established a library with ten books in India, three of which were works by Edwards, the *HWR* among them.[18] Furthermore, the *American Tract Society* (1825) published and distributed between the years 1838 and 1875 over sixty thousand copies of the *HWR*,[19] and the society supported missionary printing houses such as the American Mission Press at Beirut, Syria, which published in 1868 the Arabic language version of the *HWR*.[20] The Dutch edition, moreover, reflected the growing mission consciousness in the Dutch

---

14. On John Erskine, see, Yeager, *Enlightened Evangelicalism*. Edwards, *Geschiedenis van het Werk der Verlossing*.

15. See Johnson and Lesser, *Printed Writings*, 126–40.

16. Ibid., 134–35.

17. Drew, *Imperial Magazine*, 191. See also Fyfe, "Industrialised Conversion," 16–79.

18. Stuart Piggin, "The Expanding Knowledge of God," 279.

19. The American Tract Society was rooted in the New York Tract Society (1812), the New England Tract Society (1814) and the London-based Religious Tract Society.

20. See for example, Freidinger, "Centennial," 163–66; Antakly, "American Protestant Educational Missions"; Malikck, *American Mission Press*, 11.

Republic that contributed to the founding of the *Nederlands Zendingsgenootschap* (1797). One of the co-founders, Cornelis Brem, was a translator of many works of "evangelical revival," including some by Edwards.[21] The Welsh edition (1829, 1830), to illustrate another example, can be situated within the rise of the Calvinist Methodist movement, contributing to the founding of the LMS, as well as the Baptist mission movement. Finally, the American Board of Commissioners for Foreign Missions (1810) contributed to the Arabic edition. In summary, the reception of the *HWR*, and in particular the translations of the *HWR*, were intimately connected to the rise of the worldwide Protestant evangelical mission movement of the early nineteenth century. And so, in a similar way the French edition of the *HWR* finds itself in the context of *Le Réveil* movement and the PEMS.

The sermon series preached during the post Connecticut Valley awakening was intended to bring the Northampton church back in doctrine and life to the times of revival. Edwards envisioned the entire Redemption Discourse becoming part of a much larger project—a systematic theology in the form of a history—and his later editors promoted the printed publication as such. In spite of—or thanks to—them, the worldwide reception of the work and its translations was primarily in the context of missions, but not as a work of systematic theology. Mabille's reference to Edwards in his *Dogmatique* in a French missionary context, however, changed that.

## Edwards's *HWR* and Nineteenth-Century French Missions

The outlook of nineteenth-century Protestant French evangelicals regarding the advancement of mission work and religious literature resonated with and resembled that of their English-speaking counterparts.[22] However, and particular to France, the Napoleonic Concordat of 1801—guaranteeing religious freedom, in particular with respect to the Protestants—together with *Le Réveil* may have been a greater stimulus to the rise of the Protestant church, the foundings of a theological faculty at Montauban, a Protestant mission

---

21. Boone, "Zending en gereformeerd," 34.

22. Stephen J. Gill observes, "the story of the French Evangelical missionaries and their work in Lesotho can be told from a number of different perspectives. For example, one can portray the evolution of the church in Europe, how a spiritual re-awakening swept through these church at the beginning of the 19th century, strengthening their awareness of the need to make disciples at home and in all nations . . . Alternatively, one can focus on how Moshoeshoe the Great, after creating a fledging nation . . . sought 'teachers of peace' in order to strengthen himself." In Gill, *Mekolokotoane Kerekeng*, 45.

society, and a religious book enterprise in France.[23] The intellectual endeavors of French evangelicals at the time are mirrored in the library catalogue of the Protestant faculty of Montauban.[24] The majority of this library consisted of works pertaining to biblical exegesis,[25] church history, patristics, medieval and early modern theology, and homiletics, and included works of Augustine, the Roman Catholic polemicist Robert Bellarmine (1542–1621), and the covenant-history theologian Johannes Cocceius (1603–69). Furthermore, the library catalogue lists the *Institutio Theologiae Elencticae* of Francis Turretin (1623–87) and *Theologia Christiana* of Bénédict Pictet (1655–1724), whose works show the architecture of Post-reformation Reformed intellectual thought that included six *loci* of theology: theology proper (doctrine of God), anthropology, Christology, soteriology, ecclesiology, and eschatology. Last but not least, the library contained the works of Edwards, Samuel Hopkins (1721–1803), and Samuel Mather (1706–85) of New England. This eclectic theological landscape, as well as the establishment of the missionary and book publishing societies, is related in particular to the reception of Edwards's thought in Basutoland.

Proponents of *Le Réveil* in France founded the PEMS in 1822 with the assistance of the LMS. Missionaries for the PEMS were trained at the Mission house at Paris, similar to the LMS, which trained their own missionaries.[26] As such, the Mission house was instrumental in the formation of many French missionaries throughout the nineteenth century. After a stumbling start, the Mission house was re-opened on November 1, 1856 and directed by the former missionary to Basutoland, Eugène Casalis (1812–91). Among the first five students was Adolphe Mabille (1836–94), who was educated in classical studies at the Paedagogium at Bâle, Switzerland. Having studied biblical Hebrew and Greek under Samuel Thomas (d. 1867), the former principal of the Vaudois missionary school, Mabille had left for The Hague in 1854—a center for the Réveil movement in Holland—traveled to and taught in England, and was admitted to the PEMS Mission House in 1856.

---

23. The movement was rooted in the Society of Friends (*Société des Amis*, 1810) at Geneva, led by César Malan (1787–1864). The *Société* strongly influenced by Robert Haldane (1764–1842), an exponent of the Scottish awakenings of the 1790s prompted in part when John Erskine (1720–1803) re-published in 1784 Edwards's *Humble Attempt to Promote Explicit Agreement and Visible Union of God's People in Extraordinary Prayer for the Revival of Religion and the Advancement of Christ's Kingdom* (1747) to promote revival prayer. Haldane, then, was familiar with Edwards, as attested in his published lectures at the *Société*.

24. Bolliger et al., *Histoire et richesses*, 15.

25. *Bibliothèque universitaire*, 13–87. Bolliger et al., *Histoire et richesses*, 77.

26. Parker, *Dissenting Academies*.

A comprehensive approach to theological studies was followed through classical studies, biblical exegesis, dogmatics ("dogmatique"), and church history relevant for the mission field, as reported by the director, reminding the board members of the work of other missionaries such as Edwards.[27] Mabille occasionally substituted for Casalis, lecturing in systematic theology during his stay at the Mission house until April 1859, before leaving that same year for Basutoland. Edwards's exposition of the redemptive drama through history with attention to France and Africa might have been appealing to the students at the PEMS Mission House.[28] Edwards showed deep acquaintance with the history of the church in France, attesting that

> the Protestant church of France was great part of the glory of the Reformation. But now it is far otherwise; this church is all broken to pieces and scattered,[29] . . . in some respects perhaps more than any other, has been a scene of dreadful cruelties suffered by the Protestants there.[30]

Edwards also added encouragingly, "the church will be revived"—something that the Protestants in France, and those attending the PEMS Mission House in particular, may have understood for their own time, as attested by the expansion of the Protestant enterprise of church, mission society, theological education, and printing of religious books. In addition, Edwards's work on redemption history, and in particular addressing missionary and mission endeavors, might have been inspiring as well. He demonstrated clearly a global interest in the propagation of the gospel, turning his attention to China, the East Indies, and South America. However, he expected the most from Africa, declaring that it would not only,

> be enlightened with glorious light, and delivered from all their darkness, and shall become a civil, Christian and an understanding and holy people,[31]

---

27. *Société des missions*, Mf. No. 32, April 23, 1857. The reference to Edwards may also refer to the Wesleyan missionary John Edwards (1804–87).

28. Edwards, *History of the Work of Redemption*, WJE 9:428, 472, 480. See Edwards, *Histoire de l'oeuvre de la Rédemption*, chapitre V, De la Réformation à nos jours, 343; chapitre VII, Du temps présent à la chute d'antéchrist, 387–88; chapitre VIII, Succès de la rédemption, 396.

29. Edwards, *History of the Work of Redemption*, WJE 9:437; *Histoire de l'oeuvre de la Rédemption*, chapitre V, De la Réformation à nos jours, 351.

30. Edwards, *History of the Work of Redemption*, WJE 9:428; *Histoire de l'oeuvre de la Rédemption*, chapitre V, De la Réformation à nos jours, 343.

31. Edwards, *History of the Work of Redemption*, WJE 9:472; *Histoire de l'oeuvre de la Rédemption*, chapitre VII, Du temps présent à la chute d'antéchrist, 387–88.

in that order, but also,

> shall be full of light and knowledge. Great knowledge shall prevail everywhere. It may be hoped that then many of [them] will be divines, and that excellent books will be published in Africa—and not only very learned men, but others that are more ordinary men, shall then be very knowing in religion.[32]

Finally, Mabille's preaching, teaching, translating, printing, and publishing at Morija was in essence an exceptional and exemplary working out of Edwards's vision as expounded in the *HWR*, laying out a holistic vision for missionary work, in which the gospel proclamation coincided with "set[ing] up schools among them, and a printing press to print Bibles and other books for their instruction in their own language."[33] Many of Mabille's printed and published works have been carefully preserved at the Morija Archives, Lesotho, among them the recently discovered manuscript containing the outlines of systematic theology.

The founders of the missionary society, furthermore, became involved in establishing in 1836 the *Société des Livres Religieux* for the distribution of religious publications. Works of Baxter, Bunyan, Calvin, Ryle, and Spurgeon were translated into French, published and distributed.[34] As such, the *Société* was solely responsible for the *HWR*'s French translation of 1858, *Histoire de l'oeuvre de la Redemption,* and its distribution in the French-speaking world. The French translation accords with the English edition of 1774—an edition reprinted for and by the English missionary and tract societies—but differs in a shortened title, the absence of the preface by Jonathan Edwards Jr., and omission of introductions, opening and transition paragraphs, and other passages.[35] The main distribution centers for the *Histoire de l'oeuvre*

---

32. Edwards, *History of the Work of Redemption,* WJE 9:480; *Histoire de l'oeuvre de la Rédemption,* chapitre VIII, Succès de la rédemption, 396.

33. Edwards, *History of the Work of Redemption,* WJE 9:435; *Histoire de l'oeuvre de la Rédemption,* chapitre V, De la Réformation à nos jours, 349.

34. *Catalogue général de la Société des livres religieux de Toulouse* (1878).

35. Omitted in Edwards, *Histoire de l'oeuvre de la Rédemption* but present in Edwards, *A history of the work of redemption* (1774), 1–15 (General Introduction); 16, "My first talk . . . were preparatory to it;" 37, "I proceed now . . . redemption for his people;" 46, "I proceed now to show . . . extending to Moses;" 61, "I proceed to the fourth period . . . this also;" 88, "I come now to the fifth period . . . through this period also;" 94, "We have no certain account of the time . . . by an induction of particulars;" 114, "I have taken notice . . . reign of Solomon;" 122, "I come now to the last period . . . through this period;" 130, "Thus I have taken notice . . . on in particulars;" 171, "First, I would consider . . . for us;" 194, "The third distribution . . . in them;" 218–19, "Not but that there . . . before him;" 244, "In showing how the success . . . church tribulation

*de la Redemption* were found in Brussels, Geneva, London, Lyon, Paris, and Toulouse.[36] Even more, the work was distributed in Paris at three locations, including the library at Place d' Oratoire belonging to Mr. J. Cherbuliez , a member of the congregation of Frédéric Monod (1794–1863) and secretary of the PEMS;[37] and in London by Partridge and Oakey, at 34 Paternoster Row, next to the main distribution depot of the Religious Tract Society.[38]

Edwards's works, moreover, were not unfamiliar in early nineteenth-century France.[39] The preface of the 1823 French translation of *Humble Attempt* (*L'union dans la prière pour la propagation de l'Evangile: abrégé d'un humble essai*) contains an introduction to Edwards's writings and demonstrates a historical awareness of the Scottish revival of the 1880s, so influential to the rise of mission work and missionary societies. The preface also stated:

> Thus the plan of union in prayer, so strongly recommended by President Edwards is pretty much adopted by the Christian world. But there are probably too many reasons to awaken among the faithful zeal for this important duty of prayer, and, to this end, the editor choosing the most essential parts of the Essay of Edwards, the reduced to one dimension, it would hope, will reach a greater number of readers. Happy if these pages could engage millions of Christians in France to unite to present to God fervent prayers for the propagation of the Gospel and mission success![40]

If this publication aimed at the promotion of revival, another translation of Edwards's work in 1838, *The Life of David Brainerd* (*Quelques réflexions sur la vie du missionnaire Brainerd*)—cited by Mabille in a letter to his

---

and travail end;" 255, "To show how . . . Christ's coming to judgment;" 265, "Inference. From what has been said . . . several ways;" 269, " . . . and the destruction of Satan's visible kingdom on earth . . . ;" 283, "Thus having gone through . . . .to the destruction of Antichrist, I come now;" 298, "Thus I have mentioned . . . in the world," and 315, "It has already been shown . . . to the present time."

36. Edwards, *Histoire de l'oeuvre de la Rédemption*, back page.

37. *Société des missions évangéliques de Paris*, Ms 94, H–2107 / 43, Mf. No. 26.

38. The distributors in Genève, London and Toulouse are also the disseminators of other evangelical literature.

39. Edwards, *Histoire de l'oeuvre de la Rédemption* 1854. Other nineteenth century works published in the French language include *L'union dans la prière pour la propagation de l'Evangile: abrégé d'un humble essai*, and *Quelques réflexions sur la vie du missionnaire Brainerd*.

40. Edwards, *L'union dans la prière*, v–vi.

wife Adèle Casalis (1840-1923)[41]—was meant to inspire missionary work. With the reading of Brainerd's life, according to the preface, "the church could get a lot of instruction and edification . . . of one of the first Protestant missionaries."[42] Moreover, Edwards's works, such as the *Doctrine of Original Sin Defended*, was cited in *Evangelical Magazine* (*Magasin évangélique*), and *Freedom of the Will* was familiar to Roman Catholics such as Abbé Grégoire (1750-1831).[43] According to French biographer L. G. Michaud, William Gordon (1729-1807) translated an abridged version of Edwards's *A Treatise concerning Religious Affections* into French together with "some sermons, and two pamphlets."[44]

The French familiarity with these writings, then, resulted for some in "the celebrated Edwards,"[45] while for others, such as the French historian L. M. Chaudon, Edwards was a "Savvy metaphysician but a rigid Calvinist."[46] In sum, the French edition of Edwards's *HWR* is closely connected to the rise of the Protestant French missionary movement of the nineteenth century, whereby the founding of the missionary and religious book societies played an indispensible role. The reception of Edwards's thought in Mabille's *Dogmatique*, therefore, is remarkable, and warrants further investigation.

## Mabille's *Dogmatique*: Structure, Content, and Sources

Mabille's *Dogmatique* is a quarto-sized manuscript notebook of 592 pages, in which the author consistently places the pagination in the right top corner of each page. The document also contains the word "dogmatique" accompanied by a number placed on the right and bottom of some pages. The opening chapter commences with page one but is identified as "dogmatique 52," and concludes with "dogmatique 88" on page 577. Each of

41. "As Brainerd says somewhere, *we shall never think it enough to live at the rate of ordinary Christians*." (Smith, *Mabilles of Basutoland*, 83). See Edwards: "don't think it enough to live at the rate of common Christians!" Edwards, *Life of Brainerd*, WJE 7:495.

42. " . . . convaincu que nous sommes que l'Eglise pourrait retirer beaucoup d'instruction et d'édification de la lecture d'une vie aussi fidèle et bien remplie . . . l'on peut certainement l'appeler le premier des missionaires protestants." Edwards, *Quelques réflexions sur la vie du missionnaire Brainerd*, 4.

43. *Magasin évangélique*, 285; Grégoire, *Histoire des sectes religieuses*, 237.

44. Michaud and Michaud, *Biographie universelle*,133

45. Edwards, *Quelques réflexions sur la vie du missionnaire Brainerd*, 4.

46. Chaudon et al., *Dictionnaire universel*, VI:172: "Savant métaphysicien, mais rigide calviniste." See also Grégoire, *Histoire des sectes religieuses*, 87.

the "dogmatiques" is fifteen to seventeen pages, which may indicate the length of each lecture—taking about 50 minutes to read. The inference can be made, then, that these thirty-six extant lectures comprise an extended semester, commencing in November 1856 and ending June the year following, amounting to a partial presentation of systematic theology.[47]

Mabille's *Dogmatique* actually outlines a Protestant theology consisting of topics usually found in seventeenth-century Reformed theology, divided into three main sections: On Election (*De L'Élection*),[48] On the Work of Redemption (*De L'Œuvre de la Rédemption*),[49] and On the Church (*De L'Église*).[50] The middle section of over four hundred pages, moreover, covers topics such as "Calling and Faith," "Grace," "Justification"—topics that were also identified by Edwards in "A Rational Account." These sections, along with ones on the doctrines of adoption and sanctification,[51] are arranged by the missionary to Basutoland under the heading *The personal application of redemption* (*Des effets personnels de la Rédemption*), and understood by the author as the application of Christ's redemptive benefits, which commence on earth by grace and consummate in heaven in glory.[52] In sum, only two of the six *loci* of the Reformed *systema* are presented in the *Dogmatique*: soteriology and (succinctly) ecclesiology.[53]

The notebook reveals, furthermore, a wide-ranging array of sources, and an extensive exegetical use of Scripture. Concerning the former, Mabille referred to more than fifty different authors and publications from various theological traditions.[54]

---

47. This assumption is underscored by Mabille's pattern of handwriting, which is fairly consistent, though breakpoints between lectures coincide with a slight change of ink color and change of the slope of the letters and spacing between letters.

48. Mabille, *Dogmatique*, 1–146.

49. Ibid., 146–574.

50. Ibid., 574–92.

51. Ibid., 381–405, *De la Vocation et de la Foi*; 405–16, *La Grâce*; 416–92, *De la Foi*; 492–553, [*De la*] *Justification*; 533–35, *De l'adoption*; 553–74, *De la Sanctification*.

52. Mabille, *Dogmatique*, 381: "Les bienfaits personnels de la Rédemption commencent ici-bas par la grâce, et consommeront dans le ciel par la gloire."

53. Ibid., 574–80 (De L'Église), 581–88 (Des membres de l'église), and 589–92 (De l'unité de l'église).

54. Ibid., 13, 406, 428, 431, 432, 481, 495, 497, 508, 511, 515, 526, 531, 536, 542, 547, 581 (docteurs de Rome); 22 (Franciscans, Dominicans), 24 (Brochmand); 23 (Calixt); 112, 506, 562, 565 (Jesuits); 565, 569 (Wesleyans); 434, 435, 450, 511, 515, 536, 562 (Socinians); 589 (Arminians); 443, 536 (Remonstrants); 14, 21, 23, 34, 108, 109, 111, 114, 415, 450, 562, 565 (Pélagiens, semi-Pélagians).

A comment is in order on Augustine of Hippo (354–430), Jean Calvin (1509–64) and Francis Turretin (1623–87), in order to illustrate Mabille's use of theological sources and the missionary's theological orientation. First, Augustine is the leading and most positively referenced author (twenty-two per cent of the citations). Moreover, the cited works of Augustine include: *On Admonition and Grace* (*De correptione et gratia*, 7x), *On the Gift of Perseverance* (*De dono perseverantiae*, 1x), *On The Grace of Christ and On Original Sin, contra Pelagius* (*De Gratia Christi et de Peccato Originali, contra Pelagium*, 2x), and *On the Predestination of the Saints* (*De praedestinatione sanctorum*, 2x).[55] Secondly, there are only three references to Calvin: one to the Latin edition of the *Institution of Christian Religion* and two citations of the treatise *Concerning the Eternal Predestination of God* (*De aeterna Dei praedestinatione*).[56] Mabille's references to the *Doctor gratiæ* and the pastor of Geneva are found in the section discussing the doctrine of election, and the missionary to Basutoland's orientation of this doctrine stands unmistakably in an Augustinian-Calvinist theological trajectory. Thirdly, Mabille gave prominence to Turretin in discussing the doctrine of justification. Following the opening sentences of the chapter on justification, he approvingly quoted a Latin phrase, which he attributed to Martin Luther. Justification, Luther states, was

> the article by which the church stands or falls; For other Christians, it is the basis of Christianity, the principal bulwark of the Christian religion (*Articulus stantis, & cadentis Ecclesiae; Christianorum peculium, Christianismi basis, religionis Christianae propugnaculum*).[57]

However, the informed reader observes immediately that Mabille cited verbatim, if only in part, from Turretin's *Institute of Elenctic Theology* (*Institutio Theologiae Elencticae*).[58] Moreover, Mabille exactly followed Turretin in structure and theological content in eight of the ten *quaestiones* in the chapter *On Justification*, excluding the two last questions on the time and assurance of this doctrine.[59] This exposition of fifty-five pages (ten percent of

---

55. Ibid., 90, 108, 414 (2x), 468, 587 (*De correptione et gratia*); 90 (*De dono perseverantiae*); 410, 412 (*De Gratia Christi* . . . ); 414 (*De praedestinatione sanctorum*).

56. Ibid., 442 (2x, *De aeterna Dei praedestinatione*); 91 (*Inst.* lib. II, ch. 22).

57. Mabille, *Dogmatique*, 492.

58. Turretin, *Institutio*, 691: "Luthero dicitur *Articulus stantis, & cadentis Ecclesiae;* aliis Christianorum peculium, & Christianismi basis non abs re vocatur, praecipuúmque Religionis Christianae propugnaculum, quo adulterato vel subverso impossibile est puritatem doctrinae in aliis locis retinere."

59. Mabille, *Dogmatique*, 493, 1re question, Du sens du mot Justifier. Cf. Turretin,

the entire notebook) includes identical primary source references as found in Turretin's *Institutio* on the same doctrine. On the one hand, this finding may temper any possible enthusiasm about the many and various sources Mabille employed, leading to a more modest but noteworthy remark: Turretin's work is characterized by opposing Roman Catholic teaching, especially that of Bellarmine, who Mabille nonetheless also cites prominently, especially his work *On Justification (De Justificatione)*.[60] Furthermore, Turretin's work mediated sources of the Patristic and Medieval era—a distinct feature of many *systema* of the Post-reformation Reformed period.[61] On the other hand, Turretin's work may have been instrumental in the training of the PEMS missionaries for the purpose of Christian apologetics. Taking all of these factors together, we can say that Mabille's *Dogmatique* relies on Patristic, Medieval, Roman Catholic, and Protestant theology, with an orientation to Augustine and attention to the doctrine of justification—a theological subject reappraised during the era of the sixteenth-century Protestant Reformation, dexterously defended from the Roman Catholic side by Bellarmine. This attention can be explained in part by the position of nineteenth-century Protestantism in France, within a predominantly Roman Catholic society, which renounced what they saw as the pronounced predestinarianism of Reformed theology.[62]

Finally, all these source references, whether *via* Turretin's *Institutio* or not, are found outside of the section of Mabille's notebook entitled *On the Work of Redemption (De L'Œuvre de la Rédemption)*. In 235 pages (forty per cent of the entire *Dogmatique*), the author does not refer to any other author, with one exception: Edwards of eighteenth-century New England.[63]

---

*Institutio*, XVI.1, 691; *Dogmatique*, 503, 2e question, La cause de la justification. Cf. *Institutio*, XVI.2, 695; *Dogmatique*, 511, 3e question. De la justice imputée de Jésus-Christ. Cf. *Institutio*, XVI.3, 705; *Dogmatique*, 522, 4e question, La justification consiste-t-elle seulement dans la rémission des péchés. Cf. *Institutio*, XVI.4, 716; *Dogmatique*, 525, 5e question, la rémission des péchés consiste-t-elle . . . Cf. *Institutio*, XVI.5, 720; *Dogmatique*, 533, 6e question, De L'adoption. Cf. *Institutio*, XVI.5, 727; *Dogmatique*, 535, 7e question. De la justification par la foi. Cf. *Institutio*, XVI.7, 731; *Dogmatique*, 546, 8ème question, Est-ce la foi seule qui justfie? Cf. *Institutio*, XVI.8, 738.

60. Mabille, *Dogmatique*, 22, 114, 115, 481, 482, 494, 508, 515, 537, 565, 567, 581 (Bellarmine); 428, 437, 481, 482, 515, 537, 565 (*De Justificatione*).

61. Muller, *Reformed Dogmatics*, 46–49.

62. See for example, Muller, *After Calvin*, 63–65.

63. Mabille, *Dogmatique*, 147–381.

## Mabille's *Dogmatique* and Edwards's *HWR*

A closer examination of this part of the notebook, *De L'Œuvre de la Rédemption*, preceding *Des effets personnels de la Rédemption*,[64] reveals a division of three major parts dealing with the history of the work of redemption. These parts or periods are entitled "From the fall to the incarnation of Christ," "The time of Christ's humiliation," and "From Christ's resurrection to the end of the world"[65]—mirroring Edwards's major dispensations. This chronological presentation of the redemptive drama is further subdivided, with the first period, in six epochs, addressing divine redemptive activity "From the fall to the flood," "From the flood to the calling of Abraham," "From the calling of Abraham to Moses," "From Moses to David," "From David to the Babylonian captivity," and "From the Babylonian captivity to the coming of Christ."[66] The second period, focusing on Christ's life on earth, contains, besides a historico-doctrinal exposition of the centrality of Christ's salvific work, a contemporary practical application encouraging readers to trust in Christ for salvation.[67] In the third period, the author moves from the time of Christ, through the Constantinian era, the sixteenth-century Reformation, and into the "present state," concluding with an eschatological dimension dealing with the future Millennium and Kingdom of God.[68] This tripartite outline of redemptive history, treated at length in Mabille's *Dogmatique*, corresponds identically with the French edition of Edwards's *HWR*.

Edwards's original treatment, as noted before, was an ambitious series of sermons, preached in 1739, casting a broad vision of salvific history. The

---

64. Mabille, *Dogmatique*, 381.

65. Ibid., 163–251 (*Depuis la chute de l'homme jusqu'à l'incarnation de Jésus-Christ*), 251–88 (*De l'incarnation du Christ à sa résurrection*), 288–381 (*De la résurrection de Christ jusqu'à la consummation du siècle*).

66. Mabille, *Dogmatique*, 165–75 (Iere Epoque. *De la chute au Déluge*), 175–81 (IIe Epoque. *Du Déluge à l'appel d'Abraham*), 181–90 (IIIe Epoque. *D'Abraham à Moïse*), 191–209 (IVe Epoque. *De Moïse à David*), 209–29 (Ve Epoque. *De David à captivité de Babylone*), 229–46 (VIe et dernière Epoque. *De la captivité de Babylone à la venue du Christ*).

67. Ibid., 252–88. This part is entitled by Mabille as "epoch" instead of "period."

68. Ibid., 288–381, 302–8 (1ere Époque. *De la résurrection de Christ à la destruction de Jérusalem*), 309–15 (2e Époque. *De la destruction de Jérusalem au règne de Constantin*), 315–17 (3e Époque. *De Constantin au commencement de l'Antéchrist ou de l'homme de péché*), 317–23 (4e Époque. *De l'Antéchrist à la Réformation*), 323–28 (5e Époque. *De la Réformation jusqu'à nos jours*), 328–37 (6e Époque. *Du temps présent à la ruine de l'Antéchrist*), 337–44 (7e et dernière Époque. *Depuis l'avènement de Jésus-Christ jusqu'à la fin*), 344–51 (*Du Millénium*), 352–59 (*Du Royaume de Christ*), 366–81 (*Les derniers jugements de Dieu*).

history of redemption, according to Edwards, was organized in distinct phases from the fall of Adam to the final judgment. Here, Edwards, though unique in his time, nevertheless resonated with earlier figures within seventeenth-century Reformed orthodoxy, such as Turretin and Petrus van Mastricht (1630–1706)—whose works, we know, Edwards admired.[69] Turretin, for example, expounded the administrations of the covenant of grace in his *Institutio Theologiae Elencticae*,[70] from Adam to Abraham, "the first age,"[71] Abraham to Moses,[72] followed by the era of Moses to Christ.[73] In his Redemptive Discourse, Edwards may have followed Mastricht more than Turretin, as the German-Dutch theologian offered a detailed account of the dispensations of the covenant of grace (*De Dispensatione Foederis Gratiæ*), divided in three major sections from the dispensation under the patriarchs and Moses to Christ, ending with a treatment on the dispensation of eternity. In the first section, he is concerned with the propagation, theology and heresies of the covenant of grace in the era from Adam to Noah to Abraham to Moses,[74] followed by the discussion of the progress and regress of this covenant during the period from Moses to David; from David to the Babylonian captivity;[75] and then to the coming of Christ. In the section on the dispensation of Christ, the largest part, Mastricht blends theology, sacred and world history, typology and shadows, confessions and creeds, heresies, persecutions, schisms, the rise and fall of the antichrist, and Roman Catholic and Islamic theology, into one and continuing and expanding narrative.[76] Mastricht's view on theology and history, or the development of the covenant of grace, then, is based on the work of redemption. He noted that the exposition of the dispensation of redemptive history rests upon and extends the discussion of the personal appropriation of the work of redemption.[77]

69. "They [Mastricht and Turretin] are both excellent. Turretin is on polemical divinity; on the Five Points, and all other controversial points; and is much larger in these than Mastricht; and is better for one that desires only to be thoroughly versed in controversies." Edwards, "Letter to the Reverend Joseph Bellamy," *WJE* 16:217.

70. Turretin, *Institutio*, II:239.

71. Ibid., 240, questio vii, xi.

72. Ibid., 243, questio vii, xvii: "Secunda aetas ab Abrahamo protenditur usque ad Mosem … "

73. Ibid., 245, questio vii, xxiv. Edwards may have oriented his outline of redemptive history more to Mastricht who provide a more detailed account than Turretin.

74. Mastricht, *Theoretico-practica theologia*, VIII.1.xi, 66; Ibid.,875, xx; Ibid., xxii, 879.

75. Ibid., VIII.2.xxvi, 908.

76. Ibid., VIII.2.xxv, 906; VIII.3.xliii, 1051; VIII.2.xxvii, 918.

77. Ibid., V.1.i, 389.

In other words, the work of redemption, for Mastricht, has two intertwined dimensions: historical and personal—an understanding Edwards adhered to in his major treatise on the subject, and which Mabille followed as well. The use of Edwards's *HWR* by the missionary to Basutoland shows that both Edwards and Mabille were appreciative of Turretin's work and paid attention to salvation history.[78]

The architecture of the dispensations of redemptive history, as found in Mabille's *Dogmatique*, rests on Edwards's exposition of the history of the work of redemption: an exposition that is rooted in the Reformed orthodoxy of the seventeenth century, but was also foundational for Mabille's first catechism for the Basutos of the nineteenth century.

## Mabille's *Dogmatique* and *Katakisma ea Litaba tsa Bibele*

Upon arrival at Morija, Lesotho, in 1860, Mabille was appointed by the missionaries to succeed Thomas Arbousset (1810–77), who belonged with Casalis to the first generation of French Protestant missionaries in Basutoland.[79] These missionaries had not only learned the Sesotho language since 1833, but also taught the Basutos to read and write their own language. Their next step was to compile and translate a Catechism of the Language of Basuto.[80] These developments led to the translation of the first and second catechisms of Isaac Watts (1674–1748) by Arbousset in the mid-1840s.[81] Arbousset stressed, in particular, the need to attend catechism classes and the teaching of Scripture "as they were mediated by the missionaries." In the Catechism, for example, he inquires of a Basuto:

> Why, Mokhanoi do you never come to catechism? Several people have been brought there by you. Aren't you like the bell that call everyone to prayer, but without ever taking part in it yourself?[82]

Mabille continued to stress the importance of catechetical teaching, but in contrast to French translations of Watts's writings, Mabille wrote in 1865

---

78. McClymond points out that Edwards's sermons on redemptive history falls within the "genre of the Christian "universal chronicle," as exemplified by such books as Augustine's *City of God* and Bishop Bosuet's *Discourse on Universal History* (1681)." McClymond, "A Different Legacy," 21.

79. Smith, *Mabilles of Basutoland*, 99.

80. See *Katekismaniane ka Puo*.

81. See *Katekhisma ea Pele* and *Katekhisma ea Boberi*.

82. Gill et al., *Mekolokotoane Kerekeng*, 51.

the first catechism in the vernacular Basuto language, entitled *Katekisma ea Lipolelo tsa Bibele* (*Catechism of Sayings of the Bible*), published by the PEMS at Strasbourg.[83] This catechism became the cornerstone of religious instruction in Basutoland. It was reprinted by Mabille, between 1875 and 1896 in five editions, as *Katekisma ea Litaba tsa Bibele* (*Catechism of the Tidings of the Bible*), once he had made his printing press operational.[84] This influential catechism, in a question-and-answer format, was divided into chronological periods: "The first 1656 years, to the deluge";[85] "From the time of the flood to the calling of Abraham"; "Abraham to Moses"; "Exodus to [David] Salomon"; "David to Babylonian Captivity"; "Babylonian Captivity to Christ"; "Christ"; "Christ after resurrection"; and, "To the end of the world."[86] In fact, the structure of the catechism follows closely Mabille's outline of redemptive history (*De L'Œvre de la Rédemption*) as found in his *Dogmatique*.[87] Moreover, the content of the catechism also resonates with Mabille's work, though in some cases it follows Edwards's exposition of redemptive history, appropriated for a Basuto context. For example, in chapter two of the *Katekisma ea Litaba tsa Bibele*, one reads:

- What did Noah do after he had disembarked the ark? He build God an altar and thanked Him by sacrificing cows as burnt offering;

- Did God bless Noah? Yes, God, full of grace, accepted Noah's sacrifice and gave him authority over everything on earth;

83. See *Katekisma ea Lipolelo*.

84. See *Katekisma ea Litaba*. Note that between 1846 and 1865, no catechism was published due to the limited finances of the PEMS and to the Boer-Basuto wars of 1858 and early 1865.

85. Mabille, *Katekisma ea Litaba*, 3: "Go thlōga pōpong ea lefatše isa morallong oa metsi, ki lilemo tse 1656."

86. Ibid., 45.

87. Ibid., 3: "Go thlōga pōpong ea lefatše isa morallong oa metsi, ki lilemo tse 1656." Cf. Mabille, *Dogmatique*, 165–75 (Iere Epoque. *De la chute au Déluge*); Mabille, *Katekisma ea Litaba*, 10: "Go thlōga nakong ea morallo, go isa pitsong ea Abrahama, ki lilemo tse 430." Cf. Mabille, *Dogmatique*, 175–81 (IIe Epoque. *Du Déluge à l'appel d'Abraham*); Mabille, *Katekisma ea Litaba*, 13: "Go thlōga isa pitsong ea Abrahama, go fitlela go tsueng ga Iseraela Egepteng, ki lilemo tse 430." Cf. Mabille, *Dogmatique*, 181–90 (IIIe Epoque. *D'Abraham à Moïse*); Mabille, *Katekisma ea Litaba*, 18: "Go thlōga ha Baiseraele ba tsuile Egepet eng, go fitla lefung la Salomone, ki lilemo tse 500." Cf. Mabille, *Dogmatique*, 191–209 (IVe Epoque. *De Moïse à David*); Mabille, *Katekisma ea Litaba*, 26: "Go thlōga lefung la Salomone go isa motla Baiseraele ba isoang Babylona ki lilemo tse 400." Cf. Mabille, *Dogmatique*, 209–29 (Ve Epoque. *De David à captivité de Babylone*); Mabille, *Katekisma ea*, 29: "Go thlōga motla Bayode ba isoang Babylona go isa go tsualoeng ga Yesu Kreste, ki lilemo tse 580." Cf. Mabille, *Dogmatique*, 229–46 (VIe et dernière Epoque. *De la captivité de Babylone à la venue du Christ*).

- Did Noah's descendents hold on to God? No, they turned against God...;
- What did they try to do? They came together to build a city and high tower...;
- How did God preserve true religion on earth? God chose for himself a nation...;
- Who was the father of that nation? It is Abraham who was born in [the land of] Chaldees...[88]

This narrative trajectory from the deluge to the calling of Abraham, again, in question-and-answer format, is briefly identified in Mabille's *Dogmatique*, but is followed in a similar order and detail as found in Edwards's *Histoire*.[89] Therefore, we cannot automatically conclude that the missionary's systematic theology was solely responsible for the content of the catechism. Chapter five of *Katekisma ea Litaba tsa Bibele*,[90] for example, on the period from David to the Babylonian captivity, articulates the decline of religion, the rise of idolatry, and the warnings of the prophets. Although these notions are found in Mabille's *Dogmatique* and Edwards's *Histoire*, there is here a lesser dependence on either one.[91] Examination of the Mabille's *Katekisma*, moreover, shows that the author actually may have relied more on the French edition of Edwards's discourse on redemptive history in writing the first catechism in the Sesotho language than his own work.

---

88. Mabille, *Katekisma ea Litaba*, 10–13: "Go thlōga nakong ea morallo, go isa pitsong ea Abrahama, ki lilemo tse 430." Cf. Mabille, *Dogmatique*, 175–81 (IIe Epoque. *Du Déluge à l'appel d'Abraham*) and Edwards, *Histoire*, 42–53 (Chapitre II. *Du Déluge à la vocation d'Abraham*).

89. Mabille, *Katekisma ea Litaba*, 10. Cf. Edwards, *Histoire*, 47, and Edwards, *History of the Work of Redemption*, WJE 9:152. Mabille, *Katekisma ea Litaba*, 11. Cf. Edwards, *Histoire*, 49, and Edwards, *History of the Work of Redemption*, WJE 9:153. Mabille, *Katekisma ea Litaba*, 12. Cf. Edwards, *Histoire*, 54, and Edwards, *History of the Work of Redemption*, WJE 9:158. Mabille, *Katekisma ea Litaba*, 12. Cf. Edwards, *Histoire*, 54, and Edwards, *History of the Work of Redemption*, WJE 9:158.

90. Mabille, *Katekisma ea Litaba*, 26: "Go thlōga lefung la Salomone go isa motla Baiseraele ba isoang Babylona ki lilemo tse 400." Cf. Mabille, *Dogmatique*, 209–29 (Ve Epoque. *De David à captivité de Babylone*).

91. Only four out of the fifteen questions and answers in chapter five related to Mabille's *Dogmatique* and Edwards's *Histoire*. Mabille, *Katekisma ea Litaba*, 26. Cf. Edwards, *Histoire*, 126, and Edwards, *History of the Work of Redemption*, WJE 9:224–25; Mabille, *Katekisma ea Litaba*, 27. Cf. Edwards, *Histoire*, 141–42, and Edwards, *History of the Work of Redemption*, WJE 9:238; Mabille, *Katekisma ea Litaba*, 28. Cf. Edwards, *Histoire*, 144, and Edwards, *History of the Work of Redemption*, WJE 9:239.

## Conclusion

The recently discovered manuscript in Lesotho, Mabille's *Dogmatique*, sheds light on religious education in Basutoland, and the reception, translation, and appropriation of Edwards's *HWR* in a nineteenth-century French missionary context. Edwards's Redemption Discourse (1739) was published as a "body of divinity" (1788), translated into French (1854), and appropriated in a systematic theology (1856) and Sesotho catechism (1875). Preached as a sermon series with the aim to awaken New England's congregation of Northampton to the times of revival, it was first published in Edinburgh, Scotland, with the hope that it, "may assist in studying with greater pleasure and advantage the historical and prophetical books of scripture; and excite to a conversation becoming the gospel."[92] The work then found its way from America to Africa through French missionary endeavors in relgious educational training (Paris) and teaching (Basutoland).

Edwards's original aim, and the subsequent publication of "outlines of a body of divinity," converged in nineteenth-century France, where the *HWR* was translated in the context of revival (*Le Réveil*) and taught in the course of systematic theology at the PEMS Mission house, exemplified by Mabille's *Dogmatique*. The appropriation of Edwards's *HWR* in the combined context of missions and religious education, moreover, was extended in Basutoland as seen in the *Katekisma*. The outline of the catechism may be due to Mabille's classical training and acquaintance with "universal chronology" and Scripture, but it also reflected his intimate knowledge of Edwards's work. The reception of Edwards's exposition of redemptive history in the catechism of Basutoland resonates, then, in part with Mabille's *Dogmatique*—a text transmission of Edwards's *Histoire*. The transmission of this text remained the same in structure, was shortened in content, and modified over time, but continued as intended by Edwards: to show "a work that God is carrying on from the fall of man to the end of the world."[93]

## Bibliography

Antakly, Waheeb G. "American Protestant Educational Missions: Their Influence on Syria and Arab Nationalism, 1820–1923." PhD diss., The American University, 1976.

---

92. Preface written Feb. 25, 1773 by Jonathan Edwards Jr.

93. Edwards, *History of the Work of Redemption*, *WJE* 9:119, and Edwards, *History of the Work of Redemption* (1774), 5; Ibid. *Histoire*, 7. Cf. Mabille, *Dogmatique*, 147; Ibid., *Katekisma*, 3.

Bebbington, David W. "Remembered Around the World." In *Jonathan Edwards at Home and Abroad: Historical Memories, Cultural Movements, Global Horizons*, edited by David W. Kling and Douglas A. Sweeney, 177-200. Columbia: University of South Carolina Press, 2003.

Bellarmine, Roberto. *De Scriptoribus ecclesiasticis*. Paris: Sebastian Cramoisy, 1617.

Berg, Johannes van den. *Constrained by Jesus' Love: Inquiry into the Motives of the Missionary Awakening in Great Britain in the Period between 1698-1815*. Kampen: J. H. Kok, 1956.

*Bibliothèque universitaire, Section de théologie protestante à Montauban: catalogue*. Université de Montpellier, Montauban: Université, 1890.

Bolliger, Daniel, et al., eds. *Histoire et richesses de la Bibliothèque de théologie protestante de Montauban*. Toulouse: S.I.C.D, 2007.

Boone, A. Th. "Zending en gereformeerd Piëtisme in Nederland: een historisch overzicht." *Documentatieblad Nadere Reformatie* 14.1 (1990) 1-31.

*Catalogue général de la Société des livres religieux de Toulouse*. Toulouse: Société des livres religieux, 1878.

Chamberlain, Ava. "Editor's Introduction." In *The "Miscellanies" (Entry Nos. 501-832)*, edited by Ava Chamberlain, The Works of Jonathan Edwards 18:1-48. New Haven: Yale University Press, 2000.

Chaudon, Louis M. et al., eds. *Dictionnaire universel, historique, critique, et bibliographique; ou, Histoire abrégée et impartiale des hommes de toutes les nations qui se sont rendus célèbres, illustres ou fameux . . . depuis la plus haute antiquité jusqu'à nos jours; avec les dieux et les héros de toutes les mythologies; enrichie des notes et additions des abbés Brotier et Mercier de Saint-Leger*. Paris: De Mame Frères, 1810.

Cocceius, Johannes. *Opera Omnia theologica*. Amsterdam: Johannes à Someren, 1675.

Davies, Ronald E. "'Prepare Ye the Way of the Lord': The Missiological Thought and Practice of Jonathan Edwards (1703-1758)." PhD diss., Fuller Theological Seminary, 1988.

Davies, Ronald E. *Jonathan Edwards and His Influence of the Development of the Missionary Movement from Britain*. Cambridge: Currents in World Christianity Project, 1996.

Drew, Samuel, ed. *The Imperial Magazine and Monthly Record of Religious, Philosophical, Historical, Biographical, Topographical and General Knowledge*. London: Fisher, Son, & Jackson, 1831.

Edwards, Jonathan. "A City on a Hill." In *Sermons and Discourses, 1734-1738*, edited by Max X. Lesser, The Works of Jonathan Edwards 19:537-59. New Haven: Yale University Press, 2001.

―――. *The Distinguishing Marks of a Work of the Spirit of God . . . A Discourse Delivered at New-Haven, September 10th 1741*. Boston: S. Kneeland and T. Green, 1741.

―――. *Geschiedenis van het Werk der Verlossing: Bezielende de Schetsen van een Zamenstel van Godgeleerdheid, in een geheel nieuwe order*. Translated by Engelbert Nooteboom. Utrecht: Abraham van Paddenburg, 1776.

―――. *Histoire de l'oeuvre de la Rédemption*: Toulouse: Société des Livres Religieux, 1854.

―――. *History of the Work of Redemption, Comprising a Summary of the History of the Jews up to the Destruction of Jerusalem, by President Edwards*. London: Printed for the Religious Tract Society, 1831.

———. *A History of the Work of Redemption*. Edited by John F. Wilson. The Works of Jonathan Edwards 9. New Haven: Yale University Press, 1989.

———. *The Life of Brainerd*. The Works of Jonathan Edwards 7. Edited by Norman Pettit. New Haven: Yale University Press, 1985.

———. *L'union dans la prière pour la propagation de l'Evangile: abrégé d'un humble essai*. Paris: H. Servier, Libraire, 1823.

———. "'Misc.' 832." In *The "Miscellanies" (Entry Nos. 501–832)*, edited by Ava Chamberlain, The Works of Jonathan Edwards 18:546–47. New Haven: Yale University Press, 2000.

———. "Outline of a 'Rational Account.'" In *Scientific and Philosophical Writings*, edited by Wallace E. Anderson, The Works of Jonathan Edwards 6:396–97. New Haven: Yale University Press, 1980.

———. *Quelques réflexions sur la vie du missionnaire Brainerd*. Lausanne: M. Ducloux, 1838.

———. *Some Thoughts Concerning the Present Revival of Religion in New-England*. Boston: S. Kneeland and T. Green, 1742.

———. "To the Reverend Joseph Bellamy." In *Letters and Personal Writings*, edited by George S. Claghorn, The Works of Jonathan Edwards 16:216–18. New Haven: Yale University Press, 1998.

———. "To the Trustees of the College of New Jersey, October 19, 1757." In *Letters and Personal Writings,* edited by George S. Claghorn, The Works of Jonathan Edwards 16:725–30. New Haven: Yale University Press, 1998.

———. *A Treatise Concerning Religious Affections*. Boston: S. Kneeland and T. Green, 1746.

———. *United Prayer for the Spread of the Gospel . . . an Abridgement of "An Humble Attempt . . . "* London: R. Williams, 1814.

———. *United and Extraordinary Prayer for the Revival of Religion and the Advancement of Christ's Kingdom, Earnestly Recommended*. Andover: Printed for the New England Tract Society by Flagg and Gould, 1815, 1816, and 1820.

Freidinger, W. A. "Centennial of the American Mission Press-Beirut, Syria." *The Muslim World* 13.2 (1923) 163–66.

Fyfe, Aileen Kennedy. "Industrialised Conversion: The Religious Tract Society and popular science publishing in Victorian Britain." PhD diss., University of Cambridge, 2000.

Gill, Stephen J., et al., eds. *Mekolokotoane Kerekeng ea Evangeli Lesotho. Jubilee Highlights 1833–2008*. Morija: Morija Museum and Archives, 2009.

Goen, Clarence C. "Editor's Introduction." In *The Great Awakening*, edited by Clarence C. Goen, The Works of Jonathan Edwards 4:1–95. New Haven: Yale University Press, 1972.

Grégoire, Henri-Baptiste. *Histoire des sectes religieuses*. Paris: Baudouin Frères editeurs, 1829.

Hopkins, Eziekel. *The doctrine of the two covenants, wherein the nature of original sin is at large explain'd . . . : with a discourse of glorifying God in his attributes*. London : Richard Smith, 1712.

Johnson, Thomas H., and M. X. Lesser, eds. *The Printed Writings of Jonathan Edwards, 1703–1758: A Bibliography*. Princeton: Princeton Theological Seminary, 2003.

Mabille, Adolphe. *Dogmatique* [1856]. Morija: Morija Archives and Museum, 2010.

———. *Katekhisma ea Boberi le Katekhisma ea Liketsogalo.* Second Catéchisme de I. Watts traduit en Sessouto et imprimé pour la Société des Missions Evangéliques de Paris. Cape Town: Pike & Philip for the "Young Men's Christian Association," 1846.

———. *Katekhisma ea Pele le Katekhisma ea Mabito a Mangolo a Bibele.* Premier Catéchisme de I. Watts, D.D., traduit en Sessouto et imprimé pour la Société des Missions Evangéliques de Paris: par T. Arbousset. Cape Town: Pike & Philip for the "Young Men's Christian Association," 1845.

———. *Katekisma ea Lipolelo tsa Bibele.* Imprimé pour la Société des Missions Evangéliques de Paris; Strasbourg: Imp. De Veuve Berger-Levault, 1865.

———. *Katekisma ea Litaba tsa Bibele.* Morija: Kathiso ea A. Mabille, 1875, 1884, 1885, 1895, and 1896.

———. *Katekismaniane ka Puo ea Basuto.* Imprimé pour la Société des Missions Évangeliques de Paris; Cape Town: G. J. Pike, 1839.

*Magasin évangélique.* Genève: Emile Guers fils, 1821.

Malikck, David G., *The American Mission Press. A Preliminary Bibliography.* N. p.: ATOUR Publications, 2008.

Manor, James. "The Coming of Britain's Age of Empire and Protestant Mission Theology." *Zeitschrift für Missionswissenschaft und Religionswissenschaft* 61 (1977) 38–54.

Marsden, George M. "Jonathan Edwards, the Missionary," *Journal of Presbyterian History* 81 (2003) 5–17.

Mastricht, Petrus van. *Theoretico-practica theologia.* Amsterdam: Sumtibus Societatis, 1715.

Mather, Samuel. *A Vindication of the Holy Bible, wherein the arguments for, and objections against, the divine original, purity and integrity of the Scripture, are proposed and considered.* London: Printed for John and Barham Clark, 1723.

McClymond, Michael J. "A Different Legacy." In *Jonathan Edwards at Home and Abroad: Historical Memories, Cultural Movements, Global Horizons,* edited by David W. Kling and Douglas A. Sweeney, 16–39. Columbia: University of South Carolina Press, 2003.

Michaud, Joseph Fr., and Louis Gabriel Michaud. *Biographie universelle, ancienne et moderne . . .* Paris: L.G. Michaud, 1816.

Minkema, Kenneth P. "Jonathan Edwards in the Twentieth Century." *Journal of the Evangelical Theological Society* 47.4 (2004) 661–66.

Muller, Richard A. *After Calvin: Studies in the Development of a Theological Tradition.* Studies in Historical Theology. Oxford: Oxford University Press, 2003.

———. *Reformation and Post-Reformation Reformed Dogmatics.* Grand Rapids: Baker, 1987.

Parker, Irene. *Dissenting Academies in England: their Rise and Progress, and their Place Among the Educational Systems of the Country.* Cambridge: Cambridge University Press, 1914, 2009.

Payne, Ernest A. *The Prayer Call of 1784.* London: Baptist Laymen's Missionary Movement, 1941.

Piggin, Stuart. "The Expanding Knowledge of God: Jonathan Edwards's Influence on Missionary Thinking and Promotion." In *Jonathan Edwards at Home and Abroad: Historical Memories, Cultural Movements, Global Horizons,* edited by D. W. Kling

and Douglas A. Sweeney, 266–96. Columbia: University of South Carolina Press, 2003.
Rooy, Sydney H. *The Theology of Missions in the Puritan Tradition: A Study of Representative Puritans: Richard Sibbes, Richard Baxter, John Eliot, Cotton Mather, and Jonathan Edwards*. Grand Rapids: Eerdmans, 1965.
Smith, Edwin W., *The Mabilles of Basutoland*. London: Hodder and Stoughton, 1939.
*Société des missions évangéliques de Paris*. Leiden: IDC Microform Publishers, 1987.
Turretin, Francis. *Institutio Theologiae Elencticae*. 2 vols. Geneva: Apud Samuelem De Tournes, 1688.
Yeager, Jonathan M. *Enlightened Evangelicalism: The Life and Thought of John Erskine*. Oxford: Oxford University Press, 2011.

# 5

# Jonathan Edwards, Christian Zionist

### Gerald R. McDermott[1]

It is commonly assumed that Christian Zionism was an invention of nineteenth-century dispensationalists. But Christian Zionism is actually part of the warp and woof of the New Testament, and was common in the early church until Augustine's amillennial eschatology became accepted in the medieval church. It was not until the Reformation and later that renewed vision for a future Israel gained momentum. The stimulus for a renewed Zionism came from British Puritans, and as early as the sixteenth century. It was developed by Thomas Brightman, John Cotton, and Increase Mather.

Jonathan Edwards provided further momentum, predicting that the Jews would one day return to their homeland. This would happen, he reasoned, because the prophecies of land being given to them had been only partially fulfilled. In the mid-eighteenth century the majority of Jews were still living in the diaspora. It was also necessary for God to make them a "visible monument" of his grace and power at their return and then conversion. Canaan once again would be the spiritual center of the world. Although Israel would again be a distinct nation, Christians would have free access to Jerusalem because Jews would look on Christians as their brethren.

The eighteenth century marked the beginning of a reevaluation of Judaism. The deists, who dominated intellectual life in England at the beginning of the century and were the leaders of this reappraisal, portrayed Judaism as

1. This paper was taken and adapted from McDermott, *New Christian Zionism*.

unnecessary, and indeed damaging, to Christianity. They learned this from Johann Buxtdorf the Elder (1564-1629), whose guide to synagogue life depicted Judaism as a "confused" and "disorderly" religion obsessively devoted to empty ritual. Partly as a result Voltaire, who studied the deists when in London in the 1720s, Bolingbroke, Gibbon, and other Enlightenment thinkers began to regard Jews as simply another political entity, unprotected by divine covenant. Pogroms against them were considered natural consequences of their creation of a cruel and irrational god. Gibbon, for example, argued that Rome fell because of the Jewish character in the Christian religion that had infected the Empire.[2] It was against this background of deist severance of the religious link between Christians and Jews that Jonathan Edwards argued for one covenant binding the two religions.

## Zionism in the New Testament

Zionism is the idea that Jews should have their own *politeia* to protect the covenant people from persecution. Religious Zionism adds that a *politeia* on the land of Israel is needed for the people of Israel to be able to realize the ideals of the covenant to which the God of Israel had bound them. Some secular Zionists and all religious Zionists point to the predictions of the prophets of Israel that one day the people of Israel would return from the four corners of the earth to the land of Zion. Some scholars have suggested that these prophecies of return were fulfilled when some of the Babylonian exiles returned to rebuild Jerusalem toward the end of the sixth century BC.

But Jesus and the apostles give evidence that they were still expecting a future return. When Jesus quotes Isaiah's prediction that the temple would become "a house of prayer for all nations" (Mark 11:17; Is 56:1), he seems to concur, as Richard Hays suggests, with Isaiah's vision of "an eschatologically restored Jerusalem" where foreigners would come to God's holy mountain to join the "outcasts of Israel" whom God has "gathered" (Is 56:7-8).[3] Hays adds that John's figural reading of Jesus' body as the new temple (John 2:21) "should be read neither as flatly supersessionist nor as hostile to continuity with Israel."[4] It does not deny the literal sense of Israel's Scriptures—that the temple was God's house—"but completes it by linking it typologically

---

2. For eighteenth-century attitudes to Judaism, see Manuel, *The Changing of the Gods*; Manuel, *The Broken Staff*; Goldman, *Hebrew and the Bible in America*; and Pailin, *Attitudes to Other Religions*. For this paragraph, see Manuel, *Broken Staff*, 85–90, 166, 175, 291, and Gibbon, *Decline and Fall*, 1:384-91, 446-48; 2: 804, 807.

3. Hays, *Reading Backwards*, 6–7.

4. Ibid., 102.

with the narrative of Jesus and disclosing a deeper prefigurative truth within the literal historical sense."[5] That the apostles saw the temple as both God's continuing house and *also* a figure for Jesus' body is shown by their participation in temple liturgies even after the Temple's leaders had helped put their Messiah to death (Acts 2:46).

There is more evidence that Jesus looked to a future return of Jews and a restored Jerusalem. In Matthew 24 he says that when the Son of Man returns, "all the tribes of the land will mourn," quoting Zechariah's prophecy about the inhabitants of Jerusalem mourning when "the Lord will give salvation to the tents of Judah" (Zech 12:7, 10). Then in Matthew 19 Jesus tells his disciples that "in the new world, when the Son of Man shall sit on his glorious throne, you who have followed me will also sit on twelve thrones, judging the twelve tribes of Israel" (v. 28). James Sanders has observed that these repeated references to the twelve tribes imply restoration of Israel, particularly in Jerusalem.[6] Luke records Anna speaking of the baby Jesus "to all who were waiting for the redemption of Jerusalem" (Luke 2:38), and Jesus' expectation that when he returns Israel will welcome him: "You will not see me again until you say, 'Blessed is he who comes in the name of the Lord'" (Luke 13:34–35; Matt 23:37–39). Luke suggests that the return will be in Jerusalem (Luke 21:24–28). And when his disciples asked Jesus just before his ascension, "Lord, are you at this time going to restore the kingdom to Israel?" (Acts 1:6), Jesus did not challenge their assumption that one day the kingdom would be restored to physical Israel. He simply said the Father had set the date, and they did not need to know it yet. It was these sorts of indications in the gospels and Acts that caused Markus Bockmuehl to write that "the early Jesus movement evidently continued to focus upon the restoration of Israel's twelve tribes in a new messianic kingdom."[7]

Paul, Peter, and the writer of the book of Revelation had similar expectations. Paul uses Isaiah's prophecy of restoration in Isaiah 59 to declare that "the deliverer will come from Zion, he will banish ungodliness from Jacob" (Rom 11:26). In Acts 3 Peter looks forward to "the times of restoration of all things which God spoke through the mouth of his holy prophets from ancient time" (Acts 3:21). The word Peter uses for "restoration" is the same word (*apokatastasis*) used in the Septuagint (which the early church used as its Bible) for God's future return of Jews from all over the world to Israel.[8]

---

5. Ibid.

6. Sanders, *Jesus and Judaism*, 98.

7. Bockmuehl, *Jewish Law*, xi.

8. Jer 16:15: I will bring them back [*apokatastēso*] to their own land that I gave to their fathers; Jer 24.6 I will set my eyes on them for good, and I will bring them

In Revelation, the Lamb draws his followers to Zion in the final stage of history (14.1), and the new earth is centered in Jerusalem, which has twelve gates named after "the twelve tribes of the sons of Israel" (Rev 21:2, 12).

## Zionism in Early and Medieval Christianity

Justin Martyr (100–165), one of the best-known second-century Christian apologists, expected that the millennium would be centered in Jerusalem. Although he was one of the first replacement theologians, his vision of the church's future included a particular city in the particular land of Israel.

> But I and others, who are right-minded Christians on all points, are assured that there will be a resurrection of the dead, and a thousand years in Jerusalem, which will then be built, adorned and enlarged, [as] the prophets Ezekiel and Isaiah and others declare . . . [such as] John, one of the apostles of Christ, who prophesied, by a revelation that was made to him, that those who believed in our Christ would dwell a thousand years in Jerusalem.[9]

Irenaeus (d. ca. 202) was similar. Like Justin, he believed "the church is the [true] seed of Abraham," and those who will return "from all the nations" will be Christians rather than Jews.[10] But he also believed there will be a future for Jerusalem in the end days. It will be "rebuilt after the pattern of the Jerusalem above," but not in allegorical fashion. Those who "allegorize [prophecies] of this kind . . . shall not be found consistent with themselves," for the new earth "cannot be understood in reference to supercelestial matters."[11]

Tertullian (160–225) also saw a future for the people and land of Israel. Although he decried "Jews" for their ignorance in putting Jesus to death, and thought that God punished them by tearing "from [their] throat[s] . . . the very land of promise," he believed that they would one day be returned to their land.

---

back[*apokatastēso*] to this land; Jer 50 [27 LXX]:19: I will restore Israel [*apokatastēso*] to his pasture; Hos 11.11 They shall come trembling like birds from Egypt, and like doves from the land of Assyria, and I will return [*apokatastēso*] them to their homes, declares the Lord.

9. Justin Martyr, *Dialogue with Trypho*.
10. Irenaeus, *Against Heresies* V, 34.1.
11. Irenaeus, *Against Heresies* V, 35.1, 2.

> It will be fitting for the Christian to rejoice, and not to grieve, at the restoration of Israel, if it be true, (as it is), that the whole of our hope is intimately united with the remaining expectation of Israel.[12]

A bit later in the third century, the Egyptian bishop Nepos, who "was a respected and admired Christian leader," foresaw a restoration of Jerusalem and rebuilding of the temple. Millennial teaching was prevalent in that area of third-century Egypt, and had been so for a long time, along with, presumably, faith in a restored Israel.[13]

But this early church Zionism came screeching to a halt with Origen (184–254). He possessed a brilliant mind and was called by Jerome the greatest teacher of the church after the apostles. But when it came to the Jewish messiah and the promise of the land, Origen regarded their relationship as a zero-sum game. Either one or the other could be fulfilled, not both. As Robert Wilken puts it, "If Jesus of Nazareth was the Messiah, the prophecies about the messianic age had already been fulfilled, and it was the task of biblical interpreters to discover what the spiritual promises meant in light of this new 'fact.' For Origen the essential feature of the holy land was not its location but its quality and character."[14] In Origen's words,

> therefore the prophecies relating to Judaea and Jerusalem, and to Israel, Judah and Jacob indicate to us, because we do not interpret them in a fleshly sense, various divine mysteries . . . [15]

Hence prophecies about the land of Israel and the future of the Jewish people on the land would be "emptied of their spiritual content" if they were permitted to refer in any literal sense to Jerusalem or the land. So Jerusalem "does not designate a future political center but a spiritual vision of heavenly bliss." When the psalmist says "the meek shall possess the land" he means the "pure land in the pure heaven" not somewhere on planet earth.[16]

Augustine was willing to call soil taken from Israel "holy land,"[17] but he spiritualized the promises of land in a way similar to Origen. Once Augustine's amillennial eschatology became accepted in the medieval church, with its assertion that the millennium is simply the rule of Christ

---

12. Tertullian, *On Modesty*, chapter 8.

13. Wilken, *Land Called Holy*, 76–77, drawing on Eusebius, *The History of the Church* 7.24, and other sources.

14. Ibid.

15. Origen, *On First Principles*, 301–02 (IV, III, 9).

16. Wilken, *Land Called Holy*, 70, 72, 77–78.

17. Ibid., 125.

through the existing church, few medieval thinkers saw a future for the people or land of Israel. All Old Testament prophecies of future Israel were interpreted to be predictions of the Christian church that came after the resurrection of Christ.

It was not until the Reformation and later, however, that renewed vision for a future Israel gained momentum. Calvin's amillennialism and replacement theology prevented him from imagining such a thing. Something similar is routinely said of Luther, and for good reason. Yet there is the curious remark by the great Reformation scholar Heiko Oberman that Luther once quipped that if the Jews were to reestablish themselves in the holy land, he would be the first to go there and have himself circumcised![18] Even if this was a sarcastic counterfactual,[19] it suggests that the return of Jews to their ancient land would have had theological significance to the great Reformer.

## Sixteenth-Century Groundwork

The stimulus for a new kind of Zionism came from Britain, and as early as the sixteenth century. In part, this was because of its cultural memory. By the sixteenth century, the Bible had already become "the national epic of Britain," as Julian Huxley put it.[20] The earliest surviving essay from England's history is the Epistle of Gildas, which dates from AD 550. After every battle is an Old Testament analogy, and on every page are quotes from the Pentateuch, Prophets, or Psalms. The Venerable Bede, author of the eighth-century *Ecclesiastical History of the English People*, linked the earliest Britons to the Cymbri of Scythia (near the Black Sea), believed to be descended from Noah's sons. Later English medieval tradition held that Joseph of Arimathea, an Israelite, was the founder of Christianity in England.[21]

Another reason for England's eschatological singularity was that "England enjoyed relative political and religious tranquility in contrast to Europe's constant wars," political intrigues, economic distress, and growing spiritual despair in the sixteenth and seventeenth centuries. When the English looked across the Channel at the wars and counter-reformations of

---

18. Burrell, "How Christians Share," 13. Burrell reports this from a lecture by Oberman in Jerusalem May 24, 1982.

19. In other words, it is not going to happen—something like the snowball in hell. This is Lutheran theologian Paul Hinlicky's surmise; private conversation, March 25, 2015.

20. Tuchman, *Bible and the Sword*, xiv.

21. Ibid., 3–4, 13–14.

Europe, it became easy for Englishmen to think they were providentially favored. This was, "to a people steeped in Scripture, analogous to that special place held by the ancient Israelites." It was also congruent with the prevailing Calvinism, which "suggested the idea of Divine Election as belonging to the privileged and faithful nation."[22] Thus their own sense of election helped English Christians imagine that God had elected Israel to a permanent role in redemptive history.

Three influential English books in the sixteenth century helped focus this cultural memory and sense of privilege in ways that would resemble Zionism. John Bale (1495–1563) was "one of the best-known polemicists in the first generation of English Protestantism."[23] He was a supersessionist, but without the anti-Jewish polemics of a Martin Luther. His 1570 edition of *The Image of Both Churches* includes what was then innovative—hope for the national conversion of Jews to Protestantism, and assigning to them a place at the throne of the Lamb at the end of history. This meant they would have a central role in Christian eschatology.[24]

Bale was building on what had been suggested just ten years before in the Geneva Bible, first published in 1560 and more popular than the King James Bible for generations, especially among Presbyterian Scots and English Puritans. The notes of the Geneva Bible at Romans 11 predict that one day Israel as a people "shall embrace Christ" and then "the worlde shal be restored to a newe life." When it speaks at Revelation 1:7 of "they whiche pearced him [Christ]," it "deliberately does not single Jews out for condemnation or persecution." Historian Donald Lewis suggests that it was the Geneva Bible's vision of Israel's spiritual "return" or "turning" that prepared its huge readership for the associated idea of a literal return of Jews to their ancestral homeland.[25]

The third book of sixteenth-century Britain that helped prepare the English mind for Christian Zionism was John Foxe's *Book of Martyrs* (1563). After the Bible and John Bunyan's *Pilgrim's Progress*, it was the most widely read book in English for several centuries.[26] Foxe's book is not without its own denunciations of Jews and Judaism, yet he assures his readers that God's promises to Jews are "remaining still in their force."[27] God has

---

22. This and other quotes in this paragraph are from Culver, *Albion and Ariel*, 30–31.

23. Smith, *More Desired*, 55.

24. Ibid., 58–59.

25. Ibid., 60; Lewis, *Origins of Christian Zionism*, 29.

26. Ibid., 47.

27. Smith, *More Desired*, 64.

decreed that the time of the gentiles will end, and then "the Jewes also after that fulnes of time shall returne unto the faith."[28] Once again, British readers were told that there is a future for the Jewish people that is distinct from that of gentiles (even if Jews would eventually change their faith!), and that they will play a role in God's drama at the end.

## Seventeenth-Century Puritan Restorationism

Beginning in the seventeenth century, British thinkers started connecting Jewish conversion to Jewish return to Zion. Most had some connection to the Puritan movement, and some thought Jews would return to Zion without converting to Christianity first. Thomas Draxe (d. 1618), a disciple of the Puritan theologian William Perkins, held a view of Jews that for his day was remarkably generous. Even if their usury and rejection of Christianity was to be criticized, gentiles were "in many respects inferior unto them" because the Jews were still "God's chosen nation." Christians "must therefore acknowledge our selves debters unto the Iewes."[29] Draxe believed that Jesus would not come again until "the dispersed Jewes generally converted to Christianitie," but that in the meantime they "would be temporally restored into their owne Country, [would] rebuild Jerusalem, and have a most reformed, and flourishing, Church and Commonwealth." Their attempts to return will cause "the great Turke, the King of the North," to try to exterminate them, but "Michaell the great Prince" will defend them. Then they will reach their ancient homeland, become "an Exemplary Church of all the world, and all Nations shall flow unto it, and it shall bee, as it were, a visible heaven upon earth."[30]

Thomas Brightman (1562–1607) laid the foundation for much ensuing thought about eschatology and Israel, particularly by Puritans. In his commentary on the book of Revelation, published posthumously in 1611, Brightman said that Jews were the "kings of the east" of Revelation 16:12 who would destroy Islam. He was certain they would be restored to the land of Zion: "Shal they returne agayn to Jerusalem? There is nothing more sure: the Prophets plainly confirme it, and beat often upon it." Brightman rebuked gentile hatred for Jews, and "laid out a political program by which well-meaning gentiles will seek to advance Jewish interests."[31]

---

28. Ibid., 65.

29. Draxe, *Worldes Resurrection*, 3, 63–64. Smith's *More Desired* is the best guide to Puritan Zionism in the seventeenth century.

30. Draxe, *Last Judgement*, 22, 74–76, 76–77.

31. Brightman, *Revelation*, 440; cited in Smith, *More Desired*, 75.

Toward the beginning of the next decade Henry Finch (c. 1558-1625) expanded the British imagination on Zion. Finch was a legal scholar, Member of Parliament, and strong advocate of Puritan causes. In *The Worlds Great Restauration, or, The Calling of the Iewes* (1621), Finch asserted that after the Jews defeated Gog and Magog (the forces of Islam), they would "sit as a Lady in the mount of comelenesse, that hill of beautie, the true *Tsion*." Then the gentiles will be their servants, and their land would become more fertile and populous than ever before. Making explicit what Brightman and others had assumed, Finch argued against the supersessionist assumption that all references to Israel and Zion in the Bible could be interpreted as references to the gentile church:

> Where *Israel, Iudah, Tsion, Ierusalem,* &c. are named in this argument, the Holy Ghost meaneth not the spirituall Israel, or Church of God collected of the gentiles, no nor of the Iewes and Gentiles both (for each of these have their promises severally and apart) but Israel properly descended out of *Iacobs* loynes.[32]

The widely respected biblical scholar at Cambridge, Joseph Mede (1586-1638), was another Puritan sympathizer who advanced these same Zionist themes of the Jews being restored to the land of Israel after the destruction of the Turkish Empire. One of Mede's students was John Milton, who in *Paradise Regained* wrote in 1670 of the return of the people of Israel to their ancient land:

> Yet He at length, time to himself best known,
> Remembering Abraham, by some wondrous call
> May bring them back, repentant and sincere,
> And at their passing cleave the Assyrian flood,
> While to their native land with joy they haste,
> As the Red Sea and Jordan once he cleft,
> When to the Promised Land their fathers passed.
> To his due time and providence I leave them.[33]

Between Mede and Milton was John Cotton, the Puritan who helped shepherd the adventurous souls of the Massachusetts Bay Colony. Cotton's 1642 commentary on Canticles (the Song of Solomon) followed Brightmans's suggestion that the armies of the Jews "shall bee terrible to the Turkes and Tartars," but goes further by urging gentiles to prove their

---

32. Finch, *Worlds Great Restauration*, A2-A3, 5-6.

33. Milton, *Paradise Regained* (1671), cited in Lewis, *Origins of Christian Zionism*, 33.

faithfulness by actively helping Jews return to Palestine. They should be willing "to convey the Jewes into their owne Countrie, with Charets, and horses, and dromedaries."[34]

Another Puritan development of Christian Zionism came in Increase Mather's *The Mystery of Israel's Salvation* (1669), which was "the most comprehensive work on the restoration of Israel published" in this period. Writing from Boston in the Bay Colony, Mather wrote that the future conversion of "the Jewish Nation" was "a truth of late [that] hath gained ground much throughout the world." This widespread acceptance was a sign that the times of the end were near, a time when "the *Israelites* shall again possesse . . . the Land promised unto their *Father Abraham*."[35]

One of Mather's innovations was to charge that the Jews would regain their ancient land *before* they would convert. It would be only "after the Israelites shall be returned to their own Land again" that the Holy Spirit would be poured out on them. Mather also warned against a supersessionist spiritualization of promises made to Israel: "Why should we unnecessarily refuse literal interpretations?" Like Finch, Mather insisted that promises about earthly inheritance should not be spiritualized away.[36]

## Eighteenth-Century Zionist Postmillennialists

At the turn of the eighteenth century, the Dutch Reformed theologian Wilhelmus à Brakel (1635–1711) published a four-volume systematic theology that decisively broke with Calvin's supersessionism and presented a Christian Zionism that was more nuanced than what we have seen heretofore. Brakel insisted that the church was not a New Israel, and that Paul's reference to "all Israel" in Romans 11:25 had in mind Jewish Israel as a people with a distinct future.[37] Brakel declared emphatically that Jews would return to the land.

> Will the Jewish nation be gathered together again from all the regions of the world and from all the nations of the earth among which they have been dispersed? Will they come to and dwell in

---

34. Cotton, *Song of Solomon*, 195, 196.

35. Smith, *More Desired*, 124; Increase Mather, *Mystery of Israel's Salvation*, 43–44, 53–54.

36. Mather, *Mystery*, 54, 56–57; cited in Smith, *More Desired*, 126, 125.

37. VanGemeren, "Israel as the Hermeneutical Crux," 142–43.

Canaan and all the lands promised to Abraham, and will Jerusalem be rebuilt? We believe that these events will transpire.[38]

Jonathan Edwards (1703–58) agreed with Brakel that Calvin's supersessionism used a hyper-spiritualist hermeneutic that rode rough-shod over Scripture's plain sense. Like Brakel, he felt that the development of rabbinic Judaism had departed from the Old Testament's soteriological trajectory, but Edwards waxed lyrical over the theological continuity between the Jewish Bible and the New Testament. He did so in the midst of his life-long battle against deism, which he considered to be the greatest enemy to Christian orthodoxy.

For the first time since Marcion (d. ca. 160), in the eighteenth century Jews were regarded as religiously unrelated to Christians. Deists launched the attack, charging that Judaism was essentially pagan, unspiritual, unnecessary to Christianity, and in fact the source of all that was wrong with traditional Christianity.[39] Edwards argued strenuously against the deist severance of the religious link between Jews and Christians by positing one covenant binding the two religions. The Old Testament and New Testament covenants, he asserted, are different but integrally-related modes of a single plan of redemption. The Old Testament covenant was the "cortex" or "shell" that "envelops" the "medulla" of the gospel or covenant of grace.

For Edwards, the two covenants were two phases or ways of performing the same one covenant. As Edwards put it early in his career, "The gospel was preached to the Jews under a veil."[40] The process of conversion was the same for Jews in the Old Testament as for Christians in the New. They were "convinced so much of their wickedness that they trusted to nothing but the mere mercy of God." Christ saved the Old Testament saints just like their cohorts in the New, and they believed in Christ, but under the name of the "angel of the Lord" or "messenger of the covenant." In fact, Christ appeared to Old Testament Jews; Moses saw his back parts on Mount Sinai, and he appeared in human form to the seventy elders (Exod 24:9–11) as well as to Joshua, Gideon, and Manoah. For that matter, every time God was said to have manifested himself to humans in a voice or otherwise tangible form, it was always through the second person of the Trinity.[41]

---

38. Brakel, *Reasonable Service*, 4: 530–31. I am grateful for Horner's work on Brakel, *Future Israel*, 153–55.

39. McDermott, *Jonathan Edwards Confronts the Gods*, 9–11, 26–28, 150–52.

40. Edwards, "Profitable Hearers of the Word," *WJE* 14:247.

41. Edwards, "'Misc.' 39," *WJE* 13:221–22; Edwards, "'Misc.' 1283," *WJE* 23:229–30; Edwards, "'Controversies' Notebook," *WJE* 21:372–73, 375–76; Edwards, *History of the Work of Redemption*, *WJE* 9:197, 131.

Though the two covenants had two federal heads, Adam and Christ, and one was a "dead" way but the other "living," "in strictness of speech" they were not two but one. For they shared the same mediator, the same salvation (which means the same calling, justification, adoption, sanctification, and glory), and the same medium of salvation: the incarnation, suffering, righteousness, and intercession of Christ. The Holy Spirit was the same person applying Christ's redemption in both dispensations, and the method of obtaining salvation was the same: faith and repentance. The external means (the word of God and ordinances such as prayer and praise, sabbath and sacraments) were not different. Nor were the benefits—God's Spirit by God's mere mercy and by a divine person (the angel of the Lord or Mediator)—and future blessings. For both, the condition was faith in the Son of God as Mediator, expressed with the same spirit of repentance and humility. This is why all parts of the Old Testament point to the future coming of Christ. In sum, the religion of the church of Israel is "essentially the same religion with that of the Christian church."[42]

However, Jews were no longer a seed of Abraham, "no more than Ishmaelites or Edomites." Edwards believed that their rare conversions to Christianity and continued refusals to accept Christ were two clear signs that "the Spirit of God left them and their day of grace was past."[43] After all, they have persisted in their "obstinate Jewish infidelity."[44]

So, *sounding* like a typical Reformed supersessionist, Edwards wrote that the Christian church is the true Israel that inherits *most* of the promises made to Jews in the Old Testament. "The Christian church is grafted on to their [Israelites'] root," but "we are not to imagine that the old walls of separation [between Jew and gentile] will be set up again."[45] Now that Christ has come and the early church, which was entirely Jewish at first, has gradually been displaced by a mostly gentile church, the "Mosaic ordinances" have also been displaced.[46] They are defunct for those who recognize that the Jewish messiah has already come.

Gentiles have so replaced the Jewish church that their blood has been mixed. Edwards was convinced that most Christians have traces of Jewish

42. Edwards, *History of the Work of Redemption*, WJE 9:443, 283. See also Edwards, "'Misc.' 35," WJE 13:219; "'Misc.' 874," WJE 20:117–18; "'Misc.' 1353," WJE 23:502–03.

43. Edwards, *History of the Work of Redemption*, WJE 9:383; Edwards, "Living Unconverted under an Eminent Means of Grace," WJE 14:369.

44. Edwards, *History of the Work of Redemption*, WJE 9:469.

45. Edwards, "Notes on the Apocalypse," WJE 5:135; Edwards, *History of the Work of Redemption*, WJE 9:443.

46. Edwards, "'Misc.' 597," WJE 18:132.

blood. Why? Because the early Jewish Christians "were dispersed all over the world" and intermarried with gentiles.[47] So there are even genetic reasons now why the true church of Christ is the new spiritual Israel.

So for Edwards, the Christian church was the New Israel: "They have the essentials of Israelites, the circumcision of the heart, and are the spiritual Israel of God, of which the Israelite nation are but a mere type and shadow."[48] Besides, all through the history of Old Testament Israel, foreigners who submitted to the God of Israel were taken to be Jews: Uriah the Hittite, Obil the Ishmaelite, Araunah or Ornan the Jebusite, Zelek the Ammonite, Ithmah the Moabite, Obed-edom the Gittite, Ittai the Gittite, the six hundred men who came up with David from Gath, many of the Jebusites, the Kenites in Numbers 10, Jethro, the Gibeonites, and Ruth.[49] Isaiah predicted that gentiles would be many more than Jews in the new, spiritual Israel. Therefore "there can be no reason why people now that join themselves to the God of Israel, and embrace the religion that he has instituted for Israel, should not be accounted true Israelites, as well as those Edomites."[50]

## Future Christians

But if Edwards appeared to be a typical Reformed supersessionist—in swallowing up "spiritual" Jews into the New Israel that was overwhelmingly gentile, and setting Mosaic law aside so that Jews for all intents and purposes disappear—he brought Jews back in through the eschatological door. There was, he insisted, to be a second day of grace. God would not reject Jewish Israel forever. God had abandoned them because their idolatry had moved him to jealousy, and now he was moving *them* to jealousy by casting them off and taking another people for himself. Just before the millennium commenced, God would remove the veil over their eyes and soften their hearts with grace. All Israel will then be saved. "Nothing is more certainly foretold than this national conversion of the Jews in the eleventh chapter of Romans."[51]

Edwards was not innovative on this score. As we have seen, Increase Mather and Joseph Mede had both predicted that Israel would be restored,

---

47. Edwards, "'Misc.' 49," *WJE* 13:228.
48. Ibid.
49. Edwards, "'Misc.' 597," *WJE* 18:132–33.
50. Ibid., *WJE* 18:134.
51. Edwards, *History of the Work of Redemption*, *WJE* 9:189, 469.

politically and spiritually, before the millennium would begin.⁵² Cotton Mather spent his life yearning expectantly for the conversion of the Jews.⁵³ But Edwards seemed as energized as any. He made entries into his notebooks of articles in the press reporting conversions of Jews. In 1748, for example, he noted that a Jew was baptized in London, a German Christian had led six hundred Jews to Christian faith, and fifty-three Polish Jews and one rabbi had converted in Germany.⁵⁴ He calculated the timing of this national conversion; it would be before the wholesale conversion of the heathen, and after the "first main" destruction of the Antichrist.⁵⁵

Edwards also determined that the Jews would return to their homeland. This was inevitable, he reasoned, because the prophecies of land being given to them had been only partly fulfilled. It was also necessary in order for God to make them a "visible monument" of his grace and power at their conversion. At that moment, religion and learning would be at their respective peaks, and Canaan once again would be a spiritual center of the world. Although Israel would again be a distinct nation, Christians would have free access to Jerusalem, because Jews would look on Christians as their brethren.⁵⁶

As we have seen, on this score too Edwards was not unique, at least for the Puritan tradition. But just as some of the most distinctive innovations have come from thinkers who are removed from bastions of intellectual power,⁵⁷ new arguments and impetus came from this theologian on the frontier.

For example, he became convinced that there would be a massive Jewish conversion "before the glory of the gentile part of the church shall be fully accomplished," because Paul says in Romans 11 that "their [Jews'] coming in shall be life from the dead for the Gentiles."⁵⁸ It would be after the conversion of the "civilized" world and Europe (and even Turkey!) in

---

52. Manuel, *Broken Staff*, 160–61.
53. Goldman, *Hebrew and the Bible in America*, xvii.
54. Edwards, "Notes on the Apocalypse," *WJE* 5:287, 292–93, 295–96.
55. Ibid., 140, 195–96.
56. Ibid., 134, 135.
57. Think of Einstein who conducted a scientific revolution while, unable to get a teaching post, toiled as a patent clerk, and Barth who preached to a resistant congregation within imaginative hearing of "the sound of the guns booming away in the north." Karl Barth, *Romans*, v.
58. Edwards, *History of the Work of Redemption*, *WJE* 9:470.

the latter-day glory before the millennium, but before "the converting and enlightening of all the nations of Asia."[59] These are the true "heathen."[60]

Edwards also entertained some novel reasoning about the return of Jews to the land in those latter days that were to come. He said that this *had* to happen because "they never have yet possessed one quarter of that land, which was so often promised them, from the Red Sea to the river Euphrates." This promise was partly fulfilled in Solomon's time, but that time was very short, and besides, Israel only *governed* other lands then—she did not *possess* them.[61] Furthermore, he argued, it makes sense that corporate redemption would follow the pattern of individual redemption. Or, as Edwards would put it, there is *harmony* between corporate and individual redemption. In his Blank Bible he wrote that just as the "restoration" of an individual at first involves only his soul but then later his body at the general resurrection, the same applies for Israel: "not only shall the spiritual state of the Jews be hereafter restored, but their external state as a nation in their own land"[62] will be restored as well.

And what a restoration it shall be! Edwards said that the "remains of the Ten [Lost] Tribes" of Israel would also come to the land with the rest of the Jews returning from all over the world. They will be showered with a "more eminent share" of the "benefits" of the latter-day glory than perhaps any other people. Their learning and messianic religion shall be the "highest" of all, and their books will be "more excellent" than others. Their ancient connections to their fathers Abraham, Isaac, and Jacob shall be exceedingly "visible and conspicuous" to all the world. And then, after this latter-day glory, their land would be the center of the millennium.

We might wonder why. Why would God shower what seems to be greater glory on Israel than on any other people of the world, especially after thousands of years in which Jewish Christians have lost their identity in a gentile church? Edwards's answer is God's faithfulness, which he identified elsewhere as God's righteousness, and which, in view of his understanding of the end of creation, means God's glory. God would bring further glory to himself by showing the cosmos that he was faithful after all to the promises he made to the fathers of Israel—Abraham, Isaac, and Jacob. By showing "respect to the Fathers," God would gain glory for himself.

59. Edwards, "Notes on the Apocalypse," *WJE* 5:116.

60. Ibid., *WJE* 5:140. At the same time, Edwards believed that ancient China was the closest of all nations in the ancient world—Israel excepted of course—to knowing the true God. McDermott, *Jonathan Edwards Confronts the Gods*.

61. Edwards, "Notes on the Apocalypse," *WJE* 5:134.

62. Edwards, *WJE* 24:1028.

## American—and Edwardsean—Exceptionalism

According to Arthur Hertzberg, this American linkage of Jewish conversion to end-time glories and the millennium was why "American intellectual anti-Semitism never became as virulent as its counterparts in Europe."[63] Christians in Europe believed the End was in the indefinite future. But in America the End seemed near because of the influence of Puritan theology and its foregrounding of Israel, and according to these Puritans the End would not come without major changes in the fortunes of the Jews. So in the colonies, the Jewish question moved "to center stage."[64]

So Edwards declined the invitation of the intellectual elites to minimize Christianity's debt to Judaism. If Christianity was the logical end of Judaism, its meaning could be found only through Judaism. The antitype was to be fully understood only by reference to its types. Hence, tension in the Jewish-Christian relationship was a family quarrel. Edwards exercised a certain hubris by claiming that his Jewish brethren were less favored by their common Father, and indeed had been disowned. But he believed they would someday be reconciled to their divine Parent, regain their ancient homeland, establish a polity there, and regain their status as children in full favor.

But we might ask what led Edwards to develop Puritan Zionism to the lengths that he did. Here we can only guess, but I think our guesses are plausible. First, Edwards was overwhelmingly driven by the conviction that deism was the greatest threat to orthodoxy that the modern world had seen. This fueled his battles with Arminianism, because he believed that the latter was only a way-station on the road to the former. He knew the vicious anti-Semitism of the deists (Voltaire, for example, wrote that Jews ought to have inscribed on their foreheads, "Fit to be hanged"), and he also knew that anti-Judaism was the tip of the spear that deists used to pierce what they thought to be the fragile balloon of Christian orthodoxy.

Second, Edwards was a master of the biblical text like few others in the history of Christian thought. He was fully aware that two-thirds of the Bible came from and was about Israel; it is no surprise that two-thirds of his commentary in the Blank Bible was on the Old Testament. He also knew that Romans 11 predicted a future for Jews and Israel that was distinct from the gentile world and church. It was for this reason, among others, that he could not abide the rest of the Reformed tradition's obliteration of ethnic Israel after AD 33.

---

63. Hertzberg, "New England Puritans," 116.
64. Ibid.

Third, Edwards was a virtuoso typologist. He was fully aware of the distinction that Erich Auerbach drew between allegory and type/antitype, in which the latter are events and persons in history rather than free-floating ideas linked by imagined similarities.[65] This commitment to the fleshiness of the antitype, combined with his Reformation commitment to the plain sense of Scripture, prevented him from so spiritualizing the biblical prophecies that their earthy fulfillments were evaporated. To be sure, Edwards believed the New Jerusalem was part of the new earth that was not on this earth but beyond this solar system.[66] And he also recognized the abundance of metaphorical "similitudes" in the book of Revelation.[67] Nevertheless, just as, according to Bill Danaher, Edwards went beyond his Reformed predecessors in his conviction that the humanity of Christ was really present at the Lord's Supper,[68] so too in his Zionist eschatology Edwards put new emphasis on the carnal dimensions of biblical prophecies about the land of Israel.

## Conclusion

Why am I exploring this topic? Why is this significant, other than uncovering perhaps a little bit more about "America's theologian" than some of us might have known? In other words, is this just another kind of antiquarianism with a sensationalist edge?

I would suggest that it is not, and for three reasons. First, I explore this topic to correct misperceptions. As I said at the start, far too many historians and theologians think Christian Zionism is recent and dispensationalist—another zany fundamentalist myth. Or that all Christian Zionisms forbid criticisms of the present state of Israel, or assume that this state is the last polity of the Jewish people before the eschaton. Or that it precludes seeking justice for Palestinians. I hope I have shown, albeit briefly, why none of these descriptors apply to Edwards's Zionism. And that Zionism goes back to the early church and has been embraced by many before Edwards, but indeed also *by* Edwards.

---

65. Auerbach, "Figura"; *Mimesis*.

66. Stein, "Editor's Introduction," *WJE* 5:67; Edwards, "Nothing Upon Earth Can Represent the Glories of Heaven," *WJE* 14:138; Edwards, "Notes on the Apocalypse," *WJE* 5:141.

67. Edwards, "Nothing Upon Earth Can Represent the Glories of Heaven," *WJE* 14:138.

68. Danaher, "By Sensible Signs Represented," 279–80.

Second, although it has been well known for some time that Puritan eschatology took a different direction from the rest of the Reformed tradition, its Zionism has been less well known. It *needs* to be known that this is a significant contribution of the Reformed tradition—no matter what we think of Zionism. For the sake of our knowledge of the Reformed tradition, it is important to add that that other great luminary of modern Reformed theology—Karl Barth—was also a Christian Zionist. He respected millenarian attempts to take seriously God's sovereignty over world events, including the appearance of Israel as a nation-state in 1948. This was a "secular parable," as was the rise of socialism in modern history. The sudden reappearance of Israel was a type of resurrection and the kingdom of God. It was a "little light" that bore witness to the Light of the World in Jesus Christ. The modern history of Israel "even now hurries relentlessly" toward the future of God's redemptive purposes. According to Barth, biblical revelation points to a threefold parousia of Jesus—the Incarnation, Pentecost, and Christ's eschatological coming in Israel and the church. This last coming is the meaning of a long string of Old Testament prophecies that speak of the return of Jews to the land, a time when gentiles shall come to Israel to learn Torah.[69] Israel would be involved in a global spiritual renewal at the end of history, and in the meantime God's promise to Abraham that in him all the earth would be blessed meant that "*any* national regime set up in deliberate opposition to the existence of Israel as a nation will not fare very well in the long run."[70]

Finally (third), while we must avoid presentist or Whiggish history in which we distort the past to serve our version of the future, it is not illegitimate to point out the timeliness or relevance of history to current concerns. In fact, I would argue that most, or all, theology and historiography are done with an ear to background events and conversations. In this case, it is important to recall that just as in the heyday of deism, Israel is once again being vilified and detached from its first child, the Christian tradition. The nation-state itself is being targeted by a national BDS (boycott, divest, sanction) movement, while at the same time it faces neighbors dedicated to its extinction. Christians are once again making Marcionite objections to the inspiration of the Old Testament, and deist-like complaints about the thuggery of the God of Israel.

For these reasons, Edwards's Zionism is of more than antiquarian interest.

69. Moseley, *Nationhood, Providence, and Witness*, 221–22. On Barth's notion of "secular parable," see *Church Dogmatics* 4.3.1; on Israel as a "little light," Moseley cites *CD* 4.3.1, 55–58; for "even now hurries relentlessly," ibid., 59; for the long string of Old Testament prophecies, she cites ibid., 58–59.

70. Moseley, *Nationhood, Providence, and Witness*, 226; emphasis original.

# Bibliography

Auerbach, Eric. "Figura." In *Scenes from the Drama of European Literature*, translated by Ralph Manheim, 11–76. Minneapolis: University of Minnesota Press, 1984.

———. *Mimesis: The Representation of Reality in Western Literature*. Translated by Willard Trask. Princeton: Princeton University Press, 2003.

Barth, Karl. *Church Dogmatics*. Translated by G. T. Thomson et al. Edinburgh: T. & T. Clark, 1936–77.

———. *Church Dogmatics* 4.3.1. Reprint. Translated by G.W. Bromiley. Peabody, MA: Hendrickson, 2010.

———. *Epistle to the Romans*. Translated by Edwyn C. Hoskyns. New York: Oxford University Press, 1968.

Bockmuehl, Markus. *Jewish Law in Gentile Churches: Halakhah and the Beginning of Christian Public Ethics*. Grand Rapids: Baker Academic, 2000.

Brakel, W. *The Christian's Reasonable Service*. 4 vols. Ligonier, PA: Soli Deo Gloria, 1992.

Brightman, Thomas. *A Revelation of the Apocalyps*. Amsterdam: Hondius & Laurenss, 1611.

Burrell, David. "How Christians Share in the Destiny of Israel." In *Voices from Jerusalem: Jews and Christians Reflect on the Holy Land*, edited by David Burrell and Yehezkel Landau, 5–17. New York: Paulist, 1992.

Cotton, John. *A Brief Exposition of the whole Book of Canticles, or, Song of Solomon*. London: Philip Nevil, 1642.

Culver, Douglas J. *Albion and Ariel: British Puritanism and the Birth of Political Zionism*. New York: Peter Lang, 1995.

Danaher, William J. Jr. "By Sensible Signs Represented: Jonathan Edwards's Sermons on the Lord's Supper." *Pro Ecclesia* 7 (1998) 279–80.

Draxe, Thomas *An Alarum to the Last Judgement*. London: Nicholas Oakes and Matthew Law, 1615.

Draxe, Thomas. *The Worldes Resurrection, or The general calling of the Iewes*. London: G Eld and John Wright, 1608.

Edwards, Jonathan. "The 'Controversies' Notebook." In *Writings on the Trinity, Grace, and Faith*, edited by Sang Hyun Lee, The Works of Jonathan Edwards 21:291–413. New Haven: Yale University Press, 2003.

———. *A History of the Work of Redemption*. Edited by John F. Wilson. The Works of Jonathan Edwards 9. New Haven: Yale University Press, 1989.

———. "Living Unconverted under an Eminent Means of Grace." In *Sermons and Discourses 1723–1729*, edited by Kenneth P. Minkema, The Works of Jonathan Edwards 14:357–70. New Haven: Yale University Press, 1997.

———. "'Misc.' 35." In *The "Miscellanies" (Entry Nos. a–z, aa–zz, 1–500)*, edited by Thomas A. Schafer, The Works of Jonathan Edwards 13:219. New Haven: Yale University Press, 1994.

———. "'Misc.' 39." In *The "Miscellanies" (Entry Nos. a–z, aa–zz, 1–500)*, edited by Thomas A. Schafer, The Works of Jonathan Edwards 13:221–22. New Haven: Yale University Press, 1994.

———. "'Misc.' 49." In *The "Miscellanies" (Entry Nos. a–z, aa–zz, 1–500)*, edited by Thomas A. Schafer, The Works of Jonathan Edwards 13:227–28. New Haven: Yale University Press, 1994.

———. "'Misc.' 597." In *The "Miscellanies" (Entry Nos. 501-832)*, edited by Ava Chamberlain, The Works of Jonathan Edwards 18:131-40. New Haven: Yale University Press, 2000.

———. "'Misc.' 874." In *The "Miscellanies" (Entry Nos. 833-1152)*, edited by Amy P. Pauw, The Works of Jonathan Edwards 20:115-18. New Haven: Yale University Press, 2002.

———. "'Misc.' 1283." In *The "Miscellanies" (Entry Nos. 1153-1360)*, edited by Douglas A. Sweeney, The Works of Jonathan Edwards 23:229-30. New Haven: Yale University Press, 2004.

———. "'Misc.' 1353." In *The "Miscellanies" (Entry Nos. 1153-1360)*, edited by Douglas A. Sweeney, The Works of Jonathan Edwards 23:492-506. New Haven: Yale University Press, 2004.

———. "'Notes on the Apocalypse.'" In *Apocalyptic Writings*, edited by Stephen J. Stein, The Works of Jonathan Edwards 5:95-305. New Haven: Yale University Press, 1977.

———. "Nothing Upon Earth Can Represent the Glories of Heaven." In *Sermons and Discourses, 1723-1729*, edited by Kenneth P. Minkema, The Works of Jonathan Edwards 14:134-60. New Haven: Yale University Press, 1997.

———. "Profitable Hearers of the Word." In *Sermons and Discourses, 1723-1729*, edited by Kenneth P. Minkema, The Works of Jonathan Edwards 14:243-77. New Haven: Yale University Press, 1997.

———. "Romans 11:11." In *The "Blank Bible,"* edited by Stephen J. Stein, The Works of Jonathan Edwards 24/2:1027-28. New Haven: Yale University Press, 2006.

Finch, Henry. *The Worlds Great Restauration, or, The Calling of the Iewes*. London: Edward Griffin and William Bladen, 1621.

Gibbon, Edward. *The Decline and Fall of the Roman Empire*, 3 vols. New York: Modern Library, n. d.

Goldman, Shalom, ed. *Hebrew and the Bible in America: The First Two Centuries*. Hanover, NH: University Press of New England, 1993.

Hays, Richard. *Reading Backwards: Figural Christology and the Fourfold Gospel Witness*. Waco: Baylor University Press, 2014.

Hertzberg, Arthur. "The New England Puritans and the Jews." In *Hebrew and the Bible in America: The First Two Centuries*, edited by Shalom Goldman, 105-21. Hanover, NH: New England University Press, 1993.

Horner, Barry E. *Future Israel: Why Christian Anti-Judaism Must Be Challenged*. Nashville: B&H Academic, 2007.

Irenaeus, *Against Heresies* V, 34.1, http://www.newadvent.org/fathers/0103534.htm.

Justin Martyr, *Dialogue with Trypho*, chapters LXXX & LXXXI in *Christian Classics Ethereal Library*, http://www.ccel.org/ccel/schaff/anf01.viii.iv.lxxx.html.

Lewis, Donald M. *The Origins of Christian Zionism: Lord Shaftesbury and Evangelical Support for a Jewish Homeland*. Cambridge MA: Cambridge University Press, 2010.

Manuel, Frank Edward. *The Broken Staff*. Cambridge: Harvard University Press, 1992.

———. *The Changing of the Gods*. Providence: Brown University Press, 1983.

Mather, Increase. *Mystery of Israel's Salvation*. London: John Allen, 1669.

McDermott, Gerald R. *Jonathan Edwards Confronts the Gods: Christian Theology, Enlightenment Religion, and Non-Christian Faiths*. New York: Oxford University Press, 2000.

McDermontt, Gerald R., ed. *The New Christian Zionism*. Downers Grove, IL: InterVarsity, 2016.
Moseley, Carys. *Nationhood, Providence, and Witness: Israel in Protestant Theology and Social Theory*. Eugene, OR: Cascade, 2013.
Origen, *On First Principles*. Gloucester, MA: Peter Smith, 1973.
Pailin, David Arthur. *Attitudes to Other Religions: Comparative Religion in Seventeenth- and Eighteenth-century Britain*. Manchester: Manchester University Press: 1984.
Sanders, James. *Jesus and Judaism*. Philadelphia: Fortress, 1985.
Smith, Robert O. *More Desired than Our Owne Salvation: The Roots of Christian Zionism*. Oxford: Oxford University Press, 2013.
Stein, Stephen J. "Editor's Introduction." In *Apocalyptic Writings*, edited by Stephen J. Stein, The Works of Jonathan Edwards 5:1–93. New Haven: Yale University Press, 1977.
Tertullian, *On Modesty*, chapter 8, http://www.newadvent.org/fathers/0407.htm
Tuchman, Barbara W. *The Bible and the Sword: England and Palestine from the Bronze Age to Balfour*. New York: Ballantine, 1956.
VanGemeren, Willem A. "Israel as the Hermeneutical Crux in the Interpretation of Prophecy." *Westminster Theological Journal* 45 (1983) 142–43.
Wilken, Robert L. *The Land Called Holy: Palestine in Christian History and Thought*. New Haven: Yale University Press, 1992.

# 6

# Revivals in Eighteenth-Century Poland
## *Jonathan Edwards and the Conversion of Polish Jews*

JOEL BURNELL

## Introduction

IN HIS WORKING JOURNAL, "Notes on the Apocalypse," Jonathan Edwards transcribed a letter written in 1752, which describes the conversion of fifty-three rabbis and 15,000 Jews in Roda, Poland. Why would Edwards bother to make note of such an event? The answer to that question is rather easy. A more difficult question is whether such a large conversion of Jews to Christianity actually took place in Poland at that time. The main body of this article will focus on determining the historical facts behind the report and considering its significance.

Edwards was an avid student of history as well as contemporary events, but his particular interest in both was piqued by his view of salvation history and eschatology. As seen in his sermon, "A History of the Work of Redemption," he saw revivals as a work of God: both the means God would use to redeem the world, and signs of the coming victory of Christ. Searching for signs of the coming Millennium, he followed events in Europe, including the Pietist revivals in Halle, and revivals in England sparked by John and Charles Wesley, George Whitefield, and the Methodists. When revivals came to Poland, he was particularly intrigued by reports of the conversion of Jews to Christianity. In 1750 Edwards wrote the following in a letter to John Erskine:

> We have had published here an extract of a letter, written by Dr. [Philip] Doddridge to Mr. [Richard] Pearsall, of Taunton in Somersetshire, and transmitted by him to Boston, in a letter to Mr. [Thomas] Prince; giving a surprising account of a very wonderful person, a German by nation, a preacher of the gospel to the Jews, lately in London; whom he (Dr. Doddridge) saw and conversed with and heard preach (or rather repeat) a sermon there; who had had great success in preaching to those miserable people in Germany, Poland, Holland, Lithuania, Hungary, and other parts; God having so blessed his labors that in the various parts through which he had traveled, he had been the instrument of the conversion of about 600 Jews; many of whom are expressing their great concern to bring others of their brethren to the knowledge of the great and blessed Redeemer, and beseeching him to instruct their children, that they may preach Christ also. I should be glad, if you hear anything further of the affair, to be informed of it by you.[1]

This letter is of interest in its own right, particularly in relation to Dr. Doddridge and the identity of the German evangelist to the Jews. Edwards's unfortunate reference to the Jews as "those miserable people," politically incorrect in our day, was not unusual for his time, and with some discomfort can be taken as a reference to their religious faith and practice rather than as an expression of anti-Semitism.

## "Notes on the Apocalypse"

An even more interesting reference to events in Poland appears in "Notes on the Apocalypse," one of Edwards's many working journals. In this journal Edwards copied a translation of a letter written in 1752 by a baptized rabbi, Leopold Jacob de Dors, describing the imminent conversion of fifty-three rabbis and 15,000 Jews in the city of Roda, Poland. This letter presents us with an historical riddle, namely, who were these Jews from Poland who sought to convert to Christianity in 1752? To answer this question, we need to first examine the letter itself, along with the note Edwards made to himself concerning its contents and source.

---

1. Edwards, "Letter to John Erskine," *WJE* 16:350.

*New York Gazette* of August 26, 1754.² A paragraph of a letter of a baptized rabbi, Leopold Jacob de Dors, written at Osnaburg in Germany, to a gentleman at Loen, by which a speedy conversion of the Jews is presaged. Translated out of the Dutch *Monthly State Secretary* for the month of March, 1754.

The above-named rabbi sets forth in the course of his letter: "In a council of the scattered Jewish church, assembled on matters of faith at Roda in Poland, the 4th of August, 1752, were assembled 548 rabbis; 53 whereof, with 15,000 of the principal Jews, separated themselves and sent a learned Jewish Christian from Poland, by way of Danzig and Amsterdam, to me with full power to offer unto me their undisguised confession of faith, contained in the five following articles.

1. That the only true Godhead consists in three persons.
2. That the Messiah is the true Immanuel.
3. That this is certainly Jesus of Bethlehem.
4. That the Old Testament is a type of the New.
5. That the holy gospel is the true Word of God.

The various divisions and disputes in Christendom, put them at a stand what set of Christians to join, which made them apply to me to advise them which was the most essential way, and the Christian books [to be] brought into Hebrew when, as they promise, they would come into the true Christian dominions, with all their effects, in order to serve the Lord.

Now, sir, as I have experienced the benefit in and by the holy religion you maintain, so I beg of you to favor me and those Jewish Christians with your protection, and to aid them in translating the Scripture into Hebrew in the city of Lingen, as also to let me have a speedy answer, etc.³

Back in New England, Edwards enthusiastically commented to his congregation about this event, which he believed portrayed Jewish dialogue with Christians and the conversion of Jews in Poland to Christianity. But there is more to this matter than meets the eye. I will look first at the letter's path of transmission, before addressing historical errors it contains. Before drawing

---

2. The New York Gazette, founded in 1725, was the first newspaper published in the colony of New York. In its early years most articles contained in the Gazette consisted of texts republished from European newspapers, with a delay of several months—in this case of five months.

3. Edwards, "Notes on the Apocalypse," *WJE* 5:295–96.

conclusions, it will also prove fruitful to discuss the historical context of the events described in the letter, both in Poland and more broadly in Europe.

## The Path of Transmission

Leopold Jacob de Dors's letter was first published in Germany in 1752, in *Acta historico-ecclesiastica: oder gesammlete Nachrichten von d. neuesten Kirchen–Geschichten*.[4] It was then translated into Dutch and printed in March, 1754, in the *Monthly State Secretary*, and was translated again into English and published in the *New York Gazette* in August, 1754, before finding its way at last into Edwards's notebook, "Notes on the Apocalypse."

Such a path of transmission shows that Edwards was not alone in his lively interest in religion, nor in tracing the spread of Protestant Christianity, including reports of the conversion of the Jews. Many of his contemporaries in Europe as well as the American colonies shared Edwards's belief that the conversion of the Jews to Christianity was a necessary precursor to the return of Christ, and hence a sign that the second coming and ensuing Millennium was near.

## Errors in de Dors's Letter

### Errors in Translation and Transcription

In the original German text, the city where Leopold Jacob do Dors wrote the letter is given as Osnabrück,[5] not Osnaburg.[6] The letter is not addressed to a gentleman residing in Loen, but rather to a gentleman named "von Loen."

The first article of the five-point confession of faith of the Polish Jews professes that "The only true Godhead consists in three forms (Gestalten)," not "three persons." Although not a definitive difference, it is significant. For Christian readers, God in three persons is a clear reference to the doctrine of the Trinity. For Jewish sectarians, in particular Sabbateans (whose views we will discuss below), God in three forms provides quite a bit of theological and historical wiggle room. There is a minor issue in the translation of the

---

4. The original letter can be found in: *Acta historico-ecclesiastica*, 1093–95.

5. Osnabrück is a city in Lower-Saxony in northwest Germany.

6. This is not actually an error, since Osnaburg is the archaic English name for Osnabrück. Osnaburg was well known to settlers in the American colonies, since it referred to a coarse type of plain fabric, perhaps first imported to the British Isles from Osnaburg. Osnaburg fabric was woven in Scotland from the 1730s on and exported to England and the British Colonies in America. https://en.wikipedia.org/wiki/Osnaburg

third article, which reads, "That the Old Testament is a type of the New." A more accurate translation than "type" would be "reflection" or "image." Though less theologically significant than the distinction between person and form, one can nevertheless imagine Edwards's enthusiasm at discovering potential Jewish converts who shared his affinity for typology.

The text as copied by Edwards reads thus: "The various divisions and disputes in Christendom, put them at a stand what set of Christians to join, which made them apply to me to advise them which was the most essential way, and the Christian books [to be] brought into Hebrew when . . . ." A more accurate translation of the original text, which has obviously been shortened in transmission, would be, "which made them apply to me to instruct the sent friend and translate for him the best and most foundational Christian books into Hebrew and give them to him." This change in the text is further compounded at the end of de Dors's letter, which in Edwards's notebook reads, "to aid them in translating the Scripture into Hebrew," but in the original asks for aid in translating "these books" into Hebrew. The request was thus for aid in translating into Hebrew selected Christian literature, not specifically the Scripture, which presumably here refers to the New Testament—though of course that would likely be included.

## *The City where the Rabbinic Council Took Place*

The rabbinic council that Edwards refers to did not take place in Roda, but in Brody. It is important to note that this error does not result from mistakes in translation or transcription, but is found in the original German text. A gathering of 548 rabbis would necessarily take place in a larger town or city that boasted a significant Jewish community. Such councils were customarily held during annual trade fairs. There is no reference in Polish or Ukrainian sources to the town of Roda. Brody, in the Lwów district of Ukraine (then a part of the Polish Commonwealth), was home to a large Jewish population. One of the largest cities in the region, Brody was a thriving center of Jewish commerce, culture, and religious life, and the Brody *kloiz* was a leading center of rabbinic and kabbalistic teaching in the Polish Commonwealth.[7]

Brody was a center for both the Haskala and Chassidic movements, and tension often arose between the adherents of these groups. The Haskala movement, which spread to Poland and Galicia in the eighteenth century, was influenced by the Enlightenment, and sought to gain full civil rights

---

7. Eisenberg, "Landau, Ezekiel ben Judah," 266.

for Jews through a program of partial assimilation.[8] Brody and Ternopol were two major centers of the movement. The Chassidic movement began in the eighteenth century, and was centered in the Podole region.[9] In brief, it combined traditional Jewish beliefs and practices with elements of mysticism and Jewish folklore.

The influence of Sabbateanism and later Frankism was also strong in the region. Sabbateanism was a messianic Jewish movement with kabbalistic and mystical roots that arose in the Middle East and Europe in the seventeenth century.[10] Its founder was Sabbatai Zevi who in 1664 declared himself to be the messiah. In 1666 Sabbatai Zevi was forced to convert to Islam. Some (not all) adherents of his teaching followed their leader and outwardly converted to Islam, while secretly observing their Jewish and Sabbatean beliefs and practices. The movement had a significant influence on both Chassidic and Frankist groups. Jacob Frank (1726–91), the founder of Frankism, was influenced by Sabbateanism.[11] His followers accepted his messianic claim. In 1756 Frank and some of his followers converted to Islam, and in 1759 they were baptized in Poland as Roman Catholics. Like the Sabbateans who converted to Islam, the Frankists who outwardly converted to Christianity continued to practice their own beliefs in secret. Brody became a center of opposition to Jacob Frank and the Frankist movement. In 1756 a council was held in the Brody Synagogue that resulted in their excommunication (*herem*), and this was followed in 1772 by excommunication of the followers of the Chassidic movement.[12]

## *The Number of Jewish Converts in Brody*

What historical data do we have regarding the scale, causes, and other characteristics of Jewish conversion in eighteenth-century Poland? Notable among other sources is Adam Kaźmierczyk's 2015 book, *Rodziłem się Żydem (I Was Born a Jew)*,[13] which focuses on Jewish conversion to Catholicism in the Polish Commonwealth in the seventeenth and eighteenth centuries.

---

8. "Haskala." http://www.sztetl.org.pl/pl/term/60,haskala/ See also "Brody" in Skolnik and Berenbaum, *Encyclopedia Judaica vol 11*, 199.

9. "Chasydyzm." http://www.sztetl.org.pl/pl/term/24,chasydyzm/ The Podole region is the west-central and south-central region of present-day Ukraine, then part of the Polish Commonwealth.

10. "Sabataim." http://www.sztetl.org.pl/pl/term/119,sabataizm/

11. "Frankisci." http://www.sztetl.org.pl/pl/term/834,frankisci/

12. Skolnik and Berenbaum. "Brody." 199.

13. Kaźmierczyk, *Rodziłem się Żydem*.

Information in this section is based on Każmierczyk's online summary, in English, of his book.[14]

Apart from genuine religious conversions, which did take place, there were several reasons Jews converted. For poorer Jews, conversion was often the only way out of the *shtetl*. This was for some an opportunity for advancement, but its possibilities were limited. Unless conversion involved one becoming part of the burgher or noble class, the convert would actually experience a drop in social status, to the level of a Christian peasant. On the other hand, when Polish nobles sponsored influential Jews, they received the noble's name and in some cases became part of the lesser gentry.

Of some interest to the question of Brody in 1752 is the matter of Catholic efforts to proselytize Jews.[15] Although this was for a time the official policy of the Roman Church, it was rarely carried out with any enthusiasm in Poland. The major exception was Bishop Franciszek Antoni Kobielski (1679–1755). Kobielski, the Bishop of Łusk, the region where Brody is located, preached in the Synagogue in Brody from 1742 onwards. In 1742 Bishop Kobielski delivered a series of sermons in the Brody Synagogue, where he conducted theological debates with Jewish leaders. The most important points of the Bishop's arguments concerned the doctrine of the Trinity (one God in three persons), the prophecies concerning the birth of Immanuel from a virgin (Is 53:4), and the person of Jesus Christ. The significance of this is perhaps already obvious, but will be discussed at the appropriate time below.

Każmierczyk notes that overall, the rate of conversion of Jews to Christianity in eighteenth-century Poland was about one per one thousand Jews. During the 1740s and 1750s (the time period under investigation in this article), this rate reached as high as three per thousand in some regions. Overall, Każmierczyk reports that hundreds and perhaps thousands of Jews converted in the eighteenth century. Conversions were mostly individuals or families. Except for the case of Jacob Frank and the Frankists in 1759, which we will discuss below, there is no record of mass conversions such as that described in de Dors's letter in 1752 or any other year.

We must also therefore call into question the numbers of Jewish "converts" in Brody. The errors in historical dates and events discussed above were typical for the time, as many writers recorded or referred to historical events from memory. Just as common was the practice of exaggeration, in this case of the numbers of converts, in order to convince the recipients

---

14  Każmierczyk, Summary: *Rodziłem się Żydem*.

15. There were also Protestant efforts to convert Jews, primarily by Lutheran Pietists.

of the letter to organize support for their cause. This leads to the conclusion that the Jewish-Christian emissary from Poland described in the letter grossly inflated the numbers of Rabbis (53 of 548) and Jews (15,000) from Brody who were seeking to convert.

Finally, it is not strange that Jewish converts, including those with Sabbatean leanings, would appeal to Protestants for assistance. As can be seen from many sources, including Edwards's own letter to John Erskine referred to above, Protestant mission efforts to evangelize Jews, most notably undertaken by Lutheran Pietists, had been going on for some time. Indeed some Frankists, rather than being baptized as Roman Catholics, would later join the Moravian Brethren.

### The Date of the Rabbinic Council Referred to in the Letter

Another issue that needs to be addressed in de Dors's original German text is the date of the rabbinic council in Brody, given as August 4, 1752. To check the historic accuracy of this event and date, we must consider key events that took place in Brody in 1752 and the years following.

Rabbi Nathan ben Levi from Brody, an important figure in the Chassidic movement, accused Rabbi Jonathan Eybeschutz of propagating Sabbatean teaching and practices. On June 11, 1752, during a rabbinic council in Brody[16], ben Levi's influence led to a declaration that Eybeschutz's teachings were "absolute heresy."[17] Later that same year, however, Rabbi Ezekiel Landau, who had earlier joined the Brody kloiz and served for ten years as the head of a rabbinic court in Brody, issued a proclamation absolving Eybeschutz of heresy. The controversy continued, and during a meeting of the Council of Four Lands held the following year (1753) in Jaroslaw a famous debate took place between Rabbi Jacob Emden and Rabbi Eybeschutz over the Sabbatean movement. Eybeschutz was acquitted of heresy, but charged to destroy amulets containing Sabbatean texts, which he had given to followers.[18] We will discuss the significance of the controversy between these two rabbis later in this paper. On June 13, 1756, a council was held in the Brody Synagogue that resulted in the excommunication of the Frankists,

---

16. Wurm, *Z dziejów Żydowstwa Brodzkiego*, 55.

17. "Jewish community of Brody," http://www.geni.com/projects/Jewish-Community-of-Brody/2250.

18. "Council of Four Lands," http://en.wikipedia.org/wiki/Council_of_Four_Lands.

Sabbatean sympathizers who accepted Frank's claim to be the reincarnation of the spirit of Sabbatai Zevi.[19]

Wurm gives an interesting though erroneous report of the tumultuous events in the Jewish community in Brody. Claiming that a second, more important rabbinic council took place in 1752, Wurm writes:

> In the same year [1752] a rabbinic court took place, made up of the most distinguished representatives of the Talmudic world in Poland. This court was called at the initiative of the Chief Rabbi of Brody, Nathan Note, with the material and moral support of the Brody Kahal (community council). The purpose of this court was to once and for all put an end to the evil that was spreading in Brody. For the emissaries of Jacob Frank had begun their campaign. The until-then proverbial purity of morals and family relations among Jews gave way to degeneration and indecency.[20]

That Jacob Frank's emissaries were already active in Brody in 1752 is indeed surprising information, given that Jakob Frank himself only arrived in the Podole region in 1755. An organized campaign by Frank's agents to prepare the way for his appearance would be news indeed! However, this report is not confirmed by other sources. It is true that Rabin Nathan Note convened a rabbinic council, composed as Wurm tells us "of the most distinguished representative of the Talmudic world in Poland," to deal with "the matter of the Frankists and their orgies,"[21] and more generally to oppose the Sabbatean practices of Frank and his followers. This council, however, took place not in 1752 but in 1756.[22]

In all likelihood Wurm's error in the date of this second council results from another mistake he made concerning the date of a decree issued by Stanisław Potocki, the Polish nobleman who owned the city of Brody and its surrounding regions. Wurm writes that Rabin Nathan Note, who initiated and led the rabbinic court in Brody (which Wurm erroneously dated in 1752), met with unpleasant consequences resulting from his struggles with the Frankists. The Sabbateans and Frankists were naturally displeased with the judgment issued against them by the rabbinic court and appealed to Potocki, the city's hereditary magnate. Wurm writes that on June 25, 1752, Potocki, under the influence of Bishop Kobielski, dismissed the rabbinic court, overturned its decrees, and issued his own edict. Potocki rehabilitated

---

19. "The Jewish Settlement of Brody," *Pinkas Hakehilot*.
20. Wurm, *Z dziejów Żydowstwa Brodzkiego*, 55.
21. "The Jewish Settlement of Brody," *Pinkas Hakehilot*, 4.
22. Ibid.

the Frankists, arrested their opponents, and removed Rabbi Note from the office of Chief Rabbi of Brody.[23]

Everything here agrees with other sources, except for the dates. The *herem* (ban) or excommunication imposed by the rabbinic court in Brody was issued on June 13, 1756,[24]—that is, twelve days before Potocki's edict of June 25, 1756 that dissolved the court, overturned its decrees, and removed Rabbi Note from his position as Chief Rabbi. Neither was Potocki's edict made under the direct influence of Bishop Kobielski, as Wurm suggested; Kobielski had died a year earlier, in 1755. Given the fact that in 1752 Jacob Frank was still in Turkey, in the process of being initiated into the secrets of the Sabbatean sect, it is also impossible to accept Wurm's claim that Frank's agents were already active in Brody in the first half of 1752. Wurm's belief that Bishop Kobielski was still alive at the time of the edict, and his declaration that Rabbi Note led the rabbinical court, is further evidence that this must be identified as the council of June 13, 1756. Therefore, we can conclude that whatever happened in 1752 in Brody concerned Sabbateans, and not Frank and his followers.

## *The Brody Jews' "Confession of Faith"*

Sabbateans had a long history of outwardly confessing Muslim and later Christian faith, while at the same time keeping their own beliefs and practice in secret. Furthermore, they frequently used kabbalah and mystical texts, and as a result Christians often understood their writings to contain hidden references to the Trinity. The "Confession of Faith" in the de Dors letter is very close in content to other Sabbatean confessions, as well Frankist declarations that appeared later in the 1750s. Hedging their bets, Sabbateans made it appear that they accepted Jesus as the Messiah, while in reality it was Sabbatai Zevi, and later Jacob Frank, whom they believed to be the messiah.

Bishop Kobielski's sermons in the Brody Synagogue focused on the doctrine of the Trinity (one God in three persons), the prophecies concerning the birth of Immanuel from a virgin (Is 53:4), and the person of Jesus Christ. Not surprisingly, the first three articles of the Confession in de Dors letter are as follows:

---

23. Wurm. *Z dziejów Żydowstwa Brodzkiego*, 56. Rabbi Nathan however did not leave the city, and the Jews continued to consider him their Rabbi. As Wurm explains, all he lost was the office of Chief Rabbi, who represented the entire rabbinical school in Brody to the outside world." Wurm, *Z dziejów Żydowstwa Brodzkiego*, 39.

24. "The Jewish Settlement of Brody," *Pinkas Hakehilot*, 4.

1. That the only true Godhead consists in three persons.
2. That the Messiah is the true Immanuel.
3. That this is certainly Jesus of Bethlehem.

Clearly, Sabbatean sympathizers in Brody (who were also called, appropriately, anti-Talmudists) were well aware of these debates, and knew only too well what points to include and emphasize in their own Confession of Faith, in order to convince church leaders that they were sincere converts to Christianity.[25] The Jewish "converts" from Brody disguised their beliefs to make it appear that they were compatible with Christianity.

Maciejko provides an example that illustrates this well, which is all the more relevant since it concerns the very charges made by Emden against Eybeschutz that were the focus of the Brody council of June 11, 1752. In 1756 Magerlin, writing in defense of Rabbi Jonathan Eybeschutz, attempted to clear Eybeschutz of charges of promoting Sabbatean belief and practice. In this context he cites "rumours that in his conversations with Lutheran clergy, Eibeschutz had voiced agreement with 'the true [viz., Lutheran] religion and claimed that the Messiah had already come."[26] His conclusion was as follows:

> Eibeschutz is not a talmudic Jew, but a moderate zoharist, or a secret proselyte and half-Christian. *Nota bene* the stubborn and intolerant Jews call such [a person] min, heretic, Sadducees, epicurian, sabbataizeviten, mumar, kopher, renegade, or blasphemer, as it happened to Jonathan from his opponents.[27]

While Magerlin's authority and scholarship have been called into question, they are still significant, since they reveal the tendency of sympathetic Christian scholars to accept Jewish claims (or even hints) that they believe in the doctrine of the Trinity. One factor that contributed to this was Christian reception and interpretation of Nehemiah Sayon's 1713 tract, 'Oz le—'Elohim. This tract was the only exposition of Sabbatean belief published by the Sabbateans, and it gave Christian scholars who could read Hebrew the opportunity to interact directly with a Sabbatean text. Jews easily recognized Hayon's text as Sabbatean, but Christians, focusing on the triune character of the Godhead, did not. As Maciejko writes,

> The Christian habit of looking for prefigurations of Christian dogmas in the Hebrew Bible and other Jewish sources formed a

25. Wurm, *Z dziejów Żydowstwa Brodzkiego*, 52–53.
26. Maciejko, "The Jews Entry into the Public Sphere," 148.
27. Ibid., 150.

firm basis for such a reading, and Hayon himself played on such Christian perceptions: for instance, he told the Spanish ambassador in Vienna that he had long been persecuted by the Jews for his belief in "another kind of trinity."[28]

Before moving to the final point and conclusion, it is interesting at the least to note the rumors of Rabbi Eybeschutz's conversations with Lutherans and speculation by many that he was a proselyte or a secret Christian. It is not unthinkable then that Eybeschutz had Sabbatean followers in Brody who appealed to Protestants for support and succor in their search for "which set of Christians to join."

## The Emden-Eybeschutz Controversy: The Broader Historical Context and Significance of the Events in Brody in the 1750s

It might seem that the discussion of a rather obscure note in one of Jonathan Edwards's numerous journals is of little significance or interest outside of rather narrow scholarly circles. However, this is not that case at all. As Paweł Maciejko demonstrates in his article, "The Jews's entry into the Public Sphere—The Emden-Eibeschutz Controversy Reconsidered," this controversy between more traditional and Sabbatean Jews in Brody was played out against the background of larger events in Europe. Of particular importance was the conflict between Rabbi Jacob Emden (1697–1776) and Rabbi Jonathan Eybeschutz (1690–1764).

The historical and religious context of this debate was the popularity at the time of a large and varied body of mystical, devotional, kabbalah, esoteric, and Sabbatean texts. As Maoz Kahana argues, members of the Jewish community, including many rabbis, found it hard to distinguish many of the texts that Emden and others considered to be heretical from ones that passed Emden's test of orthodoxy.[29] On February 4, 1751, Emden condemned amulets produced by Rabbi Jonathan Eybeschutz and given to his followers, which Emden claimed contained copies of selected Sabbateans texts.[30] In 1752 Emden went further and published a "black-list" of heretical literature. As we learned above, the rabbinical congress in Brody, of June 11, 1752, which addressed these Sabbatean teachings, led to the condemnation of Rabbi Eybeschutz and his suspicious amulets. Rabbi Ezekiel Landau

---

28. Ibid., 151
29. Kahana, "The Allure of Forbidden Knowledge," 589–616.
30. Maciejko, "The Jews Entry into the Public Sphere," 136.

(1713–93), also mentioned in the discussion above, played a mediating role, fighting against heretical literature while overlooking the person and actions of Eybeschutz. Landau tried to divert Emden's attack away from Eybeschutz in particular and steer it towards Sabbatean literature in general.

The Emden-Eybeschutz controversy thus played a crucial rule in eighteenth-century Judaism. In between the occasional rabbinic councils, the debate was conducted through published articles and books, rebuttals and counter-rebuttals. Furthermore, it attracted the attention of the non-Jewish press, for example in Poland, Germany, and Denmark, where it was examined and reported on by gentile scholars.[31] As Maciejko writes,

> The impact of the public sphere upon the Jewish world was initiated by the interest taken by sectors of the enlightened (and also less enlightened) non-Jewish public in Judaism and the theological quarrels that divided eigtheenth-century European Jewry. Once Jews and Judaism became a subject of a public debate, they had to respond to the ongoing discussion. Eagerly in some cases, reluctantly in others, they started to explain themselves to the reading public. More importantly, they started to utilise the public sphere for their own debates. The first instigance of such utilization was the Emden-Eibeschutz controversy.[32]

Many date the birth of modern journalism to the Jansenist controversy in the 1750s. This is the very time period when the Emden-Eybeschutz controversy was widely noticed and commented on in the gentile press. Jewish leaders, much chagrined, nevertheless joined in the public debate and entered the public sphere.

## Conclusion

What then is the relationship between the events in Brody in 1752 and the reported desire of a large number of Jewish rabbis with their followers to convert to Christianity? A dialogue certainly took place between Jews and Catholics in the eighteenth century, as well as between Jews and Protestants, and there were Jews who converted to Christianity. Nevertheless, as Kaźmierczyk shows, while sincere religious conversions took place, other reasons for conversions were many. Prior to emancipation of the peasants, conversion was for most Jews the only way to leave the *shtetl*. Those who received baptism received the name of the Christian protectors or sponsors,

31. Ibid., 138–44.
32. Ibid., 136.

who were usually members of the Polish nobility. In this way Jewish villagers became free citizens and (in some cases) potentially members of the lesser nobility. Nontraditional groups such as the Sabbateans and Frankists, whose beliefs and practices were rejected by traditional Jewish society, often turned to the Catholic Church for protection. Frank himself, together with his followers, was baptized in the Roman Catholic Church in 1759. His sponsor was none other than King Augustus III, King of Poland.

The rabbinic council referred to in Jacob de Dors's letter, which according to the "learned Jewish Christian from Poland" took place on August 4, 1752, cannot be identified with the 1756 council against Frank and his followers. Rather it was a follow-up effort, subsequent to the events of June of 1752, undertaken by Sabbatean sympathizers in Brody in an effort to secure support for their practices from Christian sponsors. The "converts" to Christianity, whom Edwards was so excited about, were in reality members of the Sabbatean movement. In their struggle with Haskala and traditional Jews, the Sabbateans (and later the Frankists) appealed to the Roman Catholic Church for protection; the Catholics in turn were only too glad to accept their conversion as authentic, without looking a gift horse too closely in the mouth. The Sabbateans, and later the Frankists, were able to manipulate the local bishops, the primate of Poland and the Polish king. It is no wonder then that Pastor Edwards, far away in colonial America, and so eager to discern the signs of revival that he believed signaled the imminent return of Christ, readily accepted these reports of Jewish conversion at face value.

Finally, the broader significance of these events in Brody, including the Rabbinic Council held in 1752, is best seen in light of the religious and social impact on the European Jewish community. Together with the Jansenist controversy, the Emden-Eybeschutz controversy played a key role in contributing to the birth of modern journalism. It also marked the Jews' entry in the public sphere.

## Timeline of Events

*February 4, 1751:*     *Rabbi Jacob Emden condemns amulets produced by Rabbi Jonathan Eybeschutz.*

*1752:*     *Emden publishes a "black-list" of heretical literature.*

*June 11, 1752:*     *Rabbinical Congress in Brody versus Sabbatean teachings; condemnation of Rabbi Eybeschutz.*

| | |
|---|---|
| August 4, 1752: | [?] As reported in Jacob de Dors letter: Jewish Rabbinic Council in Brody, 548 rabbis and 15,000 Jews converting to Christianity? |
| November 5, 1753: | Jacob de Dors wrote his letter. It was published in German in 1753, in Dutch in the Monthly State Secretary in March of 1754, in English in the New York Gazette on August 26, 1754. |
| December 1, 1755: | Jacob Frank enters Poland. |
| June 13, 1756: | Frankists condemned in Brody by the Rabbinic Council convened and led by Rabbi Nathan Note. |
| June 25, 1756: | Count Potocki dissolves The Rabbinic Council in Brody. |
| 1759: | The conversion of Jacob Frank and his followers (Frankists) to the Roman Catholic Church. |

## Bibliography

Acta historico-ecclesiastica:oder gesammlete Nachrichten von d. neuesten Kirchen-Geschichten. Vol 16. Weimar: 1752.

Edwards, Jonathan. "Notes on the Apocalypse." In *Apocalyptic Writings*, edited by Stephen J. Stein, The Works of Jonathan Edwards 5:95–305. New Haven: Yale University Press, 1977.

———. "To the Reverend John Erskine, July 5, 1750." In *Letters and Personal Writings*, edited by George S. Claghorn, The Works of Jonathan Edwards 16:347–56. New Haven and London: Yale University Press, 1998.

Eisenberg, Ronald L. "Landau, Ezekiel ben Judah." In *Essential Figures in Jewish Scholarship*. Maryland: Rowman & Littlefield, 2014.

Ackerfeld, Lance. "The Jewish Settlement of Brody." Pinkas Hakehilot. Page 19 on http://www.jewishgen.org/Yizkor/brody/broe019.html.

Kahana, Maoz. "The Allure of Forbidden Knowledge: The Temptation of Sabbatean Literature for Mainstream Rabbis in the Frankist Movement, 1756–1761." In *Jewish Quarterly Review* 102/4 (2012) 589–616.

Każmierczyk, Adam. *Rodziłem się Żydem . . . Konwersje Żydów w Rzeczypospolitej XVII- XVIII wieku*. Krakow: Księgarnia Akademicka, 2015.

———. Summary: *Rodziłem się Żydem . . . Konwersje Żydów w Rzeczypospolitej XVII-XVIII wieku*. Krakow: Księgarnia Akademicka, 2015.

Skolnik, Fred and Michael Berenbaum, eds. *Encyclopedia Judaica* vol 11. New York: MacMillan, 1971.

Wurm, Dawid. *Z dziejów Żydowstwa Brodzkiego za czasów dawnej Rzecypospolitej Polskiej (do r. 1772)*. Brody: Nakładem Gminy Wyznaniowej Żydowskiej, 1935.

# Part II

## Global Conversation

# 7

## The Tension between Jonathan Edwards's *"Controversies"* Notebook and *Freedom of the Will* on Whether Reality Is Open and Contingent

Philip J. Fisk

### Introduction

Any approach to the study of Jonathan Edwards must deal with the author's breadth of material, both published and unpublished. When it comes to interpreting Edwards's view of reality, there is noticeable tension between the notes on "Predestination" in his unpublished *"Controversies" Notebook* and his published work, *Freedom of the Will*. It is arguably the case that Edwards's line taken in the unpublished *Notebook* represents an open, contingent view of reality—the classic-Reformed tradition—while his approach in the published *Freedom of the Will* represents a necessitarian, closed view of reality.[1]

---

1. For the case that the Reformed tradition espouses an open, contingent view of reality, developing the innovations of the late medieval thinker John Duns Scotus (1266–1308), who arguably emancipated Christian thought on reality from the closed view of the Greek classical synthesis, see Vos, "Scotus' Significance," 173–209; Vos, *Philosophy of John Duns Scotus*, 11, 225, 281–82, 297, 390, 435, 440, 444, 459, 464–65, 610; Asselt et al., *Reformed Thought on Freedom*. For the case that Edwards reinterprets his tradition, from within his tradition, espousing a necessitarian view of reality, see

In this essay, I evidence this tension by focusing on Edwards's transcription of passages on the topic of contingency and necessity taken from the *Institutiones Theologicae Polemicae* (1743–47) of the Swiss pastor and Zurich divine Johann Friedrich Stapfer (1708–75). I report on Edwards's selective use of Stapfer and, at critical points along the way, show how Edwards's own development of thought on core concepts on this topic brings him into conflict with the view he expresses in *Freedom of the Will*.[2]

My approach to Edwards's encounter with Stapfer begins with a brief introduction to Edwards's *"Controversies" Notebook*, Part V, on predestination and its context. Second, I record Edwards's thought on Stapfer's reply to the Arminian line. Third, I report on the tension I perceive between Edwards's unpublished thoughts in the *Notebook* and his published thoughts in *Freedom of the Will* in regard to whether reality is open or closed. Finally, I draw out the significance of the tension that I find in Edwards's encounter with Stapfer, who arguably represents the classic-Reformed line on this topic of necessity, contingency, and the openness of reality.

## The *"Controversies" Notebook*, Part V, on Predestination

The editors of the Jonathan Edwards Center, Yale University, give a "headnote" that introduces the *"Controversies" Notebook*. They tell us that Edwards began to assemble these notes in the 1730s, which, by the end of his life, amounted to "120 folio leaves."[3] It is in Part V, on "Predestination," where Edwards transcribes Latin passages from Stapfer's *Institutiones* around the year 1750.[4] Edwards is collecting arguments in preparation for a major treatise on the "Arminian notion of liberty," as he calls it in the *Notebook*. His reflections on what he has extracted from Stapfer show that he finds Stapfer's reasoning compelling, particularly how Stapfer shows that the Arminians' conceptions "destroy the freedom of God himself, according to their own principles."[5] In a letter to the Reverend John Erskine, August 31, 1748, Edwards asks to be informed of the latest "best books" written "on the other

---

Fisk, *Jonathan Edwards's Turn*.

2. See Fisk, *Edwards's Turn*, 235–263.

3. See Edwards, "Predestination" in *"Controversies" Notebook*, *WJEO* 27.

4. Ibid; also Edwards, *"Controversies" Notebook* (BRBML), 262–66, 289 (Part V "Predestination," the Latin passages from Stapfer); (Part V "Predestination," 260–66, 273–91). For the argument for the date of 1750 for the transcription from Stapfer, see Fisk, *Edwards's Turn*, 237.

5. Edwards, *"Controversies" Notebook* (BRBML), 278–79.

side of the Atlantic," "in defense of Calvinism," against the Arminian notion of liberty.⁶ Perhaps Stapfer's *Institutiones* are just such a work.

The major themes in the transcript from Stapfer include the structural "order of nature" (*signum rationis*), "the order and connection of things," "sequences and series of events," "conditional decrees," "God's conditioned foreknowledge," the "representation of possible states of affairs to the mind of God," the pivotal role of God's will in relation to God's knowledge, and the "state of possibility" and of "futurition." On the top of the page that begins his Latin transcript of Stapfer, Edwards expresses his interest in these themes when he alludes to the need for any future treatise of his "to show" the regard God has to "conditions in his decree" and the "wise order and connection of things in a wise decree." Yet there is a tension in Edwards's heading between what he intends to show some day and what is contained in his extracts from Stapfer's work. Edwards's statement raises the question, "Does God decree the 'wise order and connection of things' because he regards them as wise, or are they wise because he decrees them?"⁷ One could conclude that Edwards indicates that wisdom, as such, conditions God's decree. Edwards writes, "If it were not for wise connection that is regarded, many things would not be decreed." Edwards's thought on this topic in the *Notebook* is compared with relevant passages in his *Freedom of the Will* further in the latter half of this chapter.

## *Context*

From Stapfer's five-volume *Institutiones*, Edwards extracts passages on "the Arminians, that is, Remonstrants" (volume four), and on the "Protestant consensus and dissent between the Reformed and the Lutherans" (volume five). Stapfer's concern is to highlight the differences between the Remonstrants and other movements, and between the Lutherans and the Reformed. Volume one handles the traditional loci such as the attributes and existence of God, God's knowledge, will, and power, the decrees, humankind's dependence upon God, and the Trinity. Although extracts from volume one are notably absent in Edwards's *Notebook*, I make reference to select sections on God's decrees, knowledge, and will. In what follows, I have identified the core concepts from Stapfer that Edwards himself fleshes out in his *Notebook*, and have reconstructed his interaction with Stapfer's *Institutiones*.

---

6. Edwards, *Letters and Personal Writings*, WJE 16:249.
7. Edwards, *"Controversies" Notebook* (BRBML), 262.

## Edwards on Stapfer's Reply to the Arminian Line

Edwards begins his transcript with Stapfer's formulation of the Arminian line on God's knowledge and human freedom:

> The existence of future states of affairs, that is, futurition, as the metaphysicians say, does not depend upon divine predetermination and foreknowledge, but only the free choice of the human will. Likewise, the certainty of divine foreknowledge is not antecedent and causal, but subsequent and potential . . . it infers neither necessity, nor causality.[8]

The Arminian line structures predetermination and foreknowledge in a way that conditions them upon human free choice and God's knowledge thereof. God knows and loves certain individual humans; therefore, he subsequently elects them. In other words, God elects them because he knows them. Reformed thinkers, however, hold that structurally prior to predetermination, the individual was not known as a being to be loved and elected. Stapfer adduces testimony for the Arminian position that God's knowledge is conditioned by foreseen events from Bishop Gilbert Burnet's *De praedestinatione et gratia tractatus,* 1724. Did God's foreknowledge fail when he foretold that the men of Keilah would surrender David into Saul's hands? Burnet says, "No." It is the case of an outcome dependent upon human free choice.[9]

### *Stapfer's Reply*

Edwards transcribes Stapfer's comments on the case of the men of Keilah. He points to God's knowledge of possible states of affairs that God never actualizes.

> (S1) The various series of states of affairs which represent themselves to God, but which remain in a state of pure possibility, and never become future events. He knows not only those which are future, but also those which are other possible series of states of affairs.[10]

---

8. See Stapfer, *Institutiones* 4:577 (§93); Edwards, *"Controversies" Notebook* (BRBML), 262. All translations from the Latin are my own. See Fisk, *Edwards's Turn,* 239–40.

9. Stapfer, *Institutiones* 4:578 (§93).

10. Stapfer, *Institutiones* 4: 581 (§96); Edwards, *"Controversies" Notebook* (BRBML), 263. See Fisk, *Edwards's Turn,* 247.

In his *Notebook*, Edwards skips over Stapfer's first response to the Arminian line. We give it here for the sake of the completeness of Stapfer's line of thought. Response A:

> (SA) Prior to the divine decree, if one may so speak, there are actions represented as pure possibles to the divine intellect, and these actions remain either contingent, free, or necessary, even after the predetermination of the divine will that a series of states of affairs are to be produced in actuality, and even after the foreknowledge of their certain futurition.[11]

Response A represents the classic-Reformed contingency line of thinking, that reality *ad extra*, in relation to God, is open. That is, while God is essentially good and just, possessing these attributes intrinsically and maximally, he is not essentially Creator and Redeemer, since the latter concern his contingent works and relations *ad extra*.[12] God actualizes states of affairs. But not out of necessity. God knows them as eternal possibles in contemplating his essence. God's predetermination, whereby he passes a state of affairs out of the realm of possibility into the realm of futurition, makes no inherent change in the object willed. What is necessary, remains necessary, what is contingent remains contingent in itself, and what is free remains free. For instance, God is good; and necessarily so. That created reality is contingent is not only contingently true, but necessarily so. The point to make here is that the immutability and certainty of God's decree to pass something from the realm of possibility to reality does not impose an absolute necessity

---

11. Stapfer, *Institutiones* 4: 578–9 (§94). See Fisk, *Edwards's Turn*, 241.

12. The concept of God "bringing a states of affairs out of the state of eternal possibility into the state of temporal actuality," by a decree of his will, occurs frequently in Reformed writers, including those who were well-known to Edwards and the Harvard and Yale curricula: "Similiter illis tribuitur esse possibile aeternum, quia ab aeterno fuerunt in potentia objectiva et activa Dei, cui fuerunt objectae, et per quam ad actum sunt traductae in tempore, et ex statu possibilitatis aeternae translatae in statum actualitatis temporiae," in Heereboord, *Meletemata* 305–306. (Citations are from the Amsterdam, 1665 edition, the pagination of which differs slightly from the 1654 edition). See Rutherford, *Disputatio Scholastica*, 568; Turretin, *Institutio Theologiae Elencticae*, 232, 234, 345; Twisse, *Dissertatio*, 199; Voetius, *Selectarum Disputationum Theologicarum*, 290. On the relation of God's knowledge, will, and three structurally ordered "moments," see Beck, *Gisbertus Voetius*, 298. For the medieval use of this Aristotelian concept, see Maimonides's *Moreh Nebuchim* (1190), translated into Latin by the Reformed Hebraist, Johann Buxtorf, Jr. (1599–1664), with as title *Doctor Perplexorum* (Basel, 1629), known to us as *The Guide for the Perplexed*. See Maimonides, *The Guide for the Perplexed*, Part II Introduction, Proposition 18, 250; c. 17, 302–305; c. 21, 321–323; Part III c. 20, 489–92.

upon human agents, which, as the Arminians suppose, would then deny human free choice.

Edwards does transcribe Stapfer's Response B:

> (SB) The divine intellect, seen in itself without respect to the will, is the root of the pure possibility of states of affairs. When God regards himself, his perfections, he knows himself, and his knowing himself involves no contradiction. And this is true whether what he knows be absolutely necessary, contingent, or free. But these states of affairs are not future, but only purely possible. God's will, however, is the root of the futurition of states of affairs.[13]

Response B distinguishes between God's self-knowledge, which includes all possible states of affairs, and God's will, which determines what things will be actualized. Stapfer gives God's will a pivotal role. Two paragraphs later in Stapfer's last lines, which Edwards transcribes, Stapfer makes the crucial point about the role of God's will in relation to his knowledge, namely, that "God could have elected and ordered, if he had willed, another nexus or chain of events, and other conditions, with respect to the contingency and freedom of states of affairs."[14] In the section below on God's twofold knowledge, we position the pivotal role of God's will in relation to God's knowledge with the help of scholastic terminology.

Edwards does not transcribe the following paragraphs from Stapfer, but their content complements Responses A and B above, introducing the topic of God's immutability.

> (S2) The decree of God is the determination of the divine will about the universe that it be produced in actuality. This decree, however, is immutable; hence, what God has decreed is certainly going to be. From what is aforementioned, it is certainly clear that states of affairs are only possible, as far as they are related to the intellect of God, but as far as they are related to the will, they become future; that is, they pass on from the state of pure possibility to the state of futurition by the decree.[15]

---

13. Stapfer, *Institutiones* 4: 579 (§94); Edwards, *"Controversies" Notebook* (BRBML), 262. Edwards makes an entry on "Decrees," 285: "all things . . . necessary, free, contingent, casual, are subject to his providence," which is in line with the premises in (SA) and (SB). It is taken from Millar's *Assembly's Shorter Catechism*, 18. See also Fisk, *Edwards's Turn*, 242.

14. Stapfer, *Institutiones* 4: 582–83 (§96); Edwards, *"Controversies" Notebook* (BRBML), 263. See Fisk, *Edwards's Turn*, 247.

15. Stapfer, *Institutiones* 1:107–08 (§436). See Fisk, *Edwards's Turn*, 257.

When we approach the topic of the immutability of God and his decree, we first must make a distinction between God in his Being and in his faculties. To speak of God's faculties of intellect or understanding, his will, and his affections (love, hatred) is an accommodation to our way of conceiving things. Stapfer makes clear that God contingently decrees what he decrees in relation to us, yet remains immutable. Nor does God's decree deny human freedom. Stapfer reminds us that nothing changes in the thing itself as God brings it out of the state of possibility into the state of actuality:

> (S3) Nothing in a decreed state of affairs changes by the decree of God: A state of affairs which can be seen as contingent in a state of possibility remains contingent in a state of futurition, and those which can be seen as free, remain free. The divine decree denies neither the contingency of states of affairs nor the freedom of mind-gifted actions.[16]

The immutability of the decree brings with it a certain kind of necessity which, however, is not based on the nature of the thing itself. The necessity rests upon the prior decree. The decreed event, therefore, cannot be otherwise than it is. Nevertheless, the event remains contingent, since the thing itself is contingent. The concomitant necessity does not "alter the nature of the thing itself," but establishes its *certainty*.[17]

---

16. Stapfer, *Institutiones* 1: 108–09 (§440). Fisk, *Edwards's Turn*, 241.

17. It was John Duns Scotus (1266–1308) who emancipated Christian thought from the closed view of reality of Greek necessity thinking. He concludes that this world is contingent in the sense that it is not possible that it is necessary. Indeed, whatever begins to be, is caused contingently. Scotus explains his theory by stating that (1) "there is contingency in things," (2) "God is the cause of contingency in things," and (3) "It is God's will that is the cause of contingency in things." The "conceptual core" of Scotus's innovative and emancipatory theory of "synchronic contingency" states that at the same moment of the act of God's will, it is possible that God act otherwise; that is, there is an "opposite act of willing" possible. For instance, at the moment God wills that he bring a state of affairs out of a state of possibility into a state of actuality—such as, that a universe be—there is a double alternative possibility, namely, that God will that a universe not-be, or, that God not-will that a universe be. Scotus's presentation of synchronic freedom is essential to understanding subsequent discussions of what constitutes an open view of contingent-created reality. He then demonstrates by way of the theory of "the neutral proposition" that "the immutability, certainty and infallibility of God's knowledge of the contingent future are logically compatible with the contingency of that future," in Vos et al., *John Duns Scotus: Contingency and Freedom, Lectura I 39. Introduction, Translation, and Commentary*, The New Synthese Historical Library 42 (Dordrecht: Kluwer Academic, 1994) §38, 95; §54, 127–29; §§61–68, 141–51.

## God's Twofold Knowledge

To distinguish God's intellect into two kinds of knowledge is an accommodation to our conception of God. It helps us conceive of the pivotal role of God's decreeing will. Stapfer gives the classic-Reformed definitions of God's twofold knowledge.[18] The first kind of knowledge structurally precedes the act of God's will:

> (S4) God's knowledge of simple understanding is that by which he knows what is possible and what can exist in actuality. But this does not extend to that which is going to exist in actuality. For he only knows that by his decree. Without doubt, all things are pure possibility prior to the divine decree, such that there be nothing yet to differentiate between the things which exist, and the things which do not exist.[19]

This kind of knowledge is to be conceived apart from God's will and decree, and apart from God's visionary knowledge. It is indefinite, since there is no definite object known in time. But it is also to be conceived as God's necessary knowledge of all possible states of affairs. For God to know all things, both universal and particular, is for him to know his essence. There is a second kind of knowledge that structurally follows God's will:

> (S5) By God's knowledge of vision is meant that God knows from eternity that which is going to exist in actuality in his system of the world, whether by coexistence or succession. It is also called foreknowledge.[20]

When the duality of God's knowledge collapses into one, one cannot structurally prioritize the crucial place of God's will between these two kinds of knowledge. For instance, in reprobation and election, structurally prior to God's predetermination, there was nothing for God to love or hate. God's visionary knowledge, however, is God intuitively seeing what he has decreed. There is, nevertheless, a unity when the two dimensions

---

18. Beck, *Voetius* 265–74; Muller, *Post Reformation Reformed Dogmatics* 3: 406–08. Both Beck and Muller point out that although the language of *scientia simplicis intelligentiae* and *scientia visionis* is from Aquinas, seventeenth-century Reformed theologians made these terms their own, terms which are to be identified with the Franciscan-Scotist line, which gives priority to God's will in the structural order and relation between God's will and his twofold knowledge.

19. Stapfer, *Institutiones* 1: 87 (§358). On Voetius's definition of this term, see Beck, *Voetius*, 268.

20. Stapfer, *Institutiones*, 1: 88 (§ 360). See, Beck, *Voetius*, 268.

of necessity and contingency, and God's twofold knowledge, are viewed together with his will.

## Edwards on the Pivotal Role of God's Will in Relation to His Knowledge

Edwards reflects on the crucial role that Stapfer gives to God's will, with respect to the states of possibility and futurition. He arrives at the following formulation:

> (E1) The thing in its own nature is not necessary, but only possible; and therefore it is not of itself in a state of futurition, if I may so speak, but only in a state of possibility. There must be something to bring it out of a state of mere possibility, into a state of futurition, and this must be God only... The First Being ... the things that are but merely possibility, are brought out of that state of mere possibility into a state of futurition, to be certainly future.[21]

Following Stapfer, Edwards denies the "future actual existence" of a state of affairs since that would imply an existence prior to God's decree. The effect, writes Edwards, cannot "flow from this cause before the existence of the cause."[22] In other words, God's decree is the cause that passes a state of affairs out of the state of possibility into the state of futurition. God's will and decree play the pivotal role. Like Stapfer, Edwards says, "The reason of the futurition of the thing is no other than God's decree."[23] As we saw above in (E1), "the thing in its own nature is not necessary ... but only in a state of possibility."[24]

In answer to the question, "What decides the futurition of a state of affairs?" and against the notion of the infinite regress of a "chain of events," Edwards writes, "It is as if there were a chain hung down out of the heavens

---

21. Edwards, *"Controversies" Notebook* (BRBML), 275. Block 12.
Charles Morton (1627–1698), Harvard's first Vice-President (1697–8), also passes this line of open reality on to Harvard and Yale students in a text he extracted from Heereboord's *Pneumatica*. Ebenezer Williams transcribed the text into a notebook which he passed on to Elisha Williams, Edwards's tutor. The key text is: That God by his will, "transfers a thing from an act (state) of possibility to a state of futurition," in Williams, *A System of Ethics.*). Cf. Heereboord, *Pneumatica*, 65. (Pagination from the *Pneumatica* appended to the 1665 edition of Heereboord's *Meletemata*).
22. Edwards, *"Controversies" Notebook* (BRBML), 282.
23. Ibid., 273.
24. Ibid., 275.

to the earth, and it should be inquired, 'What held up that chain?'"[25] Edwards's answer is in line with Stapfer's view in (SB). Like Stapfer, Edwards grounds futurition and God's foreknowledge thereof in the divine decree:

> (E2) The divine decree is the ground of the futurition of the events, and also the ground of the foreknowledge of it.[26]

By giving priority to God's will in the structural relation between will and knowledge, Edwards aligns himself with the classic-Reformed line in his unpublished *Notebook*. I have attempted to show that this line gives the pivotal role to God's will, which is structurally ordered between the states of possibility and actuality.

## *The Structural Order of Nature (signum rationis)*

Edwards shows interest in Stapfer's lengthy quote from Leibniz's *Theodicy*. Leibniz is writing about the question between the supralapsarians and the infralapsarians, suggesting that it comes down to understanding the "simultaneous" and "synchronism of destinations or of decrees," as well as the non-temporal, structural "order of nature" (*signum rationis*).[27] The "order of nature" is a technical term used as a conceptual tool that allows one to assign a structurally ordered and prioritized position of God's will in relation to the duality of God's knowledge. In the *Notebook*, Edwards formulates his own thoughts on the relation of the divine will and decrees in the "order of nature," to which I now turn.[28] In this next section, I show the degree to which there is tension between the unpublished *Notebook* and the published *Freedom of the Will* (1754), as he develops his own use of these technical terms.

---

25. Ibid.

26. Ibid., 282.

27. Ibid., 263–64; Stapfer, *Institutiones*, 5:185 (§77); G.W. Leibniz, *Theodicy: Essays on the Goodness of God, the Freedom of Man, and the Origin of Evil*, ed. Austin Farrer, trans. E.M. Huggard, Rare Masterpieces of Philosophy and Science (New Haven: Yale University Press, 1952), 167–68 (§84).

28. Edwards, *"Controversies" Notebook* (BRBML), 281.

## The Tension between the *Notebook* and *Freedom of the Will*

There are concepts in Edwards's *Notebook* that he develops in *Freedom of the Will*, such as, the structural "order of nature," the "self-determining power in the will," the "necessity of connection" and "indissoluble connection between the subject and predicate" of a proposition, and the question, 'What holds up the whole chain?'[29] But the notion of God willing to bring a state of affairs out of a state of possibility into a state of futurition is notably absent in *Freedom of the Will*. In the space that remains, I first show the tension between these unpublished and published works that is present in Edwards's development of the concept of the structural "order of nature." Second, I address his abandonment of the concept of "contingency." Third, I summarize Edwards's chief argument in *Freedom of the Will* and indicate its consequences for freedom of the will, and whether reality is open or closed.

First, Edwards takes up into his *Freedom of the Will* the notion of the structural "order of nature" in relation to time and acts of willing, a notion which he saw in Stapfer, and which he already had fleshed out in the *Notebook*. Edwards highlights three different levels of a structural order of nature in both the *Notebook* and *Freedom of the Will*. In the *Notebook*, the three levels of understanding the "Arminian" self-determining act of will are: (1) the will determines itself in the same act, (2) the will determines its own act by another act, which is prior to it in the order of nature, and (3) the will determines itself, but the determination is not itself an act.[30] In *Freedom of the Will*, the levels are: (1) the determining act is before the act in "the order of nature," but not in "the order of time," (2) "the determining act is not before the act, either in the order of time or nature, nor is truly distinct from it;" it is one and the same act, (3) the "volition has no cause." It "comes into existence without reason."[31]

What is new in levels one and two in *Freedom of the Will* is the factor of time. On Edwards's own evaluation, the first level is actually a logical, structural understanding of a prior act, but prior in a non-temporal sense. He allows this sense, but says it will not help the Arminian case. The second has two simultaneous acts and is thus illogical. The third claims an act comes

---

29. Edwards, *Freedom of the Will*, WJE 1:177–78, 376 and Edwards, "Controversies" *Notebook* (BRBML), 281–82 (order of nature); Edwards, *Freedom of the Will*, WJE 1: 152–53, 257–58, 265 and Edwards, "Controversies" *Notebook* (BRBML), 274 (indissoluble connection of subject and predicate); Edwards, *Freedom of the Will*, WJE 1:174 and Edwards, "Controversies" *Notebook* (BRBML), 275 (a chain).

30. Edwards, "Controversies" *Notebook* (BRBML), 281.

31. Edwards, *Freedom of the Will*, WJE 1:177.

to be without a cause, which is equally absurd. Edwards, thus, removes all three senses, calling them Arminian "evasions," none of which answers the problem Edwards perceives with the notion of a self-determining power.[32] Based on his own analysis of the order of nature, Edwards denies the notion of self-determining power in both God and humans.[33]

Second, Edwards makes clear his objection to understanding an agent, whether God or human, as having a self-determining power, by which one contingently causes something to be. For, "this contingency" is "efficient Nothing"; it is "effectual No-Cause"; it is "blind."[34] On the contrary, we saw above in (SA), (SB), and (S3) that Stapfer holds that it is possible to reconcile contingency with the divine decree and production of events *ad extra*. The moves Edwards makes in *Freedom of the Will* show an expected development of some themes found in his *Notebook*, but also a significant parting of ways with commonly used concepts in the classic-Reformed tradition.[35]

Third, Edwards's running argument against the "Arminians" in *Freedom of the Will* is that the stronger the prior inclination, the further one is removed from indifference in acts of the will, and the greater the freedom of the will is. I call this a freedom of perfection as opposed to a freedom of indifference. For Edwards, freedom and indifference are inversely proportional to one another. The greater the degree of previous bias and inclination in the will, the greater the degree of virtue, and the freer one is. He offers Jesus Christ as the greatest example hereof. The principle applies to both God and humans. "The stronger the inclination, and so the further from indifference, the more virtuous the heart . . . and the act that proceeds from it." "Indifference, contingence, and self-determination" belong to the "Arminian" view of freedom, writes Edwards.[36] What are the consequences of his theory for his understanding of whether reality is open or closed?

---

32. Ibid. The structural, non-temporal application of the order of nature, otherwise spoken of in terms of a 'previous concurrence' of the act of God's will structurally preceding the act of the human will, is made in the classic-Reformed tradition, by many authors, such as Heereboord and Stapfer. See Fisk, *Edwards's Turn*, 297–300.

33. Edwards, *Freedom of the Will*, WJE 1:375, 391, 433, 436. On Edwards's rejection of 'self-determining power', associating it with the 'Arminians', even though the Reformed use it too, see Fisk, *Edwards's Turn*, 315, 319, 350, 364, 391–93, 397, 406–08.

34. Edwards, *Freedom of the Will*, WJE 1:183–84.

35. On Edwards's use of Stapfer, see Fisk, *Edwards's Turn*, 241–42, 247–48, 256, 260–62.

36. Edwards, *Freedom of the Will*, WJE 1:281–94 (the case of Jesus Christ), 309, 320–22, 359–60, 424–25, 429. See the fuller argument for Edwards's freedom of perfection in Fisk, *Edwards's Turn*, 351–59.

From this theory, Edwards infers divine moral necessity, the impossibility that states of affairs be otherwise than they are.

From Part Four §6 of *Freedom of the Will* through the conclusion of the treatise, Edwards focuses on the moral necessity of the acts of God's will, and a "universal determining providence." While Edwards unquestionably disavows "universal fatality," he unequivocally affirms a "superior strength" of motive structurally prior to God's will, that is, in "the order of nature," as Edwards puts it.[37] On the necessity of God's will, and against his interlocutor in the text Isaac Watts, Edwards says that it is no dishonor to hold that "the will of God himself is necessary in all its determinations."[38] This includes his works *ad extra*. In the paragraph Edwards cites from Watts, Watts is calling out the "strange doctrine" of Hobbes, who makes God "an almighty minister of fate."[39] Edwards calls Watts's language "declaiming" rhetoric and even leaves out of his quote a line Watts takes from Seneca, "Thus causes run, a long connected train; not Jove himself can break the eternal chain."[40]

For Edwards, God always chooses what is "wisest and best." Edwards enlists, not Stapfer, but the support of Samuel Clarke, Andrew Baxter, and John Locke for the doctrine of a divine freedom of perfection. That is, God is always determined in his volitions by what is wisest and best. The greater the determination, the greater the perfection, the freer God is, and the further is he removed from any kind of indifference. For Edwards, the "undesigning contingence" of an open reality is antithetical to the doctrine of moral necessity, where the "superior fitness in some things" determines God's decrees. It is from this notion that he says he infers the doctrine of a "universal determining providence."[41]

## Conclusion

The result of this brief look into Edwards's unpublished *"Controversies" Notebook* is that there is significant tension between Edwards's published and unpublished views on whether reality is open and contingent, or closed and necessary. In (E1), I have shown that he was conversant with the crucial and pivotal role that the classic-Reformed line of thought assigned to God's will in relation to the duality of God's knowledge. And in (E2) he himself

---

37. Edwards, *Freedom of the Will*, WJE 1: 374–76. Here Edwards uses this technical term, "order of nature," as Stapfer had.

38. Ibid., 375.

39. Ibid.

40. Watts, *On the Freedom of Will*, 494.

41. Ibid., 375, 377, 377–79n2, 380–81, 383, 433. See Fisk, *Edwards's Turn*, 386–408.

stated as much in the *Notebook*. He understood that the complementary dimensions of necessity and contingency established the basis for holding to an open model of created reality. Nevertheless, Edwards's *published* opinion in his *Freedom of the Will* objects to the contingency dimension of God's knowledge and will. And although he developed and used the concept of the "order of nature" in *Freedom of the Will*—a concept whose differences he had highlighted in the *Notebook*, adding temporal and non-temporal dimensions—he nevertheless rejected the structural, non-temporal order used by Stapfer, among other authors. By distancing himself from the formulations (E1) and (E2) in the *Notebook*, by rejecting the non-temporal, structural order of nature, by calling it an evasive tool used by his opponents, and by developing the doctrine of freedom of perfection, which necessarily inclines God's will, he arguably promoted a closed reality in his published work *Freedom of the Will*.

# Bibliography

Asselt, W. J. van, et al., eds. *Reformed Thought on Freedom: The Concept of Free Choice in Early Modern Reformed Theology*. Texts and Studies in Reformation and Post-Reformation Thought. Grand Rapids: Baker, 2010.

Beck, Andreas J. *Gisbertus Voetius (1589-1676): Sein Theologieverständnis und seine Gotteslehre*. Forschungen zur Kirchen- und Dogmengeschichte 92. Göttingen: Vandenhoeck & Ruprecht, 2007.

Edwards, Jonathan. *"Controversies" Notebook*. Beinecke Rare Book and Manuscript Library: GEN MSS 151, Box 15, Folder 1203, block 12.

———. *Freedom of the Will*. Edited by Paul Ramsey. The Works of Jonathan Edwards 1. New Haven: Yale University Press, 1957.

———. *Letters and Personal Writings*. Edited by George S. Claghorn. The Works of Jonathan Edwards 16, 790–804. New Haven: Yale University Press, 1998.

———. "Predestination." In *"Controversies" Notebook*. The Works of Jonathan Edwards Online 27. Jonathan Edwards Center at Yale University.

Fisk, Philip J. *Jonathan Edwards's Turn from the Classic-Reformed Tradition of Freedom of the Will*. New Directions in Jonathan Edwards Studies 2. Göttingen: Vandenhoeck & Ruprecht, 2016.

Heereboord, Adriaan. *Meletemata*. Leiden, 1654. Disp. Phil. Select., D37, 2:30.

———. *Pneumatica*. Leiden, 1659, 65. Pagination from the *Pneumatica* appended to the 1665 edition of Heereboord's *Meletemata*.

Leibniz, G.W. *Theodicy: Essays on the Goodness of God, the Freedom of Man, and the Origin of Evil*. Edited by Austin Farrer. Translated by E.M. Huggard. Rare Masterpieces of Philosophy and Science. New Haven: Yale University Press, 1952.

Maimonides, Moses. *Le Guide des Égarés, Traité de Théologie et de Philosophie par Moïse Ben Maimon*. Translated by S. Munk. 3 vols. Paris: A. Franck, Libraire, 1856–66.

———. *The Guide for the Perplexed*. Translated by M. Friedländer. New York: Barnes & Noble, 2004.

Millar, David. *The Assembly's Shorter Catechism, Rescued from the late Revisor and Vindicator, being a large defence of that most excellent compend of divinity, to which is added a postscript . . . Containing a very particular answer to Mr. Gibbs's letter.* London: Joseph Davidson, 1738.

Muller, Richard A. *Post Reformation Reformed Dogmatics.* Vol. 3. Grand Rapids: Baker, 2003.

Rutherford, Samuel. *Disputatio Scholastica de Divina Providentia.* Edinburgh: Haeredes Georgii Andersoni pro Roberto Brouno, 1649.

Stapfer, Johann Friedrich. *Institutiones Theologicae Polemicae Universae, Ordine Scientifico dispositae.* 5 vols. Tiguri (Zurich): Heideggerum et socios, 1756.

Turretin, Francis. *Institutio Theologiae Elencticae.* Geneva: Samuelem De Tournes, 1688.

Twisse, William. *Dissertatio de Scientia Media Tribus Libris Absoluta.* Arnhem: Jacobum à Biesium, 1639.

Voetius, Gisbertus. *Selectarum Disputationum Theologicarum.* Utrecht: Johannis a Waesberge, 1648–69.

Vos, Antonie, et al., *John Duns Scotus: Contingency and Freedom, Lectura I 39. Introduction, Translation, and Commentary.* The New Synthese Historical Library 42. Dordrecht: Kluwer Academic, 1994.

———. *The Philosophy of John Duns Scotus.* Edinburgh: Edinburgh University Press, 2006.

———. "Scotus' significance for Western philosophy and theology." In *Lo scotismo nel Mezzogiorno d'Italia.* Edited by Francesco Fiorentino. Textes et Études du Moyen Âge 52. Porto: Fédération Internationale des Instituts d'Études Médiévales, 2010.

Williams, Ebenezer. *A System of Ethics. Of moral philosophy in general and in special.* HUC 8707.394, Harvard University Archives (seq. 64): http://nrs.harvard.edu/urn-3:HUL.ARCH:10919374?n=64.

# 8

## "An Holy and Beautiful Soul"
### Jonathan Edwards on the Humanity of Christ

Corné Blaauw

### Introduction[1]

IN THE HISTORY OF the Work of Redemption, Edwards wrote, "The creation of the world was a very great thing, but not so great a thing as the incarnation of Christ. It was a great thing for God to make the creature, but not so great as for the Creator himself to become a creature."[2] Even though Edwards ranked this event as the greatest event in history, second only to the cross, scholarship on his Christology, and specifically on the person of Christ, has not always reflected this importance. In fact, when his Christology has been studied the results have been quite diverse, with several authors presenting challenges to Edwards's orthodoxy. Despite the growing body of literature on Edwards's Christology,[3] Robert W. Caldwell III could state as recently as

---

1. A special thanks to the editors of the *Jonathan Edwards Studies* journal for their permission to republish this article from the *JES* 6.1 (2016). Additional thanks to Seng-Kong Tan, Willem van Vlastuin and an anonymous reviewer from the *JES* journal who provided helpful feedback on an earlier version of this paper.

2. Edwards, *History of the Work of Redemption*, WJE 9:299.

3. Coffin, *Some Aspects*; Carse, *Christology*; Williamson, *Excellency of Christ*; Jenson, *America's Theologian*; Stephens, *Doctrine of the Trinity*; Gerstner, *Rational Biblical Theology*; Holmes, *God of Grace*, 134–42; Michael Bush, *Jesus Christ*; Pauw, *Supreme Harmony*, 139–50; Jenson, "Christology," 72–86; Hastings, "Giving Honour to the

2006 that "The lack of consensus on the nature of Edwards's Christological views reveals that we are only in the beginning stages of understanding his complete Christology."[4] This paper will define briefly some of the problems surrounding Edwards's Christology, propose a method for constructing his Christology, place Edwards within his historical context, and then present the findings of one aspect of his Christology, namely the human nature of Christ by applying the proposed method.

## The Problem Described

What exactly is different about Edwards's theology of the person of Christ? There are various views on the matter, but all agree that Edwards has a peculiar and perhaps not altogether orthodox (at least by Reformed standards) view of the incarnation. Robert W. Jenson claims, "Jonathan Edwards' Christology is one of the most astonishing, and even eccentric, aspects of his thought. There is no doubt that he intended to be thoroughly orthodox in the matter, but he arrived at orthodoxy—if he did—on anything but usual paths."[5] Michael J. McClymond and Gerald R. McDermott's assessment is that "Edwards spent comparatively little time discussing the intricacies of the doctrine of the person of Christ."[6] W. Ross Hastings said, "For all Edwards's attention to detail with regard to the union of the Divine and the human natures of Christ in the incarnation, his emphasis on the Spirit leads him to describe a Christ who can appear ahistorical and unconnected to the humanity he came to redeem."[7] S. Mark Hamilton, in his entry in *A Jonathan Edwards Encyclopedia*, remarks that Edwards's theology of the incarnation is "Disparate, fragmentary, at times even exotic . . ."[8] Other assessments are similar.[9]

---

Spirit," 279–99 Caldwell, *Communion*; Cochran, "Creaturely Virtues"; Tan, "Trinitarian Action"; Crisp, *Revisioning Christology*; Withrow, *Becoming Divine*, 126–34, 185–92; McClymond and McDermott, *Theology of Jonathan Edwards*; Strobel, *Jonathan Edwards's Theology*, 166–71; Hamilton, "Incarnation."

4. Caldwell, *Communion*, 76.

5. Jenson, "Christology," 72.

6. McClymond and McDermott, *Theology of Jonathan Edwards*, 254–61.

7. Hastings, *Jonathan Edwards*, 10–11. This is almost exactly the same as Pauw's claim, "This distinctive role for the Spirit fuelled a tendency to describe the incarnate union in ahistorical ways, with the result that the humanity assumed by the Word seems to have no need for growth in wisdom or stature (Luke 2:40)." Pauw, *Supreme Harmony*, 147.

8. Hamilton, "Incarnation."

9. Daniel claims that Edwards's Christology is in stark contradiction to his

## Proposed Method

How, then, do we go about assessing and attempting to resolve these difficulties? First, it is necessary to identify some of the distinctive methods that Edwards's interpreters have employed, and then to propose alternative ways of reading Edwards. The methodological problems that are most common include the following: (1) Many secondary sources depend too heavily on Edwards's grand sermon *The Excellency of Christ* and on a few Miscellanies entries, in particular numbers 487 and 709. Though much can be gained from these sources, they do not tell the whole story. In response, we will be considering a broader scope of sources to describe Edwards's Christology, with specific reference to key biblical texts from his *Blank Bible*, *Notes on Scripture*, and his *Sermons and Discourses*.[10] (2) Some writers are quick to jump to ahistorical comparisons between Edwards and other theologians outside of his time.[11] Though comparisons are essential to constructive theology, there is a need first to locate Edwards in his intellectual-historical context and to examine the kind of christological questions that were being asked during his time.[12] (3) Many times when the person of Christ is treated

---

"substantialist metaphysics." In other words, he asks how Edwards could hold consistently that Christ could really have two natures and at the same time hold that there is really only one substance, namely God, in the universe. Daniel, *Philosophy of Jonathan Edwards*, 197. A recent essay by Crisp approaches the subject similarly, and rather than attempting to reconstruct Edwards's Christology from his sources, asks what can account for such peculiarities in his doctrine of the person of Christ. He wrote, "The nature of the Christological problems generated by these metaphysical commitments does not necessarily yield an unorthodox Christology. But it does yield a metaphysically exotic Christology." Crisp, *Revisioning Christology*, 44.

10. Stephen Holmes recognizes the methodological problem of merely quoting from Edwards's *Miscellanies* in constructing his Christology, but does not really rectify the problem in his discussion on it. He writes, "I have had cause to insist before now that Edwards's *Miscellanies*, significant as they are, must not be taken as finished or polished statements of his theology. They are ideas, drafts, interesting points that he thought merited further consideration in the future." Holmes, *God of Grace*, 141.

11. Richard Muller's assessment is, "'Barthian historiography' is an oxymoron." Muller, "Reflections on Persistent Whiggism," 137.

12. The basis of such theological comparisons should at least start (but not end) with William Ames, Johannes Wollebius, Francis Turretin, and Petrus van Mastricht, since these either constituted part of Edwards's education or were part of his theological staple diet. Norman Fiering states that the "reading of Ames at Harvard was mandated until at least as late as 1726, and probably for long after that." Fiering, *Moral Philosophy*, 28. Yet, "By the 1670's the Medulla was generally replaced at Harvard by John Wollebius' *The Abridgment of Christian Divinity*." Miller, *New England Mind*, 96. Yale held both these titles, yet Edwards rarely cited them directly (Wollebius never, and Ames's *Marrow* only in *WJE* 20:242). Likewise, Edwards mentions his use of

separately from his work, one of two problems occurs: either a very narrow range of topics is addressed, or, the treatment of those topics addressed only scratches the surface.[13] In light of this, there is a need for a more complete and in-depth appraisal of Edwards's Christology than has heretofore been delivered. This article will avoid the well-worn path of merely describing his oddities. Rather, we will write a more constructive account of his Christology, and will place his "oddities" in that context. A comprehensive Christology falls beyond the scope of this article; rather, the focus will be more narrowly on the humanity of Christ, which was of great importance to him and will be helpful to us in addressing some of the questions in the secondary literature.[14] The three points of method mentioned above will be applied to Edwards's thought on the humanity of Christ. This article will not suffice to answer all the challenges posed to Edwards's christological orthodoxy; but that is not its intention. Rather, it will attempt to throw fresh light on Edwards's Christology by exploring the humanity of Christ by means of the proposed method. The exact questions from the secondary literature it will address include the following. First, are McDermott and McClymond (n. 6 above) correct in asserting that Edwards spent "comparatively little time discussing the intricacies of the doctrine of the person of Christ"? Second, does Edwards present Christ as "ahistorical and unconnected with the humanity he came to redeem" (according to Hastings, n. 7 above)? Third, is Pauw correct in asserting that "the humanity assumed by the Word seems to have no need for growth in wisdom or stature" (n. 7 above)? Finally, does Edwards's presentation of Christ adequately account for Christ's humanity? Having made the intentions of this paper clear, we will now proceed to

---

Turretin and Mastricht in a letter to Joseph Bellamy dated 15 January 1747, and cited their works on numerous occasions throughout his writings. See Edwards, "To the Reverend Joseph Bellamy," *WJE* 16:217. Some of these cross-pollinations and trajectories are traced out in Vliet, *Rise of Reformed System*.

13. This, of course, is not the case with all the sources. See, for instance the excellent in-depth treatments by Caldwell and Fisk. Caldwell, *Communion*; Fisk, "Jonathan Edwards's *Freedom of the Will*."

14. This is not to say that other topics not included here are not central to Edwards's discussion on Christology; many of them are. Topics that deserve attention in their own right include: the hypostatic union, the work of the Spirit in the life of Christ, the *munus triplex*, the glory of Christ, *autotheos*, eternal generation of the Son, Old Testament christophanies and christological typologies. Some might consider it controversial that Edwards's Spirit Christology is left out of the present paper, yet this is done for two reasons: first, it is such a large topic that it deserves an appraisal in its own right (see Caldwell, *Communion*); and, second, overemphasizing it might lead one to miss features described in this essay concerning Christ's humanity in Edwards's thought.

sketch the historical setting, following which we will present the humanity of Christ from Edwards's perspective. In the process, we hope to provide answers to each of these questions.

## Historical Context

In constructing his Christology, Edwards drew from a wide range of sources, some of which he did not use in his treatment of other theological subjects. He used the English Puritan tradition, English Independents, Anglicans, New England Reformed, and Continental Reformed; meanwhile, he argued against the Unitarians (while not being entirely unwilling to learn from them as well).[15] It seems that as Edwards grew older, and as the eighteenth century wore on, the Unitarian controversy caught Edwards's attention more and more. For instance, upon hearing of the Unitarian leanings of Philip Gibbs (1696–1752), Edwards wrote of his grave concern for England in a letter to Benjamin Colman: "What you inform of Mr. Gibbs of Hackney looks very sorrowful, as many other things do respecting the present state of religion in England."[16] Edwards was right in his assessment, since controversy over the divinity of Christ had been raging on British soil throughout the seventeenth and eighteenth centuries.[17]

15. English Puritan: Richard Rawlin (1686-1757), *Christ's Righteousness of his People* (London, 1741); Thomas Goodwin (1600-80), "The Glory of Christ" in *Thirteen Sermons*, Works, vol. 1; English Presbyterian: William Harris (1675-1740), *Practical Discourses on the Principal Representations of the Messiah throughout the Old Testament* (London, 1724); English Reformed: John Hurrion, *The Knowledge of Christ Glorified* (London, 1729). Anglican: Richard Kidder (1634-1703), *Demonstrations of the Messias* (1726); Philip Skelton (1707-87), *Deism Revealed* (1751); Gilbert Burnet (1643-1715), *An Exposition of the Thirty-Nine Articles of the Church of England* (London, 1699); Joseph Edwards's *Christ God-Man. A Sermon Preached before the University of Oxford, At St. Mary's, On Sunday, July 30, MDCCXLIX. With a Preface, Occasioned by a Book lately published entitled Memoirs of the Life and Writings of Mr. Whiston, in relation to the Divinity of our Saviour, and the Controversy concerning it* (London, 1749). Independent Reformed: Philip Doddridge (1702-1751), *The Family Expositor* (1739-56); Continental Reformed: Hermann Witsius (1636-1708), *Exercitationes Sacræ in Symbolum Quod Apostolorum Dicitur*, 4th ed. (Herbornae Nassaviorum, 1712); Johann Friedrich Stapfer (1708-75), *Institutiones theologicae polemicae universae*, 5 vols (1756-57); Lutheran: Matthaus Pfaff (1686-1766), *Institutiones theologiae dogmaticae et moralis* (Tübingen, 1720); Unitarian: Thomas Emlyn (1663-1741), *An humble inquiry into the Scripture account of Jesus Christ* (1702).

16. Edwards, "To the Reverend Benjamin Colman," *WJE* 16:78. His general assessment of his own time was that there had never been such a great apostasy (See *History of the Work of Redemption, WJE* 9:437-38).

17. For the decline of trinitarian piety in England towards the end of the

Several factors led to the decline of general acceptance of the divinity of Christ, including the Racovian Catechism (1605); the anti-trinitarian writings of John Biddle (1612–62), Samuel Clarke (1675–1729), and William Whiston (1667–1752);[18] rational religion; the Johannine Comma controversy; and growing religious tolerance.[19] Edwards was appalled after reading Thomas Emlyn's *An Humble Inquiry into the Scripture-account of Jesus Christ; or, A Short Argument concerning His Deity and Glory, according to the Gospel*—so much so that it led him to write first to Thomas Foxcroft (1697–1769), and later on 11 February 1757 to Edward Wigglesworth (1693–1765), encouraging the latter to engage in controversy against the book since it might convince many against the divinity of Christ.[20] Wigglesworth declined, since he argued that although the book was debated, no one seemed to be convinced by its arguments. Emlyn's three main arguments against the divinity of Christ were: (1) Christ claims to be subordinate to the Father, whom he calls God over all; (2) Jesus did not claim to have absolute perfections as God does, and in fact denied that he possessed un-derived power, unlimited power, and unlimited knowledge; (3) the doctrine of the two natures of Christ is absurd.[21] Although Edwards read Emlyn's book only late in his life, we find scattered throughout his writings answers that could have been presented to each of these objections. Yet Emlyn's book was just one of a growing body of anti-Trinitarian literature, which met with initial resistance, but towards the end of the century met with broader acceptance.

Notwithstanding the polemical context of the eighteenth century surrounding the divinity of Christ, there were several of Edwards's theological predecessors and contemporaries who attempted to construct theologies of the person of Christ that surpassed their narrowly defined polemical context. These included: Thomas Goodwin, John Owen, John Arrowsmith,

---

seventeenth century, see Dixon, *Nice and Hot Disputes*.

18. Biddle, *Confession of Faith*; Biddle, *Apostolical and True Opinion*; Clarke, *Scripture Doctrine*; Whiston, *Primitive Christianity Reviv'd*. Many others held similar views, but some they kept them from public view until after their deaths because of state intolerance for heresy.

19. Another reason might be that the constructive content of the doctrine of the person of Christ was not making progress in the eighteenth century, since it had been "settled" by the ecumenical councils. Although there might be some truth in this, the growing body of secondary literature on Christology in the early modern period seems to suggest part of the fault lies with us who have not uncovered all there is within the period. Mark Jones wrote, "it is a great mystery why so little secondary literature has been written on Puritan Christology." Beeke and Jones, *Puritan Theology*, 336.

20. Edwards, "To Dr. Edward Wigglesworth," *WJE* 16:697–700.

21. Emlyn, "An Humble Inquiry," 81–130.

Isaac Ambrose, and Daniel Waterland, who were able to develop a distinctively Reformed Christology that went beyond mere affirmations of Chalcedonian orthodoxy.[22] The historical setting of the early modern period did not see many Docetic writers who denied the humanity of Christ while affirming his deity; rather, as was the case with Emlyn, the humanity of Christ was presented as in conflict with his simultaneous deity. The voices of the Anabaptists who sought to revive the Gnostic heresy were marginal;[23] yet, as is common in the history of Western theology, some functionally denied Christ's humanity by over-emphasizing his deity.

## The Humanity of Christ

Within this context Edwards reflected on the person of Christ. For Christ to take on real humanity, Edwards argued that there are several facets that are essential to such a nature; these fall under three headings: composition, experiences, and implications. These are not necessarily distinctions Edwards made; they are merely introduced for the convenience of arranging Edwards's material systematically.

### Human Composition

For Christ to really be fully human he has to have a real human body and soul. First, the nature of Christ's conception means Christ has a real human body. The virgin conception and birth meant for Edwards that Christ was "of the substance of her [Mary]," becoming "truly son of man" and part of the "posterity of Adam . . . Abraham . . . and David," which was "not by ordinary generation but by the power of the Holy Ghost." At the same time, "his nature was gradually perfected in the womb of the virgin in a way of natural progress."[24] This meant that Christ in his physical body did not merely appear to be human; he was human, while the glory of his deity was veiled from

22. John Arrowsmith, *Theanthropos, or, God-Man* (1660); Thomas Goodwin, *The Works of Thomas Goodwin* (1681–1704); John Owen, *Christogloria: On the Person of Christ* (1679) and *Meditations and Discourses on the Glory of Christ* (1684); Daniel Waterland, *The Works of Daniel Waterland* (1823). Incidentally, in the context of Christology, Edwards cited Goodwin's and Owen's works directly, Waterland's through John Hurrion once, and none of Arrowsmith.

23. Turretin, *Institutes*, vol. 2, topic 13, Q.5, section 2–19. Even here, Turretin can cite examples only from the sixteenth century. See Dyck, "Christology of Dirk Philips."

24. Edwards, *History of the Work of Redemption*, WJE 9:297; "'Misc.' 767," WJE 18:414.

public view.²⁵ Edwards follows Cotton Mather and Arthur Bedford in locating the birth of Christ during the feast of tabernacles (September through October), rather than the traditional dating (December).²⁶ As to the virgin birth, Edwards remarks upon the "wonderful" self-denial of Joseph who did not "know" the virgin whom he loved, but rather "abstained from her out of reverence to that divine conception that she went with."²⁷ Within Edwards's historical context, the supernatural conception was already denied by the Deists, like Thomas Chubb and John Toland;²⁸ meanwhile it was affirmed and developed by the Reformed Scholastics, like Wollebius and Ames. Edwards's formulation is strikingly similar to that of the latter group, bar some of the finer scholastic distinctions they made which Edwards does not.²⁹ The debate further unfolds as Edwards, in response to Isaac Watts (1674-1748) and Philip Doddridge (1702-51), argued (in his private notebooks and his public sermons) that the human nature of Christ was formed at the conception and did not exist before that time. In his 1741 sermon *Like Rain upon Mown Grass*, he wrote, "We are not to understand Christ's coming down from heaven in his incarnation as though his human nature came down from heaven, for his human nature never had been in heaven. It but then began to have a being."³⁰ These contours reinforce his classic formulation of the occasion of the incarnation, as opposed to those of both the Deists and writers like Watts and Doddridge.

Second, Christ has a real human soul. To Edwards, the Son of God did not merely take on an empty shell in the incarnation, but acted by his humanity in a human body and "the faculty of his soul."³¹ Why should Christ have a reasonable soul? Since it is not possible to satisfy the law "pertaining to human being except through a human being . . . in order that he might

---

25. Edwards, "Note 340," *WJE* 15:325.

26. Edwards, "Note 202," *WJE* 15:127-28.

27. Edwards, "Matthew 1:25," *WJE* 24:826.

28. Toland, *Christianity Not Mysterious*, 152.

29. Wollebius, *Compendium*, 89-90; Ames, *Marrow of Theology*, 137-38; Owen, *Christogloria*, 45-46.

30. Edwards, "Like Rain upon Mown Grass," *WJE* 22:302. For his private reflections see Edwards, "'Misc.' 1174," *WJE* 23:90. See also Caldwell, *Communion*, 80-83. Incidentally, in same sermon, Edwards also makes clear his doctrine of the *extra calvinisticum* by stating, "Nor are we to understand that the divine nature left heaven, so that heaven was empty of the divine nature of Christ." Edwards, "Like Rain upon Mown Grass," *WJE* 22:302.

31. Edwards, "'Misc.' 738," *WJE* 18:364. See also Edwards's mention of "Christ suffered in his soul . . ." McMullen, *Sermons*, vol.2, 46.

fulfil all justice in body and in spirit (Matthew 3:15)."[32] This teaching of the "rational soul" of Christ was part of the Reformed heritage that Edwards inherited. Girolamo Zanchi (1516-90) wrote, "The only-begotten Son of God did not dwell in a man formed as it were previously, but himself truly and essentially *became* man. I.e. He caused to subsist in his very own hypostasis flesh animated by a rational, intellectual soul."[33] A theologian closer to the time of Edwards, Benedict Pictet (1655-1724), understood this human soul as constituted of the faculties of knowing and willing: "The Holy Spirit also ascribes to him a soul endowed with the faculty of knowing and willing . . . "[34] Edwards also incorporated knowing and willing as not only divine but also as human faculties of the soul of Jesus. These two faculties of the soul of Christ can be traced back to Edwards's anthropology and even further to his Trinitarian thought.[35]

The first faculty of Christ's human soul is his human will. The Third Council of Constantinople (AD 680-81) argued that Christ has two wills (dyotheletism as opposed to monotheletism): one human and one divine.[36] Many texts from the Reformed Orthodox do not address the issue, but the one Edwards knew taught it: William Ames (1576-1633). He wrote, "So there were two wills, one divine, Luke 5:13, and the other human, with a natural appetite, Matt. 26:39."[37] Edwards affirms this when describing the sufferings Christ endured in the garden of Gethsemane; he argued that the garden experience was to show to Christ the terrible suffering that he would endure on the cross. He says, "Unless the human nature of Christ had had an extraordinary view given him beforehand of what he was to suffer he could not as man fully know before hand what he was going to suffer."[38] For

---

32. Edwards, "'Misc.' 1216," *WJE* 23:148.

33. Girolamo Zanchi, "De incarnate Filii Dei," as quoted in Heppe, *Reformed Dogmatics*, 419.

34. Benedict Pictet, *Theologia Christiana*, as quoted in Heppe, *Reformed Dogmatics*, 420.

35. Edwards's description of man in *Religious Affections*: "God has indued the soul with two faculties: one is . . . called the understanding. The other . . . is called the will." Edwards, *Religious Affections*, *WJE* 2:96. Strobel writes, "Any *real* attribute in God is subsumed under the categories of understanding and will." Strobel, *Jonathan Edwards's Theology*, 60 (italics in original).

36. Pelikan and Hotchkiss, *Creeds and Confession*, 225-27.

37. Ames, *Marrow of Theology*, 131. Notice that Edwards would use the same event (Matt 26:39—the garden of Gethsemane) to argue for dyotheletism. Likewise, Edwards's contemporary John Gill (1697-1771) argued for the same. See, Stamps, "John Gill's Reformed Dyothelitism."

38. Ibid.

dwelling in it, as the eternal divine Son of God is often called."[44] This idea is reinforced by the metaphors he uses for the human nature of Christ, including: "vessel," "temple," "chest," and "organ."[45] But perhaps the best evidence for this is when Edwards says, "for the incarnation was assuming flesh, or human nature, into the person of the Son, or giving communion of the divine personality to human nature, in giving that human nature being."[46] In light of this, it seems that Edwards refined his Christology away from his earlier "'Misc.' 487" Adoptionist or even Nestorian tendencies: "God hath respect to this man and loveth him as his own Son," and his Monophysite tendencies: "by the communion of understanding and communion of will, inclination, spirit or temper,"[47] towards an orthodox position by employing the distinction between *anhypostatic* and *enhypostatic* categories.[48]

Thus we have seen that the human nature of Christ, in Edwards's view, was complete, having a human body and soul with the faculties of knowing and willing, and yet it was not so complete that it could function as a person without the incarnation, since the personhood was provided for by the Logos who filled the human nature.

## *Human Experiences*

Although there is not space to deal with all Christ's human experience (including his emotional life), we will consider two prominent features. First, the sufferings of Christ were real. Edwards affirms the impassibility of God and more specifically of the Son of God, but nuances this by the doctrine of the incarnation: the incarnate Christ could, and indeed did, experience suffering, being "remarkably feeble."[49] Christ's sufferings could be described as similar to ours, but it is evident that in several places he suffered far greater than we. Edwards uses the garden of Gethsemane to illustrate the point by showing that Christ burst into a sweat all over his body on a cold night; not only sweat, but clots of blood also pushed through his pores.[50] During this time he prayed fervently, and importantly, not merely to be an example to his

---

44. Edwards, "285. Exodus 25:10–22," *WJE* 15:242–46; this quote from 245.
45. Ibid.; see also Edwards, "'Misc.' 738," *WJE* 18:364.
46. Edwards, "'Misc.' 709," *WJE* 18:334.
47. Edwards, "'Misc.' 487," *WJE* 13:529.
48. Incidentally, on this issue he used Spirit Christology throughout his writings.
49. Edwards, "521. Luke 22:44 (October 1739)," *WJEO* 54. Likewise, Edwards argues for the necessity of the incarnation in various places on the basis of the necessity of a *suffering* Savior. See Edwards, *History of the Work of Redemption, WJE* 9:295–96.
50. Edwards, "521. Luke 22:44 (October 1739)," *WJEO* 54.

Edwards this meant that before the cross, Christ had to become sensible of what he was going to suffer there; otherwise he would not be able to know, as man, what he was choosing. As God, Christ knew what he would suffer and was willing to submit to his Father, but he had to learn and choose this as man. This was important since he had to take the cup as God-man.[39] So, his death on the cross was "entirely Christ's own free and voluntary act" as both God and man.[40]

The second faculty of Christ's human soul is his human mind. Although calling this theory "the two minds" account is a modern classification, nevertheless the theology behind it is historic. William Ames wrote, "There were in Christ two kinds of understandings: a divine understanding whereby he knew all things, John 21:17, and a human, whereby he did not yet know some things, Mark 13:32."[41] Likewise, in commenting on the "wisdom" which the saints in heaven ascribe to the Lamb in Revelation 5, Edwards proposed that Christ did not only grow in wisdom on earth but advanced to such great wisdom that in heaven he is praised for his wisdom as man.[42]

At this point it would be easy to accuse Edwards of Nestorianism, as is the case with many within the Alexandrian-Reformed tradition. However, Edwards also maintains the *anhypostatic* and *enhypostatic* nature of the incarnation, that is, personhood is provided by the divine Son of God and is not also found in the human nature of Christ without the incarnation.[43] Edwards makes this point in his comments on Exodus 25:10–22 by arguing that the human nature of Christ was an empty vessel but was filled with the Logos. "The human nature of Christ had the Logos, or the Word of God,

---

39. Ibid.

40. For Edwards's most complete explanation of the volition of Christ, see "The Free and Voluntary Suffering and Death of Christ," *WJE* 19:495–514. The first half discusses his volition as God, and the second half as man.

41. Ames, *Marrow of Theology*, 131.

42. "Christ was Worthy of His Exaltation upon the Account of His Being Slain," 1732 and 1756, McMullen, *Sermons*, vol. 2, 347. For a discussion of the man Christ in heaven see, Bush, *Jesus Christ*, 225–29.

43. Reformed Orthodox writers described it in this way: Turretin wrote, "Although the human nature of Christ is a first substance (intelligent and perfect in substantial being), it is not at once a person because it does not possess incommunicability and proper substance (as the soul separated is a singular intelligent substance, yet not a person because it is a partial being, incomplete, which does not subsist, but must be adjoined to another)." Turretin, *Institutes*, 316. Similarly, Wollebius wrote, "Christ assumed manhood, not as man; not a person, but the nature." In other words, although the human nature of Christ had a soul and perfect substance, it would have been impossible for it to function as a person, since the personhood (or as some say, existence) was provided only by the incarnation. Wollebius, *Compendium*, 90.

disciples, but out of his own dire need.⁵¹ At the cross, then, it was the human nature of Christ that died and not the divine Logos: "And when his flesh was crucified, when his human nature died."⁵² Nevertheless, Edwards makes it clear that the person was involved in the death, "That life that was offered up, though it was only the human life of Christ; yet being the life of a divine person, it was that which the whole person has a priority in."⁵³ In other words, the sufferings of Christ remain real since the divine Logos remains with the human nature, although the divine Logos does not, and in fact cannot, die. Yet it is proper to speak of the person of Christ dying.

Second, Christ remained sinless through all of his real temptations since he was impeccable. Edwards's understanding of the sinless nature of Christ and impeccability has been criticized by Ross Hastings and Amy Plantinga Pauw since the Jesus he portrayed, they argue, was neither born with a fallen nature like ours, nor was he capable of sinning—therefore, they argue, he does not fully identify with us.⁵⁴ Hastings's argument is based on the accounts of Edward Irving, John Owen, and Karl Barth, all of whom expounded Christ as having a fallen human nature. At this point it has to be objected that their arguments are based on anachronistic categories that would not have been well known during Edwards's time (with the exception of Owen's) and miss the continuity between Edwards and his theological tradition. Edwards, on

---

51. Edwards, "Note 225," *WJE* 15:172–73.

52. Edwards, "Note 340," *WJE* 15:325.

53. Edwards, "The free and voluntary suffering and death of Christ," *WJE* 19:497. So also another place he attributes the crucifixion to the name of God: "they [Christians] worshipped a crucified God." Edwards, "Christ was Worthy of His Exaltation upon the Account of His Being Slain," in McMullen, *Sermons*, vol. 1, 347. This was not an uncommon practice for the Reformed variety of the *communicatio idiomatum*, and by copying out Rawlin in a late Miscellany he explains it this way (my paraphrase): it is only proper to speak of the divine nature as condescending, the human nature as dying, and the person as saving and redeeming. Edwards, "'Misc.' 1219," *WJE* 23:153–54. See Holmes, "Reformed Varieties," 70–86.

54. Hastings says that the watermark of the debate is "not whether the obedience of Christ in life and in death is vicarious, but whether it can, with integrity, be vicarious if the human nature he assumed is in any way qualified or different to our own." Hastings, *Honour the Spirit*, 290. The underlying assumption of his argument is the famous dictum by Gregory Nazianzus: "For that which He has not assumed He has not healed." But Gregory's thought is taken out of context, since he used it to argue that Christ's human composition included a mind and a soul and not a sin nature. "To Cledonius the Priest Against Apollinarius," in *Nicene and Post-Nicene Fathers*, 440. Furthermore one wonders whether it is a proper criticism of Edwards within his time, since he was following not merely within the Reformed orthodox tradition, but also the historic church which had always insisted "sin excepted." See also Heppe, *Reformed Dogmatics*, 421–28.

the other hand, argued that Christ assumed a human nature without original sin but not entirely in its pre-fall state, since the effects of the fall were so visible on his "poor, feeble, broken state."[55] This is the closest Edwards comes to explaining Christ's "likeness of sinful flesh" from Romans 8:3, but he goes beyond this and applies our sinful nature to Christ in his death, which is typified in his circumcision according to Colossians 2:11. Edwards comments on the verse, " . . . our body of sin was imputed to him. He bore it, and put it off in outward sign by his circumcision. Christ represented us: he came into the world without any original sin of his own, but with our original sin; and he was circumcised to signify the putting off our corruption of nature."[56] It is true that Edwards did not present Christ as taking on original sin in his life, but that he took it on in his death does give an adequate (and historic) account of how he could truly identify with us.

What, then, prevented Christ from sinning? Edwards presents eleven arguments in his *Freedom of the Will* for the impeccability of Christ: (1) God promised to uphold him by his Spirit;[57] (2) God promised the Messiah future glory, a kingdom, and success; (3) God promised to give the church a righteous and sinless Savior; (4) all the Old Testament promises point to a Savior perfect in holiness; (5) the Old Testament promises imply that the Savior will be perfect in the work of redemption; (6) if he could sin, it would be inconsistent with the promises made to Joseph and Mary; it would also be inconsistent with the (7) decrees of God, (8) promises made to the Son, and (9) promises the Son made to the Father; (10) if he could sin salvation would be built on a shaky foundation; and finally (11) while Christ was tempted and tried he made positive predictions about the coming kingdom.[58] After examining Edwards's doctrine of impeccability from

---

55. Edwards, "521. Luke 22:44 (October 1739)," *WJEO* 54. Unfortunately Edwards did not comment directly in either his *Blank Bible* or *Notes on Scripture* on the two key passages from which one might derive the "fallen flesh of Christ," that is, Romans 8:13, "his Son in the likeness of sinful flesh" (thought this is everywhere affirmed), and Hebrews 2:17, "Wherefore in all things it behoved him to be made like unto his brethren."

56. Edwards, "Note 69," *WJE* 15:69.

57. This point is also made elsewhere. See Edwards, "285. Exodus 25:10–22," *WJE* 15:244–45.

58. Edwards, *Freedom of the Will*, *WJE* 1:281–88. Edwards argues in other places that Christ also had other kinds of temptations since he had to be obedient to other laws that are not required of us, including moral, ceremonial and judicial laws of Moses, as well as the Father's command that he should lay down his life. All of this could be summed up as obedience to the covenant of works, which to Edwards was Christ's fulfilment of the law. "521. Luke 22:44 (October 1739)," *WJEO* 54. Edwards, *History of the Work of Redemption*, *WJE* 9:308–13.

*Freedom of the Will*, Philip Fisk argues that far from sinlessness being an external agency imposing itself on Christ so that he would not sin, it is in fact a disposition within Christ that leads him "necessarily" to act in in a holy way.[59] So the impeccability of Christ was based both on Edwards's account of the doctrine of God (specifically his faithfulness to his promises) and on the virtue of Christ.

What was the purpose of Jesus' temptations if he would by necessity not choose to sin? Edwards answers this when commenting on Hebrews 2:17–18 and 4:15, "It was required in order to his being both God and man, that he should be the subject of our calamities. That he might know, on the one hand, how to pity man who suffers or is exposed to those calamities."[60] Practically the human life of Christ was geared towards sympathizing with us, while theologically Edwards maintained the classical distinction between the active and passive obedience of Christ: where the terms of Christ's obedience are set by the covenant of redemption, and Christ's life and death accomplishes righteousness for the believer.[61] He wrote, "And so his purchase of happiness by his righteousness was also carried on through the whole time of his humiliation till his resurrection, not only in that obedience he performed through the course of his life, but also the obedience he performed in laying down his life."[62] Having said this, it is true that Edwards paid little attention to the existential realities of the wilderness temptations of Christ and does not comment on synoptic accounts in his *Blank Bible*; when he does mention it, it is usually mentioned in the context of the general sufferings of Christ rather than the lure of temptation.[63] Nevertheless, both the lure and existential realities of temptation are portrayed in Edwards's account of the Gethsemane temptation.

---

59. Fisk, "Jonathan Edwards's *Freedom of the Will*, 309–25. For more on Christ's virtue and excellency, see Edwards, "Saints Alone Dwell" *WJE* 25:57; McMullen, *Sermons* 1:167–68. Edwards argues in another place "Christ did all duty with perfect delight." McMullen, *Sermons* 2:216.

60. McMullen, *Sermons* 1:318.

61. Edwards, "'Misc.' 278," *WJE* 13:378.

62. Edwards, *History of the Work of Redemption*, *WJE* 9:307. See also Edwards, "'Misc.' 841," *WJE* 20:57. Here Pauw complains of not finding in Edwards her reading of "made perfect" (Heb 4:8–9) meaning the gradual lifelong sanctification of Christ. Yet Edwards understood such passages as referring to both Christ's lifelong obedience and his death on the cross (he cross-references Isa 50:5–6), after which he was made perfect (glorified). Edwards, "Hebrews 5:8–9," *WJE* 24:1144; "Note 142," *WJE* 15:91. Pauw, *Supreme Harmony*, 148.

63. Edwards, "'Misc.' 791," *WJE* 18:488–95.

In sum, we have seen that Edwards's portrayal of Christ's life on earth had strongly anti-Docetist impulses by portraying the sufferings of Christ throughout his life and in his death as *real* sufferings. In his depiction of the temptation of Christ, Christ initially seemed to be less than human because he was not born with original sin and because of his impeccability; but, as we have demonstrated, Edwards's portrayal here does not go beyond his tradition in which "the likeness of sinful flesh" is understood as Christ's physical sufferings, not his possessing actual "sinful flesh." Furthermore, although his discussion of the impeccability of Christ is strongly directed by his doctrine of God, it is tempered by understanding of the real virtue Christ possessed. This gives Edwards the immediate application that both the temptations and sufferings of Christ qualify him in a unique way to sympathize with our weaknesses.

## Implications

The implications Edwards drew out from the real humanity of Christ are myriad, but most of them have to do with the union of Christ's human and divine natures, or the union of the believers to Christ. Nor is there space to discuss why Jesus became man.[64] But the implication that Edwards draws out frequently, which focuses exclusively on the humanity of Christ, is that Christ serves as a real example to us. As has already been noted, some argue that if Christ is not born with original sin, he cannot serve as an example to us. But Edwards saw no contradiction between these two lines of thought. He attempted to show the great humility of Christ in his text entitled *Christ's Example*.[65] Here we meet with Edwards more as a Bible commentator than as a theologian. For instance, when he deals with the temptations of Jesus, he does not ask whether it was possible or impossible for Jesus to sin; rather, he states that Jesus' refusing Satan's offers shows his humility, meekness, self-denial and obedience to God.[66] In all this Christ acts in such a way that the Christian ought to strive to imitate him.[67]

---

64. Edwards often states, "It was chiefly for that that there was need of Christ's becoming incarnate, viz. that he might be capable of suffering and dying." Edwards, *WJE* 19:502.

65. Edwards, "Christ's Example," *WJE* 21:511–20; "'Misc.' 791," *WJE* 18:488–95 and throughout "Charity and Its Fruits," *WJE* 8:123–399.

66. Edwards, "Christ's Example," *WJE* 21:516.

67. Edwards's portrayal of Christ as an example is neither medieval (Thomas á Kempis), nor modern (Kant onwards), but typical. See for instance, Owen, *Christogloria*, 169–77.

## Conclusion

We have attempted to reappraise Edwards's Christology by taking into consideration three methodological factors have often been neglected: (1) primarily using his sermons and exegetical writings in addition to his *Miscellanies* and theological works; (2) not anachronistically comparing him to theologians outside of his time without first placing him inside his historical context, and; (3) attempting a more comprehensive Christology than has heretofore been advanced. Because of space limitations, the last factor could not be as developed as the others, so we have opted to study one aspect of his Christology (the humanity of Christ) in a more in-depth way than before. What we have discovered is that the substance of Edwards's discussion closely followed his Reformed predecessors. These writers provided him access to historic tools for examining the finer distinctions within Christology like *extra calvinisticum*, two minds and wills of Christ, *enhypostatic* and *anhypostatic*. Although Edwards does not employ this technical language, his use of these concepts is self-evident. At the same time, he incorporated many insights from a wide range of other theological traditions. Edwards's relentless artistic redressing of Reformed doctrines means that he refuses to undertake the systematization that we have attempted in this article; rather, he continually applied his theological thought to the biblical texts (and *vice versa*). But, as has already been demonstrated, this has not meant a departure from his Reformed heritage. There is no doubt from the presentation above that Edwards does not comment on all the important biblical texts and topics concerning Christology, which does leave several questions unanswered. Nevertheless, the extent of his corpus does provide not only sufficient opportunity to explore his Christology, but a window into early modern theological discussions on the person of Christ, all of which leaves the impression that there is more to be said than has been said before.

As to the questions raised in the introduction, the following answers can now be provided. First, although it is true that one has to survey most of his corpus in order to draw together his theology of the person of Christ, when this is followed through it becomes apparent that Edwards had a much more comprehensive portrayal of Christ than has previously been noticed. In this paper we have merely examined his doctrine of the humanity of Christ, and the scope has already been vast. Therefore, we will have to disagree with McDermott and McClymond, who state that Edwards wrote comparatively little on the "intricacies of the doctrine of the person of Christ."

Second, if one is looking for an Eastern model of the incarnation, where the very act of incarnation is salvific, or for a modern appropriation of the doctrine of original sin to the human nature of Christ, one must not look to Edwards. His depiction of Christ as having a fully human composition (sin excepted) and the full range of human sufferings and temptations (sin excepted) is historic and an adequate account of how Christ can function both as our sympathetic high priest and as our example. Therefore, we disagree with Hastings's account that the Jesus whom Edwards portrays is "ahistorical and unconnected with the humanity he came to redeem."

Third, although Edwards stressed the person and work of the Spirit in the life of Christ to such an extent that Jesus had access to the encyclopedic knowledge of his divine nature (not discussed in this article), he nevertheless spoke of Jesus' need to learn certain things that he would not have known merely by referencing his divine nature, and of his actual growth in wisdom to such an extent that the saints praise him in heaven for his human wisdom. Therefore, we must disagree with Pauw, who asserts that "the humanity assumed by the Word seems to have no need for growth in wisdom or stature."

Finally, there are some aspects of Edwards's theology of the person of Christ, and specifically of his humanity, that could have been explained in more detail, like the wilderness temptations, the *enhypostatic* and *anhypostatic* natures of the incarnation, and the nature of the virgin birth. Nevertheless, as far as Edwards's account of the humanity of Christ goes, it is both historic and insightful, providing many fascinating applications of his tradition to the texts of Scripture. These, of course, have not been without problems, but having taken a broader view of Edwards's Christology we could more properly put some of those problems in perspective and notice that many of them have been overstated because of wrong methodological considerations. In closing, even though progress has been made towards reconstructing Edwards's Christology, there is still room to develop other aspects as well—so it is the hope that many others would "pick it up" in order that we may advance the discussion beyond "the beginning stages."

# Bibliography

Ames, William. *The Marrow of Theology*. Translated by John Dykstra Eusden. Grand Rapids: Baker, 1968.

Arrowsmith, John. *Theanthrōpos, or, God-Man: Being an Exhortation upon the First Eighteen Verse of the First Chapter of the Gospel according to St John*. London: Printed for Humphrey and William Wilson, 1660

Beeke, Joel R., and Mark Jones, *A Puritan Theology: Doctrine for Life*. Grand Rapids: Reformation Heritage Books, 2012.

Biddle, John. *A Confession of Faith Touching the Holy Trinity, According to the Scripture.* London: n.p., 1648.

Biddle, John. *The Apostolical and True Opinion Concerning the Holy Trinity.* London: n.p., 1653.

Bush, Michael. *Jesus Christ in the theology of Jonathan Edwards.* PhD diss., Princeton Theological Seminary, 2003.

Carse, James Pierce. *The Christology of Jonathan Edwards.* PhD diss., Drew University, 1966.

Caldwell Robert W., III, *Communion in the Spirit: The Holy Spirit as the Bond of Union in the Theology of Jonathan Edwards*: Studies in Evangelical History and Thought. London: Paternoster, 2006.

Clarke, Samuel. *The Scripture Doctrine of the Trinity.* London: Printed for James Knapton, at the Crown in St. Paul's Church-Yard, 1712.

Cochran, Elizabeth Agnew. "Creaturely Virtues in Jonathan Edwards: The Significance of Christology for the Moral Life." *Journal for the Society of Christian Ethics* 27 (2007): 73-95.

Coffin, Wayne W. *Some Aspects of Jonathan Edwards' Christology.* PhD diss., Drew University, 1947.

Crisp, Oliver D. *Revisioning Christology: Theology in the Reformed Tradition.* Aldershot: Ashgate, 2011.

Daniel, Stephen H. *The Philosophy of Jonathan Edwards: A Study in Divine Semiotics.* Bloomington: Indiana University Press, 1994.

Dixon, Philip. *Nice and Hot Disputes: The Doctrine of the Trinity in the Seventeenth Century.* London: T. & T. Clark, 2003.

Dyck, Cornelius J. "The Christology of Dirk Philips." *Mennonite Quarterly Review* 31 (1957):147–55.

Edwards, Jonathan. "The Book of Job." In *Notes on Scripture*, edited by Stephen J. Stein, The Works of Jonathan Edwards 15:122–26. New Haven: Yale University Press, 1998.

———. "'Catalogue' of Reading." In *Catalogues of Books*, edited by Peter J. Thuesen, The Works of Jonathan Edwards 26:117–318. New Haven: Yale University Press, 2008.

———. "Charity and its Fruits." In *Ethical Writings*, edited by Paul Ramsay, The Works of Jonathan Edwards 8:123–397. New Haven: Yale University Press, 1989.

———. "Christ's Example." In *Writings on the Trinity, Grace, and Faith*, edited by Sang Hyun Lee, The Works of Jonathan Edwards 21:511–19. New Haven: Yale University Press, 2003.

———. "Colossians 2:11." In *Notes on Scripture*, edited by Stephen J. Stein, The Works of Jonathan Edwards 15:69. New Haven: Yale University Press, 1998.

———. *"Controversies" Notebook.* The Works of Jonathan Edwards Online 27. Jonathan Edwards Center at Yale University.

———. "Even as I Have Kept My Father's Commandments." In *The Glory and Honor of God: Volume 2 of the Previously Unpublished Sermons on Jonathan Edwards*, edited by Michael D. McMullen, 208–22. Nashville: Broadman & Holman, 2004.

———. "Exodus 25:10–22." Pages in *Notes on Scripture*, edited by Stephen J. Stein. The Works of Jonathan Edwards 15:242–46. New Haven: Yale University Press, 1998.

———. "The Free and Voluntary Suffering and Death of Christ." In *Sermons and Discourses, 1734–1738*, edited by Max X. Lesser, The Works of Jonathan Edwards 19:491–514. New Haven: Yale University Press, 2001.

———. *Freedom of the Will*. Edited by Paul Ramsey. The Works of Jonathan Edwards 1. New Haven: Yale University Press, 1957.

———. "The Glory and Honor of God Requires that His Displeasure be Manifested Against Sin." In *The Glory and Honor of God: Volume 2 of the Previously Unpublished Sermons of Jonathan Edwards*, edited by Michael D. McMullen, 34–52. Nashville: Broadman & Holman, 2004.

———. "Hebrews 5:8–9." In *The "Blank Bible,"* edited by Stephen J. Stein, The Works of Jonathan Edwards 24/2:1144. New Haven: Yale University Press, 2006.

———. "Hebrews 5:9." In *Notes on Scripture*, edited by Stephen J. Stein, The Works of Jonathan Edwards 15:91. New Haven: Yale University Press, 1998.

———. *A History of the Work of Redemption*. Edited by John F. Wilson. The Works of Jonathan Edwards 9. New Haven: Yale University Press, 1989.

———. "Jesus Christ is the Great Mediator and Head of Union in Whom All Elect Creatures in Heaven and Earth Are United to God and to One Another." In *The Blessing of God: Previously Unpublished Sermons of Jonathan Edwards*, edited by Michael D. McMullen, 311–26. Nashville: Broadman & Holman, 2003.

———. "Like Rain upon Mown Grass." In *Sermons and Discourses, 1739–1742*, edited by Harry S. Stout et al., The Works of Jonathan Edwards 22:298–318. New Haven: Yale University Press, 2003.

———. "Luke 22:44." In *Notes on Scripture*, edited by Stephen J. Stein, The Works of Jonathan Edwards 15:172–75. New Haven: Yale University Press, 1998.

———. "Matthew 1:25." In *The "Blank Bible,"* edited by Stephen J. Stein, The Works of Jonathan Edwards 24/2:826. New Haven: Yale University Press, 2006.

———. "Matthew 27:51." In *Notes on Scripture*, edited by Stephen J. Stein, The Works of Jonathan Edwards 15:324–25. New Haven: Yale University Press, 1998.

———. "'Misc.' 278." In *The "Miscellanies" (Entry Nos. a–z, aa–zz, 1–500)*, edited by Thomas A. Schafer, The Works of Jonathan Edwards 13:377–78. New Haven: Yale University Press, 1994.

———. "'Misc.' 487." In *The "Miscellanies" (Entry Nos. a–z, aa–zz, 1–500)*, edited by Thomas A. Schafer, The Works of Jonathan Edwards 13:528–32. New Haven Yale University Press, 1994.

———. "'Misc.' 709." In *The "Miscellanies" (Entry Nos. 501–832)*, edited by Ava Chamberlain, The Works of Jonathan Edwards 18:333–35. New Haven: Yale University Press, 2000.

———. "'Misc.' 738." In *The "Miscellanies" (Entry Nos. 501–832)*, edited by Ava Chamberlain, The Works of Jonathan Edwards 18:364. New Haven Yale University Press, 2000.

———. "'Misc.' 767." In *The "Miscellanies" (Entry Nos. 501–832)*, edited by Ava Chamberlain, The Works of Jonathan Edwards 18:414. New Haven: Yale University Press, 2000.

———. "'Misc.' 791." In *The "Miscellanies" (Entry Nos. 501–832)*, edited by Ava Chamberlain, The Works of Jonathan Edwards 18:488–95. New Haven: Yale University Press, 2000.

---. "'Misc.' 841." In *The "Miscellanies" (Entry Nos. 833–1152)*, edited by Amy P. Pauw, The Works of Jonathan Edwards 20:57. New Haven: Yale University Press, 2002.

---. "'Misc.' 1174." In *The "Miscellanies" (Entry Nos. 1153–1360)*, edited by Douglas A. Sweeney, The Works of Jonathan Edwards 23:89–92. New Haven: Yale University Press, 2004.

---. "'Misc.' 1216." In *The "Miscellanies" (Entry Nos. 1153–1360)*, edited by Douglas A. Sweeney, The Works of Jonathan Edwards 23:147–48. New Haven: Yale University Press, 2004.

---. "'Misc.' 1219." In *The "Miscellanies" (Entry Nos. 1153–1360)*, edited by Douglas A. Sweeney, The Works of Jonathan Edwards 23:153–54. New Haven: Yale University Press, 2004.

---. *Religious Affections*. Edited by John E. Smith. The Works of Jonathan Edwards 2. New Haven and London: Yale University Press, 1969.

---. "Saints Dwell Alone." In *Sermons and Discourses, 1743–1758*, edited by Wilson H. Kimnach, The Works of Jonathan Edwards 25:47–58. New Haven: Yale University Press, 2006.

---. "521. Sermon on Luke 22:44 (October 1739)." In *Sermons, Series II, 1739*, The Works of Jonathan Edwards Online 54. Jonathan Edwards Center at Yale University.

---. "That God is the Father of Lights." In *The Blessing of God: Previously Unpublished Sermons of Jonathan Edwards*, edited by Michael D. McMullen, 343–57. Nashville: Broadman & Holman, 2003.

---. "To Dr. Edward Wigglesworth." In *Letters and Personal Writings*, edited by George S. Claghorn, The Works of Jonathan Edwards 16:697–700. New Haven: Yale University Press, 1998.

---. "Thy Name is as Ointment Poured Forth." In *The Blessing of God: Previously Unpublished Sermons of Jonathan Edwards*, edited by Michael D. McMullen. 163–79. Nashville: Broadman & Holman, 2003.

---. "To the Reverend Joseph Bellamy." In *Letters and Personal Writings*, edited by George S. Claghorn, The Works of Jonathan Edwards 16: 216–18. New Haven and London: Yale University Press, 1998.

---. "To the Reverend Benjamin Colman." In *Letters and Personal Writings*, edited by George S. Claghorn, The Works of Jonathan Edwards 16:77–79. New Haven: Yale University Press, 1998.

Edwards, Joseph. *Christ God-Man. A Sermon Preached before the University of Oxford, At St. Mary's, On Sunday, July 30, MDCCXLIX. With a Preface, Occasioned by a Book lately published entitled Memoirs of the Life and Writings of Mr. Whiston, in relation to the Divinity of our Saviour, and the Controversy concerning it* London: New England Reformed: 1749.

Emlyn, Thomas. "An Humble Inquiry into the Scripture-account of Jesus Christ: or, A Short Argument Concerning His Deity and Glory, according to the Gospel." In *The Works of Thomas Emlyn* 1:81–130. London: John Noon, 1766.

Fiering, Norman. *Moral Philosophy at Seventeenth-Century Harvard: A Discipline in Transition*. Chapel Hill: University of North Carolina, 1981.

Fisk, Philip J. "Jonathan Edwards's *Freedom of the Will* and his Defence of the Impeccability of Christ." *Scottish Journal of Theology* 60:3 (2007) 309–25.

Gerstner, John. *The Rational Biblical Theology of Jonathan Edwards.* 2 vols. Powhatan: Berea and Ligonier, 1992.

Gregory Nazianzus. "To Cledonius the Priest Against Apollinarius." In *Nicene and Post-Nicene Fathers,* edited by Philip Schaff and Henry Wace, Second Series 8:439-42. Grand Rapids: Eerdmans, 1989.

Hamilton, S. Mark. "Incarnation." In *A Jonathan Edwards Encyclopedia,* edited by Kenneth Minkema and Adriaan Neele. Grand Rapids: Eerdmans, forthcoming.

Hastings, Ross W. "Giving Honour to the Spirit: Analysis and Evaluation of Jonathan Edwards' Pneumatological Doctrine of the Incarnation." *International Journal of Systematic Theology* 7/3 (2005) 279-99.

———. *Jonathan Edwards and the Life of God: Towards an Evangelical Theology of Participation.* Augsburg: Fortress, 2015.

Heppe, Herman. *Reformed Dogmatics.* Translated by G. T. Thompson. Reprint. Eugene, OR: Wipf and Stock, 2007.

Holmes, Stephen R. *God of Grace and God of Glory: An Account of the Theology of Jonathan Edwards.* Grand Rapids: Eerdmans, 2000.

———. "The Reformed Varieties of the *Communicatio Idiomatum.*" In *The Person of Christ,* edited by Stephen R. Holmes and Michael Rae, 70-86. London: Bloomsbury T. & T. Clark, 2005.

Hurrion, John. *The Knowledge of Christ Glorified.* London: Printed for John Clark and Richard Hett, 1729.

Jenson, Robert W. "Christology." In *The Princeton Companion to Jonathan Edwards,* edited by Sang Hyun Lee, 72-86. Oxford: Princeton University Press, 2005.

Jenson, Robert W. *America's Theologian: A Recommendation of Jonathan Edwards.* New York: OUP, 1988.

McClymond, Michael J., and Gerald R. McDermott, *The Theology of Jonathan Edwards.* New York: Oxford University Press, 2012.

McMullen, Michael D., ed. *The Blessing of God: Previously Unpublished Sermons of Jonathan Edwards.* Vol. 1. Nashville, TN: Broadman & Holman, 2003.

———. *The Glory and Honor of God: Previously Unpublished Sermons of Jonathan Edwards* Vol. 2. Nashville, TN: Broadman & Holman, 2004.

Miller, Perry. *The New England Mind: The Seventeenth Century.* Boston: Beacon Press, 1961.

Muller, Richard A. "Reflections on Persistent Whiggism and Its Antidotes in the Study of Sixteenth- and Seventeenth-century Intellectual History." In *Seeing Things Their Way: Intellectual History and the Return of Religion,* edited by Alister Chapman et al., 134-53. Indiana: University of Notre Dame Press, 2009.

Owen, John. *Christogloria: On the Person of Christ.* In *The Works of John Owen,* Vol. 1. Edinburgh: Banner of Truth Trust, 1972.

———. *Meditations and Discourses on the Glory of Christ.* London: A.M. and R.R. 1684.

Pauw, Amy Plantinga. *The Supreme Harmony of All: The Trinitarian Theology of Jonathan Edwards.* Grand Rapids: Eerdmans, 2002.

Pelikan, Jeroslav, and Valerie Hotchkiss, eds. *Creeds and Confession of Faith in the Christian Tradition.* Vol. 1. New Haven: Yale University Press, 2003.

Stamps, Robert Lucas. "John Gill's Reformed Dyothelitism." *Reformed Theological Review* 74/2 (2015) 77-93.

Stephens, Bruce Milton. *The Doctrine of the Trinity from Jonathan Edwards to Horace Bushnell: A Study in the Eternal Sonship of Christ.* PhD diss., Drew University, 1970.

Strobel, Kyle. *Jonathan Edwards's Theology: A Reinterpretation.* London: Bloomsbury T. & T. Clark, 2013.

Tan, Seng-Kong. "Trinitarian Action in the Incarnation." In *Jonathan Edwards as Contemporary: Essays in Honour of Sang Hyun Lee,* edited by Don Schweitzer. New York: Peter Land, 2010.

Toland, John. *Christianity Not Mysterious.* London: n.p., 1696.

Turretin, Francis. *Institutes of Elenctic Theology.* 3 vols. Translated by George Musgrave Giger and edited by James T. Dennison. New Jersey: P&R Publishing, 1992-97.

Vliet, Jan van. *The Rise of Reformed System: The Intellectual Heritage of William Ames.* Studies in Christian History and Thought. Eugene, Oregon: Wipf & Stock, 2013.

Waterland, Daniel. *The Works of Daniel Waterland, D.D. Formerly Master of Magdalene College.* 10 vols. Oxford: Clarendon Press, 1823.

Whiston, William. *Primitive Christianity Reviv'd.* 4 vols. London: Printed for the Author, 1711–12.

Williamson, Joseph Crawford. *The Excellency of Christ: A study in the Christology of Jonathan Edwards.* PhD diss., Harvard University, 1968.

Withrow, Brandon G. *Becoming Divine: Jonathan Edwards's Incarnational Spirituality within the Christian Tradition.* Eugene, OR: Cascade, 2011.

Wollebius, Johannes. *Compendium Theologiae Christianae,* In *Reformed Dogmatics: Seventeenth-Century Reformed Theology Through the Writings of Wollebius, Voetius, and Turretin,* edited and translated by John Beardslee III, XVI:2.I–III. Grand Rapids: Baker, 1977.

# 9

# Being Seen and Being Known
## *Jonathan Edwards's Theological Anthropology*

KYLE STROBEL

OF ALL THAT EDWARDS is known for, anthropology is not near the top of the list. Assumed at every point in his thought, Edwards's anthropology is one of the more under-studied features of his theology.[1] But it wouldn't be far-reaching to claim that the question, "What sort of beings are we?" is fundamental to his theological project *in toto*. In *Freedom of the Will*, Edwards addresses human freedom and morality in relation to God, in *The Religious Affections* he attends to the nature of human response to God's indwelling presence, in the *Two Dissertations* he develops his account of the creature in relation to God's glory, love, and beauty, and in *Original Sin* he addresses the fall and humanity, both as individuals and corporate realities. Human flourishing was at the core of all he did.

To advance an account of Edwards's theological anthropology, this chapter proceeds to two major movements.[2] First, I articulate Edwards's

---

1. This needs qualification. The areas of anthropology that are attended to are issues related to freedom of the will, religious affection, and the relation of his view to John Locke's own analysis. My statement concerns a broader picture of anthropology such as the one I am developing here.

2. This paper is substantially better because of the suggestions by Ty Kieser, Rob Price, and the ThM Seminar in theology at Talbot School of Theology.

understanding of the human person doctrinally according to the history of redemption, pausing on three main touch-points of redemption history: creation, salvation, and then glorification. The second movement of this paper will unpack the initial insights by addressing the creature's being seen and known by God. This section expands my initial analysis to extend Edwards's view to more existential realities of human actuality. In concluding, I will suggest a categorization of Edwards's anthropology based upon the structure, dynamism, and teleology of his account.

## Touch-Points of Redemption History

### Creation

By starting with creation, I address, briefly, the structure of the human person, the reality of the fall and its impact, and Edwards's understanding of the image of God. The goal of this section is to articulate a clear account of what human persons were created for, and, in light of the fall, what it now means to become human in full.

#### STRUCTURE OF THE HUMAN PERSON

In his "Discourse on the Trinity" (hereafter, "Discourse"), Edwards makes the bold declaration that, "though the divine nature be vastly different from that of created spirits, yet our souls are made in the image of God: we have understanding and will, idea and love, as God hath, and the difference is only in the perfection of degree and manner."[3] We will explore what this means for the image of God below, but here it is important to note that Edwards has ushered in a vision of personhood that can bridge the divine and human, with certain key qualifications. This psychology can be referred to as a "bipartite psychology," where the human soul has two "faculties," the understanding and the will. By the understanding, on the one hand, the soul is capable of perception and speculation; by the will, on the other hand, the soul inclines toward or away from what is perceived or considered.

While this "bipartite distinction" may be conceptually helpful, it is important to note that Edwards does not posit real faculties.[4] The person does not *have* a will, for instance, as if a part of the soul willed. Rather, *the person* wills. On Edwards's account, faculties are simply modes by which the

---

3. Edwards, "Discourse on the Trinity," *WJE* 21:113.
4. For more on this, see Ramsey, "Editor's Introduction," *WJE* 1:48.

human person engages reality, either through perception and cognition, or inclination, or repulsion. In his *Freedom of the Will*, Edwards states, "For the will itself is not an agent that has a will: the power of choosing, itself, has not a power of choosing. That which has the power of volition or choice is the man or the soul, and not the power of volition itself."[5] "To be free," Edwards continues, "is the property of an agent."[6] In Edwards's psychology there is a personal agent who has the power of understanding and perceiving on the one hand, and the power of willing on the other. These powers are not separate mechanisms the soul *has*—powers it owns but is differentiated from—these are capacities of the soul itself.

## Image of God

Building upon his development of the human person as a being (or mind) with understanding and will, Edwards develops his understanding of the *imago dei*. To do so, he draws a distinction between the *natural* image of God and the *supernatural* image. The natural image is focused on the intellectual capacities of human persons. "Man's reason," Edwards states, "is that wherein mainly consists the natural image of God. It is the noblest faculty of man; 'tis that which ought to bear rule over the other powers. It was given for that end, to govern in the soul."[7] The natural person is able to order their lives intellectually. This should not be taken to mean that Edwards values the intellect over the will or somehow divorces them radically. The excellency of the creature is not established by the intellect alone, but is primarily seated in the creature's willing.[8]

Edwards's integrated focus on the understanding and willing helps him articulate that human persons are fundamentally affective creatures, created to partake in beauty and love and to allow that beauty and love to govern their lives. Put another way, human persons were created for life with God who is the fountain of beauty and love. The very structure of persons mirrors the life of God so that creatures can partake of the divine life within themselves. In this sense, the inner life of human persons corresponds to the inner movements of God's life (i.e., the procession of understanding and will as Son and Spirit respectively). It is not irrelevant that when Edwards

---

5. Edwards, *Freedom of the Will*, WJE 1:163.
6. Ibid. See Paul Ramsey's remarks on how Edwards follows Locke in "Editor's Introduction," WJE 1:47–65.
7. Edwards, "The Pure in Heart Blessed," WJE 17:67.
8. Edwards, *Religious Affections*, WJE 2:255.

talks about the image of God he does so in relation to the divine attributes. Edwards claims,

> As there are two kinds of attributes in God, according to our way of conceiving of him, his moral attributes, which are summed up in his holiness, and his natural attributes, of strength, knowledge, etc., that constitute the greatness of God; so there is a twofold image of God in man, his moral or spiritual image, which is his holiness, that is the image of God's moral excellency (which image was lost by the fall); and God's natural image, consisting in men's reason and understanding, his natural ability, and dominion over the creatures, which is the image of God's natural attributes.[9]

The Spirit's presence was infused into the soul of the creature, but this infusion was not a necessary feature of the creature's existence. With the Spirit, the soul was sanctified space, but with the entrance of sin the soul is defiled. In this new Spirit-less condition, the natural principles reign. After the fall, human creatures are now "flesh" alone, without the Spirit reigning.

## Creation, Fall, and the Supernatural Aspect of Human Personhood

In order to explain the structure of human existence as the flesh, and the supernatural feature of humankind's "natural" state, Edwards claims,

> when God made man at first, he implanted in him two kinds of principles. There was an *inferior* kind, which may be called *natural*, being the principles of mere human nature; such as self-love, with those natural appetites and passions, which belong to the nature of man, in which his love to his own liberty, honor and pleasure, were exercised: these when alone, and left to themselves, are what the Scriptures sometimes call *flesh*. Besides these, there were *superior* principles, that were spiritual, holy and divine, summarily comprehended in divine love; wherein consisted the spiritual image of God, and man's righteousness and true holiness; which are called in Scripture the *divine nature*.[10]

Adam and Eve were created as supernatural beings because they were created with the Holy Spirit of God communicating the divine nature to

9. Ibid., 256.
10. Edwards, *Original Sin*, WJE 3:381.

them.[11] If one were to take away these supernatural principles, Edwards tells us, humans would still be human, but now they would be *merely* human, and devoid of the communion with God that allows them to thrive.[12] In this sense, the "flesh" is human nature as such, destined for ruin without the Holy Spirit's presence.[13] Prior to the fall, "These superior principles were given to possess the throne, and maintain an absolute dominion in the heart: the other, to be wholly subordinate and subservient. And while things continued thus, all things were in excellent order, peace and beautiful harmony, and in their proper and perfect state."[14] This is why humankind could still be considered "good," even with the flesh. "Flesh" is not bad as such, as long as it given order by the Spirit.

Importantly, the Spirit's presence was not external to the soul—some kind of alien power acting upon it—but was so united (i.e., infused) to the soul that together they are considered "one nature."[15] Unfortunately, this union was established by a conditional covenant and not by necessity, such that once sin entered, the Spirit's supernatural presence dissolved this union, leaving only the flesh. Edwards avers,

> Therefore immediately the superior divine principles wholly ceased; so light ceases in a room, when the candle is withdrawn: and thus man was left in a state of darkness, woeful corruption and ruin; nothing but flesh, without spirit. The inferior principles of self-love and natural appetite, which were given only to serve, being alone, and left to themselves, of course became

---

11. "Those may be called supernatural, because they are no part of human nature. They don't belong to the nature of man as man, nor do they naturally and necessarily flow from the faculties and properties of that nature. Man can be man without 'em. They did not flow from anything in the human nature, but from the Spirit of God dwelling in man, and exerting itself by man's faculties as a principle of action." Edwards, "Galatians 5:17," *WJE* 24:1086.

12. One thinks of Paul's comment about the Corinthians acting as if they were "merely human" (1 Cor 3:4).

13. "So that man's entire nature in his primitive state was constituted of flesh and Spirit. That part of his entire nature that consists in the principles of the mean human nature, or that is the human nature in its present animal state, simply and absolutely considered, is flesh. The human nature, or humanity in that animal state in which it is in this world, is often called flesh in Scripture (*Genesis 6:12*; *Psalms 65:2*; *Isaiah 40:5–6*, and *Isaiah 49:26*, and *Isaiah 66:16*; *Matthew 24:22*; *John 1:14*)." Edwards, "Galatians 5:17," *WJE* 24/2:1086.

14. Ibid.

15. Keeping in mind Edwards's distinction between nature and essence. See my *Jonathan Edwards's Theology*.

reigning principles; having no superior principles to regulate or control them, they became absolute masters of the heart.[16]

Far from being alien, the Spirit's activity functions within the structure of the human person. These principles are supernatural, but they function within the natural. The Spirit's work as holiness and love within a human person harmonizes the soul with God's created order. With the Spirit's departure, these superior principles vanished, and this creates a disordered soul. Now, selfishness reigns. Without holiness the intellect can no longer reign over the natural will because it is no longer reigned over by the presence of the Spirit.

## *Salvation*

Whereas human kind was created to commune with God, and was created with the presence of God already infused into their being, in the fall human persons are alone. In the fall the Spirit leaves, and people are left to their inferior principles. In salvation, therefore, human persons are recovered to the fullness of their humanity as they receive an infusion of the Spirit in regeneration. To understand this, we have to keep in mind that humanity, in its original condition, was partaking in the life of God as a normal feature of their existence. Edwards claims that the Spirit's infusion renews the nature "after the image of God," so that "man is raised to the heavenly life, so that he is enabled to live to God and to perform those actions that are for God's glory and for his own true happiness."[17] The Spirit's presence restores reason to its proper governing position and the new "spiritual principles" allow the person to "live to God" and "to perform those actions that are for God's glory and for his own true happiness."[18] In regeneration the new creation is similar to the old, in that the Spirit is infused within the very structure of our personhood to compose "one nature" with it. But this new creation differs from the old, not least in the fact that this is the Spirit of the crucified and risen Christ, whom believers now see as theirs. For the regenerate, therefore, "Jesus Christ is the true nourishment of the soul," Edwards tells us.[19]

> Nonetheless, self-love functions in both the believer and the unbeliever based on the reality that both are human (having

16. Edwards, *Original Sin*, *WJE* 3:382.
17. Edwards, "Honey from the Rock," *WJE* 17:136.
18. Ibid., 135–36.
19. Ibid., 136.

> a will equals loving what you love).[20] But on Edwards's view, "The main ground of true love to God is the excellency of his own nature,"[21] which can only be obtained through the Spirit's presence. With divine love living in the hearts of the saints, the saints have a "new principle of nature" united to their faculties.[22] They are "partakers of the divine nature" in that they participate in God's own love, or in other words, are partakers of God's holiness "not only as they partake of holiness that God gives, *but partake of that holiness by which he himself is holy.*"[23]

Salvation, broadly speaking, is not primarily about forgiveness or even holiness (abstractly considered). Salvation is oriented by creaturely participation in God's own life. That life is the life of the Father and Son gazing upon one another in love and existing in the Spirit's communion of love. So too, in salvation, by the Spirit we come to partake in this Father-Son relationship as we are united to the person of Christ. Edwards claims, "We shall in a sort be partakers of his [Christ's] relation to the Father or his communion with him in his Sonship. We shall not only be the sons of God by regeneration but by a kind of participation of the Sonship of the eternal Son."[24] Furthermore,

> They have spiritual excellency and joy by a kind of participation of God. They are made excellent by a communication of God's excellency: God put his own beauty, i.e., his beautiful likeness, upon their souls. . . . The saints hath spiritual joy and pleasure by a kind of effusion of God on the soul. . . . The saints have both their spiritual excellency and blessedness by the gift of the Holy Ghost, or Spirit of God, and his dwelling in them. *They are not only caused by the Holy Ghost, but are in the Holy Ghost as their principle. The Holy Spirit becoming an inhabitant is a vital principle in the soul.*[25]

Holiness, just like knowledge, is obtained by participation in God's self-giving, in this case the *Holy* Spirit. The superior faculties once again reign in God's chosen. The Holy Spirit's inhabitation is divine love wrought in the heart of the elect, from which and by which they can truly love God.[26]

---

20. Edwards, "True Virtue," *WJE* 8:575–76.
21. Edwards, "Treatise on Grace," *WJE* 21:175.
22. Ibid., 194.
23. Ibid., 195, emphasis added.
24. Edwards, "Thy Name is as Ointment Poured Forth," 177.
25. Edwards, "God Glorified in Man's Dependence," *WJE* 17:208, emphasis added. See also Edwards, "Charity and its Fruits," *WJE* 8:132.
26. Edwards, "Treatise on Grace," *WJE* 21:175.

Redemption, again, entails a true partaking in God's nature—who is love, beauty, holiness, and grace.

## *Glorification*

Human persons are so constituted that they are fully actualized in glory—where they will partake in the vision of God that Edwards calls "happifying."[27] Human reason, which is meant to order the person, is delighted, Edwards tells us, by seeing God.[28] Persons are designed to partake in the delight of God, which is why we were created in the twofold image of God. Only persons created with the capacity to partake in God's life could delight fully in seeing God. This is why it is not irrelevant that Adam and Eve were created with the Spirit infused in their being, that they were supernatural beings from the outset. This supernatural reality engrained a telos in humanity for the ecstatic delight of God's presence.

As creatures designed to partake in God's life, people were created to behold beauty, which is why fallen human persons obsess over the beautiful—taking what is ugly and deformed because what is beautiful and in-form is foreign to the fallen soul.[29] But the human person was not created to partake in beauty as an abstract concept or existential desire, but to partake in beauty as they participated in God's life of beauty. Edwards tells us, "Intellectual pleasure consists in beholding of spiritual excellencies and beauties; but the glorious excellency and beauty of God, they are far the greatest. God's excellence is the supreme excellence; when the understanding of the reasonable creature dwells here, it dwells at the fountain and swims in a boundless and bottomless ocean."[30] This beholding of God by faith, which is a true gazing upon God as beautiful, brings proper order to the soul; sinful indulgence, in contrast, is "pleasing to the senses and inferior powers," but runs contrary to reason.[31] Seeing God actualizes and humanizes the soul—it

---

27. Edwards, "The Pure in Heart Blessed," *WJE* 17:61, 63.

28. Ibid., 66.

29. Edwards notes, "For carnal delights are of that nature, that they keep the soul that places happiness in them always big with expectations and in eager pursuit, but they are ever more like shadows, never yield what is hoped for. And they that give themselves up to them, they unavoidably bring upon themselves many heavy inconveniences; wherein they promote their pleasure one way, they destroy their comfort other ways. And there is this sting accompanies them every time there is any consideration exercised: that they are but short-lived. They will soon vanish and be no more." Edwards, "The Pure in Heart Blessed," *WJE* 17:69.

30. Ibid., 67.

31. Ibid.

orders the soul according to its human and supernatural purpose, and as such it is reasonable, and a delight to the reason.

## Edwards's Theocentric Anthropology

Just as with the image of God, we see again that the form of creaturely flourishing is discovered first in the life of God. The first line of Edwards "Discourse" states, "When we speak of God's happiness, the account that we are wont to give of it is that God is infinitely happy in the enjoyment of himself, in perfectly beholding and infinitely loving, and rejoicing in, his own essence and perfections."[32] Edwards's model of the Trinity, as I have argued elsewhere, is best understood as religious affection in pure act.[33] What constitutes the divine persons in the inner life of God is the beatific vision shared among the Father and the Son, the divine Mind and Idea respectively. But without the Spirit, God would simply be gazing upon his perfect idea; he would only be engaging in infinite speculation. But with the Spirit there is true, and archetypal, beatific self-knowing in God, such that the Spirit of love, beauty, and glory pours between Father and Son uniting them in affectionate knowledge.

To know God, therefore—to *actually* know him—entails knowing him affectionately, because affectionate knowledge is the only true knowledge of God. In Edwards's conception of glory and the beatific vision, we can pick up disparate pieces from the doctrines of creation and salvation and unite them in a broad mosaic of participation. Human persons were made to partake in God's life—to be "partakers of the divine nature" (2 Pet. 1:4)— and the soul of the person was formed accordingly. In this sense, there is a twofold analogy between God's processions of understanding and willing and the human soul: one that is natural, and one that is truly religious. The first is simply the functional structure of personal existence (i.e., having an understanding and will), and the other is perceiving Christ and having the will flow forth in love to unite the believer to Christ—what we may call humanity actualized. Edwards claims, "The soul shall not be an inactive spectator but shall be *most active*, shall be in the most ardent exercise of love toward the object seen. The soul shall be, as it were, all eye to behold, and yet

---

32. Edwards, "Discourse on the Trinity," *WJE* 21:113.

33. See my *Jonathan Edwards's Theology*, 21–72. There, I tend to focus on the language of "personal beatific-delight" to talk about Edwards's "model" of the Trinity. This language was purposeful at the time, but for the sake of clarification and identification, I now prefer "religious affection in pure act."

all act to love."³⁴ Likewise, "Every faculty of the soul will be employed and exercised, and will be employed in vastly more lively, more exalted exercises than they are now, though without any labor or weariness."³⁵

The "rest" of eternity is the actualization of the creature, Edwards claims, saying specifically that the saints "shall *perpetually* behold God's glory and *perpetually* enjoy his love. But they shall not remain in a state of inactivity, merely receiving from God; but they return to him and shall enjoy him in a way of serving and glorifying him."³⁶ What Edwards is articulating is that the glorified soul is most active, never wearied, and perpetually in enjoyment of God's love, not simply receiving, but returning to God in affection. In heaven, the saint is "transformed into love, dissolved into joy, become[s] activity itself, [and] changed into mere ecstasy."³⁷ This life of ecstatic affection is synonymous with "serving and glorifying God," because religious affection is simply the will vigorously inclined to God. As an act of willing, action is inherent within it; or, in Edwards's words, "the very willing is the doing."³⁸

The perfection of human persons, therefore, entails drinking in the infinite ocean of God's love. Always satisfied, but always increasing in capacity for more, the creature moves into the life of God without circumscribing him, because God is infinite and therefore cannot be circumscribed by the creature. The glorified saints are like containers that are always full but whose capacity is always growing. There is never a moment without perpetual act; nonetheless, as the act is realized according to one's potential, potential itself increases. Therefore, Edwards is able to state, "Created spirits come nearer to [God], *or more imitate* [God], the greater they are in the powers and faculties."³⁹ The creature never disappears within God, losing their identity, nor do they become divinized, which Edwards and the New Lights were being accused of claiming.⁴⁰ Rather, Edwards states, "The way in which the saints will come to an intimate full enjoyment of the Father is not by the Father's majesty . . . but by their ascending to him by their union with Christ's person."⁴¹ In taking this line, Edwards follows

34. Edwards, "373. Romans 2:10 (December 1735)," *WJEO* 50:L. 45v, emphasis added.

35. Edwards, "Serving God in Heaven," *WJE* 17:259.

36. Ibid., emphasis added.

37. Edwards, "'Misc.' 94," *WJE* 13:260–61.

38. Edwards, *Freedom of the Will*, *WJE* 1:162.

39. Edwards, "'Misc.' 135," *WJE* 13:295.

40. See my "Jonathan Edwards and the Polemics of Theosis."

41. Edwards,"'Misc.' 742," *WJE* 18:375.

distinctively Reformed developments of *theosis*, arguing that regenerate, and then glorified, persons ascend to the Father in the *person* of Son by the Spirit.[42] This is a focus on ascent as relational union and communion rather than a participation in nature, although Edwards's account unites these two notions into one.

This ascent begins with regeneration, where the believer apprehends the sight of God by faith. This sight is of the beauty and excellency of Christ and is the sight Christians grow into in this life, anticipating the life to come. The life to come is not *essentially* different, but circumstantially so. There will be no corruption there to inhibit the sight of God, and therefore we will be perpetually in contemplation of him. In this age, we increase *toward* perfection, but in the age to come we will increase *in* perfection.[43]

## *Being Seen and Known by the Father*

While this age is not the age to come, the two are intrinsically connected. On Edwards's understanding, unlike most of his Reformed conversation partners, there is not an absolute division between faith and sight. Faith and sight are a continuum in Edwards's thinking, whereas faith is the murky sight of God and the beatific is the clear sight of glory. But for both ages of life with God, seeing God is not simply recognizing God as such, but seeing God as the One who sees you. This will be developed further below, but first we need to turn to Edwards's metaphysics and the reality of the incarnation.

Edwards believes that human persons are more substantial than the created order around them, arguing that "beings which have knowledge and consciousness are the only proper and real and substantial beings," and that "spirits are the only proper substance."[44] In this sense, "perceiving being only is properly being."[45] Furthermore, in Edwards's peculiar understanding of the God-world distinction, he claims that the universe is upheld in its existence by God's consciousness. God's perception of reality is what makes reality real.[46] Edwards's view of reality pushes perception to the forefront with a particular emphasis on the visual. God's consciousness upholds

---

42. I develop this point in my article, "Jonathan Edwards's Reformed Doctrine of *Theosis*."

43. See Edwards, "Striving after Perfection," *WJE* 19:698, for Edwards's use of "perfection" of the image in heaven.

44. Edwards, "Of Being," *WJE* 6:206.

45. Edwards, "The Mind," *WJE* 6:363.

46. Edwards, "Of Being," *WJE* 6:204.

reality, and consciousness is simply the mind perceiving what is in itself.[47] If God would cease to be conscious of the world, it would immediately cease to exist.[48] God's perception upholds and *defines* reality.

On this view of reality, the hierarchy of being is governed at the top by God, who both sees and is seen in his own life, and at bottom consists of objects seen and upheld in that sight alone. Only *perceiving* being can reside at the top end of the hierarchy of being, because substantial beings can see *and* be seen, can be known *and* can know. This parallels Edwards's conception of beauty. Primary beauty is the harmony and union of persons, first in God's own life, as the highest beauty, and then in his union with creatures in love. Secondary beauty, in contrast, is found in "inanimate things," and is the image of the spiritual. This beauty is the harmony, proportion, and order of material reality. Both of these things are upheld by God's creative perception, and both are good. But the creature's being upheld by the Creator is different. Here, God's gazing upon the creature is more deeply profound, because human persons can see, by faith, from within God's gaze ("In your light we shall see light" [Ps 36:9]).

What it means to be human, therefore, is to be seen by God and to have the capacity to see him in the Spirit. This seeing is not raw intellection, pouring forth a penetrating glare to analyze and interpret, but this is a personal gazing: it is knowledge and love, or knowledge and wrath, that pour out from God. There is no neutral with God's seeing of the creature. But God's seeing in love is efficacious. This is also evident in Edwards's development of the incarnation. Edwards claims, "The man Christ is united to the Logos these two ways: first, by the respect which God hath to this human nature. God hath respect to this man and loveth him as his own Son; this man hath communion with the Logos, in the love which the Father hath to him as his only begotten Son. Now the love of God is the Holy Ghost."[49]

God's gazing upon Jesus with the dove of God's belovedness descending upon him is the economic overflow of his eternal beatific contemplation of the Son. The love that is the Holy Spirit binds the life of the Son to the Father, because the love of the Holy Spirit is that economic paternal contemplation, and within the union of the Spirit Jesus knows God. Similarly, when God looks upon the creature in love there is an efficacious calling inherent in that sight. God's gazing upon us defines us. As God looks upon us within his Son, we too look upon the Son; and if we have seen him we have seen the Father (John 14:9). In the condescension of the Son, the image of the invisible God,

---

47. Edwards, "The Mind," *WJE* 6:345.
48. Edwards, "Of Being," *WJE* 6:204.
49. Edwards, "'Misc.' 487," *WJE* 13:529.

human persons can truly know God. Just as the Father gazes upon the Son and the Spirit billows forth between them as love, so too do we gaze upon the Son with the Spirit pouring forth in affection. God's life is the fullness of affectionate self-knowledge, so all knowledge of God is pushed into this affectionate mold, necessitating a participation in God's own knowing and willing. God's archetypal self-knowing is according to sight, as the Father gazes upon the Son within the bond of love that is the Holy Spirit. This knowledge is paralleled in salvation, where God now looks upon his people within his Son, and out of his infinite love for the Son, pours forth his love to his creatures. Recall that love is the Holy Spirit. The Father looking with love on the creature *simply is* the sending of the Holy Spirit. Creatures can see God in Christ because they are seen by him; it is the gazing of the Father upon them that illumines Christ to be seen and known.

According to this pattern, something is known as it is perceived, and right perception necessitates a movement of the heart to embrace in beauty. As we come to see God, we come to know him, but to know him is to see ourselves in a twofold manner: first, in the reality of our sin and the truth of our brokenness; and second, as we are in Christ. Our knowledge of God and our knowledge of ourselves are tied together, because "our lives are hidden with Christ in God" (Col 3:3), as Paul proclaims. Edwards upholds this same Christocentric focus, claiming, "Jesus Christ, who alone sees immediately, [is] the grand medium of the knowledge of all others; they know no otherwise than by the exhibitions held forth in and by him."[50] Both Father and believers gaze upon the Son within the Spirit; both, within that same Spirit, experience the emanating forth of the divine idea in the clear perception of truth, which the Father knows immediately and infinitely, and believers know mediately and finitely in the Son.[51] Just as the Son comes to know himself within the Father as the Father gazes upon him, so too do believers come to know the truth of themselves in the gaze of God. Accordingly, Edwards states, "Of all the knowledge that we can ever obtain, the knowledge of God, and the knowledge of ourselves, are the most important."[52]

## *The Relational Self*

We are now able to take a step back and think in broader terms about Edwards's anthropology. From the above, we can say that Edwards's

---

50. Edwards, "'Misc.' 777," *WJE* 18:428.

51. Some of this section is a slightly reworked version of my "Theology in the Gaze of the Father."

52. Edwards, *Freedom of the Will*, *WJE* 1:133.

anthropology is ordered in relation to God's own life, and that the human person was designed to mirror and partake in the overflow of *that* life. In light of this, I want to offer some broader thoughts on the nature of Edwards's doctrine, focusing our attention on what I call the "forgotten I," and the "existential self."

### The Forgotten "I"

The development of personal existence that funds Edwards's anthropology can be found right at the beginning of the "*Discourse.*" In that work, Edwards is developing an account of God's personal existence, but the structure of personhood for Edwards is, as we've seen, univocal.[53] After addressing the divine beatitude, he turns to the divine understanding, stating that "the whole of the divine understanding or wisdom consists in the mere perception or unvaried presence of his infinitely perfect idea."[54] This perfect idea must be distinguished from God's direct existence, Edwards argues, clearly seeking to distinguish between the Father and the Son. In other words, there is the agent, and the agent's idea; no matter how perfect this idea is, there is a distinction to be drawn between the two.

Edwards's ideas are mediators of reality to the mind. He claims, "Seeing the perfect idea of a thing is to all intents and purposes the same as seeing the thing; it is not only equivalent to the seeing of it, but it *is* the seeing it: for there is no other seeing but having the idea."[55] This will prove important for Edwards's soteriology, in that seeing God's idea, Jesus, is what it means to see God. In Edwards's understanding, this is what Jesus means when he claims to be the "image of the invisible God," and that if anyone had seen him, they had seen the Father. When Edwards develops his account of personhood in relation to the Trinity, "God" has a perfect idea of himself.[56]

---

53. This is how I take Edwards comment, "Though the divine nature be vastly different from that of created spirits, yet our souls are made in the image of God: we have understanding and will, idea and love, as God hath, and the difference is only in the perfection of degree and manner," Edwards, "Discourse on the Trinity," *WJE* 21:113. The structure is univocal, but the degree and manner by which a person has an idea and love differs.

54. Ibid., 113.

55. Ibid., 118.

56. Thomas Weinandy, in a helpful exposition of this section of the Discourse, argues that Edwards's Lockean epistemology hurts his doctrine of God at this point specifically. He claims, "The problem is that, being heavily influenced by Locke, he was not fully cognizant that Locke's epistemology did not allow him to say clearly what he wishes to advance—that God truly knows himself as he is in himself without

The term "God," as used here by Edwards, references the Father, but the Father, as a distinct person, is virtually ignored throughout the *Discourse*. The emphasis is on the Son and Spirit. Part of this has to do with Edwards's polemics—but in general, in Edwards's corpus, this seems to be the case. The "I," as the anthropological corollary to the Father, is rarely referenced. The emphasis in the *Religious Affections*, for instance, is on right perception and the vigorousness of the will, but not on the "I" who perceives and wills. This agent is assumed at every turn, but rarely mentioned beyond one's capacity of intellect and will. Before moving on, this is important to note. It could be that as a feature of Edwards's top-down method, the existential "I" of the human agent takes on the hiddenness of the Father. But this existential "I" is essential to all that Edwards does. The faculties, after all, are not actual faculties, but simply rhetorical devices to talk about how the agent engages reality: *I* understand, and *I* will. But, nonetheless, unlike God I do not have a perfect idea of myself; I am a creature who engages reality in and through my idea, but I also stand in a divided relation to it.

The "I" then, on Edwards's account, is not forgotten as much as it is addressed only through its faculties. This is, once again, parallel to Edwards's account of God's life (one is reminded of Irenaeus's image of God's two hands). God the Father has two attributes, understanding and will, and these two are the only *real* distinctions in God.[57] To talk about God the Father, we talk about Jesus and the Spirit. This does not mean we can't say anything more about the Father, but his depths are meditated to us through his emanating and economic life. Likewise, there is a sense where our own depths are mediated to others, and even ourselves, through the generation of our own idea and the movement of our soul in willing. It is to these depths that we now turn.

---

the mediation of an 'idea' that is a mere representation of himself." Weinandy, "Edwards: Discourse," 70 fn. 11. I think Weinandy's critique actually highlights one of the unique features of Edwards's account; a feature I believe was central to Edwards's task. Edwards does not believe that the Father knows himself within himself outside of the Son. It would be problematic, no doubt, if he isn't able, in the end, to claim that the Father knows himself fully. But this knowledge cannot be read off of Edwards's account of the processions simply, but also perichoresis. It is not simply that the Father stands in a relation to his idea, but to his Son, that matters, and that is only the case once his doctrine of perichoresis is put into play.

57. Edwards, "Discourse on the Trinity," *WJE* 21:131. For more on this distinction, see my *Jonathan Edwards's Theology*, 234–42.

## The Existential Self

The fact that we are divided within ourselves is important for the phenomenology of Edwards's account. Whereas God gazes upon his perfect contemplative idea and is filled with love and beauty, we do not necessarily have the same experience. As fallen and finite creatures we have an idea of ourselves, and that idea is faint and perhaps different from what we want to see. We do not necessarily flow out in love toward ourselves, but see aspects of our person and life we find frustrating. Edwards narrates this odd reality, claiming:

> Man is as it were two, as some of the great wits of this age have observed: a sort of genius is with a man, that accompanies him and attends him wherever he goes; so that *a man has a conversation with himself*, that is, he has a conversation with his own idea. So that if his idea be excellent, he will take delight and happiness in conferring and communing with it; he takes complacency in himself, he applauds himself; and wicked men accuse themselves and fight with themselves as if they were two. And man is truly happy then, and only then, when these two agree, and they delight in themselves, and in their own idea and image, *as God delights in his*.[58]

Two key notions emerge from this text that we should attend to. First, we see that happiness entails mirroring the life of God within one's person. Our existential "I" gazes upon our idea, and, in agreement, finds delight in it. Our will flows forth to our idea and unites it in our love. All forms of happiness find their moorings in the divine blessedness. This also means that, second, happiness is fundamental to human flourishing. Edwards notes, "It is not a thing contrary to Christianity that a man should love himself; or what is the same thing, that he should love his own happiness. Christianity does not tend to destroy a man's love to his own happiness; it would therein tend to destroy the humanity. Christianity is not destructive of humanity."[59] Because Edwards's doctrine of God assumes the divine blessedness, and personhood is developed along those lines, it is natural for Edwards to have an account of *human* personhood that focuses on the same notion.

With happiness as a defining feature of God's life and human flourishing, Edwards articulates an unusual account of self-love. Self-love, what we might call "mere" self-love, is not bad or necessarily selfish. On Edwards's account, the act of willing and self-love are virtually synonymous, because self-love is simply willing what you will. Self-love only becomes negative

---

58. Edwards, "'Misc.' 94," *WJE* 13:260, emphasis added.
59. Edwards, "Charity and its Fruits," *WJE* 8:254.

when it is an inordinate self-love. In contrast, the person who places their happiness in God or others is able to focus on the fulfillment of *their* happiness, and is, therefore, not selfish. Edwards claims, "But yet this is not selfishness, because it is not a confined self-love, because his self-love flows out in such a channel as to take in others with himself. The self which he loves is, as it were, enlarged and multiplied, so that in those same acts wherein he loves himself he loves others."[60] The movements of the human heart, in this sense, again link to Edwards's doctrine of God. Contrasting selfishness and love again, Edwards claims, "Selfishness is a principle which does, as it were, confine a man's heart to himself. Love enlarges it and extends it to others. A man's self is as it were extended and enlarged by love. Others so far as [they are] beloved do, as it were, become parts of himself."[61] The movement of the person in love mirrors God, who overflows out of himself to offer himself in love. Unlike God, creatures do not focus on their own life as the greatest good. That would be an act of selfishness for a finite being. But creatures do offer themselves in grace, and this entails an overflowing of their own inner life such that they are enlarged to take in the other.

This notion of enlargement, or what we can call "internalization," is an important facet of Edwards's understanding of anthropology. Edwards claims, "I have observed from time to time that in pure love to others (i.e., love not arising from self-love) there's a union of the heart with others; a kind of enlargement of the mind, whereby it so extends itself as to take others into a man's self: and therefore it implies a disposition to feel, to desire, and to act as though others were one with ourselves."[62] In Edwards's anthropology, relations are internalized, and to become united to someone, or something, in love, is to pull it into oneself. To internalize God and others is to bring order and proper orientation to the self so it can exist in freedom. In freedom there is a calmness of the soul, but in the brokenness of vice there is a chaos that undermines the self's ability to love.

What we see, therefore, with how the self engages reality, and with the twofold nature of the self within the human person, is that persons are called to an internal union with their selves, which allows for true love of others. A divided self will struggle to love, since loving others requires internalizing them within one's self. Similarly, a self captivated with self-interest will use the other to buttress their self, seeking an internalization to uphold their psyche rather than seeking to love the other as a member of themselves. In

---

60. Ibid., 258.
61. Ibid., 263.
62. Ibid., 589.

either case, a chaotic soul is too tied up in self-interest to enlarge in love, and does not have the capacity to pull the other within in a relation of love.

## The Teleology of Love

Before turning to some concluding remarks, I want to, briefly, note the teleology of this account. In the three touch-points of redemption history assessed earlier—creation, salvation, and glorification—we saw that God's effusive nature of love calls the creature into his own life, such that a person's true humanity is always a spiritual humanity (a *pneumatikos*). But as noted above, love, glory, and beauty are all features of the Spirit's work. Each of these three aspects of the Spirit's work could be employed to exposit the overall telos of Edwards's account. But the Christian life, the life known in this age of redemption history, is always looking ahead to the world of love. But heaven is only a world of love because the God of love reigns there, "for God is the fountain of love, as the sun is the fountain of light. And therefore the glorious presence of God in heaven fills heaven with love, as the sun placed in the midst of the hemisphere in a clear day fills the world with light."[63]

In heaven, Edwards tells us, dwells the "Father of love," and "[d]ivine love is in him not as a subject which receives from another, but as its original seat, where it is of itself."[64] Love is the ultimate end of God's own life—the intrinsic orientation of God's dynamic being. This love "flows out in innumerable streams toward all the created inhabitants of heaven,"[65] and is rebounded and returned to God. But what God has received is his own love, caught up in and through the creature, and rebounded back to the Father in Christ by the Spirit. God in his utter necessity stands free against the finitude and contingency of the creature, but it is here that the creature comes to drink of a love that does not seek to remove freedom, but give it fully. "There this glorious God is manifested and shines forth in full glory, in beams of love; there the fountain overflows in streams and rivers of love and delight, enough for all to drink at, and to swim in, yea, so as to overflow the world as it were with a deluge of love."[66]

Love is the nature of human flourishing, and love of God and neighbor is only truly known by a participation in God's own life of love. But love, as stated here, is not arbitrary or sentimental, but is a specific love

---

63. Edwards, "Charity and its Fruits," *WJE* 8:369.
64. Ibid., 373.
65. Ibid.
66. Ibid., 370.

that we are given—the same love by which the Father loves the Son (John 17:26). This relational participation in the life of God is the end of the creature, such that Edwards will say, in eternity, "the soul which only had a little spark of divine love in it in this world shall be, as it were, wholly turned into love; and be like the sun, not having a spot in it, but being wholly a bright, ardent flame."[67] Furthermore, and no less bold, Edwards continued to paint eternity as relational participation by stating, "the saints are exalted to glorious dignity, even to union and fellowship with God him[self], to be in some respects *divine* in glory and happiness."[68] This is the end of the regenerate creature, to be, in some respects, divine in glory, happiness, and we can add, *love*.

## Conclusion

To close, it may prove helpful to highlight three key features of Edwards's anthropology: the structural, dynamic, and teleological. First, the structural nature of Edwards's anthropology articulates human persons as created to partake in the life of God. Furthermore, this structure collapses without the infusion of the Spirit, such that selfishness and self-destruction will ultimately reign if God's presence is not known and internalized. Second, and building on the first, Edwards recognizes a dynamism in the *imago dei*, such that God's pure actuality is analogically mirrored in the movement of the human heart. Increasing in holiness and perfection and becoming more like God entails an increasing movement of one's will to be united to the same image that causes the eternal movement in God's own life. Religious affections, in other words, are the analogy to this movement in God, and act as the fruit of God's self-giving in love. Last, love is the teleology for the human person because God is the ultimate end.

By looking at anthropology through the lens of creation, salvation, and glorification, we can see how Edwards's anthropology can be considered a theotic anthropology. Participation in God's life and nature is the main notion, such that, in Edwards's words, "As God delights in his own beauty, he must necessarily delight in the creature's holiness; which is a conformity to, and participation of it, as truly as the brightness of a jewel, held in the sun's beams, is a participation, or derivation of the sun's brightness, though immensely less in degree."[69] Edwards's anthropology is established in creation as a supernatural reality, one that is recovered and reformed in the new creation for a participation in the emanating beams of God's life. To

---

67. Ibid., 374–75.
68. Edwards, "'Misc.' 681," *WJE* 18:241, emphasis added.
69. Edwards, "Charity and its Fruits," *WJE* 8:442.

commune with Christ in the Spirit is to become a partaker of the divine nature. The category "glory," which could easily become the main thrust of Edwards's anthropology, is the overflow of God's life of religious affection. In eternity, the creature partakes in this fully, according to their capacity, and is, therefore, fueled by the divine life of love, delight, and beauty. This anthropology, as governed by his Reformed doctrine of *theosis*, focuses on the relational self-giving of God and the necessary conditions—structural, dynamic, and teleological—that order the creature for participation in *this* God. The theological mooring for this kind of anthropology is theology proper, and the structural, dynamic, and teleological elements are all governed by the reality of God's communicable nature as his own self-giving in love, glory, and beauty.

# Bibliography

Edwards, Jonathan. "373. Unpublished Sermon on Romans 2:10 (December 1735)." In *Sermons, Series II, 1735*. The Works of Jonathan Edwards Online 50. Jonathan Edwards Center at Yale University.

———. "Charity and its Fruits." In *Ethical Writings*, edited by Paul Ramsay, The Works of Jonathan Edwards 8:123–397. New Haven: Yale University Press, 1989.

———. "Discourse on the Trinity." In *Writings on the Trinity, Grace, and Faith*, edited by Sang Hyun Lee, The Works of Jonathan Edwards 21:109–44. New Haven: Yale University Press, 2003.

———. "Dissertation II: The Nature of True Virtue." In *Ethical Writings*, edited by Paul Ramsay, The Works of Jonathan Edwards 8:537–627. New Haven: Yale University Press, 1989.

———. *Freedom of the Will*. Edited by Paul Ramsey. The Works of Jonathan Edwards 1. New Haven: Yale University Press, 1957.

———. "Galatians 5:17." In *The "Blank Bible,"* edited by Stephen J. Stein, The Works of Jonathan Edwards 24/2:1085–90. New Haven: Yale University Press, 2006.

———. "God Glorified in Man's Dependence." In *Sermons and Discourses, 1730–1733*, edited by Mark Valeri, The Works of Jonathan Edwards 17:196–216. New Haven: Yale University Press, 1999.

———. "Honey from the Rock." In *Sermons and Discourses, 1730–1733*, edited by Mark Valeri, The Works of Jonathan Edwards 17:121–38. New Haven: Yale University Press, 1999.

———. "The Mind." In *Scientific and Philosophical Writings*, edited by Wallace E. Anderson, The Works of Jonathan Edwards 6:311–93. New Haven: Yale University Press, 1980.

———. "'Misc.' 135." In *The "Miscellanies" (Entry Nos. a-z, aa-zz, 1–500)*, edited by Thomas A. Schafer, The Works of Jonathan Edwards 13:295. New Haven: Yale University Press, 1994.

———. "'Misc.' 487." In *The "Miscellanies" (Entry Nos. a-z, aa-zz, 1–500)*, edited by Thomas A. Schafer, The Works of Jonathan Edwards 13:528–32. New Haven Yale University Press, 1994.

---. "'Misc.' 681." In *The "Miscellanies" (Entry Nos. 501–832)*, edited by Ava Chamberlain, The Works of Jonathan Edwards 18:239–43. New Haven: Yale University Press, 2000.

---. "'Misc.' 742." In *The "Miscellanies" (Entry Nos. 501–832)*, edited by Ava Chamberlain, The Works of Jonathan Edwards 18:373–76. New Haven: Yale University Press, 2000.

---. "'Misc.' 777." In *The "Miscellanies" (Entry Nos. 501–832)*, edited by Ava Chamberlain, The Works of Jonathan Edwards 18:427–34. New Haven: Yale University Press, 2000.

---. "'Misc.' 94." In *The "Miscellanies" (Entry Nos. a–z, aa–zz, 1–500)*, edited by Thomas A. Schafer, The Works of Jonathan Edwards 13:256–63. New Haven: Yale University Press, 1994.

---. "Of Being." In *Scientific and Philosophical Writings*, edited by Wallace E. Anderson, The Works of Jonathan Edwards 6:202–7. New Haven: Yale University Press 1980.

---. *Original Sin*. The Works of Jonathan Edwards 3. Edited by John E. Smith. New Haven: Yale University Press, 1970.

---. "The Pure in Heart Blessed." In *Sermons and Discourses, 1730–1733*, edited by Mark Valeri, The Works of Jonathan Edwards 17:57–86. New Haven: Yale University Press, 1999.

---. *Religious Affections*. The Works of Jonathan Edwards 2. Edited by John E. Smith. New Haven: Yale University Press, 1969.

---. "Serving God in Heaven." In *Sermons and Discourses, 1730–1733*, edited by Mark Valeri, The Works of Jonathan Edwards 17:251–61. New Haven: Yale University Press, 1999.

---. "Striving after Perfection." In *Sermons and Discourses, 1734–1738*, edited by Max X. Lesser, The Works of Jonathan Edwards 19:680–703. New Haven: Yale University Press, 2001.

---. "Thy Name is as Ointment Poured Forth." In *The Blessing of God: Previously Unpublished Sermons of Jonathan Edwards*, edited by Michael D. McMullen, 163–79. Nashville: Broadman & Holman, 2003.

---. "Treatise on Grace." In *Writings on the Trinity, Grace, and Faith*, edited by Sang Hyun Lee, The Works of Jonathan Edwards 21:149–97. New Haven: Yale University Press, 2003.

Ramsay, Paul. "Editor's Introduction." In *Freedom of the Will*, edited by Paul Ramsay, The Works of Jonathan Edwards 1:1–128. New Haven: Yale University Press, 1957.

Strobel, Kyle C. "Jonathan Edwards and the Polemics of *Theosis*." *Harvard Theological Review* 105:3 (2012) 259–79.

---. "Jonathan Edwards's Reformed Doctrine of *Theosis*." *Harvard Theological Review* 109:3 (2016) 371–99.

---. *Jonathan Edwards's Theology: A Reinterpretation*. New York: Bloombury T. & T. Clark, 2013.

---. "Theology in the Gaze of the Father: Retrieving Jonathan Edwards's Trinitarian Aesthetics." In *Advancing Trinitarian Theology: Explorations in Constructive Dogmatics*, edited by Oliver D. Crisp and Fred Sanders, 147–70. Grand Rapids, MI: Zondervan, 2014.

Weinandy, Thomas. "Jonathan Edwards: Discourse on the Trinity." In *The Ecumenical Edwards: Jonathan Edwards and the Theologians*, edited by Kyle Strobel. Surrey: Ashgate, 2015.

# 10

# Learning from Jonathan Edwards
## *Toward a Trinitarian Theology of Contemplation and Action*

SENG KONG TAN[1]

THE CHRISTIAN TRADITION TOOK over the Greek notions of *theoria* and *praxis* as representative of the contemplative and active life.[2] But this assimilation was not a wholesale borrowing, for philosophy and politics were transmuted to love of God and love of neighbor.[3] How the dialectic of these two loves has played out in the spiritual tradition has revolved around interpretations of the Bethany household. At least from Origen of Alexandria onwards, Mary and Martha have been viewed as allegories of the contemplative life and the active life respectively.[4] Three interpretations have ensued in the Christian tradition: (1) The primacy of contemplation; (2) The primacy of action; (3) The reciprocity of action and contemplation.[5]

Where the Greek bias toward rationality and the speculative intellect was retained, the Christian tradition has tended to privilege contemplation

---

1. I would like to thank Professor Bruce Hindmarsh for taking his time to read and comment on an earlier version of this article.

2. Radler, "*Actio et Contemplatio*," 212.

3. Ibid. See also "Action-Contemplation," in *Dictionary of Oblate Values*.

4. Louth, *Origins of the Christian Mystical Tradition*, 54–5.

5. Grumett, "Action and/or Contemplation?" 125–39. The early Fathers generally saw action and contemplation as complementary. Constable, *Three Studies*.

over action, for example, in Augustine and Thomas Aquinas.[6] The opposite emphasis on action stands out as a minority report in the larger Christian tradition. Here, we have Meister Eckhart as a notable exception.[7] The active life is, of course, a key characteristic of evangelical piety.[8] And, without doubt, activism has become the *de facto* mark of modern urban life.

Despite the one-sided emphasis on contemplation in the Latin spiritual tradition, the notion of a "mixed life" of action-in-contemplation or contemplation-in-action finds a place, for example, in Dominican and Ignatian spiritualities.[9] Likewise, the piety of active contemplation or contemplative action has a parallel in the Reformed-Puritan tradition. I take the two traits of "receptivity" and "energy" found in Puritanism, or what J. I. Packer has termed "reformed monasticism," to be postures that attend prayer and ministry.[10]

It is rare, however, to discover a deep trinitarian ontology that underlies a Mary-and-Martha spirituality within the Christian tradition. One significant example is the medieval Flemish mystic Jan van Ruusbroek.[11] While Jonathan Edwards does not have as developed a spiritual theology as did Ruusbroek, there are recurrent themes and images in his writings that could be used to develop an Edwardsian trinitarian theology of action and contemplation. I will argue that, for Edwards, action and contemplation are mutually related yet ordered moments that are grounded in the divine being, especially so in the eternal processions of the Word and Spirit. Following that, I will trace this reciprocal nature of action and contemplation in Edwards's theological anthropology, in a human being's natural, regenerate, and glorified states.

## Action and Contemplation in the Trinity

For Edwards, rest and activity are found in the very being of God. The divine oneness and threeness are respectively the foundation for contemplation and action. Drawing from the work of Chevalier Ramsay, an Anglican

---

6. Aquinas, *Summa Theologica*, II.2, q. 182, a. 1.

7. Constable, *Three Studies*, 116.

8. As expressed in evangelism and social reform; see Holt, "Active Life and Contemplative Life," 243–44; and Howard, "Evangelical Spirituality," 170. See also Bebbington, *Evangelicalism in Modern Britain*.

9. So, Jesus' life of preaching and teaching was a higher form of the active life— an overflow of the contemplative. Aquinas, *ST* III, q. 40, a. 1, 2230–31.

10. Packer, *A Quest for Godliness*, 331.

11. Nieuwenhove, "Jan van Ruusbroec on the Trinity," 374–75.

convert to Catholicism, Edwards agrees that the "absolute infinite . . . and solitary essence" is "God's still eternity, and solitude."[12] Yet, the divine essence is not "a state of inaction and indolence" for it is "infinitely active and productive" of the divine persons.[13] Father, Son, and Spirit are not static realities but are, as it were, personal verbs or eternal events in God's own being. Because the divine persons are the one divine essence, solitude and action are found in the Son and Spirit, who proceed from the Father.

How does Edwards view the eternal generation of the Son? In contemplating the divine essence, the Father generates the Son.[14] God's self-reflection brings forth God's "reflexive or contemplative idea."[15] And God does so by perpetually "beholding himself in the Son."[16] Hence, the Father actively produces the Logos, who stands forth as a distinct Other. In the divine generation, the Son stands forth as the eternal object of the Father's vision.[17] The Son also contemplates the Father but in a different manner.[18] The Logos has an interior vision of the Father where he beholds "the Father in himself."[19] In this mutual contemplation of each other, the Son comes forth from the Father as a distinct person with the Father remaining in him. This is a shared contemplation that is both inward and outward.

The Son not only contemplates the Father eternally, he has being and personhood in this same act of contemplation. Edwards parses the apostle John philosophically: "The idea's beholding is the idea's existing."[20] Here, the eternal Word is the *hypostasis* of contemplation that is both passive and active. On the level of being, the Son is purely passive in receiving the divine essence from the Father. Yet, this reception of existence is dynamic as the Son is "begotten by [the Father] from eternity and continually through eternity."[21]

What about the procession of the Holy Spirit? Edwards, following Augustine and Aquinas, affirms the double procession of the Spirit as the mutual love of the Father and Son. The Spirit makes the contemplation of

---

12. For Ramsay, see excerpt in Edwards, "'Misc.' 1253," *WJE* 23:186–88.

13. Ibid.

14. Edwards, "Discourse on the Trinity," in *WJE* 21:116.

15. Ibid., 116, 141.

16. Ibid., 143.

17. Edwards, "Daniel 9:25," *WJE* 24:767.

18. Edwards, "Discourse on the Trinity," *WJE* 21:143.

19. Ibid.

20. Ibid. Edwards cites John 5:26 and 12:45. See also, "On the Equality of the Persons of the Trinity," *WJE* 21:148; and, "Discourse on the Trinity," *WJE* 21:118.

21. Edwards, "'Misc.' 143," *WJE* 13:298.

Father and Son into an interactive circle of loving contemplation.[22] His procession characterizes the divine vision within God as a beatific or blessed vision. Yet the Spirit is not only the principle of eternal love, enjoyment, and happiness within God, he is also "the pure and perfect act of God."[23] Though the Spirit receives being from the Father and Son, he confers activity to the Father and Son by being their pure act of mutual love.[24] The Holy Spirit is, therefore, the *hypostasis* of action.

The Spirit not only confers action, he is also the principle of communion. According to Edwards, "the Holy Ghost is that common good or fullness which they [Father and Son] partake of, in which their fellowship consists."[25] The Spirit ensures that the otherness of the Son does not lead to division. On the contrary, the Spirit unites that which is distinct through an act of love.[26] Citing Ramsay again, Edwards thinks that God the Father "must have an object on which it exerts itself . . . into which it flows, and that flows back to it again."[27] In receiving the Spirit of the Father, the Son becomes an active subject that returns the Father's love. In this act of reciprocal affection, the Son stands before the Father as another "infinite subject."[28] Here, Edwards does not explicitly state that the Father becomes a secondary object of love, but this mutuality of love does imply a sort of receptivity in the Father.[29] By their Spirit, the Father and Son are not only active and express love toward each other, but they also enjoy and rest in each other's

---

22. Edwards, "'Misc.' 94," *WJE* 13:261–62. Similarly, Nieuwenhove, "Neoplatonism, *Regiratio* and Trinitarian Theology," 180.

23. Edwards, "'Misc.' 94," *WJE* 13:261–62. Elsewhere, see Edwards, "Discourse on the Trinity," *WJE* 21:131, 121.

24. Ibid., 121. See Studebaker, *Jonathan Edwards' Social Augustinian Trinitarianism*, 62–68; and Studebaker, "Jonathan Edwards' Social *Augustinian* Trinitarianism: An Alternative to a Recent Trend," 268–85.

25. Edwards, "Treatise on Grace," *WJE* 21:188.

26. Edwards, "On the Equality," *WJE* 21:147.

27. For Ramsay, see Edwards, "'Misc.' 1253," *WJE* 23:187. See also Edwards, "Images of Divine Things," *WJE* 11:79. While the previous citation refers to the economic Trinity, Edwards's description of God as infinite ocean echoes Ruusbroek's dynamic metaphor of the Trinity as "an ebbing, flowing sea." See Marmion and van Nieuwenhove, *Introduction to the Trinity*, 126.

28. Edwards, "Charity and its Fruits," *WJE* 8:373.

29. For example: "though the Son receives the infinite good, the Holy Spirit, from the Father, the Father *enjoys* the infinite good through the Son" [italics mine]. Edwards, "On the Equality," *WJE* 21:146.

love. In this way, the Holy Spirit as the perfect act of love establishes the divine essence as an eternal I-Thou reality.[30]

As the eternal operations of self-knowledge and self-love within God, there is an ordering to the generation of the Son and procession of the Spirit. While the intellect precedes the will in the order of nature, Word and Spirit are ontologically foundational as they are eternal processions in God.[31] Edwards makes this mutuality clear in a striking statement: "Understanding is in the Holy Ghost because the Son is in Him, not as proceeding from Him but as flowing out in Him."[32] In God, then, there is no "blind love" but rather a "seeing and understanding will." In this twofold communication of the Son and Spirit in God, we find the basis of an ordering and reciprocity of contemplation and action in Edwards's theology. While action presupposes contemplation, action is the consequence of contemplation.

In the foregoing analysis, we have seen that the contemplation and action dialectic in Edwards's doctrine of God can be structured around four polarities: (1) intellect and will; (2) receptivity and activity; (3) interiority and exteriority; and, (4) I-Thou relation. These four motifs are mirrored in human beings as creatures made in the image of God.

## Action and Contemplation in Human Beings

For Edwards, the psychological model of the Trinity is the archetype of the human spirit. "There is yet more of an image of the Trinity in the soul of man: there is," he elaborates, "the mind, and its understanding or idea, and the will or the affection or love—the heart, comprising inclination, affection, etc.—answering to God, the idea of God, and the love of God."[33] The human powers of understanding and will echo the divine processions of the Word and Spirit in the divine Mind. Furthermore, it is not just the passive powers of the mind, but the operation of the human understanding and will that best mirror the divine being as active being. "Understanding and will are the highest kind of created existence. And if they be valuable, it must be in their exercise. But the highest and most excellent kind of their exercise

---

30. Edwards, "1114. Sermon on Acts 20:28(b) (Mar 1754)," in *WJEO* 72. Edwards cites Proverbs 8:30 here.

31. Edwards, "Discourse on the Trinity," *WJE* 21:134. On Edwards's intellectualism and Augustinian voluntarism, see Studebaker, *Trinitarian Vision*, 51. See my essay on Edwards's pneumatic idealism: Tan, "Jonathan Edwards's Dynamic Idealism and Cosmic Christology."

32. Edwards, "Discourse on the Trinity," *WJE* 21:133.

33. Edwards, "'Misc.' 370," *WJE* 13:442.

is in some actual knowledge and exercise of will."[34] Receptivity and activity characterizes the human person made in the image of her Creator. And, as it is within God, this dialectic is similarly an ordered one in the human being.

How is receptivity prior to activity? As noted earlier, God is at the same time Being itself and Being-in-communion, and that is why the divine essence is both the principle of solitude and action, individuality and communion. Human persons, on the contrary, are not individuals but intrinsically relational beings, both with regard to God and others.

Firstly and foundationally, all creatures are beggars in terms of being. Like other created entities, human beings are ontologically dependent and receptive inasmuch as we are gifted with existence, properties, relations, and action moment-by-moment.[35] Secondly, Edwards insists that "we are made to subsist by society and union, one with another, and God has made us with such a nature that we can't subsist without the help of another."[36] This interdependency among human persons echoes the I-Thou relation and communion within the trinitarian life.

Since we are dependent both upon God and others for our existence, it stands to reason that passive contemplation or receptivity is primordial. Bare existence is, therefore, the ground of the substantive possession of understanding and will in the sentient creature.[37] Human dependence for existence from God and through each other is prior to any innate ability to think and act. This radically relational dimension of existence makes every human being valuable whether one's substantive properties are latent, underdeveloped, declining, temporarily dysfunctional, or permanently degenerating.

Nonetheless, there are features of human existence that mirror God, which distinguish us from other animals. The contemplation of ideas is a power that only a sentient, volitional mind possesses. It gives human beings the ability not only to passively receive ideas, but also actively engage them. It enables us to compare ideas and judge among them.[38] Animal minds, on the other hand, are purely passive as they have only "direct consciousness."[39]

This power of contemplation has two aspects. On the one hand, human beings are able to self-reflect. They "are capable of viewing what is

---

34. Edwards, "Concerning the End for which God Created the World," *WJE* 8:454.
35. Edwards, "68. Daniel 4:35 (n.d.)," *WJEO* 43.
36. Edwards, "Duty of Charity to the Poor," *WJE* 17:376.
37. Bombaro, *Jonathan Edwards's Vision of Reality*, 149–50.
38. Edwards, *Freedom of the Will*, *WJE* 1:28n5; also, Edwards, "The Mind," *WJE* 6:345, 374, 384.
39. Ibid., 374.

in themselves contemplatively."[40] On the other hand, we have the ability to contemplate external things as well. This propensity to look inwards as well as outwards mirrors the Word's inward beholding and the Father's outward contemplation.

Furthermore, that which primarily differentiates us from animals is our capacity to will.[41] Without "voluntary actions about their thoughts," animals merely perceive and remember things.[42] Only humans are religious beings because we have the capacity for "spiritual exercises and enjoyments . . . to behold and contemplate spiritual things."[43]

We are, therefore, unlike other created, "passive beings" for spirits have an "active nature."[44] In this respect, human spirits image the Divine Spirit, for as the "first supreme and universal principle of things," God is "a principle of action."[45] Yet, God is a perfect unity of disposition and act.[46] As the fully actualized Being or pure act, "the acting of love and the being of love are the same in God," which is quite unlike human beings, where "the habit or principle differs from the act."[47] Yet, as we shall see below, the gap between being and doing narrows teleologically in glorified human existence. With sin, this gap has widened into a gulf as the natural image is marred and the spiritual image—knowledge and love of God—is lost.[48]

## Contemplation and Action in the Regenerate Life

A human person exists not just to exercise her understanding and will in relation to mundane reality, but firstly toward God. In conversion, therefore, God restores to the regenerate her capacity for divine knowledge and love. Infused grace in the converted is the conjunct indwelling of divine truth and love. It is "Christ's being in the creature in the name, idea or knowledge of God being in them, and the Holy Spirit's being in them in the love of God's

---

40. Ibid.
41. Ibid.
42. Ibid.
43. Ibid.
44. Edwards, *Freedom of the Will*, WJE 1:186.
45. Edwards, "'Misc.' 383," WJE 13:451–52.
46. Edwards, "Discourse on the Trinity," WJE 21:113.
47. Edwards, "528. Rom 8:29–30 [December 1739]," WJEO 54.
48. Edwards, *Religious Affections*, WJE 2:256.

being in them."[49] When divine grace is infused into the regenerate, spiritual knowledge is received by, and finds its "immediate foundation" in, the intellect.[50] At the same time, infused grace has its "immediate seat" in the human will.[51] Thus, we come to know and love the Father by the Word and Spirit respectively.[52] In this restoration of the spiritual image, the human person regains the capacity for true contemplation and action.

The desire for solitude is natural and we would have remained in a permanent state of restfulness if not for original sin.[53] Through and in the incarnate Word, the believer has found her object of salvation and happiness. The restlessness and searching of the soul—the lack of peace and contentment—is finally satisfied in Christ. Edwards explains,

> Every faculty of the believer is satisfied and at rest in Christ. The understanding rests here, it desires no other object to be its portion, to entertain in contemplation; the glory of Christ is object enough for the entertainment of that extensive faculty. The will and affections are at rest in the beauty and love of Christ; here they are immovably fixed and need no other object to entertain and fill them, and be their everlasting food. The soul of the believer is at rest in Christ, as it desires not a more glorious object, a more sweet and delightful good than Jesus Christ.[54]

While contemplation includes a kind of peace, solitude and passivity in prayer, it is not pure quietism.[55] There is both receptivity and activity in prayer because contemplation involves both vision and affection. In Sarah Pierpont's narrative, she recounts such a contemplative encounter:

> I seemed to myself to perceive a glow of divine love come down from the heart of Christ in heaven, into my heart, in a constant stream, like a stream or pencil of sweet light. At the same time,

---

49. Edwards, "'Misc.' 1084," *WJE* 20:467. See also "'Misc.' 1094," *WJE* 20:483; "'Misc.' 1084," *WJE* 20:467.

50. Edwards, "Charity and its Fruits," *WJE* 8:296.

51. Ibid., 297. Nonetheless, divine grace does not abrogate her natural activity: Edwards, "Efficacious Grace," *WJE* 21:251.

52. Ramsay, as excerpted in Edwards, "Misc." 1254, *WJE* 23:188–89.

53. Watts, "The Lord's Day, or Christian Sabbath," in *Berry Street Sermons*, vol. 2, sermon 31, as cited in Edwards, "'Misc.' 1054," *WJE* 20:394; Edwards "Charity and its Fruits," *WJE* 8:394.

54. Edwards, "283. Cant 2:3(a)," *WJEO* 48.

55. Edwards read the writings of Archbishop Fenelon, Cardinal Pirtro Matteo Petrucci, and Blaise Pascal. See Thuesen, "Editor's Introduction," *WJE* 26:54. Also Edwards, "Charity and its Fruits," *WJE* 8:384.

my heart and soul all flowed out in love to Christ; so that there seemed to be a constant flowing and reflowing of heavenly and divine love, from Christ's heart to mine . . .[56]

We have language here that is reminiscent of the Spirit's procession toward the Son and return to the Father. For Edwards, contemplation is not merely a passive experience of God. Christian contemplation is both passive and active as it corresponds to the mutual beholding and loving between Father and Son. Our contemplation is participation in the divine contemplation; it is enjoyment of and response to God's love through and in the Word-made-flesh.

Just as contemplation of God is mediated through the incarnate Word, the written Word of God is a critical means of grace in this matter.[57] In contemplating God's words through Scripture, Edwards says that the mind finds great pleasure and joy in this act of loving reception. Following meditation on Scripture, there arises "the sweetness of those holy exercises that are excited by the word of God in the heart."[58] Scripture is, therefore, the chief means by which God grants us the divine light. To be sure, the spiritual sight of God that is had through Christ in this life is similar to but much deficient from the heavenly vision. As pilgrims in the here and now, we "see something of the reflected light of the sun mingled with darkness."[59]

Yet, even in our experience of this refracted, divine light, we see the moral beauty of God and Christ.[60] The Christian is enraptured by the loveliness of Christ just as the bridegroom in Canticles is ravished by the bride.[61] Likewise, humility or "poverty of spirit" is the beauty of the soul which "peculiarly ravish[es] the heart of Christ."[62] As such, there is a mu-

---

56. Edwards, "The Narrative of Sarah Pierpont Edwards," *WJEO* 41. See Edwards, "Charity and its Fruits," *WJE* 8:377. Such spirituality on the sacred heart of Jesus might have been drawn from Thomas Goodwin. Goodwin's musings in *The Heart of Christ in Heaven towards Sinners on Earth* anticipate "the devotion of the Sacred Heart . . . [of] Paray-le-Monal . . . but a good half-century before Margaret-Mary Alacoque." See Bouyer, *History of Christian Spirituality*, 140–42.

57. For more on Scripture as a means of grace, see Kyle Strobel's excellent work: Strobel, *Formed for the Glory of God*.

58. Edwards, "132. 1 Pet. 2:2–3," *WJEO* 44.

59. Edwards, "True Saints, When Absent from the Body, are Present with the Lord," *WJE* 25:230.

60. Edwards, *Religious Affections*, *WJE* 2:256.

61. Edwards, "The Sweet Harmony of Christ," *WJE* 19:441. This spiritual beauty is manifested even in the apparently hideous crucifixion, "by far its most full and glorious manifestation": Edwards, "'Misc.' 791," *WJE* 18:494.

62. See Edwards, "Canticles 4:9," *WJE* 15:520.

tual attraction between Christ and the saint to each other's beauty. As Christ is both God and man, the contemplative person grasps the beauty of both his holiness and his humility.

Contemplation is an ascent of spiritual insight that involves a corresponding descent of humility. Edwards reminds us that our desire for contemplation is an indicator of true meekness. "Silence is mentioned as a token of humility . . . An inclination to solitude rather than a forwardness to show oneself amongst others is a genuine fruit of humility."[63] This was manifested in the earthly Jesus, who "delighted in secret contemplation and prayer and converse with God more than" fame and worldly glory.[64] Contemplation is, at once, entering into the profundity of the double knowledge of God and human, which is aesthetical.[65]

Together with an increased appreciation of proportion and harmony, one also gains a greater sense of disproportion and discord. Which is why a person who is truly captivated by the beauty of divine holiness becomes humble, as she comes to appreciate the depth of her own sinfulness.[66] This double movement in contemplation also engenders a kind of passivity where one dies to sin, the world, and the self.[67] Repentance makes one dead or inactive to sin inasmuch as its corollary is the increasing possession of the Christ-life. This is so because the actuating principle of sanctification—mortification and vivification—is the Spirit of Christ.[68]

In regeneration, an active, divine principle is infused into our souls, when the Holy Spirit indwells us as a new, holy disposition.[69] The principle of grace in the regenerate soul or "Spirit Life" cannot lie dormant, but is outwardly active, since the "divine nature that is pure act [is] not an unfruitful thing."[70] For grace, being by definition a "principle of holy action," must

---

63. Edwards, "'Misc.' 989," *WJE* 20:314. He cites Prov 30:32, Lam 3:28, Eccl 5:2, Jas 1:19, Matt 12:16–18.

64. Edwards, "Notes on Christianity," *WJEO* 28:422.

65. See Kenneth P. Minkema, introduction to "A Spiritual Understanding of Divine Things Denied to the Unregenerate," in Edwards, *WJE* 14:68.

66. Edwards, "Charity and its Fruits" *WJE* 8:330. The disciples experienced this during Jesus' transfiguration: see Edwards, *Religious Affections*, *WJE* 2:300. Such experiences of ravishment need to be discerned, where the spiritual and intellectual dimensions should be distinguished from the imagination: see Edwards, "Distinguishing Marks," *WJE* 4:236.

67. Edwards, "Living to Christ," *WJE* 10:568.

68. Ibid., 568–70.

69. Edwards, "'Misc.' p," *WJE* 13:171.

70. Edwards, "723. Deut 5:27–29," *WJEO* 54.

tend toward practice as a root brings forth a plant.[71] Infused grace must express itself as an effusion. "A true knowledge of God and divine things is a practical knowledge," and not merely a speculative knowledge confined to the intellect.[72] Because the Holy Spirit is seated immediately in the regenerate human will, practical acts of grace must arise from the "commanding acts of the will, directing the outward action."[73]

While Edwards asserts that actual practice is the chief sign of true affections, he is also equally insistent that God "looks chiefly at the heart as exercised in those acts."[74] Heart religion is, therefore, a very critical component for Puritan (and Edwardsian) spirituality. For that reason, Edwards regards such a disposition of the heart as best typified by Mary of Bethany.[75] The reality of gracious affections does not just lie in a holy principle but a good disposition-in-exercise. "True godliness," Edwards contends, "consists not in an heart to intend to keep God's commandments, but in an heart to do it."[76]

Conversely, while only God can see and judge a person's heart, Edwards argues that God does not look *only* at the heart. For, "it is plain by the tenor of the whole Bible," he reminds us, "that God has respect not only to principles and immanent acts, but also to overt and transitory acts, and especially to them."[77] Grace in practice is not merely a mechanistic act of the body but a "practice of the soul" that precede and command bodily action.[78] That is why Christian practice is "the main evidence of our true Christianity" to others and ourselves. This emphasis on the importance of inward piety that cannot remain inward is clearly spelled out in Edwards's *Treatise on the Religious Affections*. In that work, he delineates two kinds of gracious acts in human beings: immanent and practical.[79]

---

71. Edwards, "Charity and its Fruits" *WJE* 8:298.

72. Ibid., 296.

73. Edwards, *Religious Affections*, *WJE* 2:423.

74. Edwards, "'Misc.' 819," *WJE* 18:530.

75. Such a view was also found in Thomas Hooker; see Hambrick-Stowe, *Practice of Piety*, 43.

76. Edwards, "'Misc.' 790," *WJE* 18:480.

77. Edwards, "'Misc.' 819," *WJE* 18:530. Similarly, God rewards "the transitive and good fruits of grace." Ibid., 531.

78. Edwards, *Religious Affections*, *WJE* 2:423.

79. For Aquinas, both contemplation and action have interior and exterior dimensions. See Jordan Aumann, "Appendix I: Active and Contemplative Life," in Aquinas, *Summa Theologiæ*, vol. 46 (2a2æ. 179–82), 88.

Immanent acts, like contemplation, are the exercises of grace, which are not expressed externally but "remain within the soul" or human mind.[80] Immanent acts, in and of themselves, do not involve externalization of the will, remain interior, and do not produce effects.[81] By contrast, there are the "overt and transitory," effective, or practical acts, which are the external expression of grace, where the will is involved in either acts of omission or commission.[82] A good work arises from the unity of immanent and overt acts, in which the will interposes.[83] Action and contemplation, while distinct as external and internal actions, are not to be separated.

Edwards, like the Puritans in general, interprets the Bethany sisters as representative of two types of worship: the one external and liturgical, the other spiritual and interior.[84] They are representative not only of two types of ecclesiologies, but also two forms of personal pieties.[85] For Edwards, Mary's spiritual posture toward Jesus exceeds Martha's outward devotion.[86]

Furthermore, the exercise of grace has two kinds of outward expressions—ceremonial and practical—the latter being greater.[87] First, ceremonial or "outward acts of worship" include "meeting in religious assemblies, attending sacraments and other outward institutions, and honoring God with gestures, such as bowing, or kneeling before him, or with words, in speaking honorably of him in prayer, praise, or religious conference."[88] Sec-

---

80. Edwards, *Religious Affections*, WJE 2:422. With the qualification that contemplative acts "may tend to practice (as all exercises of grace do) more remotely." Other immanent acts are "the internal breathing of love to God, and exercises of faith in Christ": Edwards, "'Misc.' 573," WJE 18:111.

81. Edwards, "Signs of Godliness," WJE 21:474.

82. Edwards, "'Misc.' 819," WJE 18:530. See also Edwards, *Religious Affections*, WJE 2:423. Elsewhere, Edwards calls this a voluntary act: see Edwards, "Signs of Godliness," WJE 21:474.

83. Edwards, *Religious Affections*, WJE 2:423.

84. The practice of distinguishing Martha and Mary as two different social or religious groups has a long history. See Constable, *Three Studies*, 72. The Puritan interpretation of privileging Mary over Martha, according to Schwanda, (citing Hooker in particular) is "a less balanced understanding between the two sisters," Schwanda, *Soul Recreation*, 100.

85. In Edwards's "Notes on Scripture," Mary and Martha typify the ceremonial (Church of England) and spiritual (dissenting church) kinds of worship. See Edwards, "Christ's Example," WJE 21:515.

86. Ibid. In this piece of writing, Edwards interprets Martha treating Christ in an outward and worldly manner. Although Christ was the greatest of all persons, Mary regard to Christ was more spiritual as she truly recognized Christ's person and mission.

87. Edwards, "Some Thoughts Concerning the Revival," WJE 4:523.

88. Ibid., 524.

ond, acts of discipleship or "moral duties" include active works of charity and passively enduring persecution.[89]

Acts of ministry to our neighbor are duties greater than ceremonial worship "because there is greater self-denial in them."[90] In a sense, such practical acts include both the Mary and Martha dimensions of worship. Charity to the poor is "as one of the greater and more essential duties of religion."[91] We are actually serving Christ by serving the poor. "And though we can't now be charitable in this way to Christ in person, who in his exalted state is infinitely above the need of our charity; yet we may be charitable to Christ now, as well as they then; for though Christ is not here, yet he has left others in his room, to be his receivers; and they are the poor."[92]

While ministering to the poor is an expression of active service, contemplation must undergird all action, for grace can only be received. Hence, Christ was more delighted by Mary's receptive posture as compared to Martha's activity, though Jesus loved both sisters and acknowledged that both were loving him through "acceptable entertainment."[93] Deeds of love, like giving to the poor, are opportunities whereby God guides us into further "divine discoveries and spiritual consolations."[94] Where there is true contemplation, it will issue in genuine action. And where is there is action that flows from divine love, it will lead us back to contemplation of God. This rhythm of action and contemplation is expressed *par excellence* in the life of Jesus, whom we are called to imitate.[95]

## Action and Contemplation in Heaven

As Hans Urs von Balthasar notes, the distinction between the contemplative and active life is an earthly one.[96] Similarly, for Edwards, there is no absolute contemplative state in heaven which transcends the state of the mixed life on earth, for contemplation as well as action in the here and now are both deficient.[97] Without doubt, our present situation is due to the cor-

89. Ibid., 522.
90. Ibid., 524.
91. Edwards, "The Duty of Charity to the Poor," *WJE* 17:375.
92. Edwards, "Some Thoughts Concerning the Revival," *WJE* 4:526.
93. Edwards, "408. Cant. 7:13 (Sep 1736)," *WJEO* 51. For Edwards, Luke 10:38–42 is more about Jesus than the two sisters: Edwards, "Christ's Example," *WJE* 21:515.
94. Edwards, "Some Thoughts Concerning the Revival," *WJE* 4:525.
95. Edwards, "Christ's Example," *WJE* 21:515.
96. Balthasar, "Action and Contemplation," 2.
97. Edwards, *Religious Affections*, *WJE* 2:216, 215. Here, Edwards echoes

rupted powers of our soul. Yet, the case will be vastly different in heaven. "The understanding," Edwards surmises, "will be in its most perfect act of beholding, and the will will be in its most perfect act in loving."[98] The saints in heaven "are exceedingly affected with what they behold and contemplate, of God's perfections and work."[99] Their contemplation is purer because "they see things they are affected by, more according to their truth."[100] The preeminent object of the heavenly contemplation is God. For Edwards, the saint in heaven perceives God as the most Beautiful and Beautifying, namely, "the Trinity, the supreme harmony of all."[101]

And what is the manner of our experiencing the beatific vision of the Trinity? It is a sight that is both immediate as well as mediated. On the one hand, this intellectual vision is a direct, intuitive perception of God's beauty, while involving the understanding, does not depend on logical argumentation.[102] On the other hand, this vision is also mediated by God's Spirit and Word. Just as spiritual insight of Christ is a gift of God's Spirit on earth, the beatific vision is had through the agency of the Spirit.[103] Also, the manner the saint sees and enjoys God is through the Son's sight and love of the Father.[104] The perception of God is through the glorified Word—God's very own Idea. In the intermediate state, the beatific vision is temporary and imperfect.

However, saints in their resurrected state perceive God the Father through the glorified Christ both through a double vision—an intellectual *and* a corporeal vision.[105] "The saints in heaven, they will see the glory of the body of Christ after the resurrection with bodily [eyes] . . . "[106] They will have a visible vision of Christ's "external glory" because God has united himself

---

Augustine's typologies of vision: an external, physical sight (*visio corporalis*); a fallible, inner, imaginative sight of things mediated by images (*visio spiritualis*); and, an infallible, intellectual vision (*visio intellectualis*). See Fraeters, "*Visio*/Vision," 178–79.

98. Edwards, "373. Romans 2:10 (1735)," *WJEO* 50.
99. Edwards, *Religious Affections*, *WJE* 2:130.
100. Ibid.
101. Edwards, "'Misc.' 182," *WJE* 13:329.
102. Edwards, "The Pure in Heart Blessed," *WJE* 17:64.
103. Edwards, "373. Romans 2:10 (1735)," *WJEO* 50. See also Strobel, *Jonathan Edwards's Theology*, 142.
104. Edwards, "373. Romans 2:10 (1735)," *WJEO* 50.
105. Edwards, "True Saints, when Absent from the Body, are Present with the Lord," *WJE* 25:229–31. Edwards echoes John Owen's christological emphasis on the beatific vision. See McDonald, "Beholding the Glory of God," 141–58.
106. Edwards, "The Pure in Heart Blessed," *WJE* 17:66.

to an "external nature" in the incarnation of the Word.[107] This bodily vision of Christ is prototypical of all the theophanies that the saints in the Bible had experienced.[108] In heaven, Edwards imagines that external beauties will be "in a manner to us inconceivable . . . vastly more ravishing and exquisite . . . and probably those beauties will appear chiefly on the bodies of the man Christ Jesus and of the saints."[109] Although heaven will be illuminated by the physical glory of the saints and Christ, the unmediated, intellectual vision will be far superior to the bodily vision.[110]

In the beatific vision, there is both contemplation and enjoyment of God.[111] Like earthly contemplation, it is not merely a passive reception of God's love, but includes an active, human response.

> The saints in heaven are not merely passive in their happiness. They do not merely enjoy God passively, but in an active manner. They are not only acted upon by God, but they mutually act towards him, and in this action and re-action consists the heavenly happiness.[112]

Glorified existence is not just immanent activity but has outward expressions that are musical, communal, theological, and doxological. Heaven is both a world of silence and Word, receptivity and activity.[113] Not only do the saints participate passively in Christ's reception of the Father's love, they actively share in Christ's "blessed and eternal employment of glorifying the Father." In this regard, glorified saints are like the angels. Edwards thinks that this not only includes the business of theology, but also praise.[114]

> The angels are as a flame of fire, in their ardor and activity in God's service . . . The souls of departed saints are doubtless become as the angels of God in heaven in this respect. And Jesus Christ is the head of the whole glorious assembly; as in other things, appertaining to their blessed state, so in this of their praising and glorifying the Father.[115]

---

107. Edwards, "Notes on Scripture," 266, *WJE* 15:219.
108. Ibid., 219–20.
109. Edwards, "'Misc.' 182," *WJE* 13:328.
110. Edwards, "'Misc.' 721," *WJE* 18:351.
111. Edwards, "131. 1 Pet. 1:8(a) (July 1757)," *WJEO* 44.
112. Edwards, "344. Rev. 14:2 (Nov 1734)," *WJEO* 49.
113. See Jenson, *America's Theologian*, 195.
114. Edwards, "The Importance and Advantage of a Thorough Knowledge of Divine Truth," *WJE* 22:99.
115. Edwards, "True Saints, when Absent from the Body, are Present with the

Unlike the intermediate state, the glorified, resurrected saints will have a more complete happiness as their persons have been spiritually and physically reconstituted.[116] We become like the angels as we have now a light, glorified body and are closer to being pure, active spirits.[117] Echoing Irenaeus, Edwards thinks that the glorified, living person is full of spirit and life.[118] As the Spirit is perfect action in God, Edwards likens glorified human persons to living, created verbs. In heaven, created beings become like God such that the distance between their being and acting will grow narrower. When the divine disposition is enthroned in the created heart, loving action flows naturally from its principle without hindrance. Our inwardness becomes perfectly transparent.

> The Holy Spirit is . . . pure act . . . because that which acts perfectly is all act, and nothing but act. There is an image of this in created beings that approach to perfect action: how frequently do we say that the saints of heaven are all transformed into love, dissolved into joy, become activity itself, changed into mere ecstasy.[119]

The glorified saints approximate pure action because the pure act of God fills and indwells them more perfectly. In the world of love which is heaven, "love resides and reigns in every heart there."[120]

This divine love dwells and reigns in "the original seat" and source, which is God's heart. The ontological basis for the free, outpouring of divine love from God to creatures is found in the I-Thou relationship within the Godhead. The reason that God can relate to sentient creatures as "objects of love" is because there is both subjectivity and objectivity in God. This necessary I-Thou relation in God is the mutual love flowing between the Father and Son.

> It flows out in the first place [necessarily] and infinitely towards his only begotten Son, being poured forth without measure, as to an object which is infinite, and so fully adequate to God's love in its fountain. . . . And the Son of God is not only the infinite object of love, but he is also an infinite subject of it. He is not only the infinite object of the Father's love, but he also

---

Lord," *WJE* 25:242.

116. Edwards, "373. Rom 2:10 (Dec 1735)," *WJEO* 50.
117. Edwards, *Religious Affections*, *WJE* 2:130.
118. Edwards, "'Misc.' 1296," *WJE* 23:237.
119. Edwards, "'Misc.' 94," *WJE* 13:260–61.
120. Edwards, "Charity and its Fruits," *WJE* 8:373.

infinitely loves the Father. The infinite essential love of God is, as it were, an infinite and eternal mutual holy energy between the Father and the Son, a pure, holy act whereby the Deity becomes nothing but an infinite and unchangeable act of love, which proceed from both the Father and the Son. Thus divine love has its seat in the Deity as it is exercised within the Deity, or in God towards himself.[121]

This active I-Thou circle of love "does not remain in such exercises only, but it flows out in innumerable streams towards all the created inhabitants on heaven" through Christ. This is the same divine love that elected the church from eternity, was expressed in the incarnation and cross, and in the sanctification of the saints on earth, which is "now fully manifested to them in heaven." With Christ, and through Christ, the angels and glorified saints are the secondary "subjects of holy love."[122] The Holy Spirit or the fullness of God is received by them and returned to God the Father.[123] We have perfect communion with Christ, and in and through him, with the Father.[124] Like Christ, we become a subject that not only receives but returns love.

And just as love is mutual in God, so there will be proportional, reciprocal acts of love returned among the glorified saints in heaven.[125] Because of the reciprocity of love, the "love of the saints to one another will always be mutual and answerable," though there are different degrees of its expression in heaven.[126] The end for which God created the world is this "emanation and remanation" of divine love between God and his creatures.[127]

While the believer is satisfied in Christ, her desire and longing for Christ is ever growing.[128] This will involve an everlasting increase in desire for God and an accompanying expansion of one's capacities for Christ. For

---

121. Ibid.

122. Ibid.

123. Ibid., 377.

124. Edwards, "True Saints, when Absent from the Body, are Present with the Lord," *WJE* 25:234.

125. Edwards, "Charity and its Fruits" *WJE* 8:377.

126. Ibid.

127. Edwards, "End for Which God Created the World," *WJE* 8:531. For some Puritan writers, the term "emanation" was used interchangeably with the procession of the Spirit. See, for example, Leigh, *Treatise of Divinity*, 138; and, Cheynell, *Divine Trinunity*, 59.

128. Edwards, "283. Cant. 2:3(a)," *WJEO* 48.

Edwards, there is progress in glorification. And in sanctification, Act II, there will be contemplation and action that is ever-increasing and unending.[129]

> There remaineth a rest for the people of God; and it is a place of the reward of labour. But yet the rest of heaven does not consist in idleness, and a cessation of all action, but only a cessation of all the trouble and toil and tediousness of action. The most perfect rest is consistent with being continually employed. . . . The saints in glory are represented as employed in serving God, as well as the saints on earth, though it be without any difficulty or opposition.[130]

## Some Concluding Remarks

Contemporary Christian dictionary definitions have discarded the Hellenistic intellectualist bias in contemplation.[131] Nonetheless, in some definitions, contemplation is still seen as a passive, inner posture in relation to God and action as an active, outward posture toward the neighbor.[132] As we have seen, Edwards not only viewed contemplation as both active and passive, but he also made room for the mutual influence of immanent and practical acts.

I believe that Edwards stands in the spirit of Luther on this matter. The goal of the contemplative life does not terminate in an infused, passive contemplation—an experiential union with God reserved for the elite spiritual warriors.[133] Rather, we are to be thrust into this world of temptation ready for combat, as it were.[134] Maybe not *tentatio* all the time, but certainly, *actio*. And when temptations cease, the new heaven and earth will remain a world of contemplation *and action*.

---

129. Edwards, "God's Excellencies," *WJE* 10:417.

130. Edwards, "344. Rev. 14:2 (Nov 1734)," *WJEO* 49.

131. See Rahner, "Theory and Practice," 1702–3.

132. See Holz, "Active Life and Contemplative Life," 243–44.

133. In this essay, "contemplation" is neither to be equated with infused nor acquired contemplation in medieval spirituality. Used broadly here, it includes meditation, where one uses word and image as means during prayerful reflection. See Ward, "Contemplation," 95–96.

134. Luther subverted the *lectio divina* of the monastic tradition (*lectio, meditatio, oratio,* and *contemplatio*) into the threefold progression of *oratio, meditatio,* and *tentatio*. Kleinig, "Oratio, Meditatio, Tentatio," 255–67. The summit is not a private, ecstatic experience of God's glory but conflict with Satan in the world. See Luther, "Preface to the Wittenberg Edition," 285–88.

Contemplation or prayer is both receptive and active, in another sense. In its highest moments, it is to be captivated by God's irresistible beauty and love in Christ so that we might respond in loving attention and ecstatic praise to God. It is to be caught up into that circle of eternal emanation and remanation within the spiritual life of Father and Son. Yet, this circle of communion is not ultimately a private encounter with a monadic God, but solitude and communion with the triune God.[135] The mind of the Christian is not distracted by the multiplicity of worldly goods but attains a unitary vision of the Good, which arises from the contemplative life. Not only so, but our reception and return to God brings about enjoyment of and service to God and each other.

# Bibliography

"Action-Contemplation." In *Dictionary of Oblate Values*; available at http://www.omiworld.org/en/dictionary/dictionary-of-oblate-values_vol-1_a/1027/action-contemplation/

Aquinas, Thomas. *Summa Theologica*. Vol. 4. Translated by Fathers of the English Dominican Province. New York: Benzinger Bros., 1948.

Aumann, Jordan. "Appendix I: Active and Contemplative Life." In Thomas Aquinas, *Summa Theologiæ*, Vol. 46 2a2æ, *Action and Contemplation* 179–82. Cambridge: Cambridge University Press, 2006.

Balthasar, Hans Urs von. "Action and Contemplation." In *The Word Made Flesh*, translated by A. V. Littledale with Alexander Dru. Explorations in Theology Vol. 1. San Francisco: Ignatius Press, 1989.

Bebbington, David W. *Evangelicalism in Modern Britain: A History from the 1730s to the 1890s*. London: Unwin Hyman, 1989.

Bombaro, John J. *Jonathan Edwards's Vision of Reality: The Relationship of God to the World, Redemption History, and the Reprobate*. Eugene, OR: Pickwick, 2012.

Bouyer, Louis. *Orthodox Spirituality and Protestant and Anglican Spirituality*. A History of Christian Spirituality, vol. 3. London: Burns & Oates, 1969.

Cameron, Andrew J. B., and Brian S. Rosner, eds. *The Trials of Theology: Becoming a "Proven Worker" in a Dangerous Business*. Rosshire: Christian Focus, 2010.

Cheynell, Francis. *The Divine Trinunity Of The Father, Son, And Holy Spirit*. London: Samuel Gellibrand, 1650.

Constable, Giles. *Three Studies in Medieval Religious and Social Thought*. Cambridge: Cambridge University Press, 1995.

Edwards, Jonathan. "373. Unpublished Sermon on Romans 2:10 (December 1735)." In *Sermons, Series II, 1735*. The Works of Jonathan Edwards Online 50. Jonathan Edwards Center at Yale University.

———. "Canticles 4:9." In *Notes on Scripture*, edited by Stephen J. Stein, The Works of Jonathan Edwards 15:520. New Haven: Yale University Press, 1998.

---

135. Christian contemplation is not a "flight of the alone to the alone." See Plotinus, *Enneads* 6.9.11.

---. "Charity and its Fruits." In *Ethical Writings*, edited by Paul Ramsay, The Works of Jonathan Edwards 8:123-397. New Haven: Yale University Press, 1989.

---. "Christ's Example." In *Writings on the Trinity, Grace, and Faith*, edited by Sang Hyun Lee, The Works of Jonathan Edwards 21:511-19. New Haven: Yale University Press, 2003.

---. "Daniel 9:25." In *The "Blank Bible,"* edited by Stephen J. Stein, The Works of Jonathan Edwards 24/1:767-68. New Haven: Yale University Press, 2006.

---. "Discourse on the Trinity." In *Writings on the Trinity, Grace, and Faith*, edited by Sang Hyun Lee, The Works of Jonathan Edwards 21:109-44. New Haven: Yale University Press, 2003.

---. "Dissertation I: Concerning the End for which God Created the World." In *Ethical Writings*, edited by Paul Ramsay, The Works of Jonathan Edwards 8:399-536. New Haven: Yale University Press, 1989.

---. "The Distinguishing Marks." In *The Great Awakening*, edited by Clarence C. Goen, The Works of Jonathan Edwards 4:213-88. New Haven: Yale University Press, 1972.

---. "The Duty of Charity to the Poor." In *Sermons and Discourses, 1730-1733*, edited by Mark Valeri, The Works of Jonathan Edwards 17:369-404. New Haven: Yale University Press, 1999.

---. "Efficacious Grace." In *Writings on the Trinity, Grace, and Faith*, edited by Sang Hyun Lee, The Works of Jonathan Edwards 21:198-290. New Haven: Yale University Press, 2003.

---. "Exodus 33:18-23." In *Notes on Scripture*, edited by Stephen J. Stein, The Works of Jonathan Edwards 15:219-20. New Haven: Yale University Press, 1998.

---. *Freedom of the Will*. The Works of Jonathan Edwards 1. Edited by Paul Ramsey. New Haven: Yale University Press, 1957.

---. "God's Excellencies." In *Sermons and Discourses, 1720-1723*, edited by Wilson H. Kimnach, The Works of Jonathan Edwards 10:413-35. New Haven: Yale University Press, 1992.

---. "'Images of Divine Things' 77." In *Typological Writings*, edited by Wallace E. Anderson et al., The Works of Jonathan Edwards 11:77-80. New Haven: Yale University Press, 1993.

---. "The Importance and Advantage of a Thorough Knowledge of Divine Truth." In *Sermons and Discourses, 1739-1742*, edited by Harry S. Stout et al., The Works of Jonathan Edwards 22:80-102. New Haven: Yale University Press, 2003.

---. "Living to Christ." In *Sermons and Discourses, 1720-1723*, edited by Wilson H. Kimnach, The Works of Jonathan Edwards 10:563-77. New Haven: Yale University Press, 1992.

---. "The Mind." In *Scientific and Philosophical Writings*, edited by Wallace E. Anderson, The Works of Jonathan Edwards 6:311-93. New Haven: Yale University Press, 1980.

---. "'Misc.' p." In *The "Miscellanies" (Entry Nos. a-z, aa-zz, 1-500)*, edited by Thomas A. Schafer, The Works of Jonathan Edwards 13:171. New Haven: Yale University Press, 1994.

---. "'Misc.' 94." In *The "Miscellanies" (Entry Nos. a-z, aa-zz, 1-500)*, edited by Thomas A. Schafer, The Works of Jonathan Edwards 13:256-63. New Haven: Yale University Press, 1994.

———. "'Misc.' 143." In *The "Miscellanies" (Entry Nos. a-z, aa-zz, 1-500)*, edited by Thomas A. Schafer, The Works of Jonathan Edwards 13:298-99. New Haven: Yale University Press, 1994.

———. "'Misc.' 182." In *The "Miscellanies" (Entry Nos. a-z, aa-zz, 1-500)*, edited by Thomas A. Schafer, The Works of Jonathan Edwards 13:328-29. New Haven: Yale University Press, 1994.

———. "'Misc.' 370." In *The "Miscellanies" (Entry Nos. a-z, aa-zz, 1-500)*, edited by Thomas A. Schafer, The Works of Jonathan Edwards 13:441-42. New Haven: Yale University Press, 1994.

———. "'Misc.' 383." In *The "Miscellanies" (Entry Nos. a-z, aa-zz, 1-500)*, edited by Thomas A. Schafer, The Works of Jonathan Edwards 13:451-52. New Haven: Yale University Press, 1994.

———. "'Misc.' 573." In *The "Miscellanies" (Entry Nos. 501-832)*, edited by Ava Chamberlain, The Works of Jonathan Edwards 18:111-13. New Haven: Yale University Press, 2000.

———. "'Misc.' 721." In *The "Miscellanies" (Entry Nos. 501-832)*, edited by Ava Chamberlain, The Works of Jonathan Edwards 18:350-51. New Haven: Yale University Press, 2000.

———. "'Misc.' 790." In *The "Miscellanies" (Entry Nos. 501-832)*, edited by Ava Chamberlain, The Works of Jonathan Edwards 18:474-88. New Haven: Yale University Press, 2000.

———. "'Misc.' 791." In *The "Miscellanies" (Entry Nos. 501-832)*, edited by Ava Chamberlain, The Works of Jonathan Edwards 18:488-95. New Haven: Yale University Press, 2000.

———. "'Misc.' 819." In *The "Miscellanies" (Entry Nos. 501-832)*, edited by Ava Chamberlain, The Works of Jonathan Edwards 18:530-31. New Haven: Yale University Press, 2000.

———. "'Misc.' 989." In *The "Miscellanies" (Entry Nos. 833-1152)*, edited by Amy P. Pauw, The Works of Jonathan Edwards 20:311-15. New Haven: Yale University Press, 2002.

———. "'Misc.' 1084." In *The "Miscellanies" (Entry Nos. 833-1152)*, edited by Amy P. Pauw, The Works of Jonathan Edwards 20:467. New Haven: Yale University Press, 2002.

———. "'Misc.' 1054." In *The "Miscellanies" (Entry Nos. 833-1152)*, edited by Amy P. Pauw, The Works of Jonathan Edwards 20:394. New Haven: Yale University Press, 2002.

———. "'Misc.' 1094." In *The "Miscellanies" (Entry Nos. 833-1152)*, edited by Amy P. Pauw, The Works of Jonathan Edwards 20:482-83. New Haven: Yale University Press, 2002.

———. "'Misc.' 1253." In *The "Miscellanies" (Entry Nos. 1153-1360)*, edited by Douglas A. Sweeney, The Works of Jonathan Edwards 23:184-88. New Haven: Yale University Press, 2004.

———. "'Misc.' 1254." In *The "Miscellanies" (Entry Nos. 1153-1360)*, edited by Douglas A. Sweeney, The Works of Jonathan Edwards 23:188-90. New Haven: Yale University Press, 2004.

———. "'Misc.' 1296." In *The "Miscellanies" (Entry Nos. 1153-1360)*, edited by Douglas A. Sweeney, The Works of Jonathan Edwards 23:236-40. New Haven: Yale University Press, 2004.

Edwards, Sarah. "Narrative." In *Family Writings and Related Documents*. The Works of Jonathan Edwards Online 41. Jonathan Edwards Center at Yale University.

Edwards, Jonathan. "Notes on Christianity." In *Minor Controversial Writings*. The Works of Jonathan Edwards Online 28. Jonathan Edwards Center at Yale University.

———. "On the Equality of the Persons of the Trinity." In *Writings on the Trinity, Grace, and Faith*, edited by Sang Hyun Lee, The Works of Jonathan Edwards 21:145–48. New Haven: Yale University Press, 2003.

———. "The Pure in Heart Blessed." In *Sermons and Discourses, 1730–1733*, edited by Mark Valeri, The Works of Jonathan Edwards 17:57–86. New Haven: Yale University Press, 1999.

———. *Religious Affections*. The Works of Jonathan Edwards 2. Edited by John E. Smith. New Haven: Yale University Press, 1969.

———. "Signs of Godliness." In *Writings on the Trinity, Grace, and Faith*, edited by Sang Hyun Lee, The Works of Jonathan Edwards 21:469–510. New Haven: Yale University Press, 2003.

———. "Some Thoughts concerning the Revival." In *The Great Awakening*, edited by Clarence C. Goen, The Works of Jonathan Edwards 4:289–530. New Haven: Yale University Press, 1972.

———. "A Spiritual Understanding of Divine Things Denied to the Unregenerate." In *Sermons and Discourses, 1723–1729*, edited by Kenneth P. Minkema, The Works of Jonathan Edwards 14:67–96. New Haven: Yale University Press, 1997.

———. "The Sweet Harmony of Christ." In *Sermons and Discourses, 1734–1738*, edited by Max X. Lesser, The Works of Jonathan Edwards 19:435–50. New Haven Yale University Press, 2001.

———. "Treatise on Grace." In *Writings on the Trinity, Grace, and Faith*, edited by Sang Hyun Lee, The Works of Jonathan Edwards 21:149–197. New Haven: Yale University Press, 2003.

———. "True Saints, when Absent from the Body, are Present with the Lord." In *Sermons and Discourses, 1743–1758*, edited by Wilson H. Kimnach, The Works of Jonathan Edwards 25:222–56. New Haven: Yale University Press, 2006.

———. "68. Sermon on Daniel 4:35." In *Sermons, Series II, 1728–1729*. The Works of Jonathan Edwards Online 43. Jonathan Edwards Center at Yale University.

———. "131. Sermon on 1 Peter 1:8(a) (July 1757)." In *Sermons, Series II, 1729*. The Works of Jonathan Edwards Online 44. Jonathan Edwards Center at Yale University.

———. "132. Sermon on 1 Peter 2:2–3." In *Sermons, Series II, 1729*. The Works of Jonathan Edwards Online 44. Jonathan Edwards Center at Yale University.

———. "283. Sermon on Canticles 2:3(a)." In *Sermons, Series II, 1733*. The Works of Jonathan Edwards Online 48. Jonathan Edwards Center at Yale University.

———. "344. Sermon on Revelation 14:2 (November 1734) ." In *Sermons, Series II, 1734*. The Works of Jonathan Edwards Online 49. Jonathan Edwards Center at Yale University.

———. "408. Sermon on Canticles 7:13 (September 1736)." In *Sermons, Series II, 1736*. The Works of Jonathan Edwards Online 51. Jonathan Edwards Center at Yale University.

———. "528. Sermon on Romans 8:29–30 (December 1739)." In *Sermons, Series II, 1739*. The Works of Jonthan Edwards Online 54. Jonathan Edwards Center at Yale University.

———. "723. Sermon on Deuteronomy 5:27–29 (November 1743)." In *Sermons, Series II, 1743*. The Works of Jonathan Edwards Online 61. Jonathan Edwards Center at Yale University.

———. "1114. Sermon on Acts 20:28(b) (March 1754)." In *Sermons, Series II, 1754-1755*. The Works of Jonathan Edwards Online 72. Jonathan Edwards Center at Yale University.

Fraeters, Veerle. "*Visio*/Vision." In *The Cambridge Companion to Christian Mysticism*, edited by Amy Hollywood and Patricia Z. Beckman, 178–79. Cambridge: Cambridge University Press, 2015.

Grumett, David. "Action and/or Contemplation? Allegory and Liturgy in the Reception of Luke 10:38–42," *Scottish Journal of Theology* 59/2 (2006) 125–39.

Hambrick-Stowe, Charles E. *Practice of Piety*. Chapel Hill, NC: University of North Carolina Press, 1986.

Holt, Bradley P. "Active Life and Contemplative Life." In *Dictionary of Christian Spirituality*, edited by Glen G. Scorgie, 243–44. Grand Rapids, MI: Zondervan, 2011.

Howard, Evan. "Evangelical Spirituality." In *Four Views on Christian Spirituality*, edited by Stanley N. Gundry and Bruce Demarest, 170. Grand Rapids, MI: Zondervan, 2012.

Jenson, Robert W. *America's Theologian: A Recommendation of Jonathan Edwards*. New York: Oxford University Press, 1988.

Kleinig, John W. "Oratio, Meditatio, Tentatio: What Makes A Theologian?" *Concordia Theological Quarterly* 66/3 (2002) 255–67.

Leigh, Edward. *A Treatise of Divinity Consisting of Three Bookes*. London: William Lee, 1646.

Louth, Andrew. *The Origins of the Christian Mystical Tradition from Plato to Denys*. Oxford: Clarendon Press, 1981.

Luther, Martin. "Preface to the Wittenberg Edition of Luther's German Writings." In *Luther's Works: Career of the Reformer IV*. Vol. 34, edited by Lewis W. Spitz, 279–88. Philadelphia: Muhlenberg Press, 1960.

Mackenna, Stephen. *Plotinus: The Enneads*. London: Faber & Faber, 1969.

Marmion, Declan, and Rik van Nieuwenhove. *An Introduction to the Trinity*. Cambridge: Cambridge University Press, 2011.

McDonald, Suzanne. "Beholding the Glory of God in the Face of Jesus Christ: John Owen and the 'Reforming' of the Beatific Vision." In *The Ashgate Research Companion to John Owen's Theology*, edited by Kelly M. Kapic and Mark Jones, 141–58. Surrey, UK: Ashgate, 2012.

Nieuwenhove, Rik van. "Jan van Ruusbroec on the Trinity, Prayer, and the Nature of Contemplation." In *A History of Prayer: The First to the Fifteenth Century*, edited by Roy Hammerling, Brill's Companions to the Christian Tradition, 374–75. Leiden: Brill, 2008.

———. "Neoplatonism, *Regiratio* and Trinitarian Theology: A Look at Ruusbroec." *Hermathena* 169 (2000) 180.

Packer, J. I. *A Quest for Godliness: The Puritan Vision of the Christian Life*. Wheaton, IL: Crossway, 1990.

Pelikan, Jaroslav, et al., eds. *Luther's Works: Career of the Reformer IV*. Vol. 34. Philadelphia: Muhlenberg, 1960.

Radler, Charlotte. "*Actio et Contemplatio*/Action and Contemplation." In *Cambridge Companion to Christian Mysticism*, edited by Amy Hollywood and Patricia Z. Beckmann, 211–22. Cambridge: Cambridge University Press, 2012.

Rahner, Karl, ed. "Theory and Practice." In *Encyclopedia of Theology: A Concise Sacramentum Mundi*, 1702–3. London: Burns & Oates, 1975.

Ramsay, Chevalier. *The Philosophical Principles of Natural and Revealed Religion Unfolded in a Geometrical Order.* Glasgow: Robert Foulis, 1748.

Schwanda, Tom. *Soul Recreation: The Contemplative-Mystical Piety of Puritanism.* Eugene, OR: Pickwick Publications, 2012.

Strobel, Kyle C. *Formed for the Glory of God: Learning from the Spiritual Practices of Jonathan Edwards.* Downers Grove, IL: InterVarsity, 2013.

———. *Jonathan Edwards's Theology: A Reinterpretation.* London: Bloomsbury, 2013.

Studebaker, Steven M. "Jonathan Edwards' Social *Augustinian* Trinitarianism: An Alternative to a Recent Trend." Scottish Journal of Theology 56 (2003) 268–85.

———. *Jonathan Edwards' Social Augustinian Trinitarianism in Historical and Contemporary Perspectives.* Piscataway: NJ: Gorgias, 2008.

Studebaker, Steven M. *The Trinitarian Vision of Jonathan Edwards and David Coffey* Amherst, NY: Cambria Press, 2011.

Tan, Seng Kong. "Jonathan Edwards's Dynamic Idealism and Cosmic Christology." In *Idealism and Christian Theology*, edited by Joshua R. Farris et al., 177–96. New York: Bloombury Academic, 2016.

Thuesen, Peter J. "Editor's Introduction." In *Catalogues of Books*, edited by Peter J. Thuesen, The Works of Jonathan Edwards 26:1–113. New Haven: Yale University Press, 2008.

Ward, J. Neville. "Contemplation." In *The Westminster Dictionary of Christian Spirituality*, edited by Gordon S. Wakefield, 95–96. Philadelphia: Westminster, 1983.

# 11

# Faith and Feeling in the Theology of Jonathan Edwards

### Willem van Vlastuin

## Introduction

In Christian life, the relation between faith and feeling is an important question, determinative for the interpretation of the spiritual life and influential in how one preaches. The concept of "feeling" can include faith experience; it can also be a designation for the more emotional side of faith. Because emotional phenomena often play a role during revivals, the latter are a rewarding source for research into how the relation between faith and the various degrees of feeling functions. This article focuses on the relation between faith and feeling in the revival theologian Jonathan Edwards.[1] The current research into Edwards's doctrine of participation and spirituality underscores the relevance of this interaction with the basics of Edwards's understanding of spiritual life.[2] Edwards's spirituality can be best under-

---

1. Recent broader studies of Edwards's understanding of experience are Whitney, *Finding God in Solitude*; Strobel, *Formed for the Glory of God*.

2. Recent studies in this area are Hastings, *Life of God*; Tan, *Fullness Received*; Strobel, *Jonathan Edwards's Theology*; Strobel, "Jonathan Edwards and the Polemics of Theosis"; Withrow, *Becoming Divine*. Hastings looks for an "overarching motif or meta-thematic center for the theology of Jonathan Edwards" (*Life of God*, 1). Strobel speaks about a "top-down" interpretation of Edwards's theology (*Jonathan Edwards's Theology*, 145, 225).

stood against the historical background of revivalism. For this reason, we will first look at the local and regional revivals in Massachusetts and then the Great Awakening. In our evaluation, we will explore the question of how the relation between faith and feeling can be understood.

## Revival in Northampton

In the years 1734 to 1735 Jonathan Edwards witnessed a local revival with regional effects. As a close observer, Edwards wrote a report of this first revival called: *A Faithful NARRATIVE of the Surprising Work of God in the CONVERSION of Many Hundred Souls in Northampton, and the Neighbouring Towns and Villages of the County of Hampshire, in the Province of the Massachusetts-Bay in New-England*.[3]

What happened at this revival? Edwards describes how people forgot all about the things of this world, which had such control over them before.[4] They seized every opportunity to be saved, and dozens and even hundreds converted in a short time.[5] There was no distinction between young or old, man or woman. Sinners became deeply convicted of their sin and of being lost, and this led to surrendering themselves to God and coming to know Christ. Those who had converted earlier also experienced a deepening of their spiritual lives. The whole city seemed to be full of the presence of God. Almost every household had people who experienced a spiritual revival. The tensions between population groups disappeared, the inn was used for religious gatherings, and the revival was especially noticeable in the church services.

It seems that rumors of a revival became a means for spreading the revival movement, or so Edwards observed in that region.[6] The reports of the local revival caused the topic of revival to be brought up elsewhere, with the result that participation in this intensification of spiritual life arose there. The title of Edwards's *Faithful Narrative* also states that the revival was a

---

3. Edwards, "A Faithful Narrative," *WJE* 4:97–211.

4. Ibid., 150–53.

5. "The work of conversion was carried on in a most astonishing manner, and increased more and more; souls did as it were come by flocks to Jesus Christ. From day to day, for many months together, might be seen evident instances of sinners brought out of darkness into marvellous light," ibid., 150. Edwards describes what is "extraordinary" in a revival in ibid., 157–59.

6. "As what other towns heard of and found in this was a great means of awakening them, so our hearing of such a swift and extraordinary propagation and extent of this work did doubtless for a time serve to uphold the work amongst us," ibid., 153, 176.

regional event. Edwards cites 23 places in his report.[7] This phenomenon also appears on a larger scale.

Edwards's work was reprinted sixty times during his lifetime, while appearing in other editions as well.[8] His *Faithful Narrative* was a model for a new religious genre, the revival report. After him, a number of reports were published with a comparable structure and content.[9] Thus, the foundation for revival was laid, and George Whitefield's evangelization tours (1714-70) were prepared. Edwards's work was therefore not only a blueprint but also a catalyst for the Great Awakening that took place from around 1740 to 1745.[10]

## Affective Religion

If we ask what the spiritual characteristic for spiritual life is, we then end up with spiritual experience. Edwards describes the spiritual breakthrough in his personal life as follows:

> The first instance, that I remember, of that sort of inward, sweet delight in God and divine things, that I have lived much in since, was on reading those words, 1 Tim. 1:17: Now unto the King eternal, immortal, invisible, the only wise God, be honour and glory forever and ever. Amen. As I read the words, there came into my soul, and was as it were diffused through it, a sense of the glory of the Divine Being: a new sense, quite different from any thing I ever experienced before. Never any words of Scripture seemed to me as these words did. I thought with myself, how excellent a Being that was, and how happy I should be, if I might enjoy that God, and be rapt up to him in heaven; and be as it were swallowed up in him forever! I kept saying, and as it were singing, over these words of Scripture to myself; and went to pray to God that I might enjoy him; and prayed in a

---

7. Goen, "Editor's Introduction," *WJE* 4: 21–25.

8. For more information and literature, see Vlastuin, *De Geest van opwekking*, 78–79.

9. Beebe's *McCulloch Examinations* has recently been published. It contains 109 reports of individual conversions.

10. Crawford, *Seasons of Grace*, 116, 120, 123–25, 164–66, 184–87. Lieburg describes the revival in Nijkerk in the international context of revivals in Lieburg, "Dutch Great Awakening," 1–19. Vlastuin describes the relation between the "Nijkerk Disturbances" (Nijkerkse beroeringen) and the revivals in Edwards's time in Vlastuin, "Nijkerk en Northampton," 59–78. Historically, it is interesting to see that the German minister Frelinghuysen witnessed revivals already before Edwards: see ibid., 61.

manner quite different from what I used to do, with a new sort of affection.[11]

Despite all his previous religious struggles, this experience was unique and incomparable because it allowed spiritual light into his dark heart. Experiential words like "sweet," "new sense," "happy," "enjoy," "rapt up," "swallowed up," and "affection" are characteristic in this account. Moreover, the words "glory" and "excellent" refer to an experienced reality.

This conception offered Edwards the chance to characterize the spiritual experience that occurred in revivals. The sudden death of a young man early in 1734 "affected" many young people.[12] When Edwards writes, just a bit further on, about the death of an older person, many are again "affected." The concept of "awakening," which Edwards used often, ultimately has to do with the fact that people are "affected" by the great things of religion and their personal participation in it.[13] Spiritual experience is interpreted from the perspective of the measure of "affections."[14]

These affections are, in the main, twofold. On the one hand, people are affected by the discoveries of the law. They become "terrified with fears" or experience "great humblings in the dust for God." They have a "sense of God's anger," a "sense of the excellency of God's justice," a "great sense of their sinfulness," or a "sense of their own helplessness." On the other hand, people are affected by the discovery of Christ in the gospel. When saved sinners speak of the discoveries of the gospel, they use words like "excellency," "gloriousness," and "sweetness."[15] Affective concepts like "delightful," "joyful," "wonderfulness," and "loveliness" occur as well.[16]

Edwards uses categories of sensory experience to interpret the spiritual life.[17] Concepts like "taste," "feel," and "see" are the most common in expressing religious reality. The use of these concepts goes back to theological reflection. In his sermon *A Divine and Supernatural Light*, preached in 1733 in Northampton, Edwards justified the use of this language.[18] He made clear that a believer has not only an "opinion" but also a "sense" of spiritual reality. The image of the taste of honey is well known: "There is

11. Edwards, "Personal Narrative," *WJE* 16:792–93.
12. Edwards, "A Faithful Narrative," *WJE* 4:147.
13. Edwards gives a general analysis of this process, ibid., 159–72.
14. Ibid., 174.
15. Edwards, "A Faithful Narrative," *WJE* 4:151–52.
16. Ibid., 171–73.
17. Ibid., 179.
18. For the sermon, see Edwards, "A Divine and Supernatural Light," *WJE* 17:405–26. See also Marsden, *Jonathan Edwards: A Life*, 156–57.

a difference between having a rational judgment that honey is sweet, and having a sense of its sweetness."[19] Thus, people can rationally conclude that God is full of glory, but through the Holy Spirit "there is a sense of the loveliness of God's holiness."[20]

His use of these categories of experience does not mean that Edwards wanted to claim that the sensory life participates in spiritual life. Rather, for him, these categories are metaphors to show how real spiritual reality is.[21] Spiritual experience is as real as sensory experience. The reality of God and Christ exists as an objective reality that the word informs us about. People can hear about it and have ideas about it, but they are convinced of the reality of through the Spirit.[22] Edwards speaks here of an immediate work of the clause: "Immediately imparted to the Soul by the Spirit of God."

This approach has consequences for the nature of spiritual life. First, it includes a deep certainty about spiritual reality. People were so convinced of spiritual reality that there could be no doubt about it.[23] Against the background of deism and the rational Enlightenment's thinking in Edwards's time, this is a striking accent.[24]

Second, this means that spiritual life is not first of all a matter of personal salvation but about knowing the glory of spiritual things.[25] People

---

19. Edwards, "A Divine and Supernatural Light," *WJE* 17:414.

20. Ibid., 413.

21. "Things now look exceeding plain to 'em, and they wonder that they did not see 'em before. They are so greatly taken with their new discovery, and things appear so plain, and so rational to 'em, that they are often at first ready to think they can convince others." Ibid., 180.

22. We could speak about the informing function of the word. With respect to the relation between word and Spirit, the following statement is important: "The notion that there is a Christ, and that Christ is holy and gracious, is conveyed to the mind by the word of God: but the sense of the excellency of Christ by reason of that holiness and grace, is nevertheless immediately the work of the Holy Spirit." Edwards, *WJE* 17:417.

23. "A true sense of the divine excellency of the things of God's Word doth more directly and immediately convince of the truth of them." Ibid., 415. Edwards also speaks on the same page of "intuitive and immediate evidence."

24. Perhaps Edwards felt the threat of deism more than Marsden thinks: Marsden, *Jonathan Edwards*, 138–39. John Erskine published Edwards's work as an "antidote to the deistical notion spreading in some parts of America," in his "Preface to Miscellaneous Observations on Important Theological Subjects," in Edwards, *Works of Jonathan Edwards* 2:459. A study of the words "deist(s)," "deism" and "deistical" produces 388 references, an indication that the problem of deism was not absent from Edwards's theology.

25. "The sweetest joy that these good people amongst us express, is not that which consists in a sense of the safety of their own state . . . The supreme attention of their

see the "excellency" of God's work of redemption, aside from the question of whether they have been saved personally. In this way, the strictly soteriological character of the Christian faith is broken open and given ontological features.

Third, this theological concept brings with it the fact that this spirituality is strongly directed at the Holy Spirit, the presence of which can be measured by the power and intensity of the spiritual experience.[26] The extent of the affection indicates the extent of the power of the Holy Spirit. Spiritual depression and spiritual tepidity are therefore characterized by weakness or the absence of spiritual experience, whereas spiritual revival is characterized by an intensification of affective religion.

This consideration leads to a fourth. It is striking that Edwards, in his description of the spiritual life, is more concerned with the affective effect of the word in us than with the participation through faith in the reality beyond us. This appears, for example, from his description of the functioning of the word in the hearts of Christians in Northampton. He does not describe this starting from the word and then proceeding to the heart, but vice versa.[27] For that matter, it seems that Edwards is very conscious of the fact that he concentrates on one aspect of faith.[28] This could mean that he assumes faith when he speaks about spiritual life. In any case, we can state that he describes spiritual life on the basis of its affective dimension and not from a perspective of the object of faith.

Fifth, in *A Divine and Supernatural Light* Edwards shows that not every affective effect is saving,[29] and this critical aspect was not or hardly present in his *Faithful Narrative*. This has to do, of course, with the nature of the latter work. Edwards wants to make a positive report of what he esteems to be a great work of the Spirit. Thus, without any reservation, he refers to

---

minds is to be the glorious excellencies of God and Christ." Edwards, "A Faithful Narrative," *WJE* 4:183.

26. "When the sense and relish of the divine excellency of these things fades, on a withdraw of the Spirit of God . . . but then at particular times, by God's help, the same sense of things revive again, like fire that lay hid in ashes. " Ibid., 180; "They for the present lose their realizing sense of those things that looked so plain to 'em, and by all that they can do they can't recover it, till God renews the influences of his Spirit." Ibid., 181.

27. Ibid., 178–79.

28. "Such a conviction of the truth of religion as this, arising . . . from a sense of the divine excellency of them, is that true spiritual conviction, that there is in saving faith." Edwards, "Divine and Supernatural Light," *WJE* 17:415.

29. Ibid., 412–13.

emotions in his sermons as signs of God's presence in the worship service.[30] For some, weeping was an expression of remorse and dread, for others one of joy and love, whereas there were also congregation members who used it to express their concern for those who did not convert. The result of this unqualified approach to emotions had effect, because precisely this work functioned as a catalyst for revival.

## Critique of Affective Religion

It is primarily the emotional aspects of the Great Awakening that led to criticism of this movement. James Davenport (1716–57), in particular, should be mentioned here.[31] Appealing to the guidance of the Holy Spirit, he ceased to engage in any kind of sermon preparation, doing everything he could to call up emotions among his audience. For him, the emotions were more important than understanding the message. There were also other extreme aspects in his work. He claimed to have special revelations. In his view, most preachers lacked grace in their souls, and he showed no hesitation in naming names. This sowed a spirit of separatism, which discredited the revival movement.

After Davenport had sowed unrest among the staff and students at Yale University in New Haven, Edwards gave the opening speech for the new school year. Those in charge at the university hoped he would provide a critique of the revival movement as such, but he did not. He distanced himself from the extreme aspects of revival and warned strongly against the spirit of judgment, but defended revival as a work of the Spirit. He also criticized opponents of the revival and reproached them for being too lukewarm regarding the progress of God's work. We no longer have the text of this speech, but we do have his further elaboration of it called *The Distinguishing Marks of a Work of the Spirit of God*.[32]

Edwards's positive approach to the revival movement reinforced the criticism. In 1742 *The wonderful Narrative: or, a Faithful Account of the French Prophets, their Agitations, Ecstacies, and Inspirations* was

---

30. Edwards, "A Faithful Narrative," *WJE* 4:151. In ibid., 75, Edwards says that there is "loud weeping" and "crying out with a loud voice."

31. See Marsden, *Jonathan Edwards*, 232–33; Vlastuin, *De Geest van opwekking*, 112–14, also for other literature. The emotions evoked resistance in Nijkerk as well: Lieburg, "Interpreting the Dutch Great Awakening," 4.

32. Edwards, "The Distinguishing Marks," *WJE* 4:213–88. See also Vlastuin , *De Geest van opwekking*, 123–28.

published.³³ It is clear that the Great Awakening was thus becoming subject to fierce criticism. Other writings and pamphlets appeared against the Great Awakening, against Whitefield, and against Edwards. Edwards responded to this with his *Some Thoughts Concerning the present Revival of Religion in New-England*.³⁴

A striking detail in this book is the description of the spiritual ecstasy of Edwards's wife Sarah.³⁵ On 20 January 1742, she entered a state of spiritual ecstasy that lasted more than two weeks in which she was regularly overwhelmed by the "unspeakable joys of the upper world." She experienced a night she called a "heavenly elysium" in which she "float[ed] or [swam], in these bright, sweet beams of the love of Christ." For Edwards, this was an example of piety, and he made clear that this was not a matter of fanaticism.³⁶

Nonetheless, Edward took a nuanced point of view in this book, and self-criticism was more strongly present here than in *Distinguishing Marks*. The largest part of *Some Thoughts* explores the dangers among the proponents of revival. It appears that Edwards saw a greater danger for the revival movement in the work of overly spiritual preachers than in the criticism of non-spiritual opponents.

Charles Chauncy (1705-87) from Boston responded publicly to this work by Edwards in his *Seasonable Thoughts on the State of Religion in New England*.³⁷ Initially, Chauncy was favorably inclined toward the spiritual movement, but when he looked more closely, he was overtaken by shock and rejection. He saw that many were misled by their emotions and he wanted to sound the alarm about the visions, physical effects, the normalizing of ecstatic states, and the mass hysteria he witnessed.

Chauncy discussed a number of aspects of revivalism in *Seasonable Thoughts*. Most pertinent here is his in-depth analysis that all emphasis in the Great Awakening lay on the immediate work of the Spirit. This promotes, on the one hand, an antinomian disposition whereby living by experiences and emotions takes precedence over serving God with zeal.³⁸

---

33. Chauncy is generally seen as the author. The book was published in Boston. In 2009 Kessinger Publishing's Rare Reprints in Whitefish, Montana published a reprint.

34. Edwards, "Some Thoughts concerning the Revival," *WJE* 4:289-530. See also Vlastuin, *De Geest van opwekking*, 128-38.

35. Edwards, "Some Thoughts concerning the Revival," *WJE* 4:331-41.

36. "Now if such things are enthusiasm, and the fruits of a distempered brain, let my brain be evermore possessed of that happy distemper." Ibid., 341.

37. Chauncy, *Seasonable Thoughts*. For the historical context, see Vlastuin, *De Geest van opwekking*, 138-45; Marsden, *Jonathan Edwards*, 268-90.

38. Chauncy saw the antinomianism of Anne Hutchinson (1591-1642) in the seventeenth century in Massachusetts in the revival movement. On this, see Winship,

Referring to Whitefield's journal, he shows that people allow themselves too much to be led by impulses they think are the inspiration of the Spirit. The emphasis on the Holy Spirit leads, on the other hand, to a contempt of external means: the liturgy in the service, the whole of the church order, and the offices of the church. Chauncy critiques, primarily, the habit of judging the spiritual state of others.

Because of these aspects, Chauncy felt compelled to take up the fight against these deviations from the true religion. According to him, the New Testament prohibits disarray and sectarianism. When Edwards expressed the expectation in *Some Thoughts* that the Great Awakening was perhaps the beginning of the millennium, this gave his contemporary every reason to defend the use of the existing order and to resist this "New Light."

It is not simply a straightforward matter to interpret Chauncy's critique of the revival as that of a defender of the "Old Light." The Erskine brothers recognized themselves in Chauncy's critique.[39] Other Presbyterian theologians also joined him.[40] Chauncy cannot simply be seen as someone who was opposed to the pietistic character of religion. In his writing, he not only defended using the Puritan church order but also appealed in a spiritual way to Puritans like Baxter, Flavel, Guthrie, Owen, and Shepard. Just like Edwards, he emphasized the necessity of spiritual rebirth, in which the "heartfelt experience" was central.[41] This emphasis on personal rebirth is found within the framework of the idea of two ways to eternity and, for that reason he also calls people to examine themselves. At the same time, he writes at the high point of the Great Awakening of the low level of religion.

What is going on here theologically? What does the fundamental difference in insight between Edwards and Chauncy hinge on? Both theologians wanted to follow the Puritan tradition, both opposed the idea of lay preachers, both pointed to extremes in revivalism—and yet they were diametrically opposed to each other with respect to their fundamental attitude to the Great Awakening. What Edwards saw as chaff among the grain, Chauncy saw as the essence of the revival movement.

If we look at this more closely, then it is apparent that it has to do with the nature of the character of the work of the Holy Spirit. For Chauncy, it is fundamental that the work of the Spirit begins with enlightening the understanding. This is an anthropological issue in which the human understanding ranks above the abilities of the human spirit, whereas the will

*The Times and Trials of Anne Hutchinson.*
  39. According to Crawford, *Seasons of Grace*, 167–74.
  40. Hodge, *Constitutional History*.
  41. See Chauncy *New Creature*.

and the affections determine the second and third levels respectively.[42] The work of the Spirit does not have to do, therefore, with "raised affections," but an "enlightened mind."[43] This makes clear that fervor and passion were not at all important for him as instruments for judging the work of the Spirit. The work of the Spirit is characterized primarily by reasonableness and not by passion. Thus, it is understandable why Chauncy argued for a more gradual rebirth, in contrast to the revivalist piety, which was characterized much more by the emphasis on the immediately experienced power of the Holy Spirit.

## The Defense of Affective Religion

Edwards felt compelled to give a theological interpretation of true religion. In 1743 he gave a series of sermons in the congregation at Northampton, which resulted in 1746 in the publication of *A Treatise concerning Religious Affections*.[44] The work consists of three main parts. In the first part Edwards grounds the affective character of the Christian religion. The basic lines we see in *Divine and Supernatural Light* and in *Faithful Narrative* are worked out further here. Edwards thus emphasizes that the greater part of the Christian religion consists of affections.[45] He supports his argument by a number of Scripture references. He thus refers to affective words like "fear," "hope," "joy," "sadness," "zeal," and "mercy" in the book of the Psalms. He finds an affective dimension in Jesus' disposition. Moreover, heavenly life can be interpreted in an affective way. The flipside is that a hard heart is characterized by the absence of affections. In the context of his situation, it probably came across quite sharply when he states that opponents of affective religion themselves probably did not know the power of religion.

Just like Chauncy, Edwards's approach has to do with his anthropology. Whereas Chauncy, a defender of intellectualism, gives the understanding pride of place in the hierarchical order of the soul's abilities, Edwards places the understanding and the will on the same level. Marsden calls Edwards a voluntarist.[46] It can be asked if that can be stated with no further qualification since Edwards does not say that the will is the primary ability of the soul. Rather, he also claims that reason is the "noblest" or "highest"

---

42. Chauncy, *Enthusiasm Described*, 18–26.
43. Chauncy, *Seasonable Thoughts*, 327.
44. Edwards, *WJE* 2. For a discussion of the content see Vlastuin, *De Geest van opwekking*, 145–60.
45. Edwards, *Religious Affections*, *WJE* 2:99–119.
46. Marsden, *Jonathan Edwards*, 282–83.

of the soul's ability.[47] In fact, Edwards rejects the dichotomy between the understanding and the will because they are both aspects of the one heart.[48]

With respect to Chauncy, he does lay much more emphasis on the will, and thus, in a relative sense, he is a voluntarist. In addition, in Edwards's understanding, the affections are an aspect of the will. This entails a major shift with respect to Chauncy. Instead of the affective dimension being secondary, it is fundamental to the work of the Holy Spirit, according to Edwards. The affective dimension of the spirituality is not under the control of the will but under that of the Spirit. Therefore, there is no work of the Spirit that is not affective, but the spiritual life always touches the affective dimension in the person.[49] It could be said that the affections indicate the orientation of the heart.

The affective dimension of personality is, at bottom, determined by the Spirit. Edwards does not only speak of the work of the Holy Spirit, but, following people like John Owen, he emphasizes the indwelling of the Spirit.[50] Given that the indwelling of the Spirit is characterized by love, the Christian life is about love.[51]

Edwards thus has a theological conception in hand to deal with the confusion regarding the Great Awakening. In the first place, this conception justifies the affective character of the Christian life, so that Edwards can completely defend the attention paid to spiritual experience in the Great Awakening.

In line with this, he can also give a place to physical effects. If the soul can be powerfully touched by the spiritual reality of God, it is—given the unity of body and spirit—not at all amazing that people are physically overcome. For Edwards, therefore, the physical effects are not essential to

---

47. Edwards, 'Charity and its Fruits,' *WJE* 8:277 and 'The Pure in Heart Blessed,' *WJE* 17:67. In a discussion of faith, the important function proves to be the understanding.

48. Edwards, *Religious Affections*, *WJE* 2:95–99. "Nor can there be a clear distinction made between the two faculties of understanding and will, as acting distinctly and separately" (ibid., 272). Hutch speaks in this connection of a "holistic view of the human personality," in Hutch, "Edwards' Analysis of Religious Experience," 125.

49. See Smith, "The Perennial Jonathan Edwards," 3. See also Lee, "Edwards on God and Nature: Resources for Contemporary Theology," 17. According to McClymond, *Encounters with God*, vi, Edwards, by the concept of "affection," gives an answer to the Enlightenment and he goes beyond the opposition between feeling and reason.

50. Owen, *Works of John Owen* 11:330–36. On this see also Kay, *Trinitarian Spirituality*, 175–78.

51. "The Scriptures do represent true religion, as being summarily comprehended in love, the chief of the affections, and fountain of all other affections." Edwards, *Religious Affections*, *WJE* 2:106.

interpreting the spiritual character of the Great Awakening. Just as feelings are secondary for Chauncy, so the physical effects are secondary for Edwards. They can figure more or they can figure less, depending on one's personal constitution.

Third, Edwards can clarify emotional deviations on the basis of his understanding. He distinguishes between "affection" and "passion."[52] "Passion" has to do with a superficial touching of the emotions that is not rooted in the heart. If the heart is touched by the Holy Spirit, both the understanding and the will are affected. If there are emotions without the enlightenment of the understanding, then the affections here are not hallowed ones. Here we can use the metaphor of fire to do justice to Edwards. Just as fire gives both light and warmth, so the work of the Spirit is characterized by "light" in the understanding and "warmth" in the heart.

This leads to the fourth consideration, namely, that Edwards agrees with Chauncy in his great appreciation for the understanding and for knowledge. Edwards's own life shows that rational reflection on the Christian faith is of the greatest importance for him.[53] He also wrote a treatment of *Christian Knowledge* in which he defends the importance and advantage of a fundamental knowledge of doctrine.[54] He emphasizes the necessity of a thorough knowledge of doctrine.[55] This means that his argument for an affective religion cannot be used to downgrade the intellectual aspect of Christian faith.[56]

Affection should always be a reasonable affection, just as love is not unacquainted with the object of love. Emotions in preaching should be called up by the content of the message and not by the emotions of the preacher. Here Edwards therefore also rejects the emotional tendencies in

52. Edwards, *Religious Affections*, WJE 2:98. For that matter, Edwards also uses the word "affection" here. The use of the word "emotion" as a synonym for "affection" is unfortunate, because emotion can have a much more superficial meaning than "affection."

53. Gerstner reconstructed a theology of Edwards called *The Rational Biblical Theology of Jonathan Edwards*.

54. Edwards, "Christian Knowledge," in *The Works of Jonathan Edwards* 2:157–63. These ideas are why Schröder interprets Edwards's theology as a "Plädoyer für die Vernunft des Glaubens"—translated "Argument for the rationality of faith" (*Glaubenswahrnehmung und Selbsterkenntnis*, 48).

55. Edwards, WJE 7:374, 570; "Narrative of the Communion Controversy," WJE 12:613; "To the Reverend Peter Clark," WJE 16:344; "Thorough Knowledge of Divine Truth," WJE 22:97, 101; "Farewell Sermon," WJE 25:490.

56. It is thus incomprehensible why some researchers hold that emotion is more important than the understanding in Edwards, such as Winslow, *Jonathan Edwards*, 216, or Miller, *Jonathan Edwards*, 184.

revivalism whereby emotion is an end in itself and the understanding is placed in opposition to the influence of the Spirit.

For that matter, it should be remarked here that Edwards provides some support for the revivalist extremists through his insight that there is a connection between the affections and the means of grace. The means of grace are, namely, directed at the promotion of the affective dimensions of religion.[57] Here Edwards is thinking of hymns, preaching, and the sacraments. This perspective offers some relativization with respect to his conviction that an affection is always reasonable in nature and is determined and processed by the content of the message.

## The Qualification of the Spiritual Affections

Fifth, Edwards's view of the affective will as determined by love offers a conception for qualifying the spiritual affections more closely.[58] In the second part of *Religious Affections* Edwards mentions twelve experiences or feelings that cannot be called spiritual,[59] in which he employs acute psychological insight into the obstinacy and complexity of the human spirit in order to distinguish between the human spirit and the mystery of the Holy Spirit. He lists the intensity of the emotions first. Second, he states that the effects on the body are not proof for or against grace. Third, he proposes that the candor that accompanies an experience is not determinative of its spiritual character; fourth, that the inexplicability of our emotions is not proof of the mystery of the Holy Spirit; fifth, the fact that we are addressed by a text from the Bible is even less decisive; and, sixth, that even the phenomena of love can be deceptive—Edwards mentions in this connection the people round Jesus who call out "Hosanna."

The seventh phenomenon that Edwards lists is the combination of various kinds of feelings. Although Edwards is a proponent of the sequence of law and gospel, he asserts that the comfort we feel after fear and unrest does not prove that the Holy Spirit is active in us. Nor are fervor and zeal definitive signs that prove their "Spirit-ual" origin. This also obtains for praise. The strong certainty people can have sometimes that they are a child of God is not a compelling sign that someone is not a hypocrite—because hypocrites can be strong in their faith. Finally, the fact that a certain person's testimony touches other Christians is not a proof of grace either.

57. Edwards, *Religious Affections*, WJE 2:114–16.

58. It came up incidentally in "A Faithful Narrative" that "affections" should be distinguished. Edwards, WJE 4:176.

59. Edwards, *Religious Affections*, WJE 2:125–90.

In the third part of *Religious Affections*, Edwards shows what is characteristic of the spiritual nature of affections.[60] The first is actually not a description but an explanation in which Edwards emphasizes that God's Spirit is its source. The second is that spiritual affections are directed to the glory of God and Christ and not primarily at one's own interest. Here, the principle that love does not seek its own is operative. Third, spiritual affections are directed to the glory of God's moral properties, such as his justice, truth, faithfulness, and goodness, summed up in his holiness. Fourth, Edwards points out that people are not only convinced by the Holy Spirit of spiritual things but also see their glory. The Spirit does not give a new intellectual knowledge, but their existing intellectual knowledge is given a new dimension because the light of God shines over it. Translated into contemporary language: two people can see the same thing, but the one has a feeling for beauty and the other not.

Fifth, spiritual affection is effective and certainly is so in us. Edwards subsequently emphasizes that spiritual affections arise from humility. He lays his finger on the problem of spiritual pride with acuity. A proud person thinks highly of his humility, but the humble person thinks highly of God and is therefore sensitive to a proud disposition. This essential characteristic of a believer is missing in those who consider themselves more spiritual than another. If the humility is foundational, it is accompanied, sixth, by a total transformation of our personality. That is why he can subsequently remark, seventh, that a Christian shows the mind of Christ in love, humility, and a disposition to forgive. This obtains, eighth, in particular for gentleness. Ninth, this revival theologian remarks that the affections of a true Christian show a balance. The tenth feature is also very important. False spiritual affections are accompanied by self-satisfaction, whereas true affection is characterized by an unquenchable thirst for God. The true believer is satisfied by God but never has enough of God. The hypocrite is satisfied to be saved, but the believer desires deeper knowledge and deeper worship of God. Affection is thus passion for God. Finally, the theologian who emphasizes the affection of the heart indicates that the most important feature of the indwelling of God's Spirit consists in its effectiveness, namely, the Christian way of life.

## The Relation between Feeling and Faith

Until now we have primarily dealt with how Edwards thinks about feeling. We should qualify the word "feeling." If "feeling" is understood as "affection

---

60. Edwards, *Religious Affections*, WJE 2:191–461.

of the heart" then Edwards is a theologian who was busy his whole life to underscore the importance of "feeling," to define it and elaborate on it. At the same time he distinguishes between the true affection of "sensitivity" or emotion.

How is this approach related to his view of faith? It is telling that Edwards does not raise this question explicitly in his works on spiritual experience. This indicates that he did not see this as a problem. We must therefore reconstruct Edwards's view from the whole of Edwards's works; to do so, we will consult his discussion of faith.[61]

Various ideas in Edwards's discussion on faith mention faith as an endorsement of the truth and reliability of a testimony. A number of expressions show that faith cannot be reduced to an intellectual matter but that all abilities of the soul are involved in it. If, in connection with the present study, we explore the relation between faith and affection, we will find that faith as such is affective in nature. Already in the third section of this discussion, Edwards speaks about faith as a "sense of glory and excellency."[62] In faith there is "a sense of the sufficiency and the reality of Christ's righteousness, and of his power and grace to save."[63] Edwards also uses other sensory expressions, such as faith is a "spiritual taste and relish of what is excellent and divine." Affection is therefore inseparably connected with faith.[64]

This affective dimension of faith becomes even clearer if we ask where the affection of the heart is directed. We could also ask ourselves what precisely the "excellency" of Christ is. In section 39 we read that holiness is the

---

61. Edwards, *Works of Jonathan Edwards* 2:578–96.

62. Ibid., 578. See also section 25: "The adhering to it, and acquiescing in it with the inclination and affection, is from the goodness and excellency of the thing revealed." See also section 32.

63. The following remark from Edwards displays a tension with his belief that the spiritual affection is without self-interest: "The Lord Jesus Christ, in the gospel, appears principally under the character of a Saviour, and not so much of a person absolutely excellent; and therefore, the proper act of reception of him, consists principally in the exercise of a sense of our need of him, and of his sufficiency, his ability, his mercy and love. . . . " (ibid., 581). This can be sensed also in section 37: "For there is implied in believing in Christ . . . that which arises from the consideration of his relation to us, and of our concern in him, his being a Saviour for such as we are; for sinful men; and a Saviour that is offered with his benefits to us" (ibid., 582). See also section 70: "To come to him for his benefits, to come for deliverance from calamity and misery, to come for safety, to come for rest, to come to eat and drink; an invitation to come into his house, to a feast" (ibid., 587).

64. "Trusting is . . . an extensive expression, comprehending many dispositions, affections, and exercises of heart." Ibid., 585.

summary of the eternal life that Christ has acquired.[65] By way of explanation Edwards immediately adds that it is "holy happiness" and that the faith is directed at this happiness in Christ. If faith shares in happiness in Christ, faith must then be an experience of this happiness.

His statement that love is the source of faith and that love is included in faith is striking.[66] Love has an unquenchable desire for the beloved.[67] In the twenty-second section Edwards expresses this through his explanation that believing is thirsting for the waters of life because of a "sense of the ability and sufficiency of Christ to save."[68]

This exploration shows that, for Edwards, faith cannot be reduced to the intellect. Rather, the will participates fully in faith, and, as a result, it is impossible to separate faith from affective love. This means that faith, as such, is affective in nature. This coheres, of course, with his anthropology, in which understanding and will can be equally appreciated. Therefore, spiritual knowledge goes together with "the disposition or will,"[69] so that faith and affection can also be used indiscriminately,[70] without these concepts being identified with each other.

## Evaluation

Having seen how Edwards deals with spiritual affection in two historical situations and having examined this in light of his concept of faith, we may now evaluate the relation between faith and feeling in his theology.

---

65. Ibid., 583.

66. "Love either is what Faith arises from, or is included in faith." Ibid., 579. "That a saving belief of truth arises from love, or a holy disposition and relish of heart." Ibid., 585. In section 57 we read: "That saving Faith implies in its nature divine love" (ibid., 586). Section 74 also takes this up: "That love belongs to the essence of saving faith" (ibid., 588). The title of a sermon also has a similar tenor: "Saving Faith and Christian Obedience Arise From Godly Love," (Edwards, *WJE* 25:494–536).

67. See also the remark in Edwards, *The Works of Jonathan Edwards* 2:580: "If it were conversant about a person only, it would be more properly called loving."

68. God reveals himself in the gospel in "his sufficiency and mercy for us, as needing, empty, helpless; and of his grace and mercy to us, as unworthy and miserable." Ibid., 586.

69. Ibid., 589. "There is, in the nature and essence of saving faith, a receiving of the object of faith, not only in the assent of the judgment, but with the heart, or with the inclination and will of the soul? . . . [F]or virtue has its special and immediate seat in the will." Ibid., 594–95 (section 88). Therefore faith cannot only be "a mere assent to the doctrines of the gospel," for that is "common to saints and sinners . . . they do judge that the doctrine is true, as the devils do." Ibid., 591–92 (section 88).

70. Edwards, "A Faithful Narrative," *WJE* 4:173.

First, in Edwards's theology, affection forms the heart of spiritual life. True religion consists in spiritual affection. Moreover, the degree of affection is also an indication of the degree of religion in the heart, so that spiritual affection becomes a gauge for the intensity of the spiritual life.

Second, Edwards's view of affective religion is closely connected with his anthropology, in which the affections are included with the will; the understanding and the will can be seen in a holistic cohesion. This characterization of the affections offers, on the one hand, the possibility of distinguishing the appearance of superficial emotion from the actuality of deep affections and, on the other, the ability to keep spiritual knowledge and spiritual affection together.

Third, there is a correlation between the relation of faith and feeling on the one hand and the relation between Christ and the Spirit on the other. Without denying the spiritual unity with Christ, Edwards emphasizes pneumatology,[71] characterized by personal application.[72] This implies that every concept of Edwards's doctrine of participation has to respect this personal character in his theology. The accent on the transforming aspect of the personal indwelling Spirit and the distinction between true and false affections demand that this personal dimension is recognizable in a current interpretation of Edwards's doctrine of participation.[73] The fact that his pneumatology is also characterized by the indwelling of the Spirit qualifies the concept of participation in such a way that participation is not only directed beyond the believer, but also inward, which gives his doctrine of participation a strong anthropological accent.

Fourth, the question of how Edwards's theology of the spiritual life is related to his own preaching merits study. In what sense is his preaching directed at the intellect and in what sense at the will? The question of whether this affective spirituality goes back to the spirituality of the early church is especially fascinating.[74] In this context, it can be asked whether

71. Compare Hastings, *Life of God*, 4, 7, 34, 272-97, and chapter 4.

72. Hastings "blames" Edwards for the lack of a universal doctrine of justification. He speaks about anthropocentrism, individualism, and introspection (ibid., 350-53, 368). Edwards's pneumatology cannot be transformed in a universal pneumatology without subverting the complete structure of Edwards's theology. It seems to me that Strobel respects this structure of personal salvation in Edwards's theology (*Jonathan Edwards's Theology*, 166-67, 227), as does Tan, *Fullness Received*, chapter 6.

73. While outside the scope of this chapter, Edwards's concept of the church underlines the personal character of his theology. See Bezzant, *Jonathan Edwards and the Church*, 259.

74. "In summary, the High Middle Ages in the West were characterized by growing divisions within theology and the gradual separation of spirituality from theology .... It was, at heart, a division between the affective side of Faith (or participation) and

Edwards offers a (conscious) correction on the more rational approach of the Reformation.[75] If we compare Edwards's approach with Brad Gregory's analysis of the fragmentation of religion, morality, science, ethics, economy, and society since the era of the Reformation,[76] it is striking that we find in Edwards an appeal for a holistic approach. Or have the roots of Edwards's affective spirituality a background in the Romantics?[77] Either way, the challenge is to search Edwards's approach against the background of the developments in culture.

## Bibliography

Beebe, Keith Edward. *The McCulloch Examinations of the Cambuslang Revival (1742): A Critical Edition*. 2 vols. Scottish History Society. Woodbridge: Boydell & Brewer, 2013.

Bezzant, Rhys S. *Jonathan Edwards and the Church*. Oxford: Oxford University Press, 2013.

Boersma, Hans. *Heavenly Participation. The Weaving of a Sacramental Tapestry*. Grand Rapids: Eerdmans, 2011.

Chauncy, Charles. *Enthusiasm Described and Cautioned Against*. Boston: J. Draper, S. Eliot, J. Blanchard, 1742.

———. *The New Creature; Describ'd and consider'd as the sure Characteristick of a Man's being in Christ*. Boston: G. Rogers, J. Edwards, S. Eliot, 1741.

———. *Seasonable Thoughts on the State of Religion in New England*. Boston: Rogers and Fowle, for Samuel Eliot, 1743.

Crawford, Michael. *Seasons of Grace. Colonial New England's Revival Tradition in Its British Context*. New York: Oxford University Press, 1991.

Edwards, Jonathan. "Charity and its Fruits." In *Ethical Writings*, edited by Paul Ramsay, The Works of Jonathan Edwards 8:123–397. New Haven: Yale University Press, 1989.

———. "The Distinguishing Marks." In *The Great Awakening*, edited by Clarence C. Goen, The Works of Jonathan Edwards 4:213–88. New Haven: Yale University Press, 1972.

———. "A Divine and Supernatural Light." In *Sermons and Discourses, 1730–1733*, edited by Mark Valeri, The Works of Jonathan Edwards 17:405–26. New Haven and London: Yale University Press, 1999.

———. "A Faithful Narrative." In *The Great Awakening*, edited by Clarence C. Goen, The Works of Jonathan Edwards 4:97–211. New Haven: Yale University Press, 1972.

———. "A Farewell Sermon Preached at the First Precinct in Northampton, after the People's Public Rejection of their Minister . . . on June 22, 1750." In *Sermons and*

---

conceptual knowledge," Sheldrake, *Spirituality and Theology*, 43.

75. Boersma, *Heavenly Participation*, 52–83.
76. Gregory, *Unintended Reformation*.
77. Sturkenboom, *Spectators*.

*Discourses, 1743–1758*, edited by Wilson H. Kimnach, The Works of Jonathan Edwards 25:457–93. New Haven: Yale University Press, 2006.

———. "The Importance and Advantage of a Thorough Knowledge of Divine Truth." In *Sermons and Discourses, 1739–1742*, edited by Harry S. Stout et al., The Works of Jonathan Edwards 22:80–102. New Haven: Yale University Press, 2003.

———. "Narrative of Communion Controversy." In *Ecclesiastical Writings*, edited by David D. Hall, The Works of Jonathan Edwards 12:507–619. New Haven Yale University Press, 1994.

———. "Personal Narrative." In *Letters and Personal Writings*, edited by George S. Claghorn, The Works of Jonathan Edwards 16:790–804. New Haven: Yale University Press, 1998.

———. "The Pure in Heart Blessed." In *Sermons and Discourses, 1730–1733*, edited by Mark Valeri, The Works of Jonathan Edwards 17:57–86. New Haven: Yale University Press, 1999.

———. *Religious Affections*. The Works of Jonathan Edwards 2. Edited by John E. Smith. New Haven: Yale University Press, 1969.

———. "Saving Faith and Christian Obedience Arise from Godly Love." In *Sermons and Discourses, 1743–1758*, edited by Wilson H. Kimnach, The Works of Jonathan Edwards 25:494–35. New Haven: Yale University Press, 2006.

———. "Some Thoughts concerning the Revival." In *The Great Awakening*, edited by Clarence C. Goen, The Works of Jonathan Edwards 4:289–530. New Haven: Yale University Press, 1972.

———. "To the Reverend Peter Clark." In *Letters and Personal Writings*, edited by George S. Claghorn, The Works of Jonathan Edwards 16:341–47. New Haven: Yale University Press, 1998.

Erskine, John. "Preface to Miscellaneous Observations on Important Theological Subjects." In *The Works of Jonathan Edwards, A.M.* by Jonathan Edwards, 2 vols, revised and edited by Edward Hickman, 459. Edinburgh: Banner of Truth Trust, 1974.

Gerstner, John H. *The Rational Biblical Theology of Jonathan Edwards*. 3 vols. Powhatan: Berea Publications, 1992.

Gregory, Brad Stephan. *The Unintended Reformation: How a Religious Revolution Secularized Society*. Cambridge: Belknap Press of Harvard University, 2012.

Hastings, William Ross. *Jonathan Edwards and the Life of God: Toward an Evangelical Theology of Participation*. Minneapolis: Fortress Press, 2015.

Hodge, Charles. *The Constitutional History of the Presbyterian Church*. Philadelphia: W. S. Martien, 1851.

Hutch, Richard A. "Edwards' Analysis of Religious Experience." *Journal of Psychology and Theology* 6/2 (1978) 123–31.

Kay, Brian K. *Trinitarian Spirituality. John Owen and the Doctrine of God in Western Devotion*. Bletchley: Paternoster, 2007.

Lee, Sang Hyun. "Edwards on God and Nature: Resources for Contemporary Theology." In *Edwards in Our Time. Jonathan Edwards and the Shaping of American Religion*, edited by Sang Hyun Lee and Allen C. Guelzo. Grand Rapids: Eerdmans, 1999.

Lieburg, Fred van. "Interpreting the Dutch Great Awakening (1749–1755)." *Church History* 77/2 (2008) 1–19.

Marsden, George M. *Jonathan Edwards: A Life*. New Haven: Yale University Press 2003.

McClymond, Michael J. *Encounters with God: An Approach to the theology of Jonathan Edwards.* New York: Oxford University Press 1998.
Miller, Perry. *Jonathan Edwards.* New York: William Morrow, 1949.
Owen, John. *The Works of John Owen.* Edited by William H. Goold. 16 vols. London: Johnstone & Hunter, 1853.
Schröder, Caroline. *Glaubenswahrnehmung und Selbsterkenntnis. Jonathan Edwards' theologia experimentalis.* Göttingen: Vandenhoeck und Ruprecht 1998.
Sheldrake, Philip. *Spirituality and Theology: Christian Living and the Doctrine of God.* London: Darton Longman & Todd, 2011.
Smith, John E. "The Perennial Jonathan Edwards." In *Edwards in Our Time. Jonathan Edwards and the Shaping of American Religion,* edited by Sang Hyun Lee and Allen C. Guelzo. Grand Rapids: Eerdmans 1999.
Strobel, Kyle C. *Jonathan Edwards's Theology: A Reinterpretation.* London: Bloomsbury T. & T. Clark, 2013.
———. "Jonathan Edwards and the Polemics of Theosis." *Harvard Theological Review* 105:3 (July 2012):259–79.
———. *Formed for the Glory of God. Learning from the Spiritual Practices of Jonathan Edwards.* Downers Grove, IL: InterVarsity, 2013.
Sturkenboom, D. *Spectators van de hartstocht. Sekse en emotionele cultuur in de achttiende eeuw.* Hilversum: Verloren, 1998.
Tan, Seng Kong. *Fullness Received and Returned: Trinity and Participation in Jonathan Edwards.* Minneapolis, MN: Fortress Press, 2014.
Vlastuin, Willem van. *De Geest van opwekking. Een onderzoek naar de leer van de Heilige Geest in de opwekkingstheologie van Jonathan Edwards (1703–1758).* Heerenveen: Groen, 2001.
———. "Nijkerk en Northampton." In *Een golf van beroering. De omstreden religieuze opwekking in Nederland in het midden van de achttiende eeuw,* edited by J. Spaans, 59–78. Hilversum: Verloren, 2001.
Whitney, Donald S. *Finding God in Solitude: The Personal Piety of Jonathan Edwards (1703–1758) and Its Influence on His Pastoral Ministry.* New York: Peter Lang, 2014.
Winship, Michael Paul. *The Times and Trials of Anne Hutchinson.* Lawrence, KS: University Press of Kansas, 2005.
Withrow, Brandon. *Becoming Divine: Jonathan Edwards's Incarnational Spirituality Within the Christian Tradition.* Eugene, OR: Cascade Books, 2011.

# 12

# A Re-Formed Understanding of Imputation in Jonathan Edwards's *Original Sin*

## Heber Campos, Jr.

THE EXTENT TO WHICH Jonathan Edwards could be described as "Reformed" is an issue that has been addressed frequently in recent scholarship, but it has a long history of discussion.[1] Such a debate has not been easily resolved for at least two reasons. First, scholars have demonstrated not to have a common definition of "Reformed" or "Calvinist." The terms been used in very different ways by Jonathan Edwards's analysts; furthermore, any attempt to quantify what is necessary in order to be considered Reformed is very subjective. Second, because Edwards both appreciates the Reformed tradition from which he is coming as well as has no fear to explore new grounds. George Marsden says that Edwards can be "simultaneously a strict conservative and an innovator" as he makes the Reformed tradition "intellectually viable in the Enlightenment era."[2] In fact, the mixture of old elements of theology with new language and philosophical undergirdings makes Edwards difficult to pinpoint.

   1. See Minkema, "A 'Dordtian Philosophe,'" 241–53; Muller, "Jonathan Edwards and the Absence of Free Choice," 3–22; Helm, "Jonathan Edwards and the Parting of the Ways?" 42–60; "A Different Kind of Calvinism?" 91–103.

   2. Marsden, *Jonathan Edwards: A Life*, 458. Minkema showed how being of "Calvinistic" principles but theologically "original" was admitted by Edwards himself and noted by his first biographer, Samuel Hopkins. Minkema, "A 'Dordtian Philosophe,'" 241–42.

The imputation of Adam's sin to his posterity is one of those topics where Jonathan Edwards is often questioned in his Reformed orthodoxy. Oliver Crisp surveys different interpretations of Jonathan Edwards's hamartiology before he comes up with his innovative read of the New Englander. The thesis of his article is that previous interpreters read Edwards as being either part of the Augustinian realist camp or the Calvinist federalist camp, but instead Edwards draws the notion of real union from the first position and the representational aspect of the second group in order to propose a new (via media) theory of imputation.[3] Realism teaches that God created a generic human nature, one numeric identity, which over the years divided itself into many distinct individuals. Since Adam encompasses the whole of humanity, his sin is in fact everybody's sin (thus, the term "realism"). Federalism, on the other hand, defends Adam in legal solidarity with the human race and, thus, his actions are representative of his posterity. Hence, his sin as our representative brings upon humanity guilt and consequent condemnation.

Among the interpreters of Jonathan Edwards surveyed by Crisp are the Presbyterian theologians who split in their understanding of him. On the one hand, Charles Hodge and William Cunningham read Edwards as a solid federalist most of the time, but one who shows himself to be a realist in the explanation of how Adam and his progeny are united.[4] They also take Edwards to have drawn from Stapfer a kind of mediate imputation. This teaching goes back to the seventeenth-century Saumur professor, Josué de la Place, who expounded that guilt is imputed to the human race by virtue of its own depravity inherited in Adam through natural generation (guilt coming through personal corruption); the human race is not born depraved for being guilty in Adam, but is considered guilty for its own depravity.[5]

---

3. Crisp, "Theological Pedigree," 308–27.

4. Hodge believes Edwards follows Placaeus (Josué de la Place) when he uses the phrase "that the evil disposition is first, and the charge of guilt consequent," but he mainly teaches a doctrine of immediate imputation and comes up with "an abstruse metaphysical discussion on the nature of oneness or identity" between Adam and his progeny (*Systematic Theology* 2:207–8). Similarly, Cunningham believes that Edwards's perspectives "do not seem to have been clear or consistent" (*The Reformers and the Theology of the Reformation*, 384). Holbrook apparently places Edwards in a sort of realism, when he compares him with Anselm and Aquinas's corrupt nature passing on from Adam to his descendants (*WJE* 3:58, footnote 8). Randall Otto also argues for a realist view in Edwards's explanation of the transmission of Adam's sin ("The Solidarity of Mankind," 205–21).

5. Macleod summarizes the difference between mediate and immediate imputation as such: "*Immediate* imputation meant that the guilt of chewing the forbidden fruit was imputed to Adam's descendants on the grounds, simply, that they are 'sons

On the other end of the spectrum, B. B. Warfield and John Murray deny that Edwards portrays mediate imputation.[6] They believe he is a consistent proponent of traditional Reformed federalism. Oliver Crisp sees Murray's discussion as insightful, but he believes that Edwards finds the federalist defense of God's justice as wanting and thus proposes new metaphysical arguments to defend the unity established by God between Adam and his descendants. Crisp concludes by recognizing federalism in Edwards, but of a different kind. Edwards took up elements of both federalism and realism "and fused them together with his own occasionalistic reading of Adam and his posterity's persistence through time, to provide a novel solution to the problem."[7]

These different interpretations confirm how difficult it was even for Reformed theologians of the nineteenth and twentieth centuries to classify Edwards in regards to the Reformed tradition. Warfield, Murray and, more recently, C. Samuel Storms,[8] have classified Edwards's doctrine of original sin as in total continuity with the tradition. Crisp also sees Edwards as within the tradition, though he widens his understanding of what the tradition encompasses.[9] On the other hand, John Gerstner, Paul Helm, and Gerald McDermott portray Edwards's doctrine of original sin as straying/deviating from the tradition. Gerstner asserts that on the doctrine of imputation of sin "Edwards is clearly departing from the reformed tradition fundamen-

---

of Adam,' and this guilt led to two punishments: privation of original righteousness and eternal death. Imputation in this sense, Placaeus denied. *Mediate* imputation, on the other hand, follows upon God's sight of our hereditary corruption, derived from Adam: 'For we share in the participation of this corruption by the sin of Adam, we habitually consent to it, as I say, and for that reason we are deserving, we who are reckoned with Adam the sinner.'" In sum, according to Placaeus the corruption comes before the guilt, whereas according to the advocates of immediate imputation the guilt comes first and corruption is its penal consequence." Macleod, "Original Sin in Reformed Theology," 141.

6. Warfield, "Edwards and the New England Theology," 515–38; Murray, *The Imputation of Adam's Sin*, 253–62.

7. Crisp, "Theological Pedigree," 325. Crisp's thesis, however, is only stated at the end of the article without undergirding it with passages from Edwards, nor detailing the fusion of models for a novel understanding of propagation of sin. Besides the fact that Edwards's "subtlety" and the doctrine's "complexities" cannot be appropriately understood by interpreters such as Helm and Murray, Crisp does not explain to the reader how Edwards's occasionalism fosters what he calls "one metaphysical unity" or how metaphysical unity differs from realism.

8. Storms, "Mediate or Immediate Imputation?"

9. Crisp argues that Reformed hamartiology underwent "reformulation and development" with Edwards, but not to conclude that there was "departure from that tradition" (*Edwards and the Metaphysics of Sin*, 1).

tally, and seems fully aware of it."[10] Helm affirms that to say Edwards was an "innovator" is too strong, but he certainly was a "re-formulator";[11] oddly enough, by the end of this chapter he does consider two of "Edwards' innovations." McDermott affirms that in the last part of *Original Sin*—where an original metaphysics is devised in which God upholds every created substance moment by moment, through immediate agency, thus leaving no room for secondary causes in the sustaining of things—"Edwards departed from this tradition."[12] So where do we place Edwards's doctrine of original sin in regards to the Reformed faith?

This essay intends to help in such assessment by first delineating the major limits of the Reformed teaching on original sin in the sixteenth and seventeenth centuries, then summarizing Edwards teaching in IV.2–3 of his treatise—regarded by some as his most original contribution to this doctrine[13]—in order to assist in any comparison. It modestly attempts to correct a few misconceptions of Edwards's intentions with his treatise and of Reformed teaching on the topic, as well as conclude that any comparison done between Edwards and his Reformed predecessors cannot be done on a whole doctrine, but different aspects of a doctrine need to be analyzed individually.

---

10. Gerstner, *Rational Biblical Theology*, 2:323. Later, Gerstner says that Edwards was "traditionally orthodox though by an untraditional route" (ibid., 2:333). He would be untraditional because he does not present a doctrine of imputation, mediate or immediate, and his teaching "is not a federal doctrine at all." His doctrine of personal identity, instead, made Adam's sin actually the sin of every one of his descendants. Thus, no one could be blamed for something done by another (ibid., 3:324–31). Along similar lines, Foster claims that Edwards made every sin "voluntary sin" and so gave "New England theology its first great distinguishing doctrine, that all sin consists in choice." (*Genetic History*, 87).

11. Helm, "Great Christian Doctrine," 177.

12. McClymond and McDermott, *Theology of Jonathan Edwards*, 351.

13. Smith highly praises Edwards's explanation: "no one can reasonably deny the philosophical originality and the brilliance with which he handles the problem. With the possible exception of the concept of religious affetions which was entirely original with Edwards, his analysis of the relation of Adam to his progeny and the consequent justification of imputing to mankind Adam's sin surpasses in insight and cogency anything he had ever written." (*Jonathan Edwards: Puritan, Preacher, Philosopher*, 93–94). Prud'homme and Schelberg Smith's analysis of Edwards praise his originality rather closely ("Disposition, Potentiality, and Beauty," 25–53). Crisp also believes that the philosophical dimension of Edwards's construct was his most significant contribution towards the understanding of the doctrine (*Jonathan Edwards among the Theologians*, 107, 123); see also Danaher, *Trinitarian Ethics*, 179.

## Original Sin in the Reformed Tradition

As I attempt to draw in broad strokes the Reformed understanding of original sin, I will highlight six of its characteristics in order to set up the context for Edwards. Some of these aspects are in continuity with a longer Christian tradition, but most of the emphasis below is in the uniqueness of Reformation and Reformed teaching on original sin in opposition to other traditions.

First, original sin is not only *privatio*, but perversion. Calvin affirms that original sin cannot be defined merely as "the lack of the original righteousness," in Anselmian fashion, for it does not express effectively enough the "power and energy" of sin. "For our nature is not only destitute and empty of good, but so fertile and fruitful of every evil that it cannot be idle." Thus, Calvin appreciates the word "concupiscence."[14] Amandus Polanus stresses how the "formal nature of sin is deformity . . . So it not mere *privatio*, but also an evil quality inherent in a soul, contrary to the good quality which conforms with the law of God."[15] Gulielmus Bucanus is even more detailed:

> Is sin something positive or privative?—Sin is not a positive, i.e. an existence created by God. Nor is it simply nothing, or a simple pure privation, as death is the *privatio* of life or darkness the *privatio* of light. It is the defect or destruction of a positive entity, namely of the divine work and ordering in a subject, which takes the blame of its depravation, namely aversion from God; like collapse in a house, blindness or loss of vision in eyes. And Paul calls it a defect or privation when he says that "all fall short of the glory of God" (Rom 3.23), although outside movements are added, which are positive entities, but yet wandering and confused, as in Cain's murder the movement or raising of his hands is a positive thing.[16]

Anthony Burgess has three chapters on why the theologians describe original sin as having both a positive as well as a privative part.[17] The Westminster Larger Catechism, question 25, sums up the common understanding saying that original sin "consisteth in the guilt of Adam's first sin, the want of that righteousness wherein he was created, and the corruption of his nature," highlighting the condition of fallen man as both "want" and "corruption."

---

14. Calvin, *Institutes*, II.i.8.
15. Heppe, *Reformed Dogmatics*, 323.
16. Ibid., 324, 340.
17. Burgess, *Doctrine of Original Sin*, 144–63.

Secondly, original sin encompasses both guilt and corruption. Calvin takes original sin to encompass the inherited corruption consequent of Adam's guilt,[18] highlighted in the definition of original sin,[19] but he also mentions children being condemned from their mother's womb, based on Ephesians 2:3.[20] Zacharias Ursinus, in his *Commentary of the Heidelberg Catechism*, describes original sin as "the guilt of the whole human race . . . corrupting our whole nature, so that all, on account of this depravity, are subject to the eternal wrath of God."[21] One can notice there is an initial guilt that corrupts and then leads to punishment. Ursinus himself says that original sin entails two things: "exposure to eternal condemnation . . . and a depravity of our entire nature."[22] Notice that he calls the two elements "condemnation" and "depravity." Seventeenth-century Reformed theology is going to be clearer on original sin being "twofold, imputed sin and inherent hereditary sin" (*Formula Consensus Helvetica*, canon XI). It was common for later puritans like Anthony Burgess, who wrote a long treatise on original sin, to talk about the twofold problem of sin (guilt and corruption) being solved by the twofold righteousness of Christ (justification taking away guilt and sanctification overcoming corruption).[23] Following the same teaching is the Dutch pastor Leonard Rijssen:

> Two effects of sin are commonly cited, *macula* and *reatus*. *Macula* is the spiritual and moral defilement with which man's soul is infected. *Reatus* is liability to punishment for a previous fault. The later corresponds to the benefit of justification, by which Christ removes liability from us by the imputation of his own righteousness. The former answers to the benefit of the sanctification of grace, by which the stain is washed out through the efficacy of the H. Spirit.[24]

---

18. Calvin, *Institutes*, II.i.5.

19. "Original sin, then, may be defined a hereditary corruption and depravity of our nature, extending to all the parts of the soul, which first makes us obnoxious to the wrath of God, and then produces in us works which in Scripture are termed works of the flesh. This corruption is repeatedly designated by Paul by the term sin (Gal. 5:19); while the works which proceed from it, such as adultery, fornication, theft, hatred, murder, revellings, he terms, in the same way, the fruits of sin, though in various passages of Scripture, and even by Paul himself, they are also termed sins." Calvin, *Institutes*, II.i.8.

20. Calvin, *Institutes*, II.i.6.

21. Ursinus, *Commentary on the Heidelberg Catechism*, 39.

22. Ibid.

23. Beeke and Jones, *A Puritan Theology: Doctrine for Life*, 205–07.

24. Heppe, *Reformed Dogmatics*, 325.

Thirdly, the inclination towards sin, not only the action, is already sinful. Discussing different late medieval and Reformation interpretations of Romans 7, David Steinmetz notes there are significantly different explanations of the struggle within the believer. Not only did the Catholics describe the believer as imperfectly just—different from the "justified though imperfectly renewed" of the Protestants—but also portrayed concupiscence as not sinful apart from the will's consent. The fall caused disorder between higher (mind or will) and lower human faculties (passions), and though baptism washed away the guilt of original sin, it did not remove concupiscence, which is not sinful in itself.[25] In response to this Roman Catholic position, the seventeenth-century theologian Bartholomew Keckermann wrote:

> [The Papists] declare that these first motions are involuntary and so are not sins. Ans. (1) The major is false. There is no involuntary sin. Sin of origin is truly sin, even if it does not include the assent of the will. (2) Moreover these motions are not altogether involuntary. We have attracted them by our will; and will, which is rational desire, is always conjoined with sense desire, even to the extent that the actual sense desire in man responds proportionally to the will.[26]

The *Westminster Confession of Faith* affirmed that not only acts are sinful, but even the corruption of nature and its motions/impulses, are "truly and properly sin" (VI.5). Keckermann also counters the papist position, as represented by Bellarmine, that concupiscence was natural for man before the fall, though under control. According to the Reformed, concupiscence is an accident to human nature.[27]

Fourthly, Adam holds both a natural and a federal relationship with his posterity. Covenant became the best framework through which to explain Adam's relationship to his posterity, not just a natural relationship. Against the Pelagians, Calvin says that Adam's sin was not propagated by imitation, but by "communication"—i.e., imputation—just like the righteousness of Christ.[28] He refers to rotten branches coming from a rotten root—the root and tree being a common analogy in the whole tradition[29]—but this contamination does not originate in the substance of the flesh or the soul, but

25. Steinmetz, *Calvin in Context*, 111.
26. Heppe, *Reformed Dogmatics*, 335.
27. Ibid., 338.
28. Calvin, *Institutes*, II.i.6.
29. "They being the root of all mankind, the guilt of this sin was imputed, and the same death in sin and corrupted nature conveyed to all their posterity, descending from them by ordinary generation." *Westminster Confession of Faith* VI.3.

by the ordinance of God.³⁰ Francis Turretin talks about a twofold connection between Adam and his descendants: a natural and a political/forensic, with imputation founded upon both.³¹ However, only the first of Adam's sin has a federal aspect to it. The remainder of Adam's sins, just like the rest of humanity's, are personal sins as taught in Ezekiel 18.³²

Fifthly, the origin of the soul is largely understood as creationist, rather than traducianist. Herman Bavinck says that the majority of the Reformed were creationists while the Lutherans showed themselves to be traducianists.³³ We have seen how Calvin denies any contamination of the substance of the soul, thus denying any traducianism or realism as an explanation of sin. Ursinus's explanation of how the soul of Adam's posterity is contaminated is, similarly to Calvin, creationist: "God, even whilst he creates the soul, at the same time deprives it of original righteousness."³⁴ Heinrich Heppe follows the same judgment of Bavinck when he writes of the Reformed Orthodoxy: "the majority after the precedent of Calvin and Ursinus taught 'that souls are created deprived of original righteousness for a punishment of the same sin.'"³⁵ Anthony Burgess is an example of a seventeenth-century theologian who holds the majority position.³⁶

30. Calvin, *Institutes*, II.i.7.

31. Turretin, *Institutes of Elenctic Theology* 1:616. Letham claims that a Reformed theology gradually shifted from a natural connection to a more forensic connection over the late sixteenth and seventeenth century (*The Westminster Assembly*, 206–23). The problem with this thesis is that even High Orthodoxy theologians, those writing in the second half of the seventeenth century, incorporate the representative element without leaving the organic relationship with Adam and Eve. Macleod writes: "This link between the federal and the biological was never broken even in fully developed covenant theology. It appears clearly, for example, in the Westminster Confession." Macleod, "Original Sin in Reformed Theology," 138.

32. Heppe, *Reformed Dogmatics*, 330.

33. Bavinck, *Reformed Dogmatics* 2:584.

34. Ursinus, *Commentary on the Heidelberg Catechism*, 41.

35. Heppe, *Reformed Dogmatics*, 347. In order to solve the problem that God would then create a corrupt soul, thus making God the author of some evil, Macleod suggests that we follow William G. T. Shedd on his traducianism (not in his realism), for it positively emphasizes the psychosomatic unity of human beings. Macleod, "Original Sin in Reformed Theology," 143–145. Herman Bavinck, however, had claimed how traducianism doesn't solve the dilemma regarding the transmission of sin, for sin is not a material substance but a moral quality. On top of that, the connection which a human being has with his descendants is not merely physical (as the animals have), nor merely moral (as angels experience). According to Bavinck, the only explanation for the communication of either sin or righteousness is to postulate a connection of a federal nature (*Reformed Dogmatics*, 2:581, 586).

36. Burgess, *The Doctrine of Original Sin*, 191–203.

Sixthly, the communication of corruption is mysterious and, thus, allows for little explanation. Heidegger says that "from the defection of Adam's heirs in his loins immediately flows the corruption of actual human nature or inherent original sin." Mastricht also says that from imputed sin "flows" inherent sin.[37] There is a sense in which corruption is a penal consequence of guilt. However, there is no hypothesis detailing how corruption is transmitted. William Whitaker, in his *De Peccato Originali*, says that the propagation of Adam's sin to his posterity "ought rather to be believed than asked, and to be asked more easily than it can be understood and better understood than explained."[38] William Perkins also affirms that propagation of sin is like a common fire in a town: "men are not so much to search how it came, as to be careful how to extinguish it."[39] Anthony Burgess, on the manner of propagating sin, an issue which he renders "the most difficult and hard to conceive" in this doctrine, he calls for a certain contentment in not knowing these details.[40] Wilhelmus à Brakel professes a certain healthy ignorance that should not dive into questions without answers in regards to the way sin is transmitted.[41] Francis Turretin says that the issue of propagation of sin is "a question of the highest difficulty" and though no explanation removes all difficulty, the truth of it should be retained with certainty.[42]

There are some who attempt minor comments on this last issue. William Ames, for example, thinks that the propagation of sin is not unfair, just like qualities of parents are passed on to their children (what he calls natural law) and weighty consequences are also transferred from father to son (hereditary law).[43]

However, there does not seem to be a metaphysics of inherent sin, to use Oliver Crisp's language, in Reformed Scholasticism. The reason for a relative silence is because Reformed Orthodoxy believed the Bible was silent about it. The early eighteenth-century Baptist theologian John Gill asserts that the *locus classicus* of Romans 5 is not teaching about the descendants of Adam receiving a corrupt nature from him, which is true, but not the truth of the passage. The biblical text is focusing on original guilt and that is

---

37. Heppe, *Reformed Dogmatics*, 334.
38. Ibid., 341.
39. Macleod, "Original Sin in Reformed Theology," 130.
40. Burgess, *Doctrine of Original Sin*, 183–84.
41. Brakel, *Christian's Reasonable Service* 1:393.
42. Turretin, *Institutes of Elenctic Theology*, IX.xii.2, 19.
43. Ames, *Marrow of Theology*, 127–28.

the foundation of the propagation of corruption.[44] This is an area in which Edwards will show some innovation.

## Jonathan Edwards on Original Sin

Edwards's work on *Original Sin* (1758) was a defense of the Reformation understanding of original sin in contrast to "the Enlightenment belief in innate goodness of the natural man."[45] John Erskine drew Edwards's attention to the controversial work of John Taylor of Norwich, published in 1740, which challenged the traditional doctrine. Edwards planned a three-part response to such tendencies: a treatise on virtue, a discussion of the character of God, and the topic of original sin. He worked on these three related topics at more or less the same time, and they became the last three major treatises of his life.[46]

But the treatise as a whole does not differ significantly from Enlightenment tendencies when he, as was his usual method, uses the argumentative tools of his day: reason, experience, and Scripture.[47] Even the structure of his work reflects the spirit of the age, though he is confronting the optimism of his days: part 1 shows the logical and empirical evidences, part 2 presents the Scriptural evidences, part 3 has a short theological grounding, and part 4 has answers to objections.

It is not complicated to show how Edwards is in continuity with some of those Reformed aspects of the doctrine, as mentioned above. He clearly understands sin to be not only a lack of original righteousness, but also a perversion of our whole being. He also takes original sin to encompass both guilt and corruption. Right at the beginning of the treatise he writes: "the topic mainly insisted on by the opposers of the doctrine of original sin, is the justice of God; both in their objections against the imputation of Adam's sin, and also against its being so ordered that men should come into the world with a corrupt and ruined nature, without having merited the displeasure of their Creator by any personal fault."[48]

Since part 4, where he constantly responds to John Taylor, is the polemical part of his treatise in regards to the Reformed tradition, this essay will focus on IV.2-3. In IV.2 Edwards deals with the transmission of corruption and in IV.3 with the transmission of guilt, both in connection

---

44. Gill, *Body of Doctrinal and Practical Divinity*, 327.
45. Smith, *Jonathan Edwards*, 82.
46. Marsden, *Jonathan Edwards*, 448-50.
47. Smith, *Jonathan Edwards*, 84-85.
48. Edwards, *WJE* 3:111; see also *WJE* 3:348.

with the accusation that the Calvinist position makes God the author of sin. After explaining how upon Adam's sin (he doesn't explain the logical mechanics of the first sin here) "the superior principles left his heart; for indeed God then left him"—God's action is thus negative, not positive—he not only concludes that Adam's nature became corrupt by God withdrawing rather than infusing evil, but also that it is the same with his posterity.[49] The comparison between Adam's corruption and ours continues when he says that what happened to Adam—God permitting sin "by withholding the gracious influences necessary to prevent it"—is not unfair just as leaving sinners in their sin in order to further it (Rom 1:24, 26, 28) does not make God the author of sin.[50] The parallel between fallen Adam and the remaining sinners will continue.

Furthermore, in connection with the majority of the Reformed tradition he presents himself as creationist, rather than a traducianist, and recognizes that, by divine will, holiness is not propagated the same way sin is. After all, the connection between Christ and his seed is of a higher kind of constitution.[51] In fact, Edwards uses the root/tree analogy to illustrate both the spiritual union between Christ and believers as well as the bond between Adam and his descendants.[52] This shows that the metaphor does not establish the nature of their connection. So it is more appropriate not to argue that the union between Christ and his people in justification is of the same nature as the identity between Adam and his progeny.[53]

Not only continuity with the Reformed tradition, but intentionality, which was touched upon earlier, should now be stressed. When Edwards says that depravity comes to Adam not only due to the course of nature, but as a penal judgment of God, and that the same thing applies to us,[54] he is focusing on the fallen Adam rather than the pristine one. Why? Because fallen Adam is paradigmatic to his posterity.

In IV.3, Edwards gets into imputed guilt. He argues that infants are born with the guilt of the first apostasy and not a guilt resulting of their depraved natures. In this, he seems to differ significantly from the mediate imputation both of de la Place and also of those New Englanders who devised an Edwardsean theology. Moreover, Edwards argues that just like there are

---

49. Edwards, *WJE* 3:382–83.

50. Ibid., 384.

51. Ibid., 385–86.

52. Ibid., 386, 389.

53. Contra Thomas Schafer and Oliver Crisp who follows him on this. See Crisp, *Jonathan Edwards among the Theologians*, 114–15.

54. Edwards, *WJE* 3:387.

two depraved dispositions in Adam—the first rising of an evil inclination and then a continuing evil disposition which is God's punishment—so is the depravity of Adam's posterity twofold: an extended pollution of Adam's sin which we inherit and a remaining established principle of corruption which itself deserves punishment (an "additional guilt"; just like his Reformed antecedents, Edwards saw the corrupt propensity itself being a fault, not just a sinful act).[55] Again, Edwards wants to look at Adam as paradigmatic in relation to his posterity.

When he comes to the nature of the union between Adam and his progeny, in order to present a sort of Lockean "reasonableness" of such a constitution, Edwards devises his idea of continued creation. Part of the reasonableness of it is in the fact that if Adam and his descendants are not identified as one and they are "in every respect perfectly innocent," then God is being unfair in bringing upon humanity the calamities of death.[56] Against the objection that it is "injurious" that Adam stand for his posterity, Edwards argues that in him we had a greater chance of success for he had stronger motives to pursue obedience (both his and his posterity's eternal welfare depended on him) and he was in a complete state of manhood (rather than being born in a state of infancy) to face the trial. Such momentary trial was no proof of evil from God, but of his goodness, for every creature owes perfect obedience to the Creator without expecting any pay.[57] And it is not "improper" to talk of the imputation of Adam's sin to his seed because the personal identity[58] created by the "arbitrary divine constitution"—the immediate upholding of creatures by God, moment by moment, as "a continued creation . . . equivalent to an immediate production out of nothing, at each moment"—allows for Adam's sin to be "truly and properly theirs" and, thus, be imputed to them.[59] Such argument for Edwards even entails "grief and humiliation . . . for the pollution and guilt which they bring into the world"—a lament not uncommon in the Reformed tradition.[60]

---

55. Ibid., 390–91. John Smith explicates this passage like this: "Our corrupt dispositions are not to be regarded as belonging to us, but to our participation in Adam's sin, what Edwards calls the "extended pollution of that sin." Depravity as an established principle in us is a punishment of the first apostasy and brings new guilt." Smith, *Jonathan Edwards*, 94.

56. Edwards, *WJE* 3:395.

57. Ibid., 396–97.

58. See Edwards, "'Misc.' 1049," *WJE* 20:391, "'Misc.' 1237," *WJE* 23:172.

59. *WJE* 3:399, 401, 402, 408.

60. Ibid., 407; see Heidelberg Cathechism, q. 60. That is, the lament is not for sinful acts themselves.

Edwards believes that with such metaphysics he has rested his case against those who accuse God of injustice. Though some might not like this philosophy, he believes that to lay the state and course of things on the sovereign constitutions of God should be sufficient to shut their mouths.[61] The sovereign constitution of Edwards's explanation matches the sovereignty of covenantal constitutions by the earlier Reformed theologians.[62] The difference, however, is in the metaphysics.

## Scrutinizing Edwards

There are two areas in which we don't find continuity between Edwards and the previous reformed tradition. The first one, in regards to the propagation of malice (IV.2), is when he attempts an explanation of the dynamics of the immediate results of the first sin. The second is in "the idealist character of his occasionalism"[63] to explain how guilt was passed on from Adam to his descendants. Both have been targets of criticism, but not equally nor with the same attentiveness. Since Edwards's occasionalism has been addressed with greater detail[64] and it apparently has no precedents in Reformed metaphysics, this section will focus on the first issue for it feeds into the dialogue with the previous tradition.

The discussion of how the first sin ocurred and the immediate results over Adam has been noted to have similarities to Thomas Aquinas's understanding of the *donum superadditum*.[65] This doctrine proposed that man in his original state had a higher nature (comprised of the intellect), which was supposed to govern the lower nature (comprised of the will and lesser appetites). A gift of grace was added so that Adam could be kept in communion with God. Richard Muller affirms, "Aquinas maintained that the *donum superadditum* was part of the original constitution of man and that its loss was the loss of the original capacity for righteousness."[66]

---

61. Edwards, *WJE* 3:409.

62. Burgess, *Doctrine of Original Sin*, 429.

63. Daniel, "Edwards' Occasionalism," 1; see also Minkema, "A 'Dordtian Philosophe,'" 245–46.

64. See Helm, *Faith and Understanding*, 152–76; Crisp, *Jonathan Edwards and the Metaphysics of Sin*, 96–112; Daniel, "Edwards' Occasionalism," 1–14.

65. The debate is not whether he was influenced by Aquinas, for scholars have shown how it was possible but not likely that Edwards engaged Aquinas directly. On top of that, "Edwards publicly invoked Aquinas only disparagingly." Thuesen, "Editor's Introduction," *WJE* 26:52.

66. Muller, *Dictionary of Latin and Greek Theological Terms*, 96.

Though a majority of scholars have seen it as an innovation and have not connected to any earlier tradition,[67] John Gerstner, Gerald McDermott and Jeffrey Waddington have delved into this debate. Gerstner explores Edwards on this issue, mainly from *Freedom of the Will*, and he writes that the Holy Spirit plays the same role as the Scholastics' *donum superadditum*. God "witheld confirming grace"—which Gerstner takes to mean the Spirit as the necessary grace to continue in holiness—and man inevitably, but culpably fell. Gerstner concludes that Edwards painted God into an ethical corner.[68] In correction to Gerstner's analysis, it should be observed that the grace prior to the fall, what Edwards calls the "superior principles," is not the Spirit himself, but the influences of the Holy Spirit. In *Original Sin*, the Spirit is never mentioned as leaving prior to the first sin, but as a result of it.[69]

McDermott also notices the similarity with Thomas Aquinas's superior and inferior powers. His criticism is that Edwards has difficulties explaining how the first sin occurred, because Adam's "superior divine principles" which were supposed to dominate the natural principles did not do so because Adam was not given efficacious grace—McDermott says that Edwards follows Ames, Turretin and van Mastricht attributing the fall of Adam to the absence of "confirming grace."[70] In *Freedom of the Will*, this anthropological description of Adam pre-fall is called an "imperfection which properly belongs to a creature" thus inevitably leading to sin.[71] Still, McDermott affirms that Edwards is in line with Calvin as to the fall being part of God's plan, even though the New Englander is less hesitant than the Reformer in offering metaphysical solutions to theological enigmas.[72]

McDermott correctly notes how Edwards is more ingenious than Calvin when it comes to the first sin, but one should note that in *Original Sin* Edwards is not concerned with explaining the logical and causal procedure

---

67. For an example, see Helm, "Great Christian Doctrine," 177, 188–89.
68. Gerstner, *Rational Biblical Theology*, 316–19.
69. Edwards, *WJE*, 3:382, 387.
70. For Edwards explanation of sufficient versus efficient grace, see Edwards, "'Misc.' 436," *WJE* 13:484–86 and "'Misc.' 501," *WJE* 18:51.
71. Edwards, *Freedom of the Will*, *WJE* 1:413.
72. McClymond and McDermott, *Theology of Jonathan Edwards*, 352–56.

that generated the first sin. Clyde Holbrook,[73] Samuel Storms,[74] and Paul Helm[75] also fault Edwards for not providing insightful and coherent explanation of how the first sin came about. They all miss Edwards's intention to focus on the transmission of sin rather than on its first occurrence.

It is true that Edwards does not solve the mystery of the first sin. In his *Miscellanies*, nos. 436–38,[76] Edwards talks about Adam's judgment being deceived. However, the argument is not as well constructed, for Adam seems to have chosen the forbidden fruit merely by ignorance or misjudgment rather than desire. In *Original Sin*, Edwards seems to complement his previous explanation like this: "although there was no natural sinful inclination in Adam, yet an inclination to that sin of eating the forbidden fruit, was begotten in him by the delusion and error he was led into; and this inclination to eat the forbidden fruit, must precede his actual eating."[77] Later he talks about "the first rising of an evil inclination in his heart, exerted in his first act of sin."[78] As much as this inclination seems logically correct, i.e., an inclination precedes the eating, still there is no explanation how rational misjudgment gives birth to evil inclination. Just like science can't explain how the laws of physics were formed, since it can only presuppose known laws, theology upon biblical revelation cannot explain the dynamics of falling from a pristine state; it just provides us with insights into how the dynamics of sin function in those who are already fallen. So, Edwards should

---

73. Holbrook thinks that when Edwards establishes Adam's original righteousness there is no way to explain how the lower faculties took over. Furthermore, Holbrook states that Edwards's reasoning could not but "lead back to Taylor's contention that the original parents sinned in the same manner in which all men do, by errors of judgment made in ignorance of consequences and with free exercise of free choice." Edwards, *WJE* 3:51–52.

74. Storms follows Schafer's judgment that Edwards could not overcome "the impossible task of accounting for both original righteousness and the fall." Storms, "The Will: Fettered Yet Free," 211–18.

75. Helm brings a cunning critical observation upon Edwards's unsatisfactory theory: "For either mankind sinned while still in possession of these supernatural principles, with all the virtuous influence they afforded, in which case it is hard to make the occurrence of the fall plausible, or alternatively, if the fall could occur while Adam had such principles and was under their influence, then they were hardly 'supernatural' in the sense that Edwards intends, for they did not succeed in preserving him . . . Edwards has done little by this innovation to cast light on the mystery of the entrance of sin into a world made good by God." Helm, "Great Christian Doctrine," 190.

76. See Edwards, *WJE* 13:485–87.

77. Edwards, *WJE* 3:228, footnote 6.

78. Ibid., 390.

not be censured for not providing explanation that the Christian tradition as a whole has not explained. Edwards was more interested in explicating how Adam's sin resulted in corruption for himself and his descendants.[79]

The third theologian who addresses Edwards in regard to Aquinas *donum superadditum* is Jeffrey Waddington. He argues that Edwards came up with the explanation of a transient act, where the first sin was not an effect without a cause, but the effect of a non-perduring cause (i.e., transient). Such transient causality was the distraction by a lesser desire. He also repeats the incorrect claim that the Holy Spirit was withdrawn before the first sin.[80] He believes that similarity in terms with Aquinas does not entail equal conceptions. Waddington establishes some fundamental distinctions between both theologians to set them apart on this issue. One particular distinction stands out:

> there is no sense in which fallen man can function adequately in Edwards whereas in Thomas it seems that natural man can, in fact, function on the horizontal plane sufficiently well. For Edwards, the loss of the presence of the Holy Spirit results in the loss of the integrity of human nature. For Thomas, the loss of the super added gift results in the natural man's inability to achieve the *visio Dei*, but it does not create any problems for man in his earthly pursuits. For Edwards, there are noetic effects with sin.[81]

Though Waddington wants to differentiate Aquinas and Edwards on the basis of their understanding of depravity, one should not pass quickly by the similarities between them on the language used to elucidate the first sin and its immediate consequences. Thomas Aquinas explained righteousness in the primitive state as consisting of Adam's "reason being subject to God, the lower powers to reason, and the body to the soul." This harmony was not maintained by nature, but was the result of "a supernatural endowment of grace," or "the grace which was added."[82] This original righteous-

---

79. See Edwards, "'Misc.' 788," *WJE* 18:473. A 1738 sermon by Edwards on Genesis 3:11 says when man first sinned, the Holy Spirit left his heart and the necessary and unavoidable consequence was the corruption of his nature. There was no need for anything positive to be done, says Edwards. He believes that the, debates throughout history about whether corruption is transmitted through the body or the soul are useless, and the best answer we have is the covenant through which we also sinned in Adam. Both guilt and corruption were transmitted by that covenant. Edwards follows the Reformed tradition very closely on this matter. See Edwards, "504. Sermon on Genesis 3:11," *WJEO* 54.

80. Waddington, "Unified Operations of the Human Soul," 74–6.

81. Ibid., 101–02.

82. Aquinas, *Summa Theologica* I.95.1.

ness, which was an accident to human nature, was "lost by his first sin."[83] Aquinas does not say how the first sin was propelled. He just focused on the tainting of nature so that it would be passed down to generations. It is true that he sees more potentiality for good than Edwards does,[84] but just like Edwards he is concerned with how "the withdrawal of original justice has the character of punishment."[85]

Edwards does not have the dichotomy between body and soul as Aquinas's more ascetic theology proposes, but they both have two immaterial principles under God. Aquinas calls them reason and inferior powers/appetites, while Edwards calls them superior/supernatural/spiritual principles versus the inferior/natural/flesh. Both talk about the superior principles controlling the inferior ones as a representation of Adam's pristine condition. Both do not have a thorough explanation for the very first impulse to sin, but they both affirm that consequent corruption was a result of God withdrawing his deterring grace. So, there is more continuity than Waddington admits.

And this places Edwards in disagreement with the previous Reformed tradition. Francis Turretin represents the tradition when he says original righteousness could be called grace but was not supernatural as the Romanists affirm.[86] He writes:

> The Romanists hold original righteousness to be a supernatural gift, superadded to the native gifts and power of the entire man. Bellarmine explains the reason why they determine this to be so. There was in man naturally a contest between the flesh and the spirit, the reason and the appetite, from which flowed a certain disease and languor of nature, arising from the condition of the material. Therefore God added original righteousness as a "golden bridle," to repress that conflict and to cover like a precious garment their nakedness, and as a remedy to heal that weakness.[87]

This kind of "chaos under control," which Edwards calls "imperfection" in *Freedom of the Will*, was totally rejected by the Reformed. Turretin affirmed

---

83. Ibid., I.100.1; I–II.81.2; I–II.85.3.

84. Ibid., I–II.85.2.

85. Ibid., I–II.85.5. See also Levering, "Jonathan Edwards and Thomas Aquinas on Original Sin," 133–48.

86. Turretin, *Institutes of Elenctic Theology*, V.xi.16.

87. Ibid., V.xi.5.

a "liability to fall" (mutable nature) by which Adam could sin, but not a "fall itself" (disease or languor) by which he must actually sin.[88]

However, Edwards has a very specific Enlightenment-related interest in his explanation that is in complete accordance with the Reformed explanation of *concursus*. Because Arminianism and other theological projects that blame Calvinism of making God the author of sin were growing during his days, Edwards intentionally shows how God did not infuse any positive influence in order for sin to occur. God does not need to give it a push. The "absence of positive good principles" leaving the common natural principles to themselves "will certainly be followed with corruption."[89] Again, Jonathan Edwards's attempt in explaining the first sin illustrates the mechanics of all later sin.

## Conclusion

This essay has attempted to evaluate Jonathan Edwards's doctrine of original sin, especially the nature of imputation, in regards to his Reformed antecedents. By laying six distinct topics that characterize the Reformed understanding of original sin, it demonstrated that Edwards follows five of them very closely, but attempts some different explanations in regard to the sixth topic. But even in the sixth topic, Edwards resonates with the Reformed understanding that God is not behind any sinful act in the same way he is behind any holy act; God does not have to infuse evil dispositions. Thus, any assessment on how Reformed was Edwards's doctrine of original sin would profit from distinctions rather than considering it as a whole.

However, his explanation of the dynamics of appetites sound more thomistic, and thus subject to criticism, since God's judgment that original creation was "very good" becomes merely moral—holy, but not perfect—with which Edwards agrees. By stating "imperfection," Edwards is saying that the pristine state was "chaos under control."

The essay has also demonstrated how a major intention for Edwards was to explain how Adam was a paradigm and, thus, Adam's misjudgment that leads to sin, sin which generates enduring corruption, and corruption as a penal judgment, are all applied to us. Adam as a paradigm for all sinners reminds us that Edwards is more interested in what we can learn from the fall story than in devising elaborate explanations on how the first sin came about.

88. Ibid., V.xi.14.
89. Edwards, *WJE* 3:381; See also Smith, *Jonathan Edwards*, 84–85.

# Bibliography

Ames, William. *The Marrow of Theology*. Translated by John Eusden. Grand Rapids: Baker, 1997.
Aquinas, Thomas. *Summa Theologica*. 5 vols. Translated by Fathers of the English Dominican Province. New York: Benzinger Bros., 1948.
Bavinck, Herman. *Reformed Dogmatics*. Edited by John Bolt. Translated by John Vriend. Grand Rapids: Baker, 2008.
Beeke, Joel, and Mark Jones. *A Puritan Theology: Doctrine for Life*. Grand Rapids: Reformation Heritage Books, 2012.
Brakel, Wilhelmus à. *The Christian's Reasonable Service*. Edited by Joel R. Beeke. Translated by Bartel Elshout. Grand Rapids: Reformation Heritage Books, 1995.
Burgess, Anthony. *The Doctrine of Original Sin*. London: Abraham Miller for Thomas Underhill, 1658.
Calvin, John. *Institutes of the Christian Religion*. 2 vols. Edited by John T. McNeill. Translated by Ford Lewis Battles. Philadelphia: Westminster, 1960.
Crisp, Oliver D. *Jonathan Edwards among the Theologians*. Grand Rapids: Eerdmans, 2015.
———. "On the Theological Pedigree of Jonathan Edwards' Doctrine of Imputation." *Scottish Journal of Theology* 56/3 (2003) 308–27.
———. *Jonathan Edwards and the Metaphysics of Sin*. Aldershot, Hampshire: Ashgate, 2005.
Cunningham, William. *The Reformers and the Theology of the Reformation*. Edinburgh: T. & T. Clark, 1862.
Danaher, William J. *The Trinitarian Ethics of Jonathan Edwards*. Louisville: Westminster/John Knox, 2004.
Daniel, Stephen H. "Edwards' Occasionalism." In *Jonathan Edwards as Contemporary: Essays in Honor of Sang Hyun Lee*, edited by Don Schweitzer, 1–14. New York: Peter Lang, 2010.
Edwards, Jonathan. *Freedom of the Will*. The Works of Jonathan Edwards 1. Edited by Paul Ramsey. New Haven: Yale University Press, 1957.
———. "'Misc.' 436." In *The "Miscellanies" (Entry Nos. a–z, aa–zz, 1–500)*, edited by Thomas A. Schafer, The Works of Jonathan Edwards 13:484–86. New Haven: Yale University Press, 1994.
———. "'Misc.' 501." In *The "Miscellanies" (Entry Nos. 501–832)*, edited by Ava Chamberlain, The Works of Jonathan Edwards 18:51. New Haven: Yale University Press, 2000.
———. "'Misc.' 788." In *The "Miscellanies" (Entry Nos. 501–832)*, edited by Ava Chamberlain, The Works of Jonathan Edwards 18:473. New Haven Yale University Press, 2000.
———. "'Misc.' 1049." In *The "Miscellanies" (Entry Nos. 833–1152)*, edited by Amy P. Pauw, The Works of Jonathan Edwards 20:391. New Haven: Yale University Press, 2002.
———. "'Misc.' 1237." In *The "Miscellanies" (Entry Nos. 1153–1360)*, edited by Douglas A. Sweeney, The Works of Jonathan Edwards 23:172. New Haven: Yale University Press, 2004.
———. *Original Sin*. The Works of Jonathan Edwards 3. Edited by John E. Smith. New Haven: Yale University Press, 1970.

———. "504. Sermon on Genesis 3:11 (February 1738)." In *Sermons, Series II, 1739*. The Works of Jonathan Edwards Online 54. Jonathan Edwards Center at Yale University.

Foster, Frank Hugh. *A Genetic History of the New England Theology*. Chicago: University of Chicago, 1907.

Gerstner, John H. *The Rational Biblical Theology of Jonathan Edwards*. 3 vols. Powhatan: Berea Publications, 1992.

Gill, John. *A Body of Doctrinal and Practical Divinity*. Paris, Arkansas: Baptist Standard Bearer, 1989.

Helm, Paul. "A Different Kind of Calvinism? Edwardsianism Compared with Older Forms of Reformed Thought." In *After Jonathan Edwards: the Courses of the New England Theology*, edited by Oliver Crisp and Douglas A. Sweeney, 91–103. New York: Oxford University Press, 2012.

———. "Jonathan Edwards and the Parting of the Ways?" *Jonathan Edwards Studies* 4/1 (2014) 42–60.

———. "The Great Christian Doctrine (Original Sin)." In *A God Entranced Vision of All Things*, edited by John Piper and Justin Taylor, 175–200. Wheaton: Crossway, 2004.

———. *Faith and Understanding*. Grand Rapids: Eerdmans, 1997.

Heppe, Heinrich. *Reformed Dogmatics*. Edited by Ernst Bizer. Translated by G. T. Thomson. Grand Rapids: Baker, 1950.

Hodge, Charles. *Systematic Theology*. 3 vols. New York: Scribner/Armstrong, 1872.

Letham, Robert. *The Westminster Assembly: Reading its Theology in Historical Context*. Phillipsburg: P&R, 2009.

Levering, Matthew. "Jonathan Edwards and Thomas Aquinas on Original Sin." In *The Ecumenical Edwards: Jonathan Edwards and the Theologians*, edited Kyle C. Strobel, 133–48. New York: Routledge, 2016.

Macleod, Donald. "Original Sin in Reformed Theology." In *Adam, The Fall, and Original Sin*, edited by Hans Madueme and Michael Reeves, 129–46. Grand Rapids: Baker Academic, 2014.

Marsden, George. *Jonathan Edwards: A Life*. New Haven: Yale University Press, 2003.

McClymond, Michael J. and Gerald R. McDermott. *The Theology of Jonathan Edwards*. New York: Oxford University Press, 2012.

Minkema, Kenneth P. "A 'Dordtian Philosophe': Jonathan Edwards, Calvin and Reformed Orthodoxy." *Church History and Religious Culture* 91/1–2 (2011) 241–53.

Muller, Richard A. *Dictionary of Latin and Greek Theological Terms*. Grand Rapids: Baker, 1985.

———. "Jonathan Edwards and the Absence of Free Choice: A Parting of Ways in the Reformed Tradition." *Jonathan Edwards Studies* 1/1 (2011) 3–22.

Murray, John. *The Imputation of Adam's Sin in Justified in Christ: God's Plan For Us in Justification*. Edited by K. Scott Oliphint. Geanies House, Fearn: Mentor, 2007.

Otto, Randall E. "The Solidarity of Mankind in Jonathan Edwards' Doctrine of Original Sin." *Evangelical Quarterly* 62/3 (1990) 205–21.

Prud'homme, Joseph, and James Schelberg. "Disposition, Potentiality, and Beauty in the Theology of Jonathan Edwards: A Defense of his Great Christian Doctrine of Original Sin." *American Theological Inquiry* 5/1 (2012) 25–53.

Smith, John. *Jonathan Edwards: Puritan, Preacher, Philosopher.* Notre Dame: University of Notre Dame, 1993.

Steinmetz, David C. *Calvin in Context.* 2nd ed. Oxford: Oxford University Press, 2010.

Storms, C. Samuel. "Mediate or Immediate Imputation?" samstorms.com, 21 Jun. 2016. http://www.samstorms.com/all-articles/post/mediate-or-immediate-imputation.

———. "The Will: Fettered Yet Free (Freedom of the Will)." In *A God Entranced Vision of All Things,* edited by John Piper and Justin Taylor, 201–20. Wheaton: Crossway, 2004.

Thuesen, Peter J. "Editor's Introduction." In *Catalogues of Books,* edited by Peter J Thuesen, The Works of Jonathan Edwards 26:1–113. New Haven and London: Yale University Press, 2008.

Turretin, Francis. *Institutes of Elenctic Theology.* Edited by James T. Dennison Jr. Translated by George Musgrave Ginger. Philipsburg: P&R, 1997.

Ursinus, Zacharias. *Commentary on the Heidelberg Catechism.* Phillipsburg: P&R, n. d.

Waddington, Jeffrey C. "The Unified Operations of the Human Soul: Jonathan Edwards' Theological Anthropology and Apologetic." Ph.D. diss. Westminster Theological Seminary, 2013.

Warfield, Benjamin Breckinridge. "Edwards and the New England Theology." In *Studies in Theology,* 515–38. Edinburgh: Banner of Truth, 1988.

*Westminster Confession of Faith.* Glasgow: Free Presbyterian Publications, 1985.

*Part III*

Global Practice

# 13

## "A Good and Sensible Man"
### *John Wesley's Reading and Use Of Jonathan Edwards*

GLEN O'BRIEN

## Introduction

THERE IS A CLEAR trend in the study of the origins of evangelicalism to stress its international dimensions. Britain and America were by no means isolated from events in central Europe that gave rise to new religious minorities—minorities that were focused on personal spiritual renewal, partly as a means of resisting absorption by church and state. As David Hempton states it,

> Religious identities in the British Isles are not as hermetically sealed as they first appear.... In [the displaced and persecuted minorities of Habsburg-dominated central Europe] a tangled web of circulating literature, itinerant revivalists and folk migrations combine to show that the great awakening of the eighteenth century was more of an international event than many have imagined, and cannot be reduced to the social and economic peculiarities of specific places, however much they may have shaped the distinctive local expression of revival enthusiasm.[1]

---

1. Hempton, *Religion and Political Culture in Britain and Ireland*, 151.

Reg Ward insisted that eighteenth-century revivalism could "only be understood in the widest possible area 'between the Russian and American frontiers of the European world.'"[2] That's a lot of territory indeed. Methodism emerged largely as a result of international networks of piety and cannot be understood apart from this global context.

In earlier histories of revival, the tendency has been to use the term "Great Awakening" for the American context and "Evangelical Revival" for the British context but using separate nomenclature obscures the international nature of the movement. The term "transatlantic" also has its limitations because it is usually understood to mean Britain on the one side and America on the other. The global dimensions of religious revival make the story more complex than that. While Britain and America were overwhelmingly Anglo and Anglo-Celtic in the eighteenth century, both were also sites of significant non-Anglo people and cultures. The rise of Methodism is inexplicable without reference to European diaspora populations in Britain and America including Moravians, Palatines, Huguenots, and Swedes. John Wesley was connected to the leaders of these movements, and his contacts open up insights into the complex web of international networks that created the evangelical revival of the eighteenth century. This paper will consider Wesley's appropriation and use of the writings of the New England revivalist Jonathan Edwards and argue that such use indicated a genuine (though qualified) respect for Edwards and at the same time served to legitimate Methodism as a genuine work of God.

## Wesley's Reading of Edwards

John Wesley first read Jonathan Edwards's *Faithful Narrative of a Surprising Work of God* on 9 October 1738 en route to Oxford. "In walking I read the truly surprising narrative of the conversions lately wrought in and about the town of Northampton in New England. Surely, 'this is the Lord's doing and it is marvellous in our eyes!'"[3] He abridged the work for Methodists in 1744, and forty years after his first reading he could still describe it as "a particular and beautiful account" of a "wonderful work of God."[4]

Albert Outler saw Wesley's reading of the *Faithful Narrative* as one of several "climactic experiences" of 1738, which included the influences of the Moravians and Salzburgers in Georgia, his Aldersgate experience on 24 May, and his pilgrimages soon after to the Moravian communities of Marienborn

2. Ward, "Power and Piety," 231.
3. Wesley, *Journals and Diaries II*, Works of John Wesley 19:16.
4. Wesley, "The Late Work of God in North-America," Works III:596.

and Hernhutt.[5] The reading of the *Faithful Narrative* "shook" him because it spoke of a revival being stirred by a form of pietism much like his own, yet at a time of instability in his own personal journey; he found himself, even after Aldersgate, still "beating the air" in trying to reconcile his theology of justification with his personal experience. According to Outler, this set of cumulative experiences drove him back to his own Anglican tradition where in the Edwardian Homilies he found an articulation of the doctrine of justification, "the theological font of his own heritage," which "remained as a fixed benchmark for the rest of his theological development."[6]

That Edwards was an important influence on Wesley is clear from the latter's publishing activity. He published an extract of Edwards's *The Distinguishing Marks of a Work of the Spirit of God* (1741) in July 1744, first preached as a commencement address at Yale College in 1741. On Monday 12 May 1746 at the Bristol Conference, both the *Faithful Narrative* and the *Distinguishing Marks* were read by the preachers (possibly out loud).[7] On Saturday 9 December 1749 Wesley read Edwards's popular *Life of David Brainerd*, which had been published that year. In 1768 he published his own abridgment of the 1765 English edition and urged the preachers at the Conference of that year to

> Let every preacher read carefully over the life of Mr. Brainerd. Let us be followers of him as he was of Christ, in absolute self-devotion, in total deadness to the world, and in fervent love to God and man. We want nothing but this. Then the word and the devil must fall under our feet.[8]

While he rejoiced at the way God had once more "surely . . . given to the Gentiles repentance unto life," Wesley also had some criticism for Brainerd.

> Yet amidst so great matter of joy I could not but grieve at this, that even so good a man as Mr. Brainerd should be "wise above that is written" [1 Cor. 4:6] in condemning what the Scripture nowhere condemns, in prescribing to God the way wherein he should work, and (in effect) applauding himself and magnifying his own work above that which God wrought in Scotland or among the English in New England; whereas in truth the work

---

5. Outler, "Introduction," 4.
6. Outler, "Introduction," 39.
7. Wesley, *Methodist Societies*, Works of John Wesley 10:170.
8. Ibid., 365.

among the Indians, great as it was, was not to be compared with that at Cambuslang, Kilsyth, or Northampton.[9]

Wesley abridged Edwards's *Treatise on Religious Affections* (1746) in 1773.[10] His most extended interaction with Edwards's ideas in print is probably *Thoughts upon Necessity* (written from Glasgow and dated 4 May 1774), in which Wesley responded to David Hume's essay, *Of Liberty and Necessity*, and its attempt to preserve human freedom within the overall framework of determinism.[11] In doing so, he drew upon Edwards's *Freedom of the Will* (1754).[12]

Wesley rejected the determinism of both Hume and Edwards because he could not "believe the noblest creature in the visible world to be only a fine piece of clockwork."[13] "Mr. Edwards of New England . . . by abundance of deep, metaphysical reasoning . . . flatly ascribes the necessity of all our actions to Him who united our souls to these bodies . . . [In this way he] connects together and confirms the . . . schemes . . . of the ancient Stoics and the modern Calvinists."[14] For Wesley, such determinism would make God the author of sin, which he cannot allow. Though he describes Edwards as a "good and sensible man," he cannot accept the latter's assertion that human actions are either commended or condemned because they are done voluntarily. If the human will is compelled to an action by an outside force then it is not truly free; therefore, no action can justly be subject to blame or punishment.[15] "There is no blame if [persons] are under a necessity of willing. There can be no moral good or evil, unless they have liberty as well as will, which is entirely a different thing. And the not adverting to this seems to be the direct occasion of Mr. Edwards's whole mistake."[16]

In a further *Thought on Necessity*, Wesley refers to "that great man, President Edwards of New-England," in his reply to Dr. Hartley's "Essay

---

9. Wesley, Journal entry for Monday 4 Dec, 1749, in *Journals and Diaries III*, Works of John Wesley 20:315.

10. Though it appeared in an edition of his Works in 1773 (vol. XXIII), it was not published separately during Wesley's lifetime. Wesley, *Journals and Diaries I*, Works of John Wesley 18:11n44.

11. Wesley, "Thoughts upon Necessity," Works of John Wesley 10:460, 463. 467, 475.

12. Edwards, *The Freedom of the Will*.

13. Wesley, "Thoughts upon Necessity," Works of John Wesley 10:456.

14. Ibid., 460, 463.

15. Ibid., 467.

16. Ibid.

on Man."[17] Hartley had reduced all human action to vibrations within the brain, giving the doctrine of necessity a physiological foundation. Wesley asked why Hartley would publish such ideas, seeing they would destroy morality by leaving no room for either vice or virtue. "Why? Because his brain vibrated in such a matter that he could not help it." Edwards, according to Wesley, makes the same error attributing all actions of the will to the effects of impression upon the pineal gland or some other part of the brain. "Where is liberty then? It is excluded. All you see, is one connected chain, fixed as the pillars of heaven . . . inevitable necessity governs all things, and men have no more liberty than stones."[18]

Wesley is not wishing to champion any doctrine of free will, however, in his rejection of this particular view of necessity. He goes on to insist that free will is as incapable of determining human action as reason. Both have no more pull over human nature "than a thread of tow that has touched the fire." The will is always subject to divine grace and two texts must always be placed together—"Without me, ye can do nothing" and "I can do all things through Christ strengthening me." In the final analysis, for Wesley, neither reason nor free will is the determining factor in human volition, but the power and the grace of God in Christ.[19]

In his journal entry for 16 June 1775, Wesley compared the awakening in England with that in Scotland and New England. God had undoubtedly "laid bare his arm" in all three places, but he considered England to be more significant for the following reasons. More people were reached and their transformation was more rapid. The change people experienced was clearer, deeper, and more long lasting. Where Scotland and New England saw God move for weeks or months at a time, in England the work has extended over eighteen years without interruption. In Scotland and New England, God used "a considerable number" of prominent and talented clergy, but in England, God had used "only two or three inconsiderable clergymen, with a few, young, raw, unlettered men" opposed by clergy and laity alike.[20] A week later, on 23 June, he took up the same line of thought, this time asking why the revival had ground to a halt in Scotland and New England. Many of the leaders of the revival became wise in their own eyes and thought that God could not work but through them. "Many of them were bigots, immoderately attached either to their own opinions or mode of worship." Somewhat uncharitably, perhaps, Wesley claims "Mr. Edwards himself was not clear of

17. Ibid., 474–80, quote on 475.
18. Ibid., 475–76.
19. Wesley, "A Thought on Necessity," Works of John Wesley 10:476–79.
20. Wesley, *Works Journals and Diaries IV*, Works of John Wesley 21:18–19.

this. But the Scotch bigots were beyond all others, placing Arminianism (so called) on a level with Deism, and the Church of England with that of Rome ... No marvel then that the Spirit of God was grieved. Let us profit by their example."[21]

In his 1773 abridgment of Edwards's *Treatise on Religious Affections* (1746), Wesley saw the many that fell away after the New England revival as proof that a believer "may make shipwreck of the faith"; Edwards determined instead that such people were never genuinely converted in the first place.

> In order to do this, he heaps together so many curious, subtle, metaphysical distinctions, as are sufficient to puzzle the brain, and confound the intellects, of all the plain men and women in the universe, and to make them doubt of, if not wholly deny, all the works which God wrought in their souls.
>
> Out of this dangerous heap, wherein much wholesome food is mixed with much deadly poison, I have selected many remarks and admonitions which may be of great use to the children of God.[22]

## "Some Account of the Late Work of God in America" (1778)

I would like now to examine in some detail Wesley's 1778 sermon "Some Account of the Late Work of God in North-America," in which he sets out a history designed to defend Methodism as a genuine work of God as well as to extend his opposition to the American Revolution. The sermon is based on Ezekiel 1:16: "The appearance was, as it were, a wheel in the middle of a wheel." Wesley notes how the text had been used by Christians in a secondary way to refer to the mysterious workings of God's providence, the purposes of which could not be understood until they had been fulfilled. "Perhaps no age ever afforded a more striking instance of this kind than the present does, in the dispensations of divine providence, with respect to our colonies in North America."[23]

> A worldwide view of the movement of grace was part of the legacy of the pietist world to the evangelicals. Exchange of

---

21. Ibid., 19–20.

22. Wesley, "List of Works Revised and Abridged," in *Works* (Jackson) 14:269–70.

23. Wesley, *Some Account of the late Work of God in North-America, in a Sermon on Ezekiel I. 16*, 4.

information of this kind was one of the ways in which expectations were created which were satisfied by the spread of the revival itself. In the 1740s John Erskine and other spokesmen for the Scots' revivals . . . exchanged correspondence and literature with Jonathan Edwards, Thomas Prince, and other American friends of Whitefield, from which developed an historical view that God's saving activity was not, as the hypercalvinists alleged, at an ebb, but at a flood tide—a view thoroughly documented in standard works such as John Gillies, *Historical Collections Relating To Remarkable Periods of the Success of the Gospel* (4 volumes, 1754–96), and its successors.[24]

Wesley traces the "first wheel" in terms of his ministry in Georgia, believing that in 1736 God had begun a work of grace in that southern colony.[25] This is an interesting description, given that historians often view Wesley's brief two years in Georgia, from 1736–37, as marked by personal and professional failure and as something of a spiritual wasteland. This suits the evangelical narrative of the religious seeker who must first reach the bottom of the barrel before finding the "glorious liberty" entailed in the new birth. It is certainly not that the established narrative is without compelling historical evidence; the problem is that historians have sometimes found it difficult to see the Georgia sojourn on its own terms, divorced from later developments. Geordan Hammond's recent study, *John Wesley in America*, presents a convincing case that Wesley's time in Georgia was not a failure or a mere prelude to greater things; rather, it provided an opportunity for Wesley to apply the disciplines and practices of primitive Christianity that had fascinated him since his days as a student at Oxford.[26] There in the

24. Wesley, *Journals and Diaries II*, Works of John Wesley 19:75n85, cited in Ward, "The Baptists and the Transformation of the Church," 170–71.

25. Wesley, *Late Work of God*, 4–12.

26. Hammond, *John Wesley in America*. One of the great strengths of this book is that it draws upon primary sources on the colony of Georgia that Wesley biographers have neglected and that are helpful in shedding new light on Wesley's time there. These include The Colonial Records of the State of Georgia and the diaries and journals of trustees of the colony such as John Perceval, first Earl of Egmont and William Stephens, trustee of the colony during Wesley's last months there. The author is careful not to rely solely on Wesley's published journals recognising that these are constructed accounts designed for public consumption. Though Henry Rack described the Georgia journals as "a selective and slanted account," (Rack, *Reasonable Enthusiast*, 113), Hammond nonetheless concludes after crosschecking Wesley's private diaries as well as the journals of Charles Wesley, Benjamin Ingham, Thomas Causton and many others, that they remain "an accurate and reliable picture." (Hammond, *John Wesley in America*, 11). This book is also the first full-length treatment of the influence of the so-called "Usager" Non-Jurors on Wesley's liturgical and sacramental practice. The

American wilderness, he was given the opportunity to apply pastoral practices that would later be adapted and developed in the Methodist movement. It is not that this was not a personally turbulent time for Wesley—his failed romance with Sophia Hopkey and his unpopularity with some of his parishioners are well known—but the greater significance of this period of Wesley's life is that it enabled him to experiment with the ideal of "Primitive Christianity" in ways that shaped the later development of Methodism. Georgia should, then, not be seen as a lacuna in Wesley's spiritual journey but as a defining period.

Wesley included the English, the Moravians, and the Germans from Salzburg as the beneficiaries of the work of grace in Georgia. At the same time, Wesley affirms that an awakening of the English took place in Savannah and Frederica and links this to the New England Awakening in Northampton, Massachusetts, and "adjoining towns," an account of which was published by Jonathan Edwards in the *Faithful Narrative*. "I suppose, there had been no influence in America, of so swift and deep a work of Grace, for an hundred years before: Nay, nor perhaps since the English settled there."[27] The following year the work spread from New England to the South and at the same time proceeded northward from Georgia in a kind of pincer movement.[28] In 1738 George Whitefield came to Georgia to assist Wesley either in preaching to the Indians or to the settlers, but because Wesley had left for England before Whitefield arrived he preached only to the settlers. He began in Georgia and then preached his way north through "South and North Carolina" and "in the intermediate provinces" until he came to New England. Whitefield made many converts along the way, so that "by his Ministry a line of Communication was formed, quite from Georgia to New England." Over several years, Whitefield made "several more journeys through the Provinces" [in fact he made seven] and God prospered the work greatly.[29]

---

"Non-Jurors" were those Anglican clergy who refused to sign the Oath of Allegiance to William (1689–1702) and Mary (1689–1694) because of their support for the deposed Stuart monarchy. Non-Jurists had a fascination for the practices of the early church and sought to re-establish many of them in the Church of England. The "Usagers" were a party of Non-Jurors who were committed to the "use" of (1) Mixing water with the Eucharistic wine (2) a prayer of oblation over the elements understood as a representative sacrifice (3) a prayer of blessing over the Eucharistic elements and (4) prayer for the faithful dead during the Eucharist.

27. Wesley, *Late Work of God*, 5.
28. Ibid., 5–6.
29. Ibid., 6–7.

This linking of Georgia with Edwards's famous revival is an interesting strategy and an instance of breathtaking hubris. Wesley describes his own work in Georgia and the awakening in Northampton as though they were two parts of a continuous and converging stream, connected by the itinerancy of his Oxford colleague George Whitefield. In doing this he smooths over the historical complexities and continuities, rewriting history to serve his own purposes.

On Whitefield's final journey, he was saddened to find that most who had formerly been awakened had now fallen away, and very few had "brought forth fruit to perfection."[30] Wesley seized upon this observation to set forth (in a back handed way) the value of the Methodist system of classes and bands:

> And what wonder? For it was a true saying, which was common in the ancient church, "The soul and the body make a man, and the Spirit and discipline make a Christian." But those who were more or less affected by Whitefield's preaching, had no discipline at all. They had no shadow of discipline; nothing of the kind. They were formed into no Societies. They had no Christian connexion with each other, nor were ever taught to watch over each other's souls. So that if any fell into lukewarmness, or even into sin, he had none to lift him up: He might fall lower and lower; yea into hell if he would; for who regarded it?[31]

Things remained like this until Wesley received several letters from America, describing the low state of religion there and requesting that he send some preachers over to help revive the work. This was considered at the 1769 Conference, and Richard Boardman and Joseph Pilmore were sent. They preached first in Philadelphia and New York. People responded, and Societies were formed with "Christian discipline introduced in all its branches." Other preachers followed, and God also raised up native-born American preachers "till there were two and twenty travelling preachers in America, who kept their circuits as regularly as those in England."[32] The work spread to North Carolina, Maryland, Virginia, Pennsylvania, and the Jerseys, and "sunk abundantly deeper than it ever had before," so that "at the beginning of the late troubles" there were three thousand in the Societies.[33]

Then "a bar appeared in the way, a grand hindrance to the progress of Religion." An increase in trade bought immense wealth to the American

30. Ibid., 7.
31. Ibid., 7–8.
32. Ibid., 8–9.
33. Ibid., 9

colonies, and many grew wealthy. This led to pride and luxury. Abundant banquets filled the tables of Americans—up to twenty dishes at a sitting—and this was not condemned but praised as generosity and hospitality.[34] Idleness and sloth sprung from this luxury. Young people in perfect health could not even put on their own clothes but had to be dressed by slaves. It is a wonder they did not get slaves to handfeed them as well, as "the lordly lubbers in China are fed by a slave standing on each side."[35] Sloth and luxury had led to sexual immorality. A letter from Philadelphia informed Wesley that if he thought the women of England did not abound in chastity, they would pass as vestal virgins compared to the women of Philadelphia![36]

Now Wesley traces the second "Wheel of Divine Providence." From the beginning of the American colonies there had been a "hankering after Independency." This is understandable, considering the connections they had formed before leaving England and the poor treatment they had received there. They were never well reconciled to the government, and they passed that attitude on to their children in their new setting. This was in spite of the many favors and benefits they had received from the English government.[37] This spirit prevailed, especially in Boston, as early as 1737, as witnessed by Charles Wesley during his visit there in that year. Many were crying for independence even then, but there was no plan to assert it since none thought they could stand against the "power of Great Britain."[38]

"Why should these English blockheads rule over us?" was the general sentiment, and this spread to the other colonies. But there was a fear of the French in Canada, against which British military power served as a buffer. Once Canada was ceded to Britain, definite plans for separation began to be drawn up.[39] An opportunity was provided by the Stamp Act of 1765, and agitators began to press their claims and spread their ideas among the people. They vilified the British Parliament, speaking as if they were the vilest wretches and villains alive. They had not yet turned to attacks upon the king, but this was soon to follow.[40] Northern and Southern Colonies then took up arms and formed a Congress. At first they spoke not of independence but only of liberty, but soon they threw off this mask and showed their true intent. Dr. Witherspoon, President of the College in New

34. Ibid., 10–11.
35. Ibid., 11.
36. Ibid., 12.
37. Ibid., 12–13.
38. Ibid., 13–14.
39. Ibid., 14.
40. Ibid., 14–15.

Jersey, addressed the Congress (published in a sermon in 1776) and made it clear that the British Parliament had not understood the extent of American claims. William Pitt's ["Lord Chatham's"] Bill of Reconciliation would never have been consented to in America, and it was clear that their agenda was Independence.[41] Once they had defected from the mother country, nine tenths of their trade was cut off and they turned to privateering (piracy). But this did not profit them because they lost as many ships as they took. Their fountains of wealth dried up, so that they are now as poor as the poorest parts of Scotland or Ireland. Goods are now in such short supply that not only luxury items but food and clothing also are scarce.[42]

So the two wheels have been observed apart:

1. Trade, wealth, pride, luxury, sloth, and wantonness on the one hand.
2. The Spirit of Independence spreading north and south on the other.

How do these two wheels relate to each other? How does a Wise Providence use one to check the other? By blocking British ships from American ports, trade declined and want ensued. The wheel began to move within the wheel. Once trade and wealth failed, so pride failed, luxury was no longer possible, poverty and want struck at the root of sloth. Now one must work in order to eat.[43] "Thus by the Adorable Providence of God, the main hindrances of this work were removed."[44] The vile disease of the spirit of independence provided a cure for all the rest. The destruction of trade has made way for humility, temperance, industry and charity. So the fierceness of the Americans turns to the praise of God and they will learn to value not independence but the genuine British liberty that their ancestors in the earliest colonies had always enjoyed as well as that greater and more glorious liberty of the sons of God.[45]

Brett C. McInnelly, in his recent *Textual Warfare and the Making of Methodism*, has investigated the manner in which eighteenth-century Methodist self-identity was formed in the context of public dispute and contestation resolved through textual discourse of various kinds.[46] McInnelly's work shows how Methodists responded in print to their many critics in such a way as to construct their own identity as a people.[47] Of course, Wes-

41. Ibid., 15–16.
42. Ibid., 16–17.
43. Ibid., 17–20.
44. Ibid., 20.
45. Ibid., 20–23.
46. McInnelly, *Textual Warfare*.
47. Ibid., 5.

ley led the way in this "textual warfare," wielding his considerable literary and polemical skills to argue for the legitimacy of Methodism as a genuine work of God. In his providential view of history, Wesley saw the American Revolution not simply in political terms. God had worked through it to teach the Americans a lesson. British Americans had been blessed by God under the crown. They had known revival in Georgia under the Wesleys and in Northampton under Edwards; southern and northern colonies, Arminian and Calvinist, linked together by George Whitefield, the "first Methodist," the "Divine Dramatist," and the "Pedlar of Divinity," who made such a successful business out of revival and stood at the center of what came to be known (whether "invented" or not) as "the Great Awakening." But the Americans had grown fat and kicked in their prosperity, rebelling against their God and their pious king, George III. So God had sent war, the "besom of destruction," to reduce them once again to poverty. In this way they would return once again to their first love.

## Conclusions

Wesley's appropriation of Edwards displays his usual mix of Christian charity and the unconquerable conviction of the rightness of his own opinions. In Edwards's *Faithful Narrative*, he was given a case study that helped confirm the doctrines he had learned from the Moravians and was surprised to find also in his own Anglican tradition. Justification brought with it a deeply felt awareness of the forgiveness of sins and a filial connection to God as Father and Christ as Savior. While such a conversion might be accompanied by deeply emotional states that could manifest in surprising and even alarming ways, the genuine fruit of revival was not in such manifestations but in the enduring qualities of holy love—in "charity and its fruits." Wesley was an astute observer and recorder of religious experience. Too much a "man of reason" to be given to flights of mystical fancy himself (remember his heart was "strangely" warmed, as if such emotional states were unusual for him), he looked upon the strange religious manifestations sometimes on display among Methodists with some concern and with perhaps even a trace of envy. His response to such manifestations—they could be either from God, the devil, or "animal spirits" (overwrought emotional states), and that one should neither promote nor prohibit them but look instead for lasting holiness as the only genuine fruit of revival—was essentially the same as the approach taken by Edwards in his *Religious Affections*. Reg Ward and Dick Heitzenrater have argued that what transformed Wesley from a failed missionary into a successful outdoor evangelist was the realistic observation that when he preached after the manner of Jonathan Edwards he got results after the manner of Jonathan Edwards; that he was saved not as Peter Bohler recommended by preaching faith till he had it, but by preaching faith till he observed that other people had it.[48]

I am not suggesting that Edwards stands out above all other influences on Wesley, but simply observing that he was an important part of the complex patchwork of religious ideas and influences that ebbed and flowed throughout the Atlantic world of the eighteenth century. Just as with George Whitefield, it was Edwards's Calvinism that came in for Wesley's most trenchant criticism. Undoubtedly Edwards was "a good and sensible man," yet for Wesley, his writings remained a "dangerous heap," a mixture of "wholesome food" with "deadly poison." Edwards was, in Wesley's view, among those whose immoderate attachment to Calvinism and bigotry toward "Arminians" had quenched the Spirit and contributed to a loss of revival momentum. (Of course, Wesley could be equally immoderate in his attachment to his own side of the argument and equally bigoted toward Calvinists.) Wesley's connection of his own work in Georgia with Edwards's famous revival in Northampton was surely a self-serving exercise, an attempt to both legitimize Methodism as a genuine work of God and provide an argument that the hand of Providence stood against the rebellious spirit of American independence. Yet it was also a form of flattery, an indication of how important Wesley saw Edwards. It also may serve as further evidence that the transatlantic evangelicalism of the eighteenth century exhibited the capacity to transcend denominational factionalism in the common cause of the gospel.

## Bibliography

Edwards, Jonathan. *The Freedom of the Will: A Careful and Strict Inquiry into the Modern Prevailing Notions of that Freedom of the Will which is Supposed to be Essential to Moral Agency, Virtue and Vice, Reward and Punishment, Praise and Blame.* http://www.earlymoderntexts.com/pdfs/edwards1754.pdf.

Hammond, Geordan. *John Wesley in America: Restoring Primitive Christianity.* Oxford: Oxford University Press, 2014.

Hempton, David. *Religion and Political Culture in Britain and Ireland: From the Glorious Revolution to the Decline of Empire.* Cambridge, UK: Cambridge University Press, 1996.

---

48. Ward and Heitzenrater, "Introduction," Journals and Diaries (BCE), 18:35 with reference to Outler, *John Wesley*, 15–17, citing Outler as having maintained this view "with some force."

McInnelly, Brett C. *Textual Warfare and the Making of Methodism*. Oxford: Oxford University Press, 2014.

Outler, Albert C. *John Wesley*. New York: Oxford, 1964.

———. *John Wesley's Sermons: An Introduction*. Nashville: Abingdon Press, 1991.

Rack, Henry. *Reasonable Enthusiast: John Wesley and the Rise of Methodism*. 3rd ed. London: Epworth, 2002.

Ward, W. Reginald, and Richard P. Heitzenrater. "Introduction." In *Journals and Diaries I, 1735–1738*, edited by W. Reginald Ward and Richard P. Heitzenrater, Works of John Wesley: Bicentennial Edition 18. Nashville: Abingdon Press, 1988.

Ward, W. Reginald. "The Baptists and the Transformation of the Church, 1780–1830." *Baptist Quarterly* 25 (1973) 170–71.

———. "Power and Piety: The Origins of Religious Revival in the Early Eighteenth Century." *Bulletin of the John Rylands University Library of Manchester* 63/1 (1980) 231–53.

Wesley, John. *Journals and Diaries I, 1735–1738*. Edited by W. Reginald Ward and Richard P. Heitzenrater, The Works of John Wesley: Bicentennial Edition 18. Nashville: Abingdon Press, 1988.

———. *Journals and Diaries II, 1738–1743*. Edited by W. Reginald Ward and Richard P. Heitzenrater. The Works of John Wesley: Bicentennial Edition 19. Nashville: Abingdon Press, 1990.

———. *Journals and Diaries III, 1743–1754*. Edited by W. Reginald Ward and Richard P. Heitzenrater. The Works of John Wesley: Bicentennial Edition 20. Nashville: Abingdon Press, 1991.

———. *Journals and Diaries IV, 1755–1765*. Edited by W. Reginald Ward and Richard P. Heitzenrater. The Works of John Wesley: Bicentennial Edition 21. Nashville: Abingdon Press, 1992.

———, "List of Works Revised and Abridged by the Rev. John Wesley, M.A., with the Prefaces by which They are Accompanied," in Vol. 14, *The Works of John Wesley* 14, edited by Thomas Jackson, 199–318. CD-ROM edition. Franklin, TN: Providence House, 1994.

———. *Some Account of the late Work of God in North-America, in a Sermon on Ezekiel I. 16*. London: at the New Chapel, 1778.

———. "Some Account of the Late Work of God in North-America." In *Sermons III*, edited by Albert C. Outler, The Works of John Wesley: Bicentennial Edition 3:592–608. Nashville; Abingdon Press, 1986.

———. "A Thought on Necessity." In *The Methodist Societies: The Minutes of Conference*, edited by Henry D. Rack, The Works of John Wesley: Bicentennial Edition 10:475–76. Nashville: Abingdon Press, 2011.

———. "Thoughts upon Necessity." In *The Methodist Societies: The Minutes of Conference*, edited by Henry D. Rack, The Works of John Wesley: Bicentennial Edition 10:456–74. Nashville: Abingdon Press, 2011.

# 14

# Training Ministers of "Light and Heat"
## Jonathan Edwards's Home-Based Educational Approach and Its Legacy

ANDREW SCHUMAN

SCHOLARS HAVE LONG NOTED the importance of the Great Awakening for the development of American higher education. Historian Douglas Sloan writes, "No attempt at an adequate understanding of colonial education can avoid a careful appraisal of the broad cultural and social impact of the Great Awakening."[1] As waves of young men experienced personal revival and entered the ministry, existing educational institutions were reshaped, and new institutions formed. Of the many new institutions created in the generation following the Awakening, the most well-known are the series of colleges established by the New Light, or for the Presbyterians, New Side, leaders: the College of New Jersey at Princeton in 1746, Rhode Island College (renamed Brown University) in 1764, Queen's College (renamed Rutgers) in 1766, and Dartmouth College in 1769.[2]

Less well-known, but critical to our understanding of ministerial education after the Awakening, was the emergence of a distinct group of men associated with Jonathan Edwards and his disciples, the so-called New Divinity. The New Divinity men saw themselves as heirs to the

---

1. Sloan, *The Great Awakening and American Education*, 1.
2. Kling, "New Divinity Schools," 185.

Edwardsean deposit, tasked with defending classical Calvinist doctrines and advancing true piety in the Revolutionary era. They valued the benefits of a Harvard or Yale education, but thought collegiate study alone insufficient for training in ministry. So they invited aspiring New Light ministers, often recent graduates of Yale, into their homes for residential study and apprenticeship. The New Divinity Schools of the Prophets, as they would come to be called, provided a curriculum of theological study and practical training in the parsonage of a seasoned minister. In time, this medium of education became part and parcel with the message. For in these schools aspiring ministers imbibed far more than a system of thought; they observed and embraced a way of life that integrated the light of the gospel with the heat of heartfelt religion.

Scholar David Kling describes the New Divinity schools of the prophets as "America's single most important source of ministerial training from the mid-eighteenth century to the establishment of seminaries in the early nineteenth century."[3] The numbers alone make a strong case: between 1750 and 1825, over five hundred clerical aspirants studied in New Divinity schools of the prophets; between 1765 and 1783, New Divinity men occupied fully one-half of New England's pulpit appointments.[4] The influence of the schools is even more impressive: they paved the way for the divinity schools in the early nineteenth century, contributed heavily to missions societies, abolitionist movements, and pro-Revolutionary causes, and preserved the revival embers that would be rekindled in the Second Great Awakening. While scholarly attention has been given to the role the schools of the prophets played in the developing American landscape, less attention has been given to the training practices and pedagogical vision employed in these schools, and what debt these practices have, if any, to Jonathan Edwards.

The purpose of this chapter is to investigate Edwards's theory and practice of ministerial training and its legacy in the schools of the prophets. To do this, I will look specifically at Edwards's education of Joseph Bellamy, Edwards's first theological student, and how Bellamy drew upon his experience in Edwards's parsonage to create his own school. Founded in the 1750s, Bellamy's parsonage seminary is considered the first and most influential school of the prophets, training over 60 ministers and becoming the pedagogical standard for the New Divinity schools. By examining the education Bellamy received in Edwards's home, and the practices he then used in his

---

3. Ibid., 186.
4. Ibid., 193.

own school, we are provided with a unique window into Edwards's vision for ministerial training.

## Bellamy Comes to Northampton

In the fall of 1736, at the age of seventeen, Joseph Bellamy moved from his hometown of Cheshire, Connecticut, to the home of Jonathan Edwards in Northampton to study theology and train for the ministry. A recent graduate of Yale College, Bellamy had taken the usual path of clerical candidates in his day: after graduation he returned to his hometown for study with a local pastor in preparation for his ordination exams.[5] It was around this time, according to his diary, that Bellamy experienced conversion and adopted New Light views on preaching and ministry. Amid circulating cautions of studying for the ministry under an unconverted clergyman, and knowing Bellamy's aspirations to be a New Light preacher, we can understand why Bellamy looked elsewhere to study. Bellamy does not record how he first learned of Edwards's ministry or resolved to study with him, but we do know that news of the 1734–35 Northampton revivals had traveled to Yale's campus when Bellamy was a senior. Additionally, students had circulated Edwards's sermon, *A Divine and Supernatural Light*, on the Yale campus. Bellamy's classmates, Aaron Burr, James Davenport, Benjamin Pomeroy, and Eleazar Wheelock, may also have shared their personal experiences of the revivals that were now sweeping through the Connecticut River Valley.[6] An aspiring New Light preacher could do no better than to study with the inaugurator of the revivals. So the young Bellamy packed his bags and headed to Edwards's home.

What Bellamy experienced when he arrived, if at all like the experience of Samuel Hopkins, David Brainerd, or many other theological students to come, was a generous integration into the full life of the family. This meant sharing meals, contributing to household work, participating in family prayer and Bible study, and—likely in imitation of Edwards—long hours of study. Additionally, we know that Edwards and Bellamy traveled together to preach and attend ministerial meetings, and when at home labored together in the Northampton congregation. While not prone to

---

5. Richard Baxter advocates this kind of training in *The Reformed Pastor*.

6. Valeri, *Law and Providence*, 12. I would like to thank Mark Valeri for letting me consult his transcription of Bellamy's notebook. His detailed transcription of the first half of the notebook was particularly helpful, as were his transcribed sections of the second half of the notebook. His work provided insights into Bellamy's shorthand that proved invaluable for transcribing the remainder of the notebook.

small talk, Edwards saw immense benefit in conversation on divine topics. In his sermon "The Importance and Advantage of a Thorough Knowledge of Divine Truth" in *The Sermons of Jonathan Edwards: A Reader* (p. 210), he concludes by exhorting his hearers: "how much might persons promote each other's knowledge in divine things if . . . all were more disposed to enter on such conversation as would be for their mutual edification and instruction." In addition to appointed times of tutorial instruction, we can assume that ongoing conversation on divine topics was a regular part of Bellamy's education.

Although different in demeanor (Bellamy rough mannered and pugnacious; Edwards serious-minded and reserved), the two men developed a deep admiration for each other. In a letter of recommendation to John Erskine, the Scottish publisher of evangelical works, Edwards wrote that Bellamy was "of very good natural abilities, of closeness of thought, of extraordinary diligence in his studies, and earnest care to know exactly the truth."[7] In 1750, on page 5 of his introduction to Bellamy's *True Religion Delineated*, Edwards wrote glowingly, "From intimate acquaintance with him [the author], which I have been favored with for many years, I have abundant reason to be satisfied that what has governed him in the publication, is no vanity of mind, no affectation to appear in the world as an author, nor any desire of applause, but a hearty concern for the glory of God, and the kingdom and interests of his Lord and Master Jesus Christ."

During their shared time in Northampton, Edwards and Bellamy developed a sense of spiritual kinship. Over the years they would share everything from visits to business ventures, from pulpits to libraries, from counsel on professional and personal decisions to support in public disputations. Their partnership ranged from editing each other's published works to divulging the joys and hardships of family life, all recorded in numerous letters. In 1750, Edwards wrote that Bellamy was "one of my most intimate friends in the world."[8] We can assume that their warm affections and depth of shared life began in Northampton. It suggests that a growing and generous friendship, united in a common love for the gospel, was the relational context of Bellamy's training.

But what do we know of Edwards's theological instruction? The best evidence we have comes from a student notebook that Bellamy kept while in Northampton. Bellamy's notebook contains a collection of reading notes on various books from Edwards's library, theological dissertations on topics ranging from heaven to regeneration to church governance, and it includes

7. Ibid., 14.
8. Ibid., 12.

example catechetical questions as well as philosophical arguments for the reasonableness of Christian doctrine.[9] It is to Bellamy's student notebook that we now turn our attention.

## Bellamy's Notebook: Contents and Theological Themes

Bellamy's notebook totals thirty-two pages, twenty-two of which contain Bellamy's writing. It is a tall but thin booklet, twelve-and-a-half by five inches, similar to those used in this period by merchants for accounting purposes. Given the value of paper in his day, its empty final pages may indicate that Bellamy retired the notebook upon leaving Northampton. Bellamy divided his notebook into distinct (usually short) entries. The notebook begins with Bellamy's name inscribed on the upper corner with the date, 1736. The rest of the first page consists of the table of contents, which continues onto the last page of the notebook, along with a short list of books that Bellamy consulted for his compositions—something of an initial bibliography.

The notebook begins much like a reading log. The first twelve pages consist, in the main, of direct excerpts from the Anglican Calvinist John Edwards's systematic theology, *Theologia Reformata*. In nearly sixteen hundred pages, this text organizes and expounds Reformed doctrines with a special view to refuting the errors of "Papists, Arians and Socinians, Pelagians and Remonstrants, Anabaptists, Antinomians, Deists, Atheists, Scepticks, Enthusiasts, and Libertines."[10] Edwards held the book in high esteem, featuring this work, as well as eight other distinct books by John Edwards, in his library.[11] Bellamy's entries trace the progression of the book, beginning with the eternal existence and attributes of God, and proceeding to the christological and soteriological doctrines of Christ's suffering and satisfaction for sin and the nature of forgiveness before concluding with church structure and the sacraments, including a lengthy entry on infant baptism. In each of these entries, Bellamy pays special attention to arguments used to defend each of the doctrines against opponents. From this first portion of the notebook we can assume Edwards considered two things of primary importance in his instruction: 1) that his student understand the systematic coherence

---

9. Bellamy, *Student Notebook, 1736*.
10. (John) Edwards, *Theologia Reformata*.
11. Edwards, "Account Book," *WJE* 26:353.

of Christian doctrine, grounded in Scripture, and 2) that his student be able to defend this system against an array of contemporary errors.

At one point in his reading notes on the *Reformata*, Bellamy skips several hundred pages ahead to make one of his longest entries before returning back to his previous place. This entry is on the nature and requirements of forgiveness relative to the unpardonable sin against the Holy Ghost. We cannot be sure what prompted this entry, but we do know that during this same period of time Edwards writes three lengthy, and nearly consecutive, entries in his *"Miscellanies,"* titled: "sin against the Holy Ghost, why unpardonable." This correspondence between the two notebooks suggests that Edwards used his *"Miscellanies,"* even at this early stage, in training ministerial candidates. It also suggests that Edwards's approach to training ministers included inviting his student into his current thought and work. If this entry was prompted by Edwards's current preoccupations, then perhaps we see early signs of conversation and collaboration between teacher and student—an invitation by Edwards to learn at his elbow.

A more careful look at the sections Bellamy excerpts from the *Reformata* reveals areas of shared interest for the two men at this time. In 1737 Edwards is drafting *A Faithful Narrative*. To little surprise, Bellamy's longest entry is on the nature of true regeneration as distinguished from both sanctification and repentance. In Bellamy's reading notes we see a course of study that is suited to the interests and needs of both student and mentor.

After Bellamy concludes his notes on the *Reformata*, his reading and writing becomes more diverse. Except for a few scattered sections of reading notes, Bellamy leaves his pattern of excerpting passages directly from other texts and begins to construct his own prose. The entries now follow the pattern of question and response. It is likely that these questions came from Edwards and comprised an early, less organized, version of the set of theological questions he uses for instruction at Princeton. Before looking at some example questions and responses, it is worth noting the wide range of books Bellamy cites in constructing his responses, all of which are included in Edwards's Catalogue of Books, and presumably in his library. It is uncertain whether Edwards guided Bellamy's course of reading or simply posed his questions and left the research up to Bellamy. In either case, integrative reading and research was an essential part of Bellamy's education.

We have already discussed John Edwards's *Theologia Reformata*. Among the other Calvinist divines in Edwards's library, Bellamy quotes most frequently from Samuel Willard's *A Complete Body of Divinity*, often considered the first systematic theology written and published in America. This comprehensive work, consisting of two hundred and fifty expository lectures on the shorter catechism, was regularly consulted by Edwards himself and likely recommended to Bellamy as a reference work.[12] Among the Non-Calvinist divines, the two most prominent figures are Edward Stillingfleet, the Anglican Latitudinarian, and Thomas Sherlock, bishop of London. For Stillingfleet, Bellamy draws most heavily upon *Origines Sacrae, A Rational Account of the Grounds of Natural and Reveal'd Religion*, and *Irenicum: The Divine Right of Particular Forms of Church Government*. In Thomas Sherlock, Bellamy draws upon *The Use and Intent of Prophesy in the Several Ages of the World*. Additionally, Bellamy cites several works that are explicitly anti-deist such as Robert Jenkin's *Reasonableness and Certainty of the Christian Religion*. Bellamy's notes also draw upon works by non-theologians, such as historian John Oldmixon's *The Critical History of England*, Sir Walter Raleigh's *History of the World*, and mathematician Humphry Ditton's *Discourse on the Resurrection of Jesus Christ*. As we see from this sampling of authors, Bellamy's reading incorporated an impressive range of material.

An example entry takes up the theme of Christ as mediator. In his table of contents, Bellamy refers to this section as a discourse on the "agreement between God and man" and the means by which Christ is able to "perform the service God required of him."[13] Bellamy proceeds systematically, according to three questions: 1) For whom was Christ mediator? 2) When was Christ made mediator? 3) What doeth Christ to bring about the treaty of peace? His answers reveal a considerable level of nuance as he answers each question according to numerous considerations. For instance, the second question he answers in a five-fold way: with respect to God's eternal plan of redemption, the inception of sin, the incarnation, the inauguration of the kingdom, and the work of the Spirit. It is worth noting the clear similarity between this entry and Edwards's third entry in his *"Miscellanies"* (on "Christ's Mediation and Satisfaction").[14] In this entry, Edwards similarly organizes his thoughts discursively according to several questions. While the questions are not identical, the two entries share the same format, reflect a similar level of theological rigor, and share a careful exegesis of Scripture. Edwards's interest, during 1736–37, in the mediatorship of Christ in 1736, reflected by two substantial entries in his *"Miscellanies"* on this topic during this time (*"Misc."* 704 and 706), strengthens our assumption that there exists a relationship between the two theological notebooks.[15] It is quite possible that Edwards encouraged Bellamy to imitate the *"Miscellanies"* as a way to organize his own theological development. That Bellamy's journal

---

12. Ibid., 3.
13. Bellamy, *Student Notebook*, 15.
14. Edwards, "'Misc.' 3," *WJE* 13:165.
15. Edwards, "'Misc.' 704," *WJE* 18:314–21, and "'Misc.' 706," *WJE* 18:322–30.

does not simply copy Edwards's reflections also indicates a certain level of autonomous thought.

Other questions Bellamy addresses range from defenses of classical doctrines—"Wherein does the greatness of sin discover itself, i.e. Adam?";[16] "Are future sins pardoned as well as the past and the present?—to speculative theology—"Will there be employment in heaven?"[17] In response to these first two questions, Bellamy's answers consist of carefully reasoned expositions of the doctrines, drawing heavily upon the exegetical use of Scripture. In response to the third question about employment in heaven, he relies on philosophical reasoning. He answers the question in the affirmative, arguing that employment is given to humans, even in their glorified state, because the "happiness of a creature consists in orthopraxy . . . [and] immediate communion with Christ will occupy their whole powers."[18] This question and response bear striking similarity to Edwards's extensive speculations in his *"Miscellanies"* on the topic "Happiness of Heaven," in entries 95, 263, 272 and elsewhere. Throughout Bellamy's notebook, his method and manner of theological reflection and the scope of his interests reflect those of his mentor, ranging from biblical exegesis, to rigorous defense of traditional doctrines, to philosophical theology.

Several other entries contain a foray into natural theology. In a section that appears to be partially reading notes and partially Bellamy's own argumentation, he provides several arguments for the immortality of the soul. The book he draws upon is William Sherlock's *Immortality of the Soul*. Bellamy's notes include several reasons arising from human conscience why the human person is an eternal being as well as speculation about the connection between the soul and the body. It is noteworthy that Edwards also included a substantial entry in his *"Miscellanies"* during this time entitled "Immortality of the Soul. Future State" (*"Misc."* 716).[19] While the two entries share a common commitment to natural theology, they consult different works. Edwards begins his reflection with reference to the positions of the Anglican Bishop John Tillotson. Again, we observe a common structure to the two notebooks while also certain autonomy of thought.

Two more sections of Bellamy's notebook contain entries on church governance. In the first section, Bellamy draws upon John Oldmixon's *The Critical History of England* to trace the establishment of the Anglican

---

16. Bellamy, *Student Notebook*, 15.
17. Ibid., 17.
18. Ibid.
19. Edwards, "'Misc.' 716," *WJE* 18:347.

Church and the conflict between the Anglicans, Puritans, and Presbyterians.[20] Much of the history reads in defense of the Presbyterians, including a strong refutation of the rumor that the Presbyterians conspired to behead King Charles. In the final section of his notebook, Bellamy draws upon John Anderson's *Defense of the Church-Government, Faith, Worship and Spirit of the Presbyterians* (no. 31 in Edwards's *Catalogues*), to recast twelve of the arguments, in discursive question and answer format, between the Episcopalians and Presbyterians regarding church governance.[21] This entry highlights Bellamy's interest in church governance, and Presbyterianism in particular, that runs throughout the notebook, beginning with quotations from the *Reformata* in the first few pages. There is some evidence that Edwards also was concerned with questions regarding Presbyterianism during this time—and possibly wanted to publish on the topic—although further research is needed to draw more specific conclusions.

In another section of Bellamy's journal, he appears to depart from theological reflection. In this section, Bellamy takes reading notes on Sir Walter Raleigh's *History of the World*. This title appears as number 142 in Edwards's *Catalogues of Books*, and we can assume it was held in his library.[22] Bellamy's notes address the fall of the Assyrian and Persian Empires, the institution of the Olympic Games, the founding of the Roman Empire, and various pagan adages and myths. It is unclear how these reading notes relate to the explicitly theological entries that comprise the rest of the journal, except to suggest that Bellamy saw a connection between world history and theology, which he certainly did. In this way he follows his mentor as well: reading all of history through the lens of the redemptive purposes of God.

Edwards's training of Bellamy was not only in doctrine but in practical ministry—this is reflected in his journal as well. One of Bellamy's entries concerns catechetical evaluation, perhaps for church membership. The entry begins with the statement: "But I must ask these people these 2 or 3 questions."[23] He goes on to write: "1. Whether they thought Christ was perfectly holy and innocent; in Christ's word whether no fault was found in his account." Then he writes in an aside "this I hope they will own." Continuing, he writes: "the next question is, whether Christ did really die upon the cross . . . . 3. Whether death be not the punishment for sin (the wages of sin is death)." Bellamy carries on with his questions until he anticipates the objection that Christ's death, since he was innocent, was unjust. In response

---

20. Bellamy, *Student Notebook*, 32.
21. Edwards, *Catalogues of Books*, WJE 26:125.
22. Edwards, *Catalogues*, WJE 26:144.
23. Bellamy, *Student Notebook*, 19.

to this objection, Bellamy outlines his best arguments from Scripture and then concludes: "Christ is God freely offered and therefore it could not be unjust." This entry suggests at least two more things: 1) that the notebook was born in the context of practical ministry activity and, 2) that the notebook was intended for use and reference in ministry, especially in catechesis and defense of right doctrine.

Another category of entries consists in the exegesis of a particular passage of Scripture with what seems a concern for homiletics. One such example is the lengthy exegesis of 2 Peter 1:19, which reads: "We have also a more sure word of prophesy, which we would do well to take heed, as a light shining in a dark place." During this time in 1737, Edwards preached two sermons on this verse, which we can assume influenced this entry.[24] Bellamy's writing traces different theological themes than Edwards's sermons on the same text. Whereas Edwards interprets the text to refer primarily to the prophetic word of the gospel that penetrates the darkness of our hearts, Bellamy focuses on the promise of Christ's return on the final day to overcome our present age of darkness—a more social and eschatological reading. At the end of this entry, Bellamy writes what seems to be a homiletical application of the doctrine. He writes: "the time will come whence the things you hope for shall be placed in a clear light, when you shall see all your expectations fully justified in the accomplishment; in the meanwhile you do well to attend to prophesy, tho' but a small glimmering light, and shining at a distance in a dark place, yet the best you have or can have at present."[25] We cannot know how he intended to use this entry, but it is possible that Bellamy was making his own notes for a sermon, or at the very least, was preparing for a conversation with Edwards on preaching. In this entry we see Edwards's commitment to keep theology and preaching together in ministerial training.

There is much more we could say about Bellamy's notebook and its themes. At this stage, though, we can make several observations about Edwards's priorities in training Bellamy as reflected in this notebook. First, we note that Edwards begins Bellamy's training by guiding his understanding of systematic theology in the Calvinist scheme, grounded in Scripture and distinguished from an array of contemporary opponents. It would seem that understanding how Christian doctrine holds together in a coherent picture was of first importance for Edwards. Secondly, we see Edwards arranging Bellamy's theological formation around a set of questions that bear a striking

---

24. They appear together as Edwards, "Light in a Dark World, a Dark Heart," *WJE* 19:704–33.

25. Bellamy, *Student Notebook*, 13.

similarity to his topics in the *"Miscellanies."* In doing this, it seems Edwards is focusing his attention on Bellamy's ability to read widely, exegete Scripture, and construct arguments, with the goal of developing something of his own *"Miscellanies."* Thirdly, we see Edwards's commitment to expose Bellamy to a wide range of thought and develop his abilities in research and writing on topics ranging from classical points of doctrine to philosophical and natural theology. Fourthly, we see Edwards's eye to train Bellamy in practical ministry, especially (as evidenced by this notebook) the work of education and catechesis. Fifthly, we see in this notebook an integration of Scriptural exegesis, systematic theology, and homiletics. This suggests that Edwards was committed not only to Bellamy's theological clarity but also his ability to apply doctrine for the edification and encouragement of his hearers. Having made these initial observations, let's see what additional insight we can gain by looking at Edwards's educational legacy in Bellamy. We turn now to the practices Bellamy instituted in his school of the prophets.

## Bellamy's Educational Practices

In the 1750s, Bellamy began receiving theological students in his home. For many of the same reasons Bellamy sought out Edwards, aspiring New Divinity ministers sought out Bellamy. Bellamy's *True Religion Delineated*, with some thanks to Edwards's endorsement, had become a bestseller in the colonies and abroad, awarding its author international acclaim, including (eventually) an honorary doctorate from the University of Aberdeen. Exceeding his reputation as a writer, however, was his famed power in the pulpit. Edwards himself said that Bellamy possessed "extraordinary gifts for the pulpit."[26] He had a large frame, a bellowing voice, and a gift for extemporaneous speech. "When the law was his theme," a hearer recalled, "Mt. Sinai was all in smoke; the thunder and the lightening issued from his lips, and all was solemn as the grave."[27] His reputation as the leading preacher of the New Divinity attracted students from across the colonies. To accommodate the steady stream of students arriving on his doorstep, he constructed a two-room classroom in his backyard and converted the third floor of his home into a dormitory. Often, he housed five or more students at a time. Drawing upon his Northampton experience, Bellamy involved his students in the full range of household activities. And, like Edwards, Bellamy won the life-long loyalty and affection of his students, many of whom founded their own schools of the prophets based on their experience in Bethlehem.

26. Minkema, "Jonathan Edwards on Education," 43.
27. Ibid.

Fortunately, we have more sources for Bellamy's educational practices than for Edwards's, which, when compiled, reveals a more-or-less complete picture of how Bellamy trained his students. Bellamy's teaching methods, like Edwards, revolved around a list of theological questions. As Tryon Edwards, Bellamy's earliest biographer, records:

> His mode of instruction was to give them, from time to time, lists of questions on such subjects as the existence, attributes, and moral government of God; our moral agency, and the law under which we are placed; the sinful state and character of mankind; the need for a divine revelation, and the fact that the one has been given; the great doctrines of revelation, especially of the gospel; the character, offices, and work of Christ; the atonement, and regeneration through the truth, and by the Holy Spirit; justification by faith; the distinguishing nature and fruits of repentance, love, and the other Christian graces; growth in grace; the perseverance of the saints; death, the resurrection, and the final judgment; heaven and hell; the nature of the church; particular churches, their officers and ordinances; the nature, uses, and ends of church discipline, etc.[28]

It was a formidable list covering the full range of theological loci in Puritan dogmatics, and bore strong resemblance to the ninety theological questions that Edwards used for instruction while president of Princeton.[29] The manner in which Bellamy distributed questions to his students reveals his commitment to the individual growth of each student. As soon as a student arrived at his house for study, Bellamy would initiate an extended conversation to discern abilities and attitude. Based on his perception of the students needs, he assigned questions and then directed their reading to the ablest resources in his library suited to the topic.

Bellamy's library was one of the largest pastoral collections in New England, containing several hundred books, pamphlets, and treatises on a broad range of subjects. Tryon Edwards remarks, "With the exception of two or three divines that might be mentioned, it is doubtful if any contemporary in America was more thoroughly read in the various departments of theology than the pastor of the small church in Bethlehem."[30] His library contained the classic Puritan systematics, catechisms, commentaries, and concordances as well as works by continental theologians such as Calvin, van Mastricht, and Moshelm. It also contained a notable quantity of

---

28. Bellamy, *Works of Bellamy*, Vol. 1, 107.
29. Minkema, "Jonathan Edwards on Education," 39.
30. As quoted in Anderson, *Joseph Bellamy*, 374.

controversial works on the Trinitarian debates in England and, especially, polemical works by Deists and Rationalists. Believing that "some light" could be discovered in any writer, and that it was important to understand the latest debates, Bellamy plunged his students into the English philosophical current of Shaftesbury, Hutcheson, and Hume. In the Bethlehem town records, it is recorded that many townsmen were shocked by the number of "infidel and heretical works" in his library.[31] Bellamy was well known for assigning a wide-ranging reading list to his students, so as to inform their responses by the strongest arguments of opponents as well as the treasuries of Puritan systematics. In his commitment to engage his students in the latest international debates and strongest arguments, Bellamy clearly reflects the education he received at Edwards's feet.

The evenings in Bellamy's school were spent in lively theological conversation and debate. During these sessions, Bellamy would examine his students' progress in their reading and answer their questions. Tryon Edwards records, "[He] generally spent his evenings in examining them as to their views, solving the difficulties they had found; suggesting and solving others;—closing by giving his opinion, and the reasons for it, and then leaving each student to digest and write out his own impressions of the entire subject."[32] The dissertations his students then prepared he would review and critique, pointing out weaknesses of argument and directing further reading often towards a more careful engagement with opposing views and a deeper engagement with Scripture. In all his instruction, Bellamy focused his attention on the strength of his student's argumentation, and frequently sent them back for revisions. It was not uncommon, as recorded by one of Bellamy's friends, for him to assume the position of the opposing view: "Then he would proceed to riddle and refute their grounds and arguments by the theories of opponents . . . leaving his pupils floored and foundering. Following this he had the students champion these various heresies and then he charged upon them with the weapons of Calvinism drawn from his ample arsenal and when the contest was over the pupils were soundly converted and established in the truth for all time."[33] In Bellamy's commitment to strength of argumentation, careful engagement with opponents, and assiduous study, we see another aspect of Edwards's legacy.

When Bellamy was satisfied with the dissertations his students produced, he then instructed them to write one or more sermons on the topic. For Bellamy, a minister's theological study must always serve his local

---

31. Ibid., 375.
32. Ibid., 107.
33. Ibid., 392.

congregation, and the proof of true understanding lay in preaching the doctrine for the conversion and edification of souls. In this practice of connecting theological study to preaching, we see Edwards's conviction that light and heat must be united in the minister of the gospel. Bellamy would engage his students in conversation throughout the process of sermon writing, guiding them to experimental and practical discourses, providing homiletical pointers, and suggesting revisions. Bellamy's chief concern in homiletics was that his students be trained not only to prepare but to properly deliver their discourses. For Bellamy, the power of the sermon lay in the gospel proclaimed, in which the disposition and affections of the minister played a major part. It was Bellamy's rule that his students should regularly preach at appointed stations around the outskirts of town and in the smaller congregations that surrounded Bethlehem. Given his wide-ranging influence in the Connecticut River Valley—he was more than once referred to as "the pope of Litchfield County"—there was no shortage of opportunities for his students to preach.

On such occasions, Bellamy would ride with all of his students to attend the service. On the ride home he would critique the sermon, often with regard to the character of the delivery and in a way not likely to be forgotten. Indeed, later in their lives, many of his students seem to have taken great pleasure in recounting his memorable critiques. To one student who had crowded too large a number of topics into his sermon, Bellamy inquired, "Sir, do you ever expect to preach again?" "Yes, sir, why?" was the response. "Because, if you do, you'll have nothing left to say: you've put your whole system of theology in today's sermon."[34] To another student who had a loud and boisterous way of speaking, he remarked: "When I was younger I thought it was the *thunder* that killed people; but when I grew older and wiser, I found out it was the *lightning*. So I determined to do what I advise to you—thunder less and lighten more!"[35] Many more examples of Bellamy's practical instruction in sermon delivery exist, but these two suffice to see his commitment to practically train his students to unite head and heart in their ministry.

When a student had graduated from Bellamy's school they would have in hand something of a systematic theology of their own making, historically and scripturally informed, and furnished with the latest and strongest polemics. It was a foundation that students could build upon for the remainder of their lives in ministry, and use to train others. Bellamy's students carried with them an appreciation for the breadth of learning, a

---

34. Ibid., 108.
35. Ibid., 109.

facility for vigorous conversation and debate, and the training to preach with light and heat for the conversion of souls. Students were prepared to connect theological reflection and homiletics for the purpose of defending right doctrine and fanning into flame vital piety in their future congregations. Furthermore, Bellamy's students left his parsonage motivated to go forth and train others likewise.

Bellamy's educational practices clearly drew upon what he learned in Edwards's home. In Bellamy's school, and in the many schools of the prophets founded on Bellamy's model, Edwards's educational legacy in ministerial education developed and grew. During the early years of the new nation, the Edwardsean mode of instruction in homes of New Divinity pastors exerted a dominant influence in pastoral training. With the founding of the divinity schools and seminaries, beginning with Andover in 1808, the schools of the prophets began to dwindle and by the mid-nineteenth century had all but disappeared. Much of the New Divinity legacy was taken up in the early divinity schools, but what happened to it there is the topic of another study. In this chapter I hope to have shed light on how Edwards trained the ministers that lived in his home, and how that approach flourished in the homes of his disciples. I would like to think we can learn from this legacy today.

## Bibliography

Anderson, Glenn Paul. *Joseph Bellamy (1719–1790): The Man and His Work*. Boston: Boston University, 1971.

Bellamy, Joseph. *Student Notebook*. 1736, Joseph Bellamy Papers, Miscellaneous Personal Papers, Ms. Group 30, Box 179, Yale Divinity School Library, New Haven, Conn.

———. *True Religion Delineated*. Edinburgh: M. Cray, 1788.

———. *The Works of the Rev. Joseph Bellamy, D. D.: in Three Volumes*. Edited by Tryon Edwards. New York: Stephen Dodge, 1811.

Edwards, John, *Theologia Reformata: or, the Body and Substance of the Christian Religion*. London: Printed for John Lawrence, John Wyat, and Ranew Robinson, 1713.

Edwards, Jonathan. "Account Book." In *Catalogues of Books*, edited by Peter J. Thuesen, The Works of Jonathan Edwards 26:319–56. New Haven: Yale University Press, 2008.

———. "'Catalogue' of Reading." In *Catalogues of Books*, edited by Peter J. Thuesen, The Works of Jonathan Edwards 26:117–318. New Haven: Yale University Press, 2008.

———. "Light in a Dark World, a Dark Heart." In *Sermons and Discourses, 1734–1738*, edited by Max X. Lesser, The Works of Jonathan Edwards 19:704–33. New Haven: Yale University Press, 2001.

———. "'Misc.' 3." In *The "Miscellanies" (Entry Nos. a–z, aa–zz, 1–500)*, edited by Thomas A. Schafer, The Works of Jonathan Edwards 13:199–200. New Haven: Yale University Press, 1994.

———. "'Misc.' 704." In *The "Miscellanies" (Entry Nos. 501–832)*, edited by Ava Chamberlain, The Works of Jonathan Edwards 18:314–21. New Haven: Yale University Press, 2000.

———. "'Misc.' 706." In *The "Miscellanies" (Entry Nos. 501–832)*, edited by Ava Chamberlain, The Works of Jonathan Edwards 18:322–30. New Haven: Yale University Press, 2000.

———. "'Misc.' 716." In *The "Miscellanies" (Entry Nos. 501–832)*, edited by Ava Chamberlain, The Works of Jonathan Edwards 18:346–48. Edited by Ava Chamberlain. New Haven: Yale University Press, 2000.

Kimnach, Wilson H., Kenneth P. Minkema, and Douglas A. Sweeney, eds., *The Sermons of Jonathan Edwards: A Reader*. New Haven: Yale University Press, 2008.

Kling, David W. "New Divinity Schools of the Prophets, 1750–1825: A Case Study in Ministerial Education." *History of Education Quarterly* 37/2 (1997): 185–206.

Minkema, Kenneth P. "Jonathan Edwards on Education and his Educational Legacy." In *After Jonathan Edwards: The Courses of the New England Theology*, edited by Oliver D. Crisp and Douglas A. Sweeney, 31–50. Oxford: Oxford University Press, 2012.

Sloan, Douglas, ed. *The Great Awakening and American Education: a Documentary History*. New York: Teachers College Press, 1973.

Sloan, Douglas. *The Scottish Enlightenment and the American College Ideal*. New York: Teachers College Press, 1971.

Valeri, Mark. *Law and Providence in Joseph Bellamy's New England*. New York: Oxford University Press, 1994.

## 15

# Hero or Herald? Agency and Authority in *The Life of Brainerd*

### Rhys S. Bezzant

IN HIS RECENT WORK *The Book that Made Your World: How the Bible Created the Soul of Western Civilization*, Indian philosopher Vishal Mangalwadi investigates the impact of the Christian Scriptures on a number of discourses and practices in the West, from rationality and technology to literature and science. He is positive about the culturally transformative power of the Bible. In his chapter on heroism, he argues that the classical view of the hero as world conqueror, or the medieval view of the hero as courageous knight, has been replaced in the modern world with the idea of the hero as someone who sacrifices him- or herself for the good of others.[1] He thereby argues that Lucifer from Milton's epic poem *Paradise Lost* is a kind of anti-hero, who said that it is "better to reign in hell, than serve in heaven."[2] In other words, worship of power is diabolical, but acts of love are divine. Heroes, so-called, resist evil and falsehood for the sake of others according to their conscience, given the example of self-sacrificing love we meet in the person of Christ.

However, the Christian church generally—but its revivalist manifestations in particular—has often succumbed to criteria for leadership which lionize the heroic big "I" leader who leads from the front with an impressive

---

1. Mangalwadi, *The Book that Made your World*, 122.
2. Ibid., 134.

personality, rather than a small "l" leader who exemplifies the development of virtue and patient endurance. Nathan Hatch has shown how the church's increasingly democratic spirit in early nineteenth-century America provoked a culture of centralized and charismatic leadership to compensate for the growth in the strength of the laity,[3] though this trend may have existed before the early national period. The cultural mood of nineteenth-century Romanticism further reinforced this trend, for, in reaction to the purported equality of all "men" by virtue of their rationality espoused in the Enlightenment, the notion of leadership now highlighted the agency of an individual who would rise above local conditions and shape the course of history in heroic terms, standing over and against the world. In our day, we may not expect military victories or the imitation of medieval systems of honor, but external competencies at the expense of the spiritual nature of discipleship in imitation of Christ can be prized nonetheless. It may be tempting to view a person's leadership gifts as universally valid or transcending culture, but leaders, too, can be trapped within cultural norms or driven unknowingly by subtle social forces.

In both the eighteenth and nineteenth centuries, David Brainerd (1718–47), missionary to Native Americans, has been presented as a big "L" leader.[4] His early association with fabled names of the Great Awakening, like Jonathan Edwards, Jonathan Dickinson, Joseph Bellamy, or Eleazar Wheelock, covered him with heroic glory. His long-suffering ministry, defying external opposition and physical frailty, suggests a martyr-like preparedness for an untimely death and reinforced his "larger than life" status.[5] Edwards's *Life of Brainerd,* his compilation of Brainerd's journal with embedded commentary—hereafter, *The Life*—functioned to create a polemical layer of heroic Reformed piety, providing a model of robust and supernatural spirituality as an alternative to Arminian and moralizing theological encroachment in America. It was a "case study of true holiness."[6] John Wesley, despite his reservations concerning Edwards's doctrine, set up Brainerd as a pious battering ram who could destroy any stronghold: "Find preachers of David Brainerd's spirit and nothing can stand before them."[7] Subsequently, *The Life*—frequently acknowledged as the only book other

3. Hatch, *Democratization of American Christianity.*

4. The common eighteenth century term "Indians" appears in much primary and secondary documentation on this topic, though in this essay I am inclined to the term "Native Americans."

5. See, for example, Edwards, *The Life of Brainerd, WJE* 7:303: "How sweet were the thoughts of death to me."

6. Conforti, "Jonathan Edwards's Most Popular Work," 188–201, especially 195.

7. Pettit, "Editor's Introduction," *WJE* 7:3.

than the Bible worth transporting—was carried to the ends of the earth to provide succor for overwhelmed and undertrained missionaries. Brainerd's model of piety was adapted to cross-cultural contexts, generating another layer of hagiography, this time framed by missiological concerns.[8] Brainerd's impact on the foundation of Australia as a European country has been recounted elsewhere.[9] Conforti, speaking of nineteenth-century America, placed Brainerd in a longer evangelical tradition, in which "ministers and parents held up both missionaries [Eliot and Brainerd] as heroic models of piety to be emulated by Christians of all ages."[10] Brainerd is not only a big "L" leader, but has spawned a big "L" legacy. If Mangalwadi is correct about Christianity undermining traditional categories of heroism, neither Edwards nor Brainerd got the memo.

The goal of this paper is to investigate Edwards's book *The Life of Brainerd* to understand Brainerd's philosophy of ministry and thereby to provide support for a counter-reading to this received heroic narrative. My interest here is in Brainerd, the "anti-revivalist," in order to understand how he represents a more embedded interaction between the individual and his context. More particularly, I want to conduct my investigation using a heuristic device that places Brainerd's sense of personal *agency* in conversation with his own often-unacknowledged appeals to ecclesiastical *authority*.[11] Individual agency, summarized as "participating actively in shaping the worldly means to be employed for realizing divine and collective purposes,"[12] must be understood in relation to Brainerd's understanding of the life of the church and its own exalted place in a vision for the future of the world. Brainerd's view of how his agency is given authority, understood as "a supervening source of legitimation," needs to be taken seriously if we are to evaluate responsibly his contribution to modern missions, personal spirituality, the writing of evangelical history, and the progress of providence.[13] Like any self-respecting federal agent in a TV show, Brainerd needs to flash a badge of authority to validate his arrest. Ecclesiology and eschatology provide his validation, while this paper attempts an explanation. This hero is not an in-

8. Grigg, *Lives of David Brainerd*, 3–4.
9. Ibid., 169.
10. Conforti, "Jonathan Edwards's Most Popular Work," 194.
11. The language of agency is frequently used as a means of understanding the individual's role within social, theological or economic developments in the eighteenth century. See, for example, Brekus, *Sarah Osborn's World*, 99, 185; or Hindmarsh, "Is Evangelical Ecclesiology and Oxymoron?" 29n30.
12. Block, *Nation of Agents*, 22.
13. Ibid., 17.

imitable outlier, but a man who provides an example of the development of the modern self, and becomes a model for the possibilities of the mentoring exchange under modern conditions. This paper functions as part of my bigger project to understand and evaluate the mentoring ministry of historical figures, especially Jonathan Edwards.

## David Brainerd: His Reception as a Hero

By the end of the 1740s, Jonathan Edwards needed friends. The movement of the Spirit of God in his church in the early 1740s had created a conflicted parish, in which spiritual impressions were valued by some, rejected by others, and adjudicated by Edwards. He was impatient with youth who had once been his greatest supporters, but who now appeared more interested in worldly distractions. His avowed goal was now to fence the table, to distinguish at the Lord's Supper between those who could recount their experience of grace and those who could not, overturning a venerable Northampton tradition. Wars and rumors of wars in the American colonies could at any moment create further social splintering in a town which, though once a picture of revived harmony,[14] was now fragile and easily torn into rival parties. Though Edwards had probably only met Brainerd once in New Haven in 1743, when delivering the Commencement address and counseling him concerning his dalliance with revivalist religion, he was glad to welcome an ailing friend into his busy home on May 28, 1747. Within a year, though nursed supportively by Jerusha, Jonathan and Sarah's second child, Brainerd would die of consumption. Brainerd was a supporter of Edwards's views on spirituality, and Edwards was a supporter of Brainerd's views on principled activism.[15] This was a mutually encouraging match.

Edwards was looking not only for friends but also for heroes to sustain the Awakening against the odds. Serendipitously, during the 1740s, Edwards was called upon to preach at the ordination services of various young men whom he had mentored into ministry, the sermons of which offer insights into his own developing construction of the criteria for ministry. These sermons provided an outlet for Edwards's yearning for heroic achievement. For example, he preached the sermon *The Great Concern of a Watchman of Souls* (1743) at the ordination of Jonathan Judd, *The True Excellency of a Minister of the Gospel* (1744) for Robert Abercrombie, *The Church's Marriage to her Sons,*

---

14. Edwards, "Faithful Narrative," *WJE* 4:151.

15. For example, Brainerd's activism is in stark evidence here: "My soul longed exceedingly for death, to be loosed from this dullness and barrenness, and made forever active in the service of God." Edwards, *The Life of Brainerd*, *WJE* 7:272.

*and to her God* (1746) for Samuel Buell, *Sons of Oil, Heavenly Lights* (1747) for Joseph Ashley, and *Christ the Great Example of Gospel Ministers* (1749) for Job Strong. Wilson Kimnach points out that Edwards wanted "to make the legacy of the Great Awakening more practical and institutional ... to bring his church to a more stable and enduring holiness, providing pure religious affections a habitation that would foster their growth and sustain their purity."[16] Settled ministers, not lay itinerants, would play a key part in the solution and guide the victorious onward march of the movement.

Though not an ordination sermon, Edwards also preached at the funeral of Brainerd in Northampton in 1748, and positioned Brainerd in similarly heroic terms. Picking up a profoundly eschatological theme, Edwards preached his doctrine from 2 Corinthians 5:8, that "the souls of true saints, when they leave their bodies at death, go to be with Christ."[17] Brainerd is thereafter described as "that eminent servant of Jesus Christ," "a singular instance, of a ready invention, natural eloquence, easy flowing expression, sprightly apprehension, quick discerning, and very strong memory; and yet of a very penetrating genius, close and clear thought, and piercing judgment."[18] Brainerd's melancholy is recognized and critiqued, and his rejection of extreme enthusiasm and separatism also affirmed.[19] Neither conformism nor license was Brainerd's aspiration. Even when allowing for the hyperbole of a eulogy, Brainerd is presented as an example in prayer, "almost inimitable; such ... as I have very rarely known equaled."[20] Perhaps it is then not surprising that when Edwards published Brainerd's literary remains in 1749, these sentiments should reappear in the "Author's Preface." Helen Westra comments that Brainerd functioned in Edwards's reflection as a "case study of authentic religious piety" and "an exemplary messenger in Christ's great work of redemption."[21] Here was a young man who stood powerfully, perhaps heroically, against the theological spirit of the age and the pernicious nominalism of the church.

It was not, however, just against eighteenth-century perversions of the Great Awakening that Brainerd functioned as symbol of heroic resistance. His celebrity as a big "L" leader was feted elsewhere. Christian Friedrich Schwarz (1726–98), Francis Asbury (1745–1816), Thomas Coke (1747–1814), William Carey (1761–1834), Samuel Marsden (1764–1838),

16. Kimnach, "Preface to the Period," *WJE* 25:17–18.
17. Edwards, "True Saints," *WJE* 25:226.
18. Ibid., 244, 245.
19. Ibid., 244, 247, 248.
20. Ibid., 245.
21. Westra, *Minister's Task and Calling*, 192.

Henry Martyn (1781–1812), David Livingstone (1813–73), and Jim Elliot (1927–56) all named Brainerd as a significant model for their missionary labors.[22] His example had impact on women, too, through the ministry of Mary Lyon at Mount Holyoke College in Massachusetts, who trained women to be missionary wives in a holy calling.[23] *The Life* encouraged Calvinists to be activists, and it later rode the wave of the New Divinity Movement into the antebellum period, offering real-life substantiation of the motto of disinterested benevolence.[24] In Britain too, as the century progressed, the needs of the Empire changed, so Brainerd even became a pin-up boy for "muscular Christianity," by virtue of which his physical weaknesses were cauterized and his spiritual altruism highlighted:

> Rooted in a sense of cultural superiority, these men and women were offering a sort of evangelized imperialism. Change would not come from gunboats, diplomats, and treaties, but from the gospel of Christ preached by highly committed men and women imbued with a deeply spiritual character. David Brainerd, then, at the turn of the nineteenth century had once more evolved. He was now a rugged young man who . . . had turned his back on the material rewards of a colonial pastorate and plunged into the howling wilderness to bring the gospel to heathens.[25]

Derivatively, Edwards's book became a model for the new genre of missionary (auto-) biography.[26] Brainerd's agency provided the shape for others' ministry expectations, or at least the template for their written recollections. Further and further removed from the original reflections of a man *in extremis*, a kind of normative picture of ministry prevailed.

## David Brainerd: His Identity as a Herald

Of course, there is a case to be made for heroic themes in Edwards's *The Life*, using even Brainerd's own words. The construction of Brainerd's heroic identity is a function of his individual agency, in which he shapes a ministry according to his own insights and capacities beyond the direct supervision of church or society. Many powerful emotions are left intact in the text to

---

22. Pettit, "Editor's Introduction," *WJE* 25:3–4; Grigg, *Lives of David Brainerd*, 164–87.

23. ibid., 174–75.

24. Conforti, "Jonathan Edwards's Most Popular Work," especially 190.

25. Grigg, *Lives of David Brainerd*, 181.

26. Conforti, "Jonathan Edwards's Most Popular Work," 197.

reinforce Brainerd's sense of self, despite Edwards's extirpation of passages that smacked of enthusiasm. Brainerd's cries of joy, but more surprisingly his confessions of melancholy, are packaged in terms that assume a life in which the most recent recording of an emotion must reach deeper depths or higher heights than experiences previously recounted. There seems to be no steady Christian walk, but impressive dramatic escalation: "[November 25, 1742] Was made sensible of my great ignorance and unfitness for public service: I had the most abasing thoughts of myself, I think, that ever I had; I thought myself the worst wretch that ever lived." Or: "[February 17, 1745] I think I was scarce ever enabled to offer the free grace of God to perishing sinners with more freedom and plainness in my life." Or: "[August 10, 1746] Afterwards baptized six persons; three adults and three children. Was in a comfortable frame in the evening, and enjoyed some satisfaction in secret prayer. I scarce ever in my life felt myself so full of tenderness, as this day."[27] This is a model of non-diminishing return.

Further, Brainerd's agency can be highlighted in battling against the natural environment, which was a "hideous and howling wilderness," through which he traveled on horseback like a "pilgrim or hermit,"[28] not in sweet rapture with nature, as Edwards had himself exemplified in his *Personal Narrative*,[29] but energetically defying it. He preached out of doors if there was a need and despite its inconvenience.[30] Time also was an enemy:

> But oh, with what reluctancy did I find myself obliged to consume time in sleep! . . . Oh, how precious is time! And how guilty it makes me feel when I think I have trifled away and misimproved it, or neglected to fill up each part of it with duty to the utmost of my ability and capacity![31]

Recognizing the power of the auditory, Brainerd approaches the act of preaching as re-establishing the authority of the preacher: "[Lord's Day, October 17, 1742] I went into the assembly trembling, as I frequently do, under a sense of my insufficiency to do anything in the cause of God . . . I scarce ever preach without being first visited with inward conflicts and sure trials."[32] Edwards makes special reference to Brainerd's ability in preaching

---

27. Edwards, *The Life of Brainerd*, WJE 7:188, 287–88, 418.

28. Ibid., 267, 401.

29. See for example Edwards, "Personal Narrative," *Letters and Personal Writings*, WJE 16.

30. Edwards, *The Life of Brainerd*, WJE 7:287.

31. Ibid., 402, 433.

32. Ibid., 183.

to "engage the attention" of those listening, no doubt an extraordinary gift when teaching those Indians on the Susquehanna who were most reluctant to listen.[33] Brainerd makes a parallel between his own ministry and that of Abraham, Joseph, Moses, Elijah, Samson, Nehemiah, and Ezra, which, while demonstrating inadequate hermeneutics by placing himself ahistorically in their moment in salvation history, more importantly for our purposes demonstrates existentially Brainerd's exalted sense of self.[34] He could frame his revivalist agency through the common practice of singing out of doors,[35] itinerating like Whitefield,[36] or expecting dramatic results: "The power attending divine truths seemed to have the influence of the earthquake rather than the whirlwind upon them."[37] To cap it all off, Brainerd's poor health, with regular reference towards the end of *The Life* to coughing up blood as a sign of consumption, sets in relief his determination to labor in the cause of the gospel without counting the cost and with the potency of individual agency. But this is only one side of the story.

## *Submission to Ecclesiological Authority*

The vision of the heroic individual, however, must not be viewed apart from Brainerd's appeal to ecclesiastical authorization. As Griggs so effectively argues, Brainerd's revivalist energy must not be understood without relation to his part in the Connecticut establishment, which defended social and theological order, though it had to make room in the end for spiritual ardor as well. I have argued elsewhere that Edwards's *Life of Brainerd* provides a window into ecclesiological themes, even if they are muted and only tangentially honored in the text.[38] In this section, I shall not demonstrate how we might dig to discover those themes; instead, assuming those themes, I shall show how Brainerd's identity is built upon them and in what sense they are needed to make sense of his ministry, and offer a corrective to the frequently one-sided heroic revivalist interpretation of his life.

The first thing that needs to be pointed out is how Brainerd's personal situation rendered him socially marginal. His failure to achieve academic qualification, having been expelled from Yale in 1741–42 for association

---

33. Ibid., 90.
34. Ibid., 226, 225, 259, 260, 237, 255.
35. Grigg, *Lives of David Brainerd*, 55; Edwards, *The Life of Brainerd*, WJE 7:369.
36. Hall, *Contested Boundaries*, 80.
37. Edwards, *The Life of Brainerd*, WJE 7:348.
38. Bezzant, *Jonathan Edwards and the Church*, 157–69.

with enthusiasts, along with his dubious status as an unmarried man, circumscribed his capacity for social influence. In eighteenth-century Massachusetts, for example, "manhood was tied closely to ownership of property and to marriage . . . marriage was a crucial part of achieving (and maintaining) full manhood . . . the ideal man was married, strong, and controlled . . . [W]eak bodies were considered evidence of degenerate natures."[39] Not surprisingly, Brainerd is aware more of his passivity than his potency, for example in the following parable:

> I am obliged to let all my thoughts and concerns run at random; for I have neither strength to read, meditate, or pray: And this naturally perplexes my mind. I seem to myself like a man that has all his estate embarked in one small boat, unhappily going adrift down a swift torrent. The poor owner stands on the shore and looks, and laments his loss.[40]

We must recall that Brainerd had given up on worldly possessions, fought debilitating sicknesses, was cared for in his dying months by someone who was not his wife—even traveling with her to Boston for recuperation—and in earlier days had succumbed to extreme notions concerning spiritual experience, which were regarded as dangerously labile to those in authority. Overcoming these disadvantages might be seen as heroic in some measure, but they placed the power of his agency in jeopardy nonetheless. There are even times when Brainerd speaks as if he were dispensable: "I never saw the work of God appear so independent of means as at this time . . . God's manner of working upon them appeared so entirely supernatural, and above means, that I could scarce believe that he used me as an instrument."[41] Lovejoy makes the point eloquently:

> He [Brainerd] was amazed to discover [in New Jersey] that there was little for him to do, for God worked upon them supernaturally, he wrote, and he was scarcely conscious of being an instrument at all. Brainerd stood still and watched God's grace descend upon them. God would work with extraordinary means in America, and the Awakening was his sign.[42]

Brainerd's emotional life was shaped, perhaps not surprisingly, around the search for ministerial validation. The very headings of *The Life* are built around the process of regaining authority from institutions of the standing

39. Foster, *Sex and the Eighteenth Century Man*, x, 5, 123.
40. Edwards, *The Life of Brainerd*, WJE 7:264.
41. Ibid., 315.
42. Lovejoy, *Religious Enthusiasm in the New World*, 194.

order of his day. The first of the eight parts ends with his period of *study* in New Haven. The second part ends with his licensure to *preach* bestowed by the Association of Ministers belonging to the Eastern District of the County of Fairfield. The third part concludes with an interview in New York with the Commissioners of an *organization* that sponsored missions among the Native Americans, the Society in Scotland for Propagating Christian Knowledge. The fourth ends with his first experience of *missionary work* among Native Americans at Kaunaumeek, some twenty miles west of Stockbridge. It is his *ordination*, perhaps a surprising achievement without formal study that concludes part five. The sixth part sees Brainerd serving as *pastor* among Native Americans at Crossweeksung. Part seven, the longest of all, takes in a period of great fruitfulness, including many testimonies of grace from Native American converts, until he retires from *active service* due to illness. The last part, number eight, tracks Brainerd in the last months of his life in Northampton, in one sense receiving semi-official *imprimatur* from Edwards himself for his faithful ministry, until his final promotion home. His revivalist ambitions and achievements are structured around ongoing ecclesiastical validation or authorization.

Brainerd's agency in the heroic reading of his ministry also needs to be balanced by insights gained from post-colonial historiography. His relationships enjoyed a notable measure of reciprocity.[43] It would be demeaning to the Native Americans with whom he worked to assume that they were powerless in any transactions with Europeans, leaving Brainerd's potency unchecked. He was influenced by the various groups among whom he ministered in New York, Pennsylvania, and New Jersey. It is true that Brainerd was ahead of his time in acknowledging that Native Americans were worthy of gospel ministrations. He rethought his ministry philosophy in response to his context: the way he used narratives to preach, his living and travel arrangements, and his preparedness to live within the Native American community despite disliking their food. He was variously encouraged or discouraged by their deeds and conversation. Some were described as magnificent examples of vital piety, exceling even European witness.[44] Brainerd's translator, Tatamy, was a highly intelligent man, on whom Brainerd depended for communication and friendship. Sometimes we learn that there was no response to his preaching from Native American leaders, acknowledging their power to resist. Just as he cared for them in spiritual and material circumstances, they were asked to care for him as their minister in his travels: "Exhorted my people to pray for me that God

---

43. Grigg, *Lives of David Brainerd*, 120.
44. Edwards, *The Life of Brainerd*, WJE 7:330.

would be with me in that journey."⁴⁵ They are presented as exercising an influence on and power over him.

Working hand in glove with more subtle assumptions of sacred time, references to institutions provide a concrete structure for *The Life*, bookending its individual sections and narrating stages of Brainerd's life and career. The theological institution of the Sabbath, for example, denotes a Puritan approach to social arrangements and sacred time, by which God is honored through regular community accountability. No doubt due to the distinctive activity of the Sabbath day, kept by Brainerd from Saturday night to Sunday night, his diary entries describing the Lord's Day are more numerous than for any other day of the week. In one notable sequence, Brainerd comments on Sunday May 24, Sunday May 31, and Sunday June 7 without interposing reflection from other days of the week, at least in Edwards's version.⁴⁶ Brainerd's time, though precious, is measured ultimately not against effectiveness or productivity, but against the recurring rhythm of the account of the creation in seven days. Perhaps surprisingly for a Puritan New Englander, he also makes reference to the church calendar. Falling on a Wednesday in 1745, he decides to take up the challenge of Christmas "to call them together and discourse to them upon divine things," even if this was chiefly to provide an alternative entertainment to drunkenness with other Europeans.⁴⁷

The sacramental seasons are likewise enormously important to Brainerd. These accounts are more numerous towards the end of *The Life*, when Brainerd pastored a congregation of Indians, which comprised some who were visibly converted—achieving what Edwards in Northampton could not. Brainerd writes:

> Saturday, July 12. This day was spent in fasting and prayer by my congregation, as preparatory to the sacrament . . . Afterwards led them to a solemn renewal of their covenant, and fresh dedication of themselves to God . . . Lord's Day, July 13 . . . Administered the sacrament of the Lord's Supper to thirty-one persons of the Indians. God seemed to be present in this ordinance; the communicants were sweetly melted and refreshed, most of them. Oh, how they melted, even when the elements were first uncovered! There was scarcely a dry eye amongst them when I took off the linen and showed them the symbols of Christ's "broken body." Having rested a little, after the administration of

---

45. Ibid., 414.
46. Ibid., 445–47.
47. Ibid., 347–48.

> the sacrament, I visited the communicants and found them generally in a sweet loving frame; not unlike what appeared among them on the former sacramental occasion.[48]

Time is marked by the regular expectation of observance of the Lord's Supper, nested within a regular sequence of preparation and follow-up. Perhaps taking their cues from the Scottish "holy fairs," prolonged occasions for receiving the Lord's Supper, often in remote locations, Brainerd learns this pastoral craft from William Tennent, whom he assisted in the distribution of the Supper on certain occasions.[49] These opportunities highlight predictable pathways of grace, based not on the potency or personality of the liturgical president, but drawing institutional authority into the wilderness. He himself, however, does not preside until authorized to do so by virtue of his ordination. His experience of deep unity between fellow Christians, for example at Elizabethtown, is amplified at the Lord's Supper, which provides a counterpoint to revivalist market-share.[50] He is keen to acknowledge that the profound impact of the Supper on the Indians was "notwithstanding agreeably regulated and kept within proper bounds ... without any indecent or boisterous commotion of the passions."[51]

The picture of the solitary individual staring down all opposition is not even accurate in Brainerd's telling of the story. Of course, wilderness necessarily entails removal from cities and companionship, but it is also striking how Brainerd needs the sustenance of networks, friendships, and mentoring opportunities for self-care. The connectional nature of church is greatly appreciated by Brainerd and taken with him on his itinerating rounds. He uses the model of the local parish as a template for ministry among the Native Americans.[52] Furthermore, his sponsorship by the Society for Propagating the Gospel ties him into a transatlantic network, which promoted interdenominational outreach, and which required structures of accountability, which his journal or diary would validate when he sent them to his overseers.[53] His son-like relationship with Joseph Bellamy, pastor at Bethlehem in Connecticut, with whom he boarded for a time after his eviction from Yale, provides evidence of Brainerd's longing for community:

48. Ibid., 413.

49. See Schmidt, *Holy Fairs*, and Long, *Eucharistic Theology*. For an example of Brainerd assisting Tennent, see Edwards, *The Life of Brainerd*, WJE 7:405.

50. Ibid., 441.

51. Ibid., 387.

52. Grigg, *Lives of David Brainerd*, 62.

53. See O'Brien, "Transatlantic Community of Saints." Also Grigg, *Lives of David Brainerd*, 87.

"Friday October 22 [1742] ... Dear Mr. Bellamy came in while I was making the first prayer (being returned home from a journey) and after meeting we walked away together and spent the evening in sweetly conversing on divine things, and praying together, with sweet and tender love to each other, and returned to rest with our hearts in a serious spiritual frame."[54] And some years later: "Wednesday, March 6 [1745] ... Oh, how kind has God been to me! How has he raised up friends in every place where his Providence has called me! Friends are a great comfort" and "'tis God that gives them; 'tis he makes them friendly to me."[55] He even rejoices in the company of the Indian Delaware King, who eased his "solitary circumstances."[56] This is not a man who is content with his own company *tout court*.

His ministry philosophy and his need of Christian fellowship point us to the substantial place of mentoring in his missionary practice. He relied on external validation for his ministry, but others might have exercised their own agency by validating or questioning his authority. For example, labors in public preaching are supplemented by one-on-one ministries, which sought to make truth particular to individuals or families. Brainerd encouraged the practice of private meetings or conferences with Native Americans, which reflect a less efficient but more personally effective strategy for propagating the gospel, often pursued in times of rapid social transition.[57] His agency is direct, expressed in the relationship of face-to-face fellowship, but the negotiation that private conversation embodies relativizes his agency, and assumes other authority by which his contributions might be tested or resisted. These personal encounters function as adaptive mechanisms,[58] to which he brings his own experience, his "assistance of an experienced spiritual guide,"[59] which is then appropriated in a variety of ways. He desires to educate potential candidates for the ministry,[60] and dignifies his hearers through intentional instruction: "August 10 [1745]. Rode to the Indians and began to discourse more privately to those who had obtained comfort and satisfaction; endeavoring to instruct, direct, caution, and comfort them."[61] Whereas Brainerd's heroic leadership is often pictured with him out of

54. Edwards, *The Life of Brainerd*, WJE 7:184.

55. Ibid., 289.

56. Ibid., 324.

57. Holifield, *History of Pastoral Care in America*, 70. For medieval parallels, see McNeill, *A History of the Cure of Souls*, 138.

58. Block, *Nation of Agents*, 206.

59. Edwards, *The Life of Brainerd*, WJE 7:365.

60. Ibid., 190.

61. Ibid., 311.

doors, preaching, he himself recognizes that this was not always the most productive: "And the Lord seemed to smile upon my private endeavors, and to make these particular and personal addresses more effectual upon some than my public discourses."[62] It is likely that he saw Jonathan Dickinson, the first president of the College of New Jersey (soon to be known as Princeton) as a mentor to him, even if we remain skeptical of the tradition that made of Brainerd the first student to matriculate there.

Given all these disclaimers concerning Brainerd's heroic agency, it may not come as a surprise that Edwards himself expresses some concern about lionizing the subject of *The Life*. Edwards is walking a tightrope: providing an isolated example of piety to emulate, without reinforcing the revivalist notion that separation from ecclesiastical authority is either acceptable or beneficial. To confirm such a model of piety without pretension, Edwards wrote:

> I found him remarkably sociable, pleasant, and entertaining in his conversation; yet solid, savory, spiritual, and very profitable; appearing meek, modest, and humble; far from any stiffness, moroseness, superstitious demureness, or affected singularity in speech or behavior, and seeming to nauseate all such things.[63]

Edwards knows the kind of heroes whom he does not respect, outlining in exquisite prose that type of "flaming Christian," with the "glare of outward appearances," who with "earnest talk, strong voice, assured looks, vast confidence, and bold assertions . . . are overborn, lose the possession of their judgment."[64] Edwards goes on to provide a vivid illustration of the person who goes into a shop and cannot determine the relative value of anything, or who presumes all things in the shop to be of equal value.[65] Brainerd is not to be counted among them, for he can discriminate between spiritual experiences and can teach in a way that honors the individual in front of him. Edwards does ultimately authorize the example and legacy of Brainerd, which Brainerd himself craved and would have supported, though Edwards does this not without discrimination.

### *Motivation by Eschatological Vision*

In *The Life*, we witness both the exercise of significant moral agency, and the commitment of Brainerd to live at the same time as a man under authority,

62. Ibid., 381.
63. Ibid., 445.
64. Ibid., 518.
65. Ibid., 519.

who in turn empowered others. However, in the end, both these categories must be read within a still larger framework. Any human agency or institutional authority in this world is to be viewed against an eschatological horizon. The ultimate purposes of God provide the final frame within which to position Brainerd's putative heroism.

Brainerd is not the isolated individual of Romantic imagination, but is the herald of a new age, for which he finds himself the vanguard. He is not pushing his way back into Eden with superhuman strength, but rather is allowing the Spirit, now freshly poured out, to sweep him along towards the heavenly destination. John Wesley's primitivism may have attempted to recreate the early church in Georgia,[66] but eschatological expectation in New England at the same time highlighted the effusion of the Spirit in order to prepare for the arrival of the millennium.[67] The whole mission to the Native Americans is soaked in eschatological assumptions, even when they don't peep through to the surface of *The Life*. One of the chief clues is Brainerd's frequent use of the category of Zion's interest, or advancement, or enlargement. Edwards writes: "In his [Brainerd's] prayers, he insisted much on the prosperity of Zion, the advancement of Christ's kingdom in the world, and the flourishing and propagation of religion among the Indians."[68] Here, several key theological tropes come together, for the city of Zion represents God's promises embodied, his presence secured, and his purposes for world transformation exemplified. Richard Hall has recognized the theme of Zion's interest in *The Life*, but my argument goes one step further.[69] Eschatology serves in Edwards's presentation of Brainerd's example of piety and ministry as the category which unites Edwards and Brainerd to generations to come, and serves to soften claims to personal agency and to promote the abiding value of the church in the purposes of God, securing ecclesiastical authority as seminal to the success of the revivals. Agency, yes; autonomy, no. De Jong picks up the significance of eschatological themes animating the legacy of Brainerd, drawing some distance from Ola Winslow's reductionist piety:

> If the main motive of men like Brainerd and Hawley had been the pursuit of sainthood, as Ola E. Winslow suggests, the diary would never have rung a responsive chord in the hearts of so many others. The truth is that the new era in missions was the

---

66. Hammond, *John Wesley in America*, 13, 147.
67. De Jong, *As the Waters Cover the Sea*, 119, 120.
68. Edwards, *The Life of Brainerd*, WJE 7:446.
69. Hall, *Neglected Northampton Texts*, 176–80.

result of a new vision of the fulfilment of God's promises for the universal spread of Christianity.[70]

Brainerd is more a herald of a kingdom dawning than a hero struggling to shake off a church that must be left behind. He is a church planter with an eschatological wind behind his back rather than a rugged individualist facing the storms of ministerial life blowing in his face.

## David Brainerd: Providence and Virtue

David Brainerd lay dying in the Northampton manse. As an act of care, he requested that those present should read to him Psalm 102, which describes the physical ailments of a man who trusted in God, juxtaposed with the eternal character of the divine kingdom: "But you, O LORD, are enthroned forever; you are remembered throughout all generations. You will arise and have pity on Zion; it is the time to favor her; the appointed time has come." (Psalm 102:12–13). His feeble life was ebbing; God's purposes within which his own identity had been formed were nonetheless robust and enduring. This moment, in which the present and the future were contrasted, relativized questions of agency and authority, and pointed Edwards to the providential part Brainerd had played in his own life. Edwards saw Brainerd as a man of eminent piety and noble example, to *him* as well as to others, in a kind of inverted mentoring relationship:

> I would not conclude my observations on the merciful circumstances of Mr. Brainerd's death without acknowledging with thankfulness the gracious dispensation of Providence to me and my family in so ordering that he (though the ordinary place of his abode was more than 200 miles distant) should be cast hither to my house, in his last sickness, and should die here: So that we had opportunity for much acquaintance and conversation with him, and to show him kindness in such circumstances, and to see his dying behavior, to hear his dying speeches, to receive his dying counsels, and to have the benefit of his dying prayers.[71]

While it was more normal for the minister to assure the dying, here we see a counter-cultural posture, in which the dying reassured the minister.[72] We may not choose to highlight the heroic virtues of the man, but we can recognize his transgressive example, in which his *weaknesses* served as a

---

70. De Jong, *As the Waters Cover the Sea*, 123.
71. Edwards, *The Life of Brainerd*, WJE 7:541.
72. Grigg, *Lives of David Brainerd*, 134–39, 155, 163.

new framework for the negotiation of agency and authority. He was a leader, though initially not ordained; a teacher, though not formally graduated; a man, though not married; an activist, despite poor health, and persevering even when apparently unsuccessful. These qualities give us permission to aspire to emulation more than heroic virtues might have achieved. Edwards does not want us merely to emulate Brainerd's actions, which by repetition can never produce virtue, but to recognize their place in a world being turned upside down and redefined eschatologically, which suggests the possibility of renewed moral excellence.[73] The limitations of human agency, and the transience of every kind of authority, point us to the inadequacy of seeing Brainerd in heroic terms alone, and point us to the value of providing leadership training which acknowledges and appropriates both.

Every generation needs leaders to clear the undergrowth and blaze a trail, which is perhaps even more the case under postmodern conditions, when a sense of order and direction are missing in an ironically fragmented though globalized world. We seek out leaders who are characterized by managerial competency in an organization, entrepreneurial risk-taking in a start-up, or inspiring vision setting in a not-for-profit, but we don't naturally ask about the character or soul-life of an applicant for a job, figuring that their private life has little bearing on their output at work or achievements in their career. In a world where big "L" leaders are celebrities, we need the reminder of the impact and virtues of small "l" leaders, and seek out through the dynamic of mentoring the next generation of teachers, missionaries, academics, and pastors, for the sake of the health of the church.

## Bibliography

Bezzant, Rhys S. *Jonathan Edwards and the Church*. New York: Oxford University Press, 2014.

Block, James E. *A Nation of Agents: The American Path to a Modern Self and Society*. Cambridge: The Belknap Press of Harvard University Press, 2002.

Brekus, Catherine A. *Sarah Osborn's World: The Rise of Evangelical Christianity in Early America*. New Directions in Narrative History. New Haven: Yale University Press, 2013.

Cochran, Elizabeth Agnew. *Receptive Human Virtues: A New Reading of Jonathan Edwards's Ethics*. University Park, PA: The Pennsylvania State University Press, 2011.

Conforti, Joseph. "Jonathan Edwards's Most Popular Work: *The Life of David Brainerd* and Nineteenth-Century Evangelical Culture." *Church History* 54/2 (1985) 188–201.

---

73. Cochran, *Receptive Human Virtues*, 111–12, 117.

De Jong, James A. *As the Waters Cover the Sea: Millennial Expectation in the Rise of Anglo-American Missions 1640–1810.* Laurel: Audubon Press, 2006.

Edwards, Jonathan. "A Faithful Narrative." In *The Great Awakening*, edited by Clarence C. Goen, The Works of Jonathan Edwards 4:97–211. New Haven: Yale University Press, 1972.

———. *The Life of Brainerd.* Edited by Norman Pettit. The Works of Jonathan Edwards 7. New Haven: Yale University Press, 1985.

———. "Personal Narrative." In *Letters and Personal Writings*, edited by George S. Claghorn, The Works of Jonathan Edwards 16:790–804. New Haven: Yale University Press, 1998.

———. "True Saints, when Absent from the Body, are Present with the Lord." In *Sermons and Discourses, 1743–1758*, edited by Wilson H. Kimnach, The Works of Jonathan Edwards 25:222–56. New Haven: Yale University Press, 2006.

Foster, Thomas A. *Sex and the Eighteenth Century Man: Massachusetts and the History of Sexuality in America.* Boston: Beacon Press, 2006.

Grigg, John A. *The Lives of David Brainerd: The Making of an American Evangelical Icon.* Religion in America Series. New York: Oxford University Press, 2009.

Hall, Richard A. S. *The Neglected Northampton Texts of Jonathan Edwards: Edwards on Society and Politics.* Studies in American Religion 52. Lewiston: Edwin Mellen, 1990.

Hall, Timothy D. *Contested Boundaries: Itinerancy and the Reshaping of the Colonial American Religious World.* Durham: Duke University Press, 1994.

Hammond, Geordan. *John Wesley in America: Restoring Primitive Christianity.* Oxford: Oxford University Press, 2014.

Hatch, Nathan O. *The Democratization of American Christianity.* New Haven: Yale University Press, 1989.

Hindmarsh, Bruce. "Is Evangelical Ecclesiology an Oxymoron? A Historical Perspective." In *Evangelical Ecclesiology: Reality or Illusion?* edited by John G. Stackhouse, Jr, 15–37. Grand Rapids: Baker Academic, 2003.

Holifield, E. Brooks. *A History of Pastoral Care in America: From Salvation to Self-Realization.* Eugene, OR: Wipf & Stock, 1983.

Kimnach, Wilson H. "Preface to the Period." In *Sermons and Discourses, 1743–1758*, edited by Wilson H. Kimnach, The Works of Jonathan Edwards 25:3–46. New Haven: Yale University Press, 2006.

Long, Kimberly Bracken. *The Eucharistic Theology of the American Holy Fairs.* Louisville: Westminster John Knox Press, 2011.

Lovejoy, David S. *Religious Enthusiasm in the New World: Heresy to Revolution.* Cambridge: Harvard University Press, 1985.

Mangalwadi, Vishal. *The Book that Made your World: How the Bible Created the Soul of Western Civilization.* Nashville: Thomas Nelson, 2011.

McNeill, John T. *A History of the Cure of Souls.* New York: Harper & Row, 1951.

O'Brien, Susan. "A Transatlantic Community of Saints: The Great Awakening and the First Evangelical Network, 1735–1755." *American Historical Review* 91/4 (1986) 811–32.

Pettit, Norman. "Editor's Introduction." In *The Life of Brainerd*, edited by Norman Pettit, The Works of Jonathan Edwards 7:1–85. Edited New Haven: Yale University Press, 1985.

Schmidt, Leigh E. *Holy Fairs: Scotland and the Making of American Revivalism.* 2nd ed. Grand Rapids: Eerdmans, 1989.
Westra, Helen P. *The Minister's Task and Calling in the Sermons of Jonathan Edwards.* Studies in American Religion 17. Lewiston/Queenston: Edwin Mellen, 1986.

# 16

## The Abolitionism of Samuel Hopkins
### *An Application of Edwards's Doctrine of True Virtue*

Richard Hall

On June 7, 1731, four men gathered around a table in a southern New England seaport, possibly at a tavern, to transact some business. Three of them . . . had the look of experienced sailors. . . . The fourth was an apparently fragile man in his late twenties, so thin as to look "emaciated, and impair'd in his Health." He was dressed in the wig, black suit, and Geneva tabs that he always made a point of wearing in public. To see this fourth man, with all the distinguishing marks of a clergyman, in such company must have struck onlookers as odd, and perhaps the other three men covertly shared bemused looks over the serious, thin-lipped minister as he watched one of his companions take up a quill, dip it into a well, and fill out a bill of sale—a receipt for a slave, "a Negro Girle named Venus," whom this man of God was buying.[1]

THE CLERGYMAN IN KENNETH P. Minkema's imaginative reconstruction of an actual historical event was none other than Jonathan Edwards, America's premier philosopher and arguably the greatest English-speaking theologian.

---

1. Minkema, "Defense of Slavery," 23.

He was also a slave owner. In extenuation of this fact, it cannot be said that Edwards was a child of his time, his attitudes and behavior limited and sanctioned by the ideas and customs then prevailing. John Wesley, Edwards's ally in promoting the Great Awakening, was an ardent abolitionist, as was Benjamin Franklin, in some ways Edwards's nemesis.

In fairness, though, Edwards was ambivalent about slavery. This is shown by his actions in a case brought against a neighboring clergyman, Benjamin Doolittle of Northfield, by Benjamin Wright. Wright, a renowned Indian fighter, and two others, remonstrated with Doolittle about his ownership of a slave. Edwards was requested by the Hampshire County Ministerial Association to reply to this charge against a fellow minister. Edwards, a Calvinist and revivalist, was thus put in an awkward position. He had to defend Doolittle, a suspected Arminian and opposer of the revivals then sweeping New England. Yet, ever mindful of human solidarity in sin, Edwards turned the tables on Wright and his confederates. He accused them of hypocrisy in criticizing Doolittle because, though they themselves did not own slaves, they indirectly benefited from the slave trade and so were "partakers" of slavery and "may have their slaves at next step." Although Edwards defended the legitimacy of the domestic trade in slaves born in captivity in America, he roundly condemned the international slave trade, "a far more cruel slavery than that which they [Wright et al.] object against in those that have slaves here." He opposed the importation of slaves from Africa, denying that "nations have any power or business to disfranchize all the nations of Africa."[2]

Moreover, Edwards was the first Northampton minister to baptize Africans and confer on them full membership in the church, which entailed significant political privileges such as the franchise.[3] He evidently had no trace of racial prejudice, for he looked forward to the millennium when "many of the Negroes and Indians will be divines, and . . . excellent books will be published in Africa, in Ethiopia, in Turkey."[4] In a sermon, *Christian Liberty*, Edwards reminds his congregation that when Christ returns at the millennium, "he should proclaim a universal liberty to all servants, captives, vassals, [and] imprisoned [or] condemned persons."[5]

   2. Ibid., 36.

   3. Ibid., 34. "Of the 11 blacks baptized by Edwards in Northampton from 1735 to 1741, 2 did not become full members, 2 others apparently died in infancy, and 7 went on to become full members." (Ibid., 54 n. 49).

   4. Edwards, *WJE* 9:480.

   5. Edwards, "Christian Liberty," *WJE* 10:621. In the original manuscript of the sermon, "slaves" is included in the list of the liberated. However, on second thoughts, he deleted "slaves" from his manuscript before actually delivering the sermon. Minkema,

Now Edwards had a student and disciple, Samuel Hopkins, who also owned slaves, but would later free them, and would risk his livelihood and reputation by himself becoming a militant abolitionist, even taking his case to the Continental Congress. The question I shall address here is, why did Hopkins change from being a slave owner to an abolitionist? There is no way, of course, of knowing for sure; however, one can speculate on the basis of evidence.

Three reasons may be adduced to explain Hopkins's moral conversion. One is that while resident in Newport, Rhode Island, the commercial hub of the slave trade in North America, he had the opportunity of observing close at hand the rigors and cruelty of the trade, which he did not have when, say, residing in Northampton with Edwards or preaching in Stockbridge. A second reason is that he had occasion to reflect more deeply on the practical implications of Edwards's doctrine of disinterested benevolence as found in the latter's *Dissertation on True Virtue*. Evidence for this is that Hopkins himself in 1773 reprises the substance of Edwards's dissertation under the title, *Inquiry Concerning the Nature of True Holiness*. (Hopkins's title, replacing Edwards's "true virtue" with "true holiness," is a subtle shift from a philosophical to a theological vocabulary with a bearing on pastoral or practical theology.) Third, the climate of political opinion had changed drastically since the time of his pastorate in Stockbridge. During his ministry in Newport, the thirteen British colonies became the American Republic dedicated to the equality and freedom of all human beings, at least on paper. This may have prompted Hopkins to see the blatant contradiction between the high-flown ideals of the Declaration of Independence and the brute fact of American slavery. It may be that any or all—or none—of these reasons caused his moral sea change; alternatively, it may have been other factors, or these in combination with the aforementioned. The actual cause (or causes) of Hopkins's change of heart may not be ascertainable. However, the three reasons taken together constitute at least a reasonable explanation for it.

The remainder of this paper is in three parts. In the first, I briefly give some biographical background on Hopkins and his association with Edwards. In the second part, I consider Hopkins's argument against slavery. And in the third, I discuss how both Edwards and Hopkins were concerned with determining the nature of true religion, thereby to differentiate it from its counterfeits. In so doing, they made disinterested benevolence, which they understood to be the nature of true virtue as well as religion, maximally inclusive. Edwards did this by making God the supreme object of benevolence, in contradistinction to the moral sense theorists, and Hopkins

---

"Defense of Slavery," 41.

by emphasizing that *all* human beings, even African slaves, should also be included as proper objects of benevolence. Thus Hopkins made explicit the humanitarian implications of Edwards's theory of virtue, which he fully accepted and actually applied through his abolitionist efforts. For it is here in Edwards's conception of true virtue as a radically inclusive benevolence to all rational and volitional beings that Hopkins, I believe, may have found the inspiration and philosophical justification for his abolitionism.

## Hopkins under Edwards

Hopkins was born in Waterbury, Connecticut, in 1721. A Yale graduate, he lived with Jonathan Edwards in Northampton, Massachusetts during the latter's pastorate there. Later he himself pastored a church in another Massachusetts town, Great Barrington. While there, together with Joseph Bellamy, another Yale student of divinity, he had occasion again to discuss theology with Edwards who had lately moved to Stockbridge as missionary to the Housatonic Indians after his dismissal from the Northampton church. Given the high caliber of mentor and disciples, these three formed perhaps the finest seminary in New England at the time. In tribute to his mentor, Hopkins would write the first biography of Edwards. Unpopular with the congregation because of his uncompromising Calvinism, Hopkins was dismissed by them in 1769. In 1770, he became pastor of the First Congregational Church of Newport, Rhode Island, which he served until his death in 1803. His tenure there was interrupted only by the outbreak of the revolution when British soldiers occupied the town and damaged the church.

Together with other disciples of Edwards—Bellamy and Jonathan Edwards the younger—Hopkins became a leader of the New Lights who promulgated Edwards's evangelical Calvinism, or the New Divinity, as it became known. It was Hopkins who codified it. Among its defining doctrines are: (1) God is absolutely sovereign, and acts solely to glorify himself and promote the happiness of all beings; (2) evil occurs with God's permission since it makes possible a greater good than would otherwise be possible by providing the occasion for God to display his mercy and justice; (3) the regeneration of the soul is in no way effected by human efforts but by God alone, the sole author of salvation; (4) evidence of regeneration is a necessary qualification for full church membership; (5) the world is a divinely ordered and harmonious system where all people should take their appointed places, live for the good of the whole creation, and love God supremely and unconditionally; (6) true virtue or holiness consists in a disinterested benevolence to being in general, or the benevolent love for God and all his creatures wherein one's self-interest is subordinated to the interest of the whole system of beings.

The key idea here for our purposes is disinterested love or benevolence, which Hopkins received from Edwards, and Edwards in turn from the moral sense theorists, particularly Francis Hutcheson.

## Hopkins on Slavery

In Newport, Hopkins witnessed first hand the horrors of the slave trade, which he attempts to describe as follows:

> But it is in vain to attempt a full description of the oppression and cruel treatment these poor creatures receive constantly at the hands of their imperious, unmerciful, worse than Egyptian taskmasters. Words cannot utter it. Volumes might be Written, and not give a detail of a thousandth part of the shockingly cruel things they have suffered, and are constantly suffering. Nor can they possibly be conceived of by any one who has not been an eye witness. And how little a part does he see![6]

Hopkins had become an eyewitness, which could well explain his change of heart over slavery. Moreover, Hopkins notes that Newport's economic prosperity depended on the slave trade:

> The inhabitants of Rhode Island, especially those of Newport, have had by far the greater share in this traffic of all these United States. This trade in the human species has been the first wheel of commerce in Newport, on which every other in business has chiefly depended. That town has been built up, and flourished in times past, at the expense of the blood, the liberty, and happiness of the poor Africans; and the inhabitants have lived on this, and by it have gotten most of their wealth and riches.[7]

After deep reflection, Hopkins freed his own slaves and demanded that slave owners in his congregation do likewise, on pain of excommunication. He came to realize that slavery is an abomination, in his own words, "a national sin, and a sin of the first magnitude—a sin which righteous Heaven has never suffered to pass unpunished in this world."[8] Indeed, Hopkins attributes the woes brought on by the American War of Independence as God's judgment against slavery: "if the slavery in which we hold the blacks

6. Hopkins, *A Dialogue concerning the Slavery of the Africans*, 555–56.
7. Hopkins, *The Slave Trade and Slavery*, 615.
8. Ibid., 614–15.

is wrong, it is a very great and public sin, and, therefore, a sin which God is now testifying against in the calamities he has brought upon us."[9] Hopkins had become a militant abolitionist.

Hopkins's polemic against slavery is contained in these four related texts. The first two, which he dedicated to the Continental Congress of 1776, are *A Dialogue Concerning the Slavery of the African* and *An Address to the Owners of Negro Slaves in the American Colonies*. The third text is *A Discourse upon the Slave Trade and the Slavery of the Africans*, delivered before the Providence Society for Abolishing the Slave Trade at their Annual Meeting on May 17, 1793. The fourth text is, *The Slave Trade and Slavery*. But Hopkins's appeal to the Congress fell on deaf ears, and the Constitution of the United States would eventually allow slavery in the new republic.

Quakers, though, were his fellow travelers in the cause of emancipation. In 1775, the Third Society for Abolition was founded in Philadelphia with Benjamin Franklin being elected its president 1787. And Hopkins's plea may have influenced the New York Manumission Society's petition of May 1786 to the New York legislature to prohibit the exportation of slaves. It is noteworthy that the petition was drafted and headed by John Jay and signed by Alexander Hamilton, who became president of the society in 1790, succeeding Jay who became Supreme Court Chief Justice.

In the aforementioned polemical works against slavery, Hopkins appeals to both his readers' reason and divine revelation. In his appeal to their reason, he argues that slavery should be abolished on the grounds of logical consistency. Americans are guilty of a vile and absurd inconsistency on three counts. For one, their denying inalienable rights to some is inconsistent with their expounding them for all:

> The Africans, and the blacks in servitude among us, were really as much included in these assertions [viz., *The Declaration of Independence*] as ourselves, and their right, unalienable right to liberty, and to procure and possess property, is as much asserted as ours, if they be men; and if we have not allowed them to enjoy these unalienable rights, but violently deprived them of liberty and property, and still taking as far as in our power all liberty and property from the nations in Africa, we are guilty of a ridiculous, wicked contradiction and inconsistence, and practically authorize any nation or people, who have power to do it, to make us their slaves.[10]

---

9. Hopkins, *A Dialogue concerning the Slavery of the Africans*, 551.
10. Hopkins, *The Slave Trade and Slavery*, 617.

For another, Hopkins argues, Americans' keeping of Africans in bondage is inconsistent with their fighting for freedom from bondage to the British crown:

> The very inconsistent part you act while you are thus enslaving your fellow-men, and yet condemning and strenuously opposing those who are attempting to bring you and your children into a state of bondage much lighter than that in which you keep your slaves, who yet have at least as good a right to make slaves of you and your children as you have to hold your brethren in this state of bondage.[11]

(Interestingly, this inconsistency was also not lost on Samuel Johnson, who once quipped, "How is it that we hear the loudest yelps for liberty among the drivers of Negroes?"[12])

And finally, Hopkins asserts, Americans' enslaving of Africans is inconsistent with the religion they profess:

> Consider also how very inconsistent this injustice and oppression is with worshipping God through Christ, and attending on the institutions of religion, and how unacceptable and abominable these must be while you neglect to let the oppressed go free, and refuse to do justice and love mercy.[13]

And in his appeal to revelation, Hopkins warns Americans are courting the wrath of God who shows solicitude to the victims of misfortune. He entreats them "seriously to consider how very offensive to God unrighteousness and the oppression of the poor, the stranger, and the fatherless is represented to be in the Holy Scripture. This is often spoken of as the procuring cause of the calamities that came on God's professing people of old, and of their final ruin." Hopkins goes on to ask rhetorically, "Are not the African slaves among us the poor, the strangers, the fatherless, who are oppressed and vexed, and sold for silver? And will not God visit and punish such oppression? Are you willing to be the instruments of bringing judgments and ruin on this land, and on yourselves and families, rather than let the oppressed go out free?"[14] Furthermore, Hopkins puts the American institution of slavery in eschatological perspective and interprets it as a sign

---

11. Hopkins, *An Address, to the Owners of Negro Slaves in the American Colonies*, 590.

12. Johnson, "Taxation no Tyranny," 89.

13. Hopkins, *An Address, to the Owners of Negro Slaves in the American Colonies*, 593.

14. Ibid., 591, 592.

of the end-time. Mindful of Revelation, he believes that in the last days human wickedness will be intensified by Satan and his minions who will "excite men, especially in the Christian world, to extraordinary and wonderful degrees of wickedness" of which slavery is an egregious example, of where "the hand and power of Satan has been in an extraordinary degree exerted and manifested." Yet, Hopkins looks forward to the millennium when "all these works of the devil shall be destroyed, and that the time is hastening on, when all the people shall be righteous and benevolent, and there shall be none to destroy or hurt in all the earth."[15]

Apart from its violation of the dictates of logic and Scripture, there is, I believe, a more profound reason for Hopkins's uncompromising condemnation of the institution of slavery: his reading of Edwards's *True Virtue*. It perhaps was his recognition of the practical import of Edwards's conception of true virtue as disinterested benevolence, together with his personal experience of the slave trade and his republican principles, which turned Hopkins into an ardent abolitionist. According to Joseph Conforti, "The American Revolution, the Newport slave trade, and the slave system itself presented Hopkins with opportunities to demonstrate his disinterested love of Being in general and to call for the reform of American society."[16] To understand how this happened, we shall consider Edwards's own conception of true virtue, or religion, as disinterested benevolence and Hopkins's subtle modification of it so as to make it an ethical argument against human bondage. As we shall see, the trend in both their moral philosophies is to make benevolence more inclusive: Edwards makes it inclusive of the whole Chain of Being, with God at its apex, whereas Hopkins emphasizes for inclusion the whole of humanity, particularly African slaves in America.

## The Doctrine of True Virtue: A Comparison of Edwards and Hopkins

### Edwards on True Virtue

"There is no question whatsoever, that is of greater importance to mankind, . . . than this, "What is the nature of true religion?"[17] With this question, which Socrates much earlier broached in *Euthyphro*, Edwards opens his *Religious Affections*, which is a sustained and rigorous answer to it. This

---

15. Hopkins, *Discourse upon the Slave Trade and the Slavery of the Africans*, 604, 605.
16. Conforti, *Samuel Hopkins*, 123.
17. Edwards, *Religious Affections*, WJE 2:84.

question was also on Hopkins's mind where, in his *True Holiness*, he writes, "Since holiness is, by the confession of all, the sum of all moral excellence and the highest and most necessary attainment, it is of the last importance that we should well understand its nature, and distinguish it from all counterfeits."[18] Both hoped that determining the nature of true religion would help resolve the religious controversies that were raging in their day.

Edwards locates the essence of true religion in the affection of love: "The Scriptures do represent true religion, as being summarily comprehended in love." The object of this love is an attribute of God, namely, the beauty of his holiness: "Those affections that are truly holy, are primarily founded on the loveliness of the moral excellency of divine things."[19] However, the later Edwards makes a subtle shift in both the language and substance of his definition of "true religion." In his posthumously published *The Nature of True Virtue*, he speaks not of "true religion" but of "true virtue." "Love" now becomes "benevolence." And its object is no longer God's "moral excellency" or beauty, a divine attribute, but the bearer of this attribute, namely, "being in general." Thus, "True virtue most essentially consists in benevolence to being in general."[20] Being in general is still to be loved for its moral beauty, but this is now only a secondary motive of a truly virtuous disposition. It depends on the primary motive, which has become love of general being for its own sake alone. He shifts from the language of theology and religion to that of metaphysics and ethics, though speaking of the same thing.

What probably accounts for Edwards's change in language and emphasis is his engagement with the moral sense theorists, namely, Anthony Ashley Cooper (third Earl of Shaftesbury) and Francis Hutcheson, with their similar conception of virtue as benevolence. In a veiled reference, Edwards signals their agreement with him by saying that virtue is "owned by the most considerable writers, to consist in general love of benevolence." However, Edwards demurs at their failure to make God the principal object of benevolence in their moral systems. He notes that, though "they don't wholly exclude a regard to the *Deity* out of their schemes of morality, but yet mention it so slightly," they instead "leave me room and reason to suspect they esteem it a less important and a subordinate part of true morality," and, further, they "insist on benevolence to the *created* system."[21]

Edwards's criticism is apposite. For Shaftesbury stipulates that "to deserve the name of *good* or *virtuous*, a Creature must have all his Inclinations

18. Hopkins, *True Holiness*, 5.
19. Edwards, *Religious Affections*, *WJE* 2:106, 253.
20. Edwards, "True Virtue," *WJE* 8:540.
21. Ibid., 541, 552–53.

and Affections, his Dispositions of Mind and Temper, sutable, and agreeing with the Good of his *Kind*, or of that *System* in which he is included, and of which he constitutes a PART." He further notes, "That PARTIAL AFFECTION, or social Love *in part*, without regard to a compleat Society or *Whole*, is in it-self an Inconsistency, and implies an absolute Contradiction."[22]

Though Hutcheson does mention God as, for example, when he stipulates that we show benevolence even to our benefactors whom we cannot possibly benefit in turn by at least expressing our gratitude to them, as in the case with all our "rational Devotion, or Religion toward a Deity apprehended as Good, which we can possibly perform." But the principal object of benevolence he has in mind seems to be the whole of humanity, as further implied by his stating that "Love, or Benevolence, is the Foundation of all apprehended Excellence in social Virtues."[23]

Edwards accuses the moral sense theorists of inconsistency on this point. As he says, "If true virtue consists partly in a respect to God [which they concede], then doubtless it consists *chiefly* in it." The reason is that "if the Deity is to be looked upon as within that system of beings which properly terminates our benevolence," then "certainly he is to be regarded as the *head* of the system, and the *chief* part of it; if it be proper to call him a *part*, who is infinitely more than all the rest, and in comparison of whom, and without whom all the rest are nothing, either as to beauty or existence."[24]

The nub of Edwards's complaint against the moral sense theorists is that their ethics is anthropocentric; Edwards's is radically theocentric: "true virtue does primarily and essentially consist in a supreme love to God."[25] The love or benevolence espoused by Edwards, no less than by Hutcheson and Shaftesbury, is entirely disinterested insofar as it is not principally motivated by self-interest but instead by the best interest, or the highest good, of all beings. And here, it should be noted, Edwards's conception of benevolence is much broader than that of the moral sense theorists. It encompasses not only humanity as its proper object, but God and angels, as well as the whole of animate nature—even worms! For Edwards, if any creature is minimally sentient then it qualifies as a constituent of the great chain of being and so is eligible for a modicum of moral regard in proportion to its degree of understanding and goodness of will. Edwards is thus advocating here a form of panpsychism that would be developed systematically by Josiah Royce and the psychologist, Gustav Fechner, in the nine-

22. Cooper, *Virtue, or Merit*, 45.
23. Hutcheson, *Beauty and Virtue*, 118, 117.
24. Edwards, "True Virtue," *WJE* 8:553–54.
25. Ibid., 554.

teenth century. By denominating its object "being in general," as in *True Virtue*, instead of simply "God," as in *Religious Affections*, Edwards makes benevolence maximally inclusive. He is including not only the Creator but all his creatures as objects deserving of benevolence in proportion to their greatness as measured by their degree of being or mental capacity and the degree of goodness of their individual wills.

### Hopkins and True Holiness

Hopkins's *True Holiness* is the fruit of his long apprenticeship under Edwards when residing with him during his student days in Northampton:

> Hopkins, especially, was so intimate with Edwards, . . . that he must have ascertained the opinions of his teacher with regard to the practical bearings of the theory [of virtue] which, more than almost any other, contains the "seeds of things." He spent much of his life in defending and applying this theory of virtue. He founded many of his peculiarities upon it. No man had enjoyed so signal an advantage for learning the varied uses which Edwards would make of it.[26]

However, the learning in this case was perhaps not a one-way street. William Ellery Channing, who was a member of Hopkins's congregation in Newport, Rhode Island, believed that Edwards learned from Hopkins: "President Edwards was a good deal indebted to Dr. Hopkins for his later views of religion, especially for those which we find in his essays on 'Virtue,' and on 'God's End in Creation.'. . . Dr. Hopkins had not the profound genius of Edwards, but was he not a man of a freer and bolder mind?"[27]

Hopkins's argument in *True Holiness* is, as he says, substantially the same as Edwards's in his *True Virtue*. (Interestingly, he substitutes the religious term "holiness" for the ethical term "virtue.") Edwards's definition of "true virtue" as "benevolence to being in general" becomes for Hopkins "love to God and our neighbor, including ourselves, and is universal benevolence, or friendly affection to all intelligent beings. This universal benevolence . . . is the whole of true holiness."[28] He had the same complaint as Edwards against the moral sense theorists for marginalizing or even excluding God from their moral systems: "Hence almost all writers on morality have made virtue to consist chiefly, if not altogether, in what they call universal benevo-

---

26. Park, *Memoir*, 218.
27. Channing, *Memoir*, 137.
28. Hopkins, *True Holiness*, 16.

lence; though many of them have left God and his kingdom, the great object of true benevolence, out of their system."²⁹

Like Edwards, Hopkins emphasizes that the universal benevolence that constitutes true virtue must be "disinterested," which means self-sacrificial living by professors of virtue.³⁰ He explains the full scale of the self-sacrifice that virtue requires in the following passage:

> He ought to be willing to give up his whole worldly interest and comfort, and live a life of poverty and want, if this were necessary to save a whole nation from ruin, and make them rich and happy; yea, he ought to be willing to expose and give up his life, if this were necessary for the good of his country, and to save the lives of millions.³¹

Hopkins held to the most stringent ideal of disinterestedness conceivable. It meant that one should be willing for one's self to be damned for the greater glory of God!

> From the Scriptures we learn that the glory of God ought to be our ultimate and highest end; that we are commanded to seek his glory in all we do, and therefore are forbid to desire or pursue any thing which is contrary to his highest glory, and required to submit to any thing, and desire it may take place, which is most for his glory. Therefore, on supposition it be most for his glory that I should not be saved, but lost, I ought to submit, and not desire to be saved.³²

And indeed, "not to be willing to be damned, in this case, is opposing God's will" no less.³³

Hopkins was able to make such an exacting demand because of the more careful distinction he makes "between benevolence and self-love,"³⁴ which he accuses the moral sense theorists of failing to do. Shaftesbury, for example, extols the "social affections" like benevolence because they redound eventually to the individual's own interest. Benevolence for him is simply

---

29. Ibid., 33–34.

30. The idea of disinterestedness has ongoing significance and operates well beyond the realm of theology, which Walter Lippmann has extensively discussed. In agreement with Hopkins and Edwards, Lippmann identifies disinterestedness as "the core of high religion." Lippmann, *A Preface to Morals*, 204.

31. Hopkins, *A Dialogue between a Calvinist and a Semi-Calvinist*, 145.

32. Ibid., 153.

33. Ibid., 148.

34. Hopkins, *True Holiness*, 34.

a matter of making one's self-love more inclusive, a form of enlightened self-interest: "That to be well affected towards the *Publick Interest* and *one's own*, is not only consistent, but inseparable: and that moral Rectitude, or *Virtue*, must accordingly be the Advantage, and *Vice* the Injury and Disadvantage of every Creature."[35] Self-love is virtuous if it does not exclude love for others. Shaftesbury focuses on the self and its interest, and his justification for benevolence is that it ultimately benefits the individual self.

By contrast, Hopkins focuses on the whole system of beings of which the self is but a miniscule part. He, like Shaftesbury, allows for a virtuous self-love. But self-love, to be genuinely virtuous, must begin with being in general, not with the self. Self-love qualifies as virtuous only if the individual loves himself *insofar as he is part of the general system* to which he is devoted:

> And as he himself is one individual part of the whole, he must of necessity by the object of this disinterested, impartial benevolence, and his own interest and happiness must be regarded and desired, as much as that of his neighbor, or any individual of the whole society; not because it is *himself*, but because he is included in the whole, and his happiness is worth as much, and as desirable as that of his neighbor, other circumstances being equal.[36]

One ought to love the system of general being first and foremost and himself second only because he is a part of it. One ought not to love one's self first, and the system of general being as an afterthought, because one stands to benefit somehow from it. For Hopkins (and Edwards) the self-love, however enlightened, that Shaftesbury and his followers extol is nothing more than a form of glorified selfishness, which is anything but virtuous because it puts self as its center instead of the system of general being.

Hopkins's aim, other than replying to Edwards's critics and determining the nature of true religion, is to make an "improvement" on Edwards, which consists, among other things, of explaining things more fully and drawing certain inferences. It is here, in his fuller—or more explicit—explanation of virtue or holiness, that he draws out a practical implication of Edwards's doctrine of virtue as it pertains to slavery. He does this in two ways. One is by making Edwards's "benevolence to being in general" to mean "*friendly affection* [emphasis added] to all intelligent beings" so as to bring out its humanitarian dimension. Another way is by clarifying the meaning of "holiness," or "virtue," by affirming that "love to God and *our neighbor* [emphasis added] . . . is the whole of true holiness." Hopkins then goes on to

---

35. Cooper, *Virtue, or Merit*, 47.
36. Hopkins, *System of Doctrines*, 380.

include slaves as neighbors, thereby enfranchising them as proper objects of love. He argues that the Golden Rule implies the manumission of slaves: "The following precept of our Lord and Savior, 'All things whatsoever ye would that men should do unto you, do ye even so to them,' which is included in loving our neighbor as ourselves, will set at liberty every slave."[37]

Hopkins was more than an armchair moralist; he put his money where his mouth was by taking action against slavery:

> He set himself against the habits and pecuniary income, of the men on whom he relied for his daily bread. He sacrificed property and immediate reputation. He was ridiculed and hated by many of his townsmen. But he threw over himself, and over his cause, the mantle of religion.[38]

His self-sacrificial behavior on behalf of manumission was simply a putting into practice of his ideal of virtue or disinterested benevolence.

Hopkins, then, has demonstrated that Edwards's "benevolence to being in general" implies "love to slaves as neighbors." He has in effect taken a metaphysical abstraction—being in general—and given it concreteness and practicability by showing that being in general includes neighbors and slaves no less. Edwards's *True Virtue* is abstract since it is rooted in the metaphysics propounded in its sister dissertation, *God's End in Creation*, after which it is placed. Hopkins simply educes what is implicit in Edwards's conception of being in general. He particularizes Edwards's generalization about virtue as benevolence to being. Thus it is that Edwards's abstract doctrine of virtue could provide a philosophical justification for the abolition of slavery. If Hopkins's abolitionism was influenced by Edwards's *True Virtue*, then it would belie Perry Miller's estimate of the moral philosophy contained therein: that it was suitable only for angels.

In sum, the chief difference between Edwards and Hopkins on virtue is in their overall orientation: Edwards's ethics is oriented vertically towards God as the head and chief part of the system of being. For Edwards, the ultimate end of the virtuous life is promoting the happiness or glory of God since he has the largest quantity and quality of being, so that the happiness of others counts far less. Without that as its primary goal there is no true virtue. Hopkins's ethics, on the other hand, is oriented horizontally towards human beings who belong no less to that general system. For Hopkins, no doubt influenced by the new climate of opinion ushered in by the Enlightenment, human happiness counted for something as well—at least that the

---

37. Hopkins, *A Discourse upon the Slave Trade and the Slavery of the Africans*, 601.

38. Park, *Memoir*, 161.

happiness of each counted equally since all human beings were created equal, that is, had the same quantity of being on average.

Ironically, Hopkins's stress on humanity as a proper object of benevolence reverts back somewhat to Hutcheson's humanistic ethics, against which Edwards—and Hopkins—had reacted. Here is an instance of a moral philosophy modified and applied out of struggle, a struggle over slavery.[39]

## Conclusion

The moral philosophy of Edwards, then, was amplified in Hopkins, and grew to shape the Abolitionist movement. As Edwards influenced Hopkins, so Hopkins influenced Channing. The young Channing, though appalled by his Calvinism and lack of elocutionary skill, nevertheless admired Hopkins the man: "I was attached to Dr. Hopkins chiefly by his theory of disinterestedness. I had studied with great delight during my college life the philosophy of Hutcheson, and the Stoical morality, and these had prepared me for the noble, self-sacrificing doctrines of Dr. Hopkins."[40] Channing was an ardent abolitionist, and it was from Hopkins, according to the former's memoirist, that Channing "first gained his convictions of the iniquity of slavery."[41] Channing, the proto-Transcendentalist, in turn influenced Emerson who, testifying to his fellow Transcendentalists' recognition of Channing's authority, conferred on him the moniker, "our Bishop." Curiously, Perry Miller in his ground-breaking essay, "From Edwards to Emerson," mentions neither Hopkins nor Channing as their intermediaries.

Hopkins, moreover, has entered the annals of American literature as a protagonist in Harriet Beecher Stowe's novel, *A Minister's Wooing*. Stowe was born into Lyman Beecher's Calvinist household and, like her brother, Henry Ward Beecher, was an Abolitionist whose plea for the manumission of African slaves received classic fictional expression in her better known novel, *Uncle Tom's Cabin*. Stowe portrays Hopkins as Edwards redivivus and as the personification of true virtue, which is most manifest when he selflessly blesses the marriage between his secret love, Mary, and her suitor. Mary herself, moreover, was drawn to Hopkins as when she "listened in rapt

---

39. The only other case I know of where an abstract moral philosophy was applied to the social and political realms and wrought significant changes was the utilitarianism of Bentham and his disciple John Stuart Mill. Bentham's principle of utility provides the philosophical justification for his advocacy of prison reform and the education of working men, among other such programs.

40. Channing, *Memoir*, 137.

41. Ibid., 32.

attention, while her spiritual guide, the venerated Dr. Hopkins, unfolded to her the theories of the great Edwards on the nature of true virtue."[42] (In reading the novel, one sometimes gets the impression that Stowe has in mind not the actual Dr. Hopkins but Jonathan Edwards himself.)

Abolitionists other than Hopkins, Channing, and Stowe were also directly or indirectly influenced by Edwards. None other than the notorious John Brown may have been subtly influenced by him in staging his raid on Harper's Ferry. Owen Brown, John's father and another Abolitionist, was deeply impressed by a sermon preached by Edwards's son, Jonathan Edwards Jr., in 1790, wherein he characterized slavery as a "Cardinal sin against God." And John Brown himself was steeped in the works of the elder Edwards.

Edwards, then, was a distant inspiration for the Abolitionist movement in ante-bellum America. However, he was not alone in this regard. It was the larger tradition of Puritanism, of which he, Hopkins, and Brown were quintessentially representative, that was foundational to American Abolitionism. And of Brown in particular, David S. Reynolds writes, "Both enemies and friends of John Brown, then, considered him a deep-dyed Puritan. They were right. He was a Calvinist who admired the works of Jonathan Edwards. He was proud of his family roots in New England Puritanism."[43] Emerson recognized this in his lecture of 1844, "New England Reformers," where he says, the "fertile forms of antinomianism among the elder puritans seemed to have their match in the plenty of the new harvest of reform."[44] And according to Reynolds, "In 1863, the Democratic congressman Samuel Cox typically blamed the Civil War on disruptive New England reform movements that he said were rooted in Puritanism. He insisted that fanatical Abolitionism caused the war, and, in his words, 'Abolition is the offspring of Puritanism.'"[45]

Abolitionism as part of the legacy of Puritanism is perhaps memorialized in Augustus Saint-Gaudens's statue, "The Puritan," which stands in Merrick Park in Springfield, Massachusetts. It has been suggested that the statue's face was modeled on John Brown's.[46] Brown lived in Springfield between 1846 and 1849: Saint-Gaudens greatly admired Brown, and the statue's face resembles Brown's. If indeed the sculptor used Brown's face as

42. Stowe, *The Minister's Wooing*, 16.
43. Reynolds, *John Brown Abolitionist*, 19.
44. Emerson, "New England Reformers," 241.
45. Reynolds, *John Brown Abolitionist*, 16.
46. See Jendrysik, "Special to the Republican."

his model, then his sculpture, "The Puritan," embodies concretely the emancipatory moral vision of Brown—shaped by the virtue theory of Edwards and his mentee Hopkins.

## Bibliography

Channing, William H., ed. *Memoir of William Ellery Channing, with Extracts from his Correspondence and Manuscripts.* Vol. 1. 4th ed. Boston: Wm Crosby and H. P. Nichols, 1850.

Conforti, Joseph. *Samuel Hopkins and the New Divinity Movement: Calvinism, the Congregational Ministry, and Reform in New England between the Great Awakenings.* The Jonathan Edwards Classic Studies Series. Eugene, OR: Wipf & Stock, 1981.

Cooper, Anthony Ashley, Third Earl of Shaftesbury. *Characteristicks of Men, Manners, Opinions, Times* [1737]. Vol. 2, *An Inquiry concerning Virtue, or Merit.* Indianapolis, Indiana: Liberty Fund, Inc., 2001.

Edwards, Jonathan. "Christian Liberty." In *Sermons and Discourses, 1720–1723,* edited by Wilson H. Kimnach, The Works of Jonathan Edwards 10:618–31. New Haven: Yale University Press, 1992.

———. "Dissertation II: The Nature of True Virtue." In *Ethical Writings,* edited by Paul Ramsay, The Works of Jonathan Edwards 8:537–627. New Haven: Yale University Press, 1989.

———. *A History of the Work of Redemption.* The Works of Jonathan Edwards 9. Edited by John F. Wilson. New Haven: Yale University Press, 2008.

———. *Religious Affections.* The Works of Jonathan Edwards 2. Edited by John E. Smith. New Haven: Yale University Press, 1969.

Emerson, Ralph Waldo. *The Works of Ralph Waldo Emerson.* Edited by Edward W. Emerson. Vol. 3, "New England Reformers." Essays: Second Series. Boston and New York: Fireside Edition, 1909.

Hopkins, Samuel. *An Address, to the Owners of Negro Slaves in the American Colonies.* The Works of Samuel Hopkins 2. Boston: Doctrinal Tract and Book Society, 1854.

———. *A Dialogue between a Calvinist and a Semi-Calvinist.* The Works of Samuel Hopkins 3. Boston: Doctrinal Tract and Book Society, 1854.

———. *A Dialogue concerning the Slavery of the Africans.* The Works of Samuel Hopkins 2. Boston: Doctrinal Tract and Book Society, 1854.

———. *A Discourse upon the Slave Trade and the Slavery of the Africans.* The Works of Samuel Hopkins 2. Boston: Doctrinal Tract and Book Society, 1854.

———. *An Inquiry into the Nature of True Holiness.* The Works of Samuel Hopkins 3. Boston: Doctrinal Tract and Book Society, 1854.

———. *The Slave Trade and Slavery.* The Works of Samuel Hopkins 2. Boston: Doctrinal Tract and Book Society, 1854.

———. *System of Doctrines.* The Works of Samuel Hopkins 1. Boston: Doctrinal Tract and Book Society, 1854.

Hutcheson, Francis. *An Inquiry into the Original of Our Ideas of Beauty and Virtue.* Edited by Wolfgang Leidhold. Indianapolis, Indiana: Liberty Fund, Inc., 2004.

Johnson, Samuel. *Taxation no Tyranny; An Answer to the Resolutions and Address of the American Congress.* London: T. Cadell, 1775, 1789.

Jendrysik, Stephen. "Special to the Republican," January 22, 2014. At http://www.masslive.com/living/index.ssf/2014/01/stephen_jendrysik_is_augustus_saint-gaudens_the_puritan_statue_really_john_brown_in_disguise.html.

Lippmann, Walter. *A Preface to Morals*. New York: The Macmillan Company, 1929.

Minkema, Kenneth P. "Jonathan Edwards's Defense of Slavery." *The Massachusetts Historical Review* 4 (2002) 23–59.

Park, Edwards A. *Memoir*. In *The Works of Samuel Hopkins. A Dialogue concerning the Slavery of the Africans*. Vol. 1, 1–266. Boston: Doctrinal Tract and Book Society, 1854.

Reynolds, David S. *John Brown Abolitionist, The Man Who Killed Slavery, Sparked the Civil War, and Seeded Civil Rights*. New York: Alfred A. Knopf, 2006.

Stowe, Harriet Beecher. *The Minister's Wooing*. Boston and New York: Houghton, Mifflin and Company, 1896.

# 17

## Preach and Print
### The Role of Printed Sermons in the Ministries of George Whitefield, John Wesley and Jonathan Edwards

IAN J. MADDOCK

As THREE OF THE most visible leaders of the eighteenth century transatlantic evangelical revival, George Whitefield, John Wesley, and Jonathan Edwards were devoted to proclaiming the gospel, not simply through the preached word, but also through the printed word. While each pursued, in varying measures, a "preach and print" strategy when it came to their sermons, this chapter seeks to explore how these forms of proclamation functioned in their respective public ministries.

Two questions in particular will shape our discussion. First, how did the sermons Whitefield, Wesley, and Edwards preached relate to the sermons they printed? Were they the same, or different, genres? As Kimnach observes, "the sermon has always labored under certain ambiguities peculiar to its genre. Most obvious is the question of exactly what the text of a sermon represents. Is it what was preached, or a literary correlative, or a separate work altogether?"[1] A second, and associated, question proceeds from the first: what function did the printed sermons of Whitefield, Wesley, and Edwards perform in their respective public ministries?

---

1. Kimnach, "Edwards as Preacher," 104.

For all of their shared commitment to furthering revival, Whitefield, Wesley, and Edwards did not have identical self-conceptions of their ministries. Nor did they publish their sermons for identical reasons. Indeed, it will become apparent that the differing manner in which each envisaged the scope of their respective ministries is in large measure encapsulated in their differing aspirations for their printed sermons, especially their volumes of collected sermons: Whitefield's *Ten Sermons Preached on Various Important Subjects*, Wesley's *Sermons on Several Occasions*, and Edwards's *Discourses on Various Important Subjects*. In short, if we desire a window into how Whitefield, Wesley, and Edwards conceived their role as revivalists, then we ought look no further than their printed sermons.

## George Whitefield: "They Contain the Sum and Substance . . . of What Was Delivered from the Pulpit"

Above all else, George Whitefield was a preacher. As he embarked on his journey to the American colonies in 1739, fresh from a phenomenally successful series of field-preaching events throughout England during the previous year, Whitefield reflected, "Everyone hath his proper gift. Field preaching is my plan. In this I am carried as on eagles' wings."[2] While he deliberately pursued a "preach and print" strategy, he privileged the former over the latter.

Nonetheless, Whitefield felt compelled to print his sermons for at least two reasons. The first was *defensive*: he printed his sermons to set the record straight. From the very earliest stages of his public career, unauthorized versions of his sermons appear to have been a source of irritation for Whitefield. He took exception to these for a number of reasons. On the one hand, there were the opportunists. In a *Journal* entry in mid 1737, Whitefield described how,

> through the importunity of friends, and aspersions of enemies, I was prevailed on to print my sermon *On the Nature and Necessity of our Regeneration or New Birth in Christ Jesus*, which under God began the awakening at London, Bristol, Gloucester, and Gloucestershire . . . A second impression was soon called for; and finding another of my sermons was printed without my leave, and in a very incorrect manner at Bristol, I was obliged to publish in my own defence.[3]

---

2. Quoted in Philip, *Life and Times*, 385.
3. Whitefield, *George Whitefield's Journals*, 86.

Likewise, in his entry for Friday, October 31, 1740, Whitefield recounts, "I . . . met with two volumes of sermons published in London, supposed to have been delivered by me, though I have never preached on most of the texts."[4]

A second reason Whitefield printed his sermons was less reactive and more pro-active; it emerged from straightforward evangelistic zeal. Whitefield conceived of his own ministry more or less exclusively in terms of evangelism. He consistently resisted overtures to diversify his ministry and assume the mantle of leadership over the Calvinistic wing of the Methodist movement, arguing on one occasion that to do so would be to "weave a Penelope's web."[5] If both he and Wesley independently declared "the whole world to be their parish," then undoubtedly Whitefield's emphasis was more on "the world" and less on "the parish"—more on evangelism and less on facilitating spiritual nurture for those converted under his preaching. Whitefield hoped that by disseminating his sermons in printed form he might thereby increase his sphere of influence to include not just auditors, but also readers. Lambert comments that, "To buyers, the evangelist's *Journals* and sermons represented an opportunity to participate in the revivals when there was no chance to hear him preach. Indeed some people knew Whitefield only through his publications."[6]

What do we know of the relationship between the sermons Whitefield preached and printed? Although on one occasion Whitefield levelled criticism against the sermons "faithfully transcribed by Joseph Gurney" on the grounds that they were "not verbatim" transcriptions of his spoken sermons, there is much evidence to suggest that even those sermons that Whitefield did authorize for publication were not precise transcriptions of his spoken sermons.[7] For instance, both editions of *Ten Sermons Preached on Various Important Subjects by George Whitefield, A .B. Carefully corrected and revised according to the best London edition* are rare among the plethora of editions of Whitefield's sermons, insofar as they commence with a preface written by Whitefield. These introductory remarks afford the reader further insight into Whitefield's aspirations for his printed sermons, especially their relationship to the sermons he preached.[8] This preface is worth quoting in full:

4. Ibid., 484.
5. Gillies, *Works of George Whitefield* 2:169–70.
6. Lambert, "*Pedlar in Divinity*," 126.
7. Jay, *Memoirs of the Life and Character*, 49.
8. The publishing details of the two editions of Whitefield's *Ten Sermons* can be found in the bibliography.

> The following Sermons, I think I may say, were given me by the Lord Jesus Christ; and according to my present light, are agreeable to the form of sound words delivered to us in the lively oracles of God. They contain the sum and substance, I will not say word for word, of what was delivered from the pulpit; for, as I had no occasion in America, Scotland, and England to preach on the same subjects, I was obliged, according to the freedom and assistance given me from above, to enlarge, or make excursions, agreeable to the people's circumstances among whom I was preaching the Kingdom of God. I had no leisure or freedom to commit any of them to writing, but during my last voyage from America to England; nor do I expect to find leisure to write down any fresh discourses, till it should please God that I embark again. May the Spirit of God, who delights out of the mouths of babes and sucklings to perfect praise, bless them to every reader, and put it into their hearts to pray for their poor unworthy servant in Jesus Christ.[9]

While admirers of Whitefield's dramatic pulpit oratory have tended to dismiss his printed discourses as comparatively unremarkable, Whitefield's prefatory remarks betray no sign of embarrassment regarding their style or content.[10] Whitefield was careful to distinguish between his spoken and printed sermons, but he was also prepared to affirm their essential substantive similarity; they existed within the same homiletical orbit. Whitefield considered his printed sermons representative of the "sum and substance" of his spoken sermons, but in the next breath he clarified that they therefore ought not be read as verbatim transcriptions of his spoken sermons. His aspirations for his printed sermons were uncomplicated: that "the Spirit of God" might "bless them to every reader." In other words, Whitefield hoped that through the medium of the printed word he might

---

9. Whitefield, *Ten Sermons*, Preface.

10. Dallimore is representative of this historiographical trend, observing, "It is necessary to remember that the difference between the spoken and the written word was more pronounced in Whitefield than in almost any other man. As he preached his whole person became alive in a powerful yet altogether natural dramatism; yet its elements—the movements of body, the expression of his countenance and modulations of his voice—are, of course, entirely lost on the printed page." Dallimore, *George Whitefield* 2:526. In a similar vein, Downey states, "that while Whitefield's sermons, reinforced by his oratorical powers, made for excellent listening, they are now rather disappointing reading. They lack variety and polish. Many of the best qualities of his preaching have been lost between pulpit and press. The repetition which proved so effective on the lips of the speaker becomes tedious when read." Downey, *The Eighteenth Century Pulpit*, 167.

extend the scope of transatlantic revival beyond those who could attend his preaching events and hear his sermons.

Whitefield's prefatory comments also indicate that although he accorded his printed sermons an important role in the advancement of transatlantic revival, the printed sermon never dislodged the spoken sermon from its position of primacy in his public ministry.[11] That is, Whitefield preached his sermons before he printed and published them, employing the printed word in order to complement the spoken word. Regardless of whether the printed word happened to take the form of a Whitefield sermon published in a newspaper or in a sermon collection,[12] an advertisement for an upcoming preaching event, glowing descriptions of transatlantic revival in his magazine *The Weekly History*, or his published journal, Whitefield used the printed word "to publicize and reinforce" his "dramatic preaching style and revolutionary meeting format."[13]

The priority Whitefield granted to his spoken sermons is perhaps nowhere better illustrated than in the manner in which he allocated his time. Whitefield's consistent practice was to write only when circumstances actively prevented him from preaching.[14] Perhaps the most regular constraint on Whitefield's itinerant preaching came in the form of the regular and lengthy sea journeys that inevitably accompanied the transatlantic scope of his public ministry, and he appears to have devoted this time to correspon-

---

11. Whitefield sought to capitalize on the overall success of his first preaching tour of the American colonies during 1740 by publishing American editions of his sermons and journals. On November 26, 1740, Whitefield wrote to his American publisher, Benjamin Franklin, "You may print my life, as you desire. God willing, I shall correct my two volumes of sermons, and send them the very first opportunity." Whitefield, *George Whitefield's Letters*, 226. Franklin would eventually publish two volumes of Whitefield's sermons later that year, entitled *Sermons on Various Subjects. In two volumes. By George Whitefield, A.B. of Pembroke College, Oxford.*

12. Lambert, "Subscribing for Profits and Piety," and Rogal, "Toward a Mere Civil Friendship: Benjamin Franklin and George Whitefield," both describe the significant role played by Benjamin Franklin in publishing and publicizing Whitefield's sermons and journals.

13. Lambert, *Inventing the "Great Awakening,"* 99.

14. Whitefield's collected works reveal that he was a faithful, though not always punctual, correspondent. He frequently cited a frantic schedule of itinerant preaching engagements as the cause for his delay in writing. For instance, in "A Letter to the Inhabitants of Maryland, Virginia, North and South Carolina," Whitefield begins by noting his preference for the spoken word over the printed word as his medium of choice: "Could I have preached more frequently among you, I should have delivered my thoughts to you in my public discourses: but, as business here required me to stop as little as possible on the road, I have no other way to discharge the concern which at present lies on my heart, than by sending you this letter." Gillies, *Works*, 4:37.

dence, composing sermons, and preparing other discourses for his printers on both sides of the Atlantic.¹⁵

## John Wesley: "Those Doctrines . . . Which I Embrace and Teach as the Essentials of True Religion"

John Wesley did not simply aspire to be *homo unius libri*, but in practice also a "preacher of one book." Nathaniel Hone's famous portrait of Wesley reinforces this self-conception, illustrating him preaching in the fields with Bible in hand. Wesley was convinced that he had been set apart to preach, well before he became convinced of the need to preach justification by faith and the new birth in 1738, and well before his successful initial forays as a field-preacher in April 1739. Wesley made a point of expressing his conviction that the tongue with which he spoke his sermons was "a devoted thing," as opposed to the pen that set them down on paper.¹⁶ Later Wesley would go so far as to proclaim, "I do indeed live by preaching!"¹⁷ He continued to preach regularly as he advanced in age and even attributed his longevity and good health in part to the rigor of his preaching schedule.¹⁸

And yet oral preaching did not exhaust Wesley's homiletical ambitions; printed sermons, too, occupied a privileged place in his public ministry. Much like Whitefield, on occasion Wesley felt compelled to print his sermons as a corrective gesture. For instance, he wrote in the preface to his sermon "Scriptural Christianity," first preached at St. Mary's, Oxford on August 24, 1744,

---

15. For example, see Whitefield, *Journals*, 111 and Whitefield, *Letters*, 294.

16. See Wesley's letter to John Burton on October 10, 1735 in *Letters I*, Works of John Wesley 25:441.

17. Wesley, *Journals and Diaries IV*, Works of John Wesley 21:118. In his comments on Acts 6:2 in his *Explanatory Notes on the New Testament*, Wesley affirmed the primacy of the preached word in general terms, stating that "the primary business of apostles, evangelists and bishops was to preach the Word of God." Wesley, *Explanatory Notes Upon the New Testament*, 290.

18. During his later years, Wesley's consistent practice was to describe the state of his health in his *Journal* on June 28, his birthday. He frequently attributes his relative good health to the invigorating effects of a busy preaching itinerary. For instance, on his 77th birthday, he wrote, "I can hardly think I am entering this day into the seventy-eighth year of my age. By the blessing of God I am just the same as when I entered the twenty-eighth. This hath God wrought, chiefly by my constant exercise, my rising early, and preaching morning and evening." Wesley, *Journals and Diaries VI*, Works of John Wesley 23:179–80. Two years later, his Journal entry for June 28, 1782 reads, "I find no more pain or bodily infirmities than at five and twenty. This I still impute . . . to my constant preaching, particularly in the morning." Ibid., 23:244–45.

> It was not my design when I wrote ever to print the latter part of the following sermon. But the false and scurrilous accounts of it which have been published almost in every corner of the nation constrain me to publish the whole, just as it was preached, that men of reason may judge for themselves.[19]

But beyond this need to respond to the appearance of unauthorized versions of his sermons, Wesley's printed sermons served a crucial function in the life of the Methodist societies. Whereas much like his spoken sermons, Whitefield's printed sermons were primarily geared towards winning converts, John Wesley's decision to print his sermons was in large measure motivated by his commitment to the task of nurture and spiritual formation among the Methodist societies.[20] In particular, Wesley understood that his printed sermons functioned in a subtly different manner when compared to his preached sermons. Wesley's sermon register indicates that he chose not to include many of the sermons he preached throughout his itinerant ministry within his *Sermons on Several Occasions*.[21] Summarizing the differences between the sermons Wesley preached versus the sermons he printed, Outler contends that Wesley "saw an important difference between the principle aims of an oral and a written sermon: the former is chiefly for *proclamation* and invitation; the latter is chiefly for *nurture* and reflection."[22]

The preface to the first volume of Wesley's *Sermons on Several Occasions* neatly articulates the role of printed sermons in his wider public ministry. Even as this collection expanded to include four volumes, Wesley continued to append this introduction unaltered. In their eventual form,

---

19. Wesley, "Scriptural Christianity" in *Sermons I*, Works of John Wesley 1:159.

20. For instance, see Harper, "Wesley's Sermons as Spiritual Formation Documents." Wesley's life-long commitment to publishing as an important means of promoting spiritual nurture among Methodists transcended the printing and distribution of his sermons. Commenting on Wesley's wider publishing activities, Boshears observes that "Wesley deliberately provided useful literature that was cheap in cost and aimed at lifting the educational and spiritual life of the eighteenth century English masses," and that his publishing patterns attest to the role he assumed as the "definitive . . . reader-advisor to the early Methodists." Boshears, "The Books in John Wesley's Life," 54–55.

21. Outler observes, "Many of Wesley's favourite texts for oral preaching do not appear at all in the corpus of his written sermons and vice versa." Outler, preface to Wesley, *Sermons I*, Works of John Wesley 1:14.

22. Ibid. Similarly, Heitzenrater concludes with regard to Wesley's sermons that, "the two homiletical forms, preached and printed, were rather different in form if not content. Many of his printed sermons were carefully developed treatises written specifically for publication and intended to be theological in nature." Heitzenrater, *Mirror and Memory: Reflections on Early Methodism*, 162.

they amounted to forty-four sermons that came to function as normative sermonic articulations of Methodist doctrines in much the same way as the Book of Homilies did within the Church of England.[23] Whereas Whitefield only took the time to prepare printed discourses when circumstances precluded him from preaching, Wesley deliberately suspended his preaching schedule in 1746 in order to devote attention to the preparation of this collection of sermons for publication.[24] Wesley began,

> The following sermons contain the sum and substance of what I have been preaching for between eight and nine years last past. During that time I have frequently spoken in public on every subject in the ensuing collection: and I am not conscious that there is any one point of doctrine on which I am accustomed to speak in public which is not here—incidentally, if not professedly—laid before every Christian reader. Every serious man who peruses these will therefore see in the clearest manner what those doctrines are which I embrace and teach as the essentials of true religion.[25]

What can we derive from this preface regarding the role of printed sermons in Wesley's public ministry? Wesley stated that his *Sermons on Several Occasions* "contain the sum and substance of what I have been preaching for between eight and nine years last past," thus incorporating the period leading up to his Aldersgate Street experience of May 1738 and beyond. Reminiscent of Whitefield's description of the relationship between his preached and printed sermons, Wesley clarified that while his printed sermons were accurate statements of the "doctrines" he embraced and taught, they were not to be confused with verbatim transcripts of his spoken sermons.

Further, just as Whitefield considered his printed sermons to be "agreeable to the form of sound words delivered to us in the lively oracles of God," and, by implication, representative expressions of the foundational truths

---

23. Commenting on this relationship, Heitzenrater suggests that Wesley used his Sermons on *Several Occasions* "with regard to his preachers in a similar fashion to the way the Church of England used the Homilies with regard to its unlicensed and uneducated preachers." *Mirror and Memory*, 179. Similarly, Outler contends that Wesley's response to the emergence of doctrinal pluralism among Methodist preachers came not in the form of "a creed or a confession, or even a doctrinal treatise, but with something analogous to a set of Methodist "Homilies"—not in this case "appointed to be read in the churches" (as Cranmer's had been) but rather to be studied and discussed by the Methodists and their critics." Outler, preface to Wesley, *Sermons I*, Works of John Wesley 1:14.

24. Ibid., 38.

25. Ibid.,103.

contained therein, so too Wesley regarded his *Sermons on Several Occasions* as encapsulating what he considered to be "the essentials of true religion." Whereas a more conventional means for disseminating doctrine might have been a systematic theological treatise, Wesley chose these published sermons as his means of conveying the doctrines he "embraced and taught." He preferred, in Outler's words, "the dialectical character of sermons" to "the didactic character of systematic treatises."[26]

But whereas, as we have previously observed, Whitefield addressed his sermons to "every reader," the very absence of a specific target audience underling his aspirations for their universal evangelistic applicability, by contrast, in the preface to his *Sermons on Several Occasions*, Wesley addressed his printed sermons to "every Christian reader." In so doing, Wesley indicated that he primarily intended his printed sermons to be read by those who had already experienced the "new birth," whether in the immediate or distant past. If Wesley's spoken sermons were "aimed at enabling people to join the Methodist societies as well as the offer of salvation,"[27] then his *Sermons on Several Occasions* were intended as instruments for nurturing spiritual growth, not just among the self-consciously regenerate, but among those Methodists who were "serious" about progressing in the Christian life. Wesley wrote,

> It is more especially my desire, first, to guard those who are just setting their faces toward heaven (and who, having little acquaintance with the things of God, are the more liable to be turned out of the way) from formality, from mere outside religion, which has almost driven heart-religion out of the world; and secondly, to warn those who know the religion of the heart, the faith which worketh by love, lest at any time they make void the law through faith, and so fall back into the snare of the devil.[28]

Thus far we have observed that just as Wesley and Whitefield understood the nature of their public ministries in different ways, these differences were translated into their respective aspirations for their printed sermons. Whereas Whitefield understood his public ministry to consist primarily in "planting" the gospel through preaching conversion-oriented sermons, Wesley was committed to a public ministry of "planting" and "watering."[29]

26. Ibid., 55.
27. Turner, *John Wesley*, 40–41.
28. Outler, preface to Wesley, *Sermons I*, Works of John Wesley 1:106.
29. Lambert observes how, "John Wesley and George Whitefield had different conceptions of their ministries: Whitefield saw his role as 'sowing' gospel seeds, while Wesley viewed his as 'reaping the gospel harvest'" (*Inventing the "Great Awakening,"*

Whitefield regarded his printed sermons in large measure simply as a means of extending the scope of spoken sermons that were primarily evangelistic. By contrast, Wesley was convinced that the proclamation of evangelistic sermons must be accompanied by discipleship and utilized his printed sermons as his foremost instrument for facilitating spiritual nurture among the Methodist societies.

## Jonathan Edwards: "To Revive the Memory of the Past Great Work of God"

The evolution of Jonathan Edwards's printed sermons mirrors the evolving nature of his role as a revivalist. Kimnach contends,

> Edwards's career as a writer of sermons can be understood as an evolution of technique, but it is also divisible into historical phases that derive from his view of the sermon in relation to his calling as one of "Christ's ambassadors" to a fallen world. While there is little evidence of any diminution of his commitment to the Christian ministry over time, there is evidence that the role of the sermon in his ministry did change.[30]

This "change" is especially evident as we compare what Kimnach styles the "second phase" of Edwards's ministry (1729–42) with the "third phase" (1743–58); a change that transpired as Edwards's gaze lifted from local revival in Northampton and shifted to that of commentator on revival on the transatlantic stage.[31] The "evolution of technique" in Edwards's preaching is neatly encapsulated in the only volume of sermons he ever published, a 1738 collection of five sermons entitled *Discourses on Various Important Subjects, Nearly Concerning the Great Affair of the Soul's Eternal Salvation*.[32] This volume had its origin in a desire to memorialize the Little Awakening that took place in Northampton in the winter of 1734 and spring of 1735. Published during the second phase of Edwards's ministry, a period when he employed his sermons primarily as instruments of awakening and

---

94). Lambert is undoubtedly correct when he suggests that Whitefield and Wesley understood the parameters of their respective public ministries in different terms. Yet we have already seen that Wesley's ministry of "watering" (not "reaping" as per Lambert) simultaneously embraced both conversion-oriented spoken sermons along with a commitment to spiritual nurture.

30. Kimnach, "Edwards as Preacher," 106.

31. For a summary of Kimnach's classification of Edwards's 37-year preaching career, see McDermott, "Theology in the Hands of a Literary Artist."

32. Published by S. Kneeland and T. Green in Boston.

pastoral leadership, it thus functioned as a tribute to Edwards's preaching during this period.

Three of the five sermons in *Discourses on Various Important Subjects*—"Pressing into the Kingdom of God," "Ruth's Resolution," and "The Justice of God in the Damnation of Sinners"—certainly embody "the minatory and hortatory elements of awakening preaching."[33] All three were selected by Edwards's congregation, which had also underwritten the cost of publication—no small thing in the circumstances given they were also in the process of building a new meetinghouse in Northampton.[34] Edwards himself chose a fourth sermon, "The Excellency of Christ," on the grounds that, "A discourse on such an evangelical subject would properly follow others that were chiefly legal and awakening, and that something of the excellency of the Savior was proper to succeed those that were to show the necessity of salvation."[35]

One question that arises is how these four sermons in their printed form (chronologically, sermons two, three, four, and five in *Discourses on Various Important Subjects*) compared with what Edwards originally preached from his Northampton pulpit. While Edwards gave the impression that they were not verbatim transcriptions of his spoken sermons, they nonetheless—to borrow the language of Wesley and Whitefield—contain the "sum and substance" of what he preached. In his Preface, Edwards described how "the practical discourses [referring to the four sermons listed above] which follow have but little added to them, and now appear in that very plain and unpolished dress in which they were first prepared and delivered."[36]

But what of the first sermon entitled "Justification by Faith Alone"? Like the ensuing four sermons, it also had its origins in the Little Awakening of 1734–35. In fact, Edwards identified the two lectures he delivered on justification as constituting the initial cause, humanly speaking, of the awakening, reflecting on how "the beginning of the late work of God in this place was circumstanced, that I could not but look upon it as a remarkable testimony of God's approbation of the doctrine of *justification by faith alone*, here asserted and vindicated."[37]

---

33. Kimnach, "Edwards as Preacher," 113.

34. Ibid.

35. Edwards, "Preface to *Discourses on Various Important Subjects*," *WJE* 19:797. See also Edwards, "Excellency of Christ," *WJE* 19:560–94.

36. Ibid.

37. Ibid., 795.

And yet "Justification by Faith Alone" was no conventional sermon—certainly not a sermon in the same sense as the other four in *Discourses on Various Important Subjects*. Most viscerally, there is its size relative to the other discourses in the collection: it occupies roughly half of the volume's total pages and is more than twice as long as any of its compatriots. Edwards initially delivered "Justification by Faith Alone" over the course of two lectures in 1734, but by the time it found its way into print in this collection it had grown in size even more, to the point that it now resembled a different genre of proclamation altogether—more treatise than sermon.[38] Kimnach indicates as much, describing "Justification by Faith Alone" not only as Edwards's first published treatise, but also "an example of [his] ability to radically expand sermons into a full-blown treatise, as he was to do most famously in *A Treatise Concerning Religious Affections*" in 1746.[39]

As we consider the evolution of Edwards's printed sermons as an encapsulation of the evolving nature of his role as a revivalist, it is even possible to extend Kimnach's illuminating observation one step further. Not only is "Justification by Faith Alone" Edwards's first sermon-come-treatise, it anticipates the major shift in the nature of Edwards's preaching and printing that occurred during the third phase of his public ministry: the shift away from pastoral and awakening sermons directed primarily towards his Northampton congregation, and towards preaching treatises in the form of lengthy sermon series. These series, though ostensibly preached to his local congregation, had a significantly broader audience and reflected Edwards's evolving self-conception as a commentator, interpreter, and critic of revival on the transatlantic stage.[40]

This evolution reached its fullest expression during the third phase of Edwards's ministry, but hints of this shift had begun to appear by the late 1730s and early 1740s. Kimnach observes how "the end of the decade [1730s] shows Edwards experiencing a kind of homiletical restlessness. He had preached sermons and lectures previously in multiple preaching units in order to accommodate more complex or comprehensive arguments from the pulpit. However, after 1735 this activity increased markedly."[41] If publications like *Discourses on Various Important Subjects* introduced Edwards as a preacher to the wider world, in retrospect they marked not simply the high

---

38. Kimnach comments on how "this modest volume of five discourses included [Edwards's] first published treatise, a sermon he had extensively reworked and hugely enlarged for print." Kimnach, "Literary Life," 141.

39. Kimnach, "Edwards as Preacher," 113.

40. Kimnach, "Literary Life," 142.

41. Kimnach, "Edwards as Preacher," 115.

point of his career as a pastoral preacher, but its culmination.[42] Thereafter he invested significantly less literary effort preparing pastoral sermons, and instead applied his creative revivalist energies producing lengthy serial sermons.[43] These extended sermon series became "increasingly obvious as treatises smuggled into the pulpit, pieces whereby Edwards preached to the town but wrote for the world."[44] As Edwards transitioned away from the second phase of his ministry and towards the third, "the trend," as Kimnach observes, "is clear enough." He "had moved from sharing a pastoral concern with the larger world to sharing a message for the larger world with his congregation as pastoral preaching" to the point that "by 1743, it seems, the literary Edwards was beginning to dominate the pastoral Edwards."[45]

This shift in the nature of Edwards's printed sermons, encapsulated in *Discourses on Several Important Subjects*, mirrors his evolution as a revivalist. While his conception of the sermon as a genre of proclamation proved to be elastic, Edwards's commitment to utilizing spoken and printed sermons as his default medium for theological utterance remained a sure constant. Edwards was a "natural proponent of print," and while "the vast majority of sermons remained oratorical events," he nonetheless embraced "the wider circulation and permanence of print" as a means of expanding his leadership role beyond the confines of colonial western Massachusetts.[46] Reflecting on Edwards's dynamic "preach and print" career, Kimnach observes, "Whether . . . taking up the practical authority of pastoral leadership in the second phase, or exploring beyond the limits of conventional pastoral preaching in the third, Edwards fully exploited the sermon genre, the essential medium through which he first published his thought throughout his life."[47]

It is finally worth observing that Edwards's *Discourses on Various Important Subjects* offers us not only a glimpse into his evolving aspirations for his public ministry, they also offer us a window into the heterogeneous nature of his intended readership. On the one hand, like Whitefield, Edwards preached and printed in order to awaken. Reflecting the second phase of his ministry, this evangelistic imperative is clearly evident in his Preface: "I declare every reader's candid acceptance and due improvement of what is

---

42. Kimnach, "Literary Life," 142.

43. For example, *Charity and its Fruits* began as a 16-part sermon series preached in 1738; *A History of the Work of Redemption* began as a 30-part sermon series preached in 1739.

44. Kimnach, "Literary Life," 142.

45. Kimnach, "Edwards as Preacher," 117.

46. Ibid., 122.

47. Ibid., 121.

here offered."⁴⁸ But on the other hand, like Wesley, Edwards was not exclusively committed to evangelism; he saw his printed his sermons as a means of edification, discipleship, and spiritual nurture. Edwards especially urges his Northampton congregation, "the people of my own charge, not to fail of improving these discourses," to "revive the memory of the past great work of God amongst us," and to "lament our declensions," in the prayerful hope that "the same work might renewedly break forth and go on amongst us."⁴⁹

Edwards's preaching had begun to undergo seismic shifts by the late 1730s when *Discourses on Several Important Subjects* was published, and his focus had begun to shift towards revival on the broader transatlantic stage. Nevertheless, come 1738 Edwards was, and would continue to be for some time to come, the shepherd of his Northampton flock, all the while the Little Awakening memorialized in this volume of sermons remaining for him *the* paradigmatic revival event.

## Conclusion

In this chapter we have begun to compare the printed sermons of George Whitefield, John Wesley, and Jonathan Edwards within the context of their wider public ministries. As three of the foremost leaders of eighteenth century evangelical revival, each vigorously pursued a "preach and print" method. And yet for all of their shared commitment to furthering revival in the transatlantic world, they did not conceive of their own ministries in precisely the same way. Nor did they publish their sermons for identical reasons. In fact, we have observed that the differing manner in which each envisaged the scope of their respective ministries is in large measure encapsulated in the differing roles played by printed sermons in their wider ministries, especially the volumes of collected sermons we have explored. How did Whitefield, Wesley, and Edwards conceive their respective roles as revivalists? We need look no further than their printed sermons as fertile ground for insights into their differing, and in Edwards's case, evolving, aspirations.

## Bibliography

Boshears, Onva K. "The Books in John Wesley's Life." *Wesleyan Theological Journal* 3 (1968) 48–56.
Dallimore, Arnold. *George Whitefield: The Life and Times of the Great Evangelist of the 18th Century Revival.* Vol. 1. Edinburgh: Banner of Truth, 1970.

48. Edwards, "Preface to *Discourses on Various Important Subjects,*" WJE 19:797.
49. Ibid., 797–98.

Downey, James. *The Eighteenth Century Pulpit: A Study of the Sermons of Butler, Berkeley, Secker, Sterne, Whitefield and Wesley.* Oxford: Clarendon, 1969.

Edwards, Jonathan. *Discourses on Various Important Subjects—Nearly Concerning the Great Affair of the Soul's Eternal Salvation.* Boston: S. Kneeland and T. Green, 1738.

———. "The Excellency of Christ." In *Sermons and Discourses, 1734–1738,* edited by Max X. Lesser, The Works of Jonathan Edwards 19:560–94. New Haven: Yale University Press, 2001.

———. "Preface to *Discourses on Various Important Subjects.*" In *Sermons and Discourses 1734–1738,* edited by Max X. Lesser, The Works of Jonathan Edwards 19:793–798. New Haven: Yale University Press, 2001.

Gillies, John. *The Works of George Whitefield.* 7 vols. Edinburgh: Kincaid and Bell, 1771.

Harper, Steve. "Wesley's Sermons as Spiritual Formation Documents." *Methodist History* 26/3 (1988) 131–38.

Heitzenrater, Richard P. *Mirror and Memory: Reflections on Early Methodism.* Nashville: Kingswood, 1989.

Jay, W. *Memoirs of the Life and Character of the Late Reverend Cornelius Winter.* New York: Samuel Whiting, 1811.

Kimnach, Wilson H. "Edwards as Preacher." In *The Cambridge Companion to Jonathan Edwards,* edited by Stephen J. Stein, 103–24. New York: Cambridge University Press, 2007.

———. "The Literary Life of Jonathan Edwards." In *Understanding Jonathan Edwards: An Introduction to America's Theologian,* edited by Gerald R. McDermott, 133–44. New York: Oxford University Press, 2009.

Lambert, Frank. *"Pedlar in Divinity": George Whitefield and the Transatlantic Revivals.* Princeton: Princeton University Press, 1994.

Lambert, Frank. "Subscribing for Profits and Piety: The Friendship of Benjamin Franklin and George Whitefield." *William and Mary Quarterly* 50/3 (1993) 529–54.

McDermott, Gerald R. "Theology in the Hands of a Literary Artist: Jonathan Edwards as Preacher." *Theologia Wratislaviensia* 7 (2012) 116–18.

Philip, Robert. *The Life and Times of the Reverend George Whitefield.* Edinburgh: Banner of Truth, 1960.

Rogal, Samuel J. "Toward a Mere Civil Friendship: Benjamin Franklin and George Whitefield." *Methodist History* 35 (1997) 233–44.

Turner, John Munsey. *John Wesley: The Evangelical Revival and the Rise of Methodism in England.* London: Epworth, 2002.

Wesley, John. *Explanatory Notes Upon the New Testament.* Reprint. Salem, OH: Schmul, 1975.

———. *Journals and Diaries IV, 1755–1765.* Edited by W. Reginald Ward and Richard P. Heitzenrater. The Works of John Wesley: Bicentennial Edition 21. Nashville: Abingdon Press, 1992.

———. *Journals and Diaries VI, 1776–1786.* Edited by W. Reginald Ward and Richard P. Heitzenrater. The Works of John Wesley: Bicentennial Edition 23. Nashville: Abingdon Press, 1995.

———. *Letters I, 1721–1739.* Edited by Frank Baker. The Works of John Wesley: Bicentennial Edition 25. Nashville: Abingdon, 1980.

———. *Sermons I.* Edited by Albert C. Outler. The Works of John Wesley: Bicentennial Edition 1. Nashville: Abingdon Press, 1984.

Whitefield, George. *George Whitefield's Journals.* Edinburgh: Banner of Truth, 1960.

———. *George Whitefield's Letters*. Edinburgh: Banner of Truth, 1976.

———. *Sermons on Various Subjects. In two volumes. By George Whitefield, A.B. of Pembroke College, Oxford*. Philadelphia: Printed and sold by B. Franklin, in Market-street, 1740.

Whitefield, George. *Ten Sermons*. First edition. Newburyport, MA: Blunt and March, 1795.

Whitefield, George. *Ten Sermons*. Second edition. Portsmouth, NH: Charles Pierce and S. Larkin, 1797.

## 18

## Visibility, Vitriol, and Vision
### The Drama of Jonathan Edwards's Refusal to Plant a Second Church in Northampton

NICK COOMBS

ON JUNE 22, 1750, Jonathan Edwards, "the most acute early American philosopher and the most brilliant of all American theologians," was dismissed from the Northampton church where he had labored for the past twenty-three years.[1] New England's foremost theological luminary was now unemployed, despised by many of his former parishioners, and dejected about the controversy that preceded his firing. More positively, Edwards was now a man with options, as invitations began arriving to secure his pastoral services. This chapter attempts to ascertain and explain the guiding thought behind Edwards's refusal of one of those options—the planting of a second church in Northampton.

Until very recently, little has been written about Edwards's thought process in relation to this decision. The research has remained at the surface, accepting Edwards's claim that, "[he] had no inclination or desire to settle over these few at Northampton, but a very great opposition in [his] mind to it," with little exploration into Edwards's reasoning.[2] However,

---

1. Marsden, *Jonathan Edwards: A Life*, 1.
2. Edwards, "To Major Joseph Hawley," WJE 16:651. Regarding the lack of depth in analysis of Edwards's reasoning, see, for example, Hopkins, *Life and Character*, 71–72.

a deeper foray into the mind of Edwards at this critical juncture will yield complications that are worth teasing out. For a man once derided as having "a head so full of divinity," yet "so empty of politics," this episode highlights that Edwards may have been more an activist than his studious stereotype seems to suggest. Indeed, after moving on from Northampton, Edwards would write in February 1752 to the leader of the minority in Northampton, Colonel Timothy Dwight, advising him:

> I beseech you not to patch up a mock reconciliation with the church, accepting of something from them that is nothing but a mere sham. Nothing ought to be accepted but proper Christian satisfaction made to you and me, and made as public as the offense committed. And I desire you never would consent to the settlement of a minister that is of principles contrary to yours; you thereby will bring yourselves into a great shame. I can't believe that Mr. [Solomon] Stoddard's principles will ever have a quiet establishment again at Northampton, or that people will ever prosper again in that way; but 'tis probable that the small company that adhered to me, if they hold their own, will prosper and prevail. I believe there will be two societies there. Yours may be the smallest at first, but if you are steadfast, and act prudently, I believe at last they will be the biggest and will get the meetinghouse.[3]

This advice reveals that Edwards was not as adverse to the separation of this minority and their desire to plant a second church as perhaps has previously been believed; yet Edwards refused to see himself as leading this initiative.

Perry Miller has famously written that "the real life of Jonathan Edwards was the life of his mind."[4] This chapter will seek to delve inside the mind of Edwards as it was concerned with the offer of his friends to install him as their pastor over a second church in Northampton. Like any decision, let alone a decision made in the mind of an intellectual of Edwards's calibre, there are many factors to explore. After briefly summarizing the factors that led to Edwards's dismissal, and the events surrounding his departure, this study will present three main influences on Edwards's refusal to plant a second church in Northampton.

---

3. Edwards, "To Col. Timothy Dwight," *WJE* 16:448.
4. Miller, *Jonathan Edwards*, xv.

## Edwards in Northampton

New England churches, since their founding, had always struggled to "hold together rival values of exclusivity and comprehensiveness."[5] The primitivist vision of a true church, inclined toward exclusivity for the sake of purity, had met challenges in the century prior to Edwards, and after a compromising Stoddardean ministry the Northampton congregation, in addition to many congregations throughout New England, was ripe for controversy. At the same time, Edwards's personal mishandling of several pastoral matters and his counter-culturally constricting convictions on access to the Lord's Supper had created a melting pot of tension that would finally reach boiling point.

On June 22, 1750, Edwards would be dismissed from his Northampton parish. The tipping point would come shortly after the publication of Edwards's convictions around the qualifications of communion. This work was fully titled *An Humble Inquiry into the Rules of the Word of God, Concerning the Qualifications Requisite to a Complete Standing and Full Communion in the Visible Christian Church* and was made public in 1749. Hopkins relays that this controversy was one Edwards foresaw, and was willing to endure:

> When he was fixed in his principles, and before they were publicly known, he told some of his friends, that if he discovered and persisted in them, it would most likely issue in his dismission and disgrace; and the ruin of himself and family, as to their temporal interests. He therefore first sat down and counted the cost, and deliberately took up the cross, when it was set before him in its full weight and magnitude, and in direct opposition to all worldly views and motives. And therefore his conduct in these circumstances, was a remarkable exercise and discovery of his conscienciousness, and his readiness to deny himself, and forsake all that he had to follow Christ.[6]

Indeed, the relationship between Edwards and his congregation, which he had once described as being "the freest of any part of the land from unhappy divisions and quarrels in our ecclesiastical and religious affairs,"[7] would now come to a sad and bitter end.

---

5. Hall, "The New England Background," 63.
6. Hopkins, *Life and Character*, 64.
7. Edwards, "A Faithful Narrative," *WJE* 4:145.

## The Unemployed Edwards

Jonathan Edwards was now unemployed. What would he do next? Edwards himself felt "thrown upon the wide ocean of the world," such was the uncertainty before him.[8] Rather awkwardly, he would continue to fill the pulpit at Northampton intermittently until November, while his former congregation looked for a replacement. It was during this time that several options arose for Edwards's next move.

As indicated by notes in his sermons, Edwards would preach in the homes of some of his friends during this time.[9] These gatherings would later be used against him, as proof that Edwards had a "desire to be settled over a few of the members of the church to the destruction of the whole."[10] More accurately, it was the adherents themselves who were leading the charge to install Edwards over them, led by Colonel Timothy Dwight. As far as we can tell from his writings, Edwards was always against being placed in this position, acknowledging it to be "a thing attended with great difficulty and darkness," and pessimistic about the possible church because they were "so small a number" and because of "their circumstances," most likely referring to the controversy in which they were still well entrenched.[11] Edwards did not want to be "a means of perpetuating an unhappy division in the town."[12]

Still, Timothy Dwight persisted, seeking counsel from some of Edwards's clergy friends about planting the second church. He asked for another council to be made up of these men, to give direction to those "that still entertain hopes of [Edwards] being installed in the work of the gospel ministry over them."[13] His reasoning for wanting Edwards to lead this initiative included the scarcity of young candidates who are not "corrupt in principles," and the work that will be lost should Edwards leave. Dwight also wanted advice about church size to ensure sustainability, and gave evidence that he'd been surveying the area for support, saying, "it may be considered that a considerable number in the neighbor towns have declared themselves

---

8. Edwards, "To the Reverend John Erskine," *WJE* 16:355.

9. One sermon notes "sabbath night at neighb. Allens" (969. Prov. 8:17(a)) (Nov. 1750); another "Sabbath day night at sergt Allyns" (970. II Cor. 3:18(b)) (Nov. 1750); and another "Private Meeting at serg Allyns," (971. John 12:13) (Dec. 1750). See Edwards, *Sermons, Series II, 1750, WJEO* 68.

10. Edwards, "To Maj. Joseph Hawley," *WJE* 16:651. See Pomeroy, "Northampton Church Committee on the Petition of the Minority, Mar. 5, 1752," *WJEO* 38.

11. Jonathan Edwards, "To the Reverends Joseph Sewall and Thomas Prince, April 10, 1751," *WJE* 16:369.

12. Hopkins, *Life and Character*, 65.

13. Dwight, "Request for a Council from the Northampton Minority," *WJEO* 38.

to be of Mr. Edwards's opinion, and several have declared they will join with this church if a church be gathered."[14]

One of the council, Edward Billing, who would later be dismissed from his own parish for similar convictions on communion and membership, would respond positively, saying: "I think it is not only advisable but duty to invite Mr Edwards to take ye pastoral care of yr Souls at NH. Reasons. NorthHampton is large enough for two parishes, and the people can without difficulty support two ministers."[15] Likewise, Thomas Prince replied: "so it will seem as if ye Church refusing such a Term as This, will have a mind to necessitate ye Dividing into Two Churches."[16] For the men around Edwards, this new initiative seemed a good and necessary endeavor that Edwards himself could ably lead.

Edwards, however, while happy to "satisfy his tender and afflicted friends" by permitting the calling of a council to give direction, was sure to advise the coming ministers, who would meet on May 16, 1751, that they give a "fair representation" of his other options, particularly at Canaan, and Stockbridge, and also hear his own preference.[17] There were also calls for Edwards to join a Presbyterian congregation in Scotland, and although their offer arrived too late, there was a group in Virginia who thought Edwards would be "most fit for this place."[18]

Evidence of how convincing Edwards's own arguments were against settling over a second church in Northampton can be seen in those ministers who, while initially positive about this move, ultimately advised Edwards to take up the position in Stockbridge as missionary to the Indians and leader of the English who were there.[19] However, this does not mean they were

14. Ibid.

15. Billing, "C104. Edward Billing to Timothy Dwight," *WJEO* 32.

16. Prince, "Thomas Prince to Timothy Dwight and the Northampton Minority," *WJEO* 32.

17. Hopkins, *Life and Character*, 65.

18. In a letter written by Davies to Bellamy, from Hanover, Virginia on July 4, 1751, it was said of Edwards: "Of all the men I know in America, he appears to me the most fit for this place; and, if he could be obtained on no other condition, I would cheerfully resign him my place, and cast myself into the wide world once more. Fiery, superficial ministers will never do in these parts: they might do good; but they would do much more harm. We need the deep judgement and calm temper of Mr. Edwards among us." Quoted in Murray, *A New Biography*, 365.

19. Edwards would later describe his comments to the council: "I had no inclination or desire to settle over these few at Northampton, but a very great opposition in my mind to it, abundantly manifested in what I continually said to them on occasion of their great and constant urgency. It was much more agreeable to my inclination to settle at Stockbridge, and though I complied to the calling of a council to advise in

against the separation of the minority to form a second church, as encouraged by their initial responses and Edwards's own writing to Dwight, quoted at the beginning of this chapter. Douglas Winiarski, who has recently shed light on this period in Edwards's life, writes:

> [Edwards] was more invested in the prospect of gathering a separate church in Northampton than previous studies acknowledge. For a brief moment, he may even have considered affiliating the proposed breakaway church with New England's scattered network of Scots-Irish Presbyterians. More important, the ex parte "anticouncil" that Edwards and Dwight jointly planned in Northampton produced an astounding judgment by eighteenth-century standards. Most Congregational church councils—even partisan meetings called solely by aggrieved factions—typically culminated in a written statement in which the assembled ministers encouraged the contending parties to reconcile their differences. The second Northampton council, by contrast, exhorted the Dwight faction to expand the conflict in order to gather enough supporters to form a separate church. The published Result may have put a final end to Edwards's pastoral career in Northampton, but the ecclesiastical turmoil that he and Dwight fomented during the spring of 1751 continued to reverberate across New England for decades.[20]

It is my contention that Winiarski goes too far in saying Edwards himself desired to lead this separate church, the primary data quite clearly suggests he was against that proposal. Yet, helpfully, Winiarski exposes the superficiality of previous survey studies that assume Edwards was against the secession completely. As his letter to Timothy Dwight highlights, Edwards believed it was the right thing to do, and was sure his adherents would gain enough support to become the primary church in Northampton.

In the end, Edwards would refuse the opportunity to plant a second church, and instead happily submit to the conclusion of the council to become missionary to the Indians at the Stockbridge post. He had already

---

the affair, it was on these terms, that it should not be thought hard that I should fully and strongly lay before 'em all my objections against it. My discourse with particular ministers applied to in their own houses, was chiefly in opposition to Col. [Timothy] Dwight; and so was my discourse before the Council when met. I earnestly argued before them against their advising me to settle there, with hopes that what I said would prevail against it, and very much with that conclusion; and what I said against it was the thing that did prevail against it, and that only." Edwards, "To Maj. Joseph Hawley," *WJE* 16:651.

20. Winiarski. "New Perspectives," 355.

preached there numerous times in early 1751, and would officially be called in February, to begin on August 8, 1751.

Stockbridge would be for Edwards a quieter pastorate, albeit not without its own controversies.[21] Perhaps the literary output of Edwards in his seven years at Stockbridge, where he wrote his four best known works, *Freedom of the Will*, *Original Sin*, *Concerning the End for Which God Created the World*, and *The Nature of True Virtue*, speaks to the relative peace he must have experienced, a welcome change to the vitriol that surrounded his leadership in Northampton.

We turn now to analyse the mind of Edwards and explore the three most pressing reasons for his decision not to lead the planting of a second church in Northampton. These include his ecclesiological convictions, the Northampton majority's treatment of him—which Edwards believed showed their true colors—and his missiological motivations.

## Reasons for Edwards's Position

### Edwards's Ecclesiological Convictions and the Question of Visibility

Jonathan Edwards was a theologian whose intellect seemed to operate on planes far higher than other minds could reach, which, coupled with his social awkwardness, often led to unintended conflict and confusion. This is obvious in the controversial work surrounding his dismissal, *An Humble Inquiry*, of which Ephraim Williams confessed: "[Edwards's] principles were such . . . that I [had] taken pains to read his book, but could not understand it, that I [had] heard almost every gentleman in the county say the same, and that upon the whole I believe he did not know them himself."[22] However difficult Edwards could be to read, it is in his theological writings, especially those concerning this controversy and his wider ecclesiastical

---

21. At Stockbridge lived the Williams family, historic rivals, even though they were related to Edwards. They were one of four English families sent to Stockbridge to live as an example of English civilization. In Ephraim Williams's opinion, Edwards was "a very great bigot for he would not admit any person into heaven, but those that agreed fully to his sentiments." In addition, Edwards battled with Abigail Williams Sergeant, the widow of his predecessor John Sergeant and daughter of Ephraim Williams, over how to best structure the mission. He also endured losing many of the Indians who left in 1754, and ultimately saw Stockbridge become an armed camp, for protection from Indian attack. See Marsden, "Biography," 35.

22. Williams, "Ephraim Williams to Jonathan Ashley," *WJEO* 32.

writings, that we find his mind and thereby can ascertain his thought applied to this situation.

The key idea of Edwards thought as it pertains to the communion controversy was the question of visibility. In *An Humble Inquiry*, Edwards's "main question" is "whether, according to the rules of Christ, any ought to be admitted to the communion and privileges of members of the visible church of Christ in complete standing, but such as are in profession, and in the eye of the church's Christian judgment, godly or gracious persons."[23] Later, Edwards clarifies that by writing "in the eye of the church's Christian judgment," he means, "a visibility to the eye of the public charity, and not of a private judgment."[24] In other words, the question of whether someone is a Christian, and therefore fit to partake in membership and communion, is a public question requiring public visibility.

One of Edwards's arguments against Stoddardean practice was that it unhelpfully and illogically created two camps, "real saints" and "visible saints," even as it sought to minimize distinctions.[25] It essentially split the church in two, between those who were genuinely converted and those who professed "visibility of sainthood without being understood to profess sainthood itself."[26] Against this, Edwards shows that visible saints must be understood to be real saints; anything less is absurdity. James Carse, in his work *Jonathan Edwards and the Visibility of God*, understands Edwards to be saying, "the church is a gathering of persons who can know each other in no other way than as they appear to each other."[27] As expressed in midweek lectures he gave on the doctrine, Edwards wanted to return to times before Stoddard, to the decision of the New England forefathers of 1662. Since then, the ecclesial landscape had "gradually brought in a notion of owning the Covenant of Grace without pretending to profess a compliance."[28] This call was a radical idea, for now, some 80 years later in Edwards's day, the "implicit principle" was that "religion was a private affair."[29] Even more so, in the early 1740s the Great Awakening had unintentionally perpetuated this understanding, making the evaluation of an individual's soul the sole responsibility of the individual. In this context, remembering Edwards's

---

23. Edwards, "An Humble Inquiry," *WJE* 12:174.

24. Ibid., 178–79.

25. Schafer, "Edwards' Conception of the Church," 60.

26. Ibid.

27. Carse, *Visibility of God*, 133.

28. Edwards, "Lectures On The Qualifications For Full Communion In The Church Of Christ," *WJE* 25:364.

29. Carse, *Visibility of God*, 130.

waning social and pastoral authority, his "challenging [his people] to reconsider their relation to the Lord" understandably caused a stir.[30]

Carse actually goes further, looking beyond *An Humble Inquiry* to argue that "when we understand what Edwards has comprehended under the term 'visibility' we shall have located the vital center of his thought."[31] His argument becomes particularly pertinent to our purposes as it is applied corporately, and is coupled with Edwards's priority on the visible union of believers in the church. Rhys Bezzant, in his seminal work on Edwards's ecclesiology, helpfully shows from Edwards's earlier treatise, *An Humble Attempt*, that the concept of "union" was a "*Leitmotif* within Edwards's ecclesiology."[32] In encouraging extraordinary prayer among the broader visible church, Edwards's argument was that:

> Union is one of the most amiable things that pertains to human society; yea, 'tis one of the most beautiful and happy things on earth, which indeed makes earth most like heaven. . . . Union is spoken of in scripture as the peculiar beauty of the church of Christ. As 'tis the glory of the church of Christ, that she in all her members, however dispersed, she is thus one, one holy society, one city, one family, one body; so it is very desirable that this union should be manifested, and become visible.[33]

In the same way that the standing of individual Christians must be made visible through profession and the partaking of communion corporately, the beauty of the church is made visible through unity. When we apply this thought to the planting of a second church in Northampton, we can understand something of why Edwards may have been hesitant to be involved. He understood God's glory to be at stake at the visible *disunity* that leading the Northampton minority would promote.

The desire for visible union among the church was an especially important conviction in the wake of the Great Awakening and the rise of separatism in New England. Like his Puritan forebears, Edwards believed the church "has to exist both as an established institution demanding the allegiance of everyone *and* as a community set apart by its disciplined life."[34] This initial Puritan tension between exclusivity and comprehensiveness continued to plague the Congregational church, and the Old and New

---

30. Bezzant, *Edwards and the Church*, 195.
31. Carse, *The Visibility of God*, 31.
32. Bezzant, *Edwards and the Church*, 154.
33. Edwards, "An Humble Attempt," *WJE* 5:365.
34. Platinga Pauw, "Practical Ecclesiology," 97.

Light responses to the Awakenings were catalytic of increasing secession. Edwards was, especially by this time, cognizant of the damage New Light separatists had rendered across New England. In *An Humble Inquiry*, he claims to be cautious in detailing his doctrine for fear that "wild enthusiastical sort of people" who have caused "unjustifiable separations ... under the pretense of setting up a pure church" would be encouraged in the "practices of theirs."[35] A significant part of Edwards's uneasiness with leading the second church in Northampton will have been the apparent visibility of his aligning with the separatists.

This more conservative position of Edwards was seemingly a reversal of his principle and practice from a decade earlier, indicating just how pertinent this tension was in his thought. As Douglas Winiarski details in his article, "Jonathan Edwards, Enthusiast?," at the beginning of the 1740s. Edwards was encouraging, and inspired by, the enthusiasm wrought at the preaching of George Whitefield and others, including his own. Edwards even presided over the acceptance of ninety-five new members at Suffield, days before preaching *Sinners in the Hands of an Angry God*, with apparently no qualms or questions concerning the visibility of their sainthood.[36] But Edwards would also publicly attack, and privately warn against, some of the "pernicious principles tending to promote and foment censoriousness and division that [had] prevailed in many parts of the land."[37] Referring to Edwards's *Some Thoughts Concerning the Present Revival of Religion in New-England*, Winiarski writes, "Edwards continued to defend the Awakening against the attacks of Old Light opposers, but he devoted the longest portion of his treatise to an extended catalog of the errors that he had witnessed in revived parishes throughout the region."[38] Edwards's strengthening resolve against the Half-Way practice he had inherited coincided, and was perhaps spurred on by, the growing visible disunity he was observing among churches across the region. Summarizing Edwards's intentions at the end of the decade, in the communion controversy, Clarence Goen writes:

> Edwards stood unalterably opposed to separatism, and hesitated to announce his view for fear of being branded as a Separate. But he was just as opposed to an artificial division of church members into professing saints and real saints, and the central

---

35. Edwards, "An Humble Inquiry," *WJE* 12:170.
36. Winiarski, "Jonathan Edwards, Enthusiast?" 730.
37. Edwards, "To the Reverend Elnathan Whitman," *WJE* 16:128.
38. Winiarski, "Jonathan Edwards, Enthusiast?" 730.

thrust of his Humble Inquiry was an attempt to restore sincerity and meaning to the profession of sainthood.[39]

The strength of Edwards's ecclesiological conviction that the visible unity of the church, made up of visibly real saints, was "the peculiar beauty of the church of Christ," inclined him away from considering leadership over the minority that adhered to him in Northampton. The contextual climate of New England during this time only reinforced Edwards's resolve.

However much this insight gives us understanding of Edwards's reluctance to plant a breakaway church in Northampton, it does not explain his apparent approval of the minority doing so without him. This seeming contradiction can best be explained by exploring the ferocity of the Northampton majority's vitriol toward him personally throughout the controversy.

## Edwards's Experience of the Northampton Majority's Vitriol

In order to understand how Edwards could advise Col. Timothy Dwight that "the small company that adhered to me, if they hold their own, will prosper and prevail," even though their prevailing would be visible disunity, we must understand the level of opposition and vitriol Edwards received as he publicized and practiced his strengthening theological convictions.

As evidence Edwards was resigned to whatever might come his way, he concluded in *An Humble Inquiry*:

> And having been fully persuaded in my own mind, what is the Scripture rule in this matter, after a most careful, painful, and long search, I am willing, in the faithful prosecution of what appears to me of such importance and so plainly the mind and will of God, to resign to his providence, and leave the event in his hand.[40]

What providence would unfold was a response to *An Humble Inquiry* by Solomon Williams, whose reply and accusations against Edwards were deemed "true absurdity" and warranted a further response from Edwards in *Misrepresentations Corrected*.[41] But the broader academic response was minor compared to the lambasting Edwards received from the local Northampton majority. In addition to the strength with which Edwards held fast to his convictions, it can also be said that his opponents in Northampton were

---

39. Goen, *Revivalism and Separatism*, 161.

40. Edwards, "An Humble Inquiry," *WJE* 12:324.

41. Edwards, "Misrepresentations Corrected, and Truth Vindicated," *WJE* 12:351.

equally passionate against Edwards. He would relate to John Erskine, just days after his dismissal, that he believed "the great power of prejudices from education, established custom, and the traditions of ancestors and certain admired teachers, and the exceeding unhappy influence of bigotry has remarkably appeared in the management of this affair.[42]"

Edwards went so far as penning a *Vindication from the Church's Accusation* that was never published, where he defends himself against each of their accusations, including that he was positioning himself to lead a second church, politically conniving and blatantly dishonest.[43] In the mind of Edwards, the church was displaying an "unchristian frame," which he verbalized before one of the councils early in the controversy. Edwards was feeling so mistreated, and witnessed such vitriol from his parishioners both before and after his dismissal, that in the same letter to Erskine he reveals he "was afraid they were in the way to ruin," and felt compelled to "bring 'em to a suitable temper."[44]

Additional evidence of Edwards's mistreatment is the detail in which he remembers his offense over four years later. Writing to Joseph Hawley, a young leader of the majority who presumptuously led the attack against Edwards, he said:

> On the whole, Sir (as you have asked my opinion), I think that town and church lies under great guilt in the sight of God. And they never more can reasonably expect God's favor and blessing till they have their eyes opened to be convinced of their great provocation of the Most High, and injuriousness to man, and have their temper greatly altered; till they are deeply humbled; and till they openly and in full terms confess themselves guilty.[45]

This opinion no doubt influenced the content and concept of his *Farewell Sermon*. The Northampton majority had so visibly transgressed against him, and against God, that Edwards concluded that sermon by challenging them to "remember, and never forget our future solemn meeting, on that great day of the Lord; the day of infallible decision, and of the everlasting and unalterable sentence. Amen."[46]

The seriousness and visibility of the "unchristian frame" with which Edwards was treated will no doubt have played into his direction to Col.

---

42. Edwards, "To the Reverend John Erskine," *WJE* 16:351.
43. Edwards, "Vindication from the Church's Accusation," *WJEO* 38.
44. Edwards, "To the Reverend John Erskine," *WJE* 16:351.
45. Edwards, "To Maj. Joseph Hawley," *WJE* 16:652.
46. Edwards, "A Farewell Sermon," *WJE* 25:488.

Timothy Dwight. While Edwards himself was not inclined to lead the minority in Northampton, partly due to his own theological convictions, this party was right to secede from the majority because they were proving themselves the more visibly Christian. In Edwards's mind a true church is none other than "those that are truly and really God's people and Christ's people, or those that truly have those outward appearances of being God's people."[47] The Northampton church had shown themselves throughout 1749 and 1750 to be "in the way to ruin," hence Edwards could encourage those who had separated that they were doing the right thing, and would one day soon "prosper and prevail." The faithfulness and principled conviction of the minority would be the light to expose the darkness of the majority. Goodness and godliness would ultimately triumph over evil. Edwards's high view of the church and its visibility inclined him to encourage Dwight, and the minority, to stick to their shared principles and hold their own.

Having explored the nuances of Edwards's ecclesiological conviction and the visible transgression of the Northampton majority, we turn now to a final influence on Edwards's refusal to plant a second church in the town and instead pursue the mission field at Stockbridge—his missiological motivation.

### Edwards's Vision and Missiological Motivation

Jonathan Edwards was a theologian, author, pastor and, less well known, a missionary. His refusal to plant a second church in Northampton was also a positive decision to lead his family elsewhere. As the historical survey of his ministry highlighted, his desire was to pursue the Stockbridge option, and this was a decision he agitated for to the council who were advising him.

The embers of Edwards's missiological motivation were likely fanned into flame by the passion of his grandfather, Solomon Stoddard himself. In 1723, Stoddard published an attack on the New England church for its neglect of evangelistic endeavor to the Indians, aptly titled *Question Whether God Is Not Angry with the Country for Doing So Little Towards the Conversion of the Indians?* It would be Stoddard's son, Colonel John Stoddard, who, in 1734, led a committee to appoint John Sargeant and found the mission at Stockbridge. This was an initiative Edwards himself was involved in, and continued to be so throughout his ministry by collecting and dispersing funds for the boarding school there.[48]

---

47. Edwards, "'Misc.' 339." *WJE* 13:414. Quoted in Schafer, "Edwards' Conception of the Church," 60.

48. Hopkins, *Historical Memoirs*, 134.

This priority for mission work, coupled with his eschatology, had compelled Edwards to pen his *Humble Attempt* in 1747, fully titled *An Humble Attempt to Promote Explicit Agreement and Visible Union of God's People in Extraordinary Prayer, for the Revival of Religion and the Advancement of Christ's Kingdom on Earth, Pursuant to Scripture—Primes and Prophecies Concerning the Last Time*. Edwards had a heart to promote the furthering of God's name among every tribe, tongue and nation.

Edwards's proximity to, and personal mentoring of, a number of missionaries further reveals his motivation and passion for mission. Over the course of his time in Northampton, the Edwardses hosted Job Strong, Joseph Bellamy, Samuel Hopkins, and Gideon Hawley, all of whom either were missionaries themselves or later developed missionary movements.[49] The most well-known case of Edwards's hospitality and influence over a missionary was his relationship with David Brainerd, and this inspired Edwards to publish Brainerd's diary, *The Life of David Brainerd*, in 1748. This work would continue to motivate missions for centuries, and was surely a motivation for Edwards himself to take up his position at Stockbridge. In fact, Edwards would write in the appendix that Brainerd's success was "a forerunner of something yet much more glorious and extensive of that kind; ... and this may justly be an encouragement to ... promote the spreading of the Gospel among them."[50] Edwards may not have known at the time that it would shape his own approach toward the mission field.

In late 1749, before Edwards would be forced to conceive of it as a realistic transition for himself, but while the controversy in Northampton was unfolding, he wrote to Thomas Foxcroft and said of Stockbridge, "I wish that the Commissioners would now take care that there may be a man sent them of sound principles, and a pious character . . . If the affair may be under the care of a missionary of good character, there seems to be the best door for gradually propagating the gospel among the Indians that is opened at present."[51] Claghorn therefore concludes, "Edwards's agreement to move to Stockbridge should not surprise us."[52]

This positivity about missionary work in Stockbridge continued as it became clear that Edwards himself could be that laborer. In a letter to William Hogg, after his dismissal, Edwards wrote regarding the Stockbridge option:

49. Gibson, "Edwards: A Missionary?" 384–85.

50. Edwards, "The Life of David Brainerd," *WJE* 7:533. Quoted in Gibson, "Edwards: A Missionary?" 386.

51. Edwards, "To the Reverend Thomas Foxcroft," *WJE* 16:301–02.

52. Claghorn, "Editor's introduction," *WJE* 16:18n9.

> There are some things remarkable in divine providence, that afford a prospect of good things to be accomplished here for the Indians, and give reason to hope that God has mercy in store for them; particularly that [of] God so enlarging the hearts of some gentlemen in England to contribute of their substance for this end.[53]

The clear inclination Edwards had toward Stockbridge has led Kenneth Minkema to conclude that "Edwards trolled for a new pastorate . . . but he had his eye on the Stockbridge post."[54]

We cannot explore this motivation without also understanding that his positivity toward Stockbridge was reinforced by his desire to write. Having been dismissed, Edwards confessed to John Erskine that he believed he was "fitted for no other business but study."[55] Edwards would go on to write some of his most influential works in the midst of a tumultuous time in Stockbridge. This does not weaken the argument that Edwards was inclined toward Stockbridge because of his missiological motivations; rather, it clarifies what Edwards understood his missiological and revivalist responsibilities to be. Edwards held youthful ambitions for venturing in great matters with his pen when he was young, and this desire would take a theological, ecclesiological and missiological bent through his writings from Stockbridge.[56]

This missiological motivation further elucidates the mind of Jonathan Edwards as he came to the crossroads of his dismissal from Northampton. Certainly, there was pressure from his friends to oversee the planting of a second church in Northampton, yet the motivation in Edwards moved beyond Northampton and focused on where he could better contribute to the wider mission of God.

## Conclusion

In today's ecclesial climate, it is surprising to hear of a theological hero and leader within church history who refused to be involved in the planting of a

---

53. Edwards, "To William Hogg," *WJE* 16:392.

54. Minkema, "Jonathan Edwards—A Theological Life," 12.

55. Edwards, "To the Reverend John Erskine," in *WJE* 16:355.

56. As a young and budding scientist, Edwards wrote, 'Before I venture to publish in London, to make some experiment in my own country; to play at small games first, that I may gain some experience in writing. For to write letters to some in England, and to try my [hand at] lesser matters before I venture in great.' Edwards, "Natural Philosophy" *WJE* 6:194. Quoted in Minkema, "Personal Writings," 43.

church. However, when one understands the threads of influence that compelled Edwards to resist those who sought to have him lead this new church, and instead head to Stockbridge to reach the Indians, it seems a wise and admirable move, corroborating his integrity. His ecclesiological convictions concerning the visible unity of the church, the transgressions he had felt personally and pastorally throughout the controversy, and the missiological motivation he had to see the advancement of the kingdom, provide us with convincing reasons as to why Edwards would make this decision. We have found that Edwards was influenced theologically, personally, and missiologically toward Stockbridge and away from church planting. Throughout this significant season of his life, Edwards's attitude, his character, and his thought, as displayed throughout this decision making process highlight one of the reasons why Edwards continues to have many more adherents today, some 250 years after the initial Northampton minority.

## Bibliography

Bezzant, Rhys S. *Jonathan Edwards and the Church*. Oxford: Oxford University Press, 2013.

Billing, Edward. "C.104. Edward Billing to Timothy Dwight, Before May 1751." In *Correspondence by, to, and about Edwards and His Family*. The Works of Jonathan Edwards Online 32. Jonathan Edwards Center at Yale University.

Carse, James P. *Jonathan Edwards and the Visibility of God*. New York: Charles Scribner's Sons, 1967.

Claghorn, George S. "Introduction." In *Letters and Personal Writings*, edited by George S. Claghorn, The Works of Jonathan Edwards 16:741–52. New Haven: Yale University Press, 1998.

Cooper Jr., James F. *Tenacious of Their Liberties: The Congregationalists in Colonial Massachusetts*. Religion in America. New York: Oxford University Press, 1999.

Davids, Peter H. "An Anabaptist View of the Church." *Evangelical Quarterly* 56/2 (1984) 81–93.

Dwight, Timothy. "Request for a Council from the Northampton Minority, [ca. 1750-1751]." In *Dismissal and Post-Dismissal Documents*. The Works of Jonathan Edwards Online 38. Jonathan Edwards Center at Yale University.

———. "Petition of the Northampton Minority, [c. 1751]." In *Dismissal and Post-Dismissal Documents*, The Works of Jonathan Edwards Online 38. Jonathan Edwards Center at Yale University.

Edwards, Jonathan. "Apostrophe to Sarah Pierpont." In *Autobiographical and Biographical Documents*, The Works of Jonathan Edwards Online 40. Jonathan Edwards Center at Yale University.

———. "A Faithful Narrative." In *The Great Awakening*, edited by Clarence C. Goen, The Works of Jonathan Edwards 4:96–210. New Haven: Yale University Press, 1972.

———. "A Farewell Sermon Preached at the First Precinct in Northampton, after the People's Public Rejection of their Minister . . . on June 22, 1750." In *Sermons and*

*Discourses, 1743–1758*, edited by Wilson H. Kimnach, The Works of Jonathan Edwards 25:457–93. New Haven: Yale University Press, 2006.

———. "An Humble Attempt." In *Apocalyptic Writings*, edited by Stephen J. Stein, The Works of Jonathan Edwards 5:307–437. New Haven: Yale University Press, 1977.

———. "An Humble Inquiry." In *Ecclesiastical Writings*, edited by David D. Hall, The Works of Jonathan Edwards 12:166–349. New Haven: Yale University Press, 1994.

———. "Lectures On The Qualifications For Full Communion In The Church Of Christ." In *Sermons and Discourses, 1743–1758*, edited by Wilson H. Kimnach, The Works of Jonathan Edwards 25:349–441. New Haven: Yale University Press, 2006.

———. *The Life of David Brainerd*. Edited by Norman Pettit. The Works of Jonathan Edwards 7. New Haven: Yale University Press, 1985.

———. "'Misc.' 339." In *The "Miscellanies" (Entry Nos. a–z, aa–zz, 1–500)*, edited by Thomas A. Schafer, The Works of Jonathan Edwards 13:414. New Haven: Yale University Press, 1994.

———. "Misrepresentations Corrected, and Truth Vindicated." In *Ecclesiastical Writings*, edited by David D. Hall, The Works of Jonathan Edwards 12:349–503 New Haven: Yale University Press, 1994.

———. "Narrative of Communion Controversy." In *Ecclesiastical Writings*, edited by David D. Hall, The Works of Jonathan Edwards 12:507–619. New Haven: Yale University Press, 1994.

———. "Natural Philosophy." In *Scientific and Philosophical Writings*, edited by Wallace E. Anderson, The Works of Jonathan Edwards 6:192–96. New Haven: Yale University Press, 1980.

———. "Notes for a Council Meeting on the Case of Elisha Hawley and Martha Root, June 1749." In *Church and Pastoral Documents*, The Works of Jonathan Edwards Online 39. Jonathan Edwards Center at Yale University.

———. "To Col. Timothy Dwight." In *Letters and Personal Writings*, edited by George S. Claghorn, The Works of Jonathan Edwards 16:447–48. New Haven: Yale University Press, 1998.

———. "To Maj. Joseph Hawley." In *Letters and Personal Writings*, edited by George S. Claghorn, The Works of Jonathan Edwards 16:645–54. New Haven: Yale University Press, 1998.

———. "To the Reverend Elnathan Whitman." In *Letters and Personal Writings*, edited by George S. Claghorn, The Works of Jonathan Edwards 16:127–33. New Haven: Yale University Press, 1998.

———. "To the Reverend John Erskine, July 5, 1750." In *Letters and Personal Writings*, edited by George S. Claghorn, The Works of Jonathan Edwards 16:347–56. New Haven and London: Yale University Press, 1998.

———. "To the Reverend Thomas Foxcroft." In *Letters and Personal Writings*, edited by George S. Claghorn, The Works of Jonathan Edwards 16:296–302. New Haven: Yale University Press, 1998.

———. "To the Reverends Joseph Sewall and Thomas Prince." In *Letters and Personal Writings*, edited by George S. Claghorn, The Works of Jonathan Edwards 16:368–69. New Haven: Yale University Press, 1998.

———. "To William Hogg." In *Letters and Personal Writings*, edited by George S. Claghorn, The Works of Jonathan Edwards 16:390–93. New Haven: Yale University Press, 1998.

---. "Vindication from the Church's Accusation." In *Dismissal and Post-Dismissal Documents*, The Works of Jonathan Edwards Online 38. Jonathan Edwards Center at Yale University.

Frazier, Patrick. *The Mohicans of Stockbridge*. Lincoln: University of Nebraska Press, 1992.

Gibson, Jonathan. "Jonathan Edwards: A Missionary?" *Themelios* 36/3 (2011) 380–402.

Goen, Clarence C. *Revivalism and Separatism in New England, 1740–1800: Strict Congregationalists and Separate Baptists in the Great Awakening*. Middletown: Wesleyan University Press, 1987.

Grasso, Christopher. "Misrepresentations Corrected: Jonathan Edwards and the Regulation of Religious Discourse." In *Jonathan Edwards's Writings: Text, Context, Interpretation*, edited by Stephen J. Stein, 19–39. Bloomington/Indianapolis: Indiana University Press, 1996.

Hall, Michael G. *The Last American Puritan: The Life of Increase Mather, 1639–1723*. Middletown: Wesleyan University Press, 1988.

Hall, Richard A. S. *The Neglected Northampton Texts of Jonathan Edwards: Edwards on Society and Politics*, Studies in American Religion 52. Lewiston: Edwin Mellen Press, 1990.

Hopkins, Samuel. *Historical Memoirs, Relating to the Housatunnuk Indians*. Boston: S. Kneeland, 1753. https://books.google.com.au/books?id=HroOAAAAQAAJ&printsec=frontcover&source=gbs_ge_summary_r&cad=0#v=onepage&q&f=false.

Hopkins, Samuel. *The Life and Character of the Late Reverend, Learned and Pious Mr. Jonathan Edwards*. Northampton: Andrew Wright for S. & E. Butler, 1804. https://books.google.com.au/books/about/The_Life_and_Character_of_the_Late_Rever.html?id=m6hIAAAAMAAJ&redir_esc=y.

Marsden, George M. "Biography." In *The Cambridge Companion to Jonathan Edwards*, edited by Stephen J. Stein, 18–38. Cambridge: Cambridge University Press, 2007.

---. *Jonathan Edwards: A Life*. New Haven: Yale University Press, 2003.

Miller, Perry. *Jonathan Edwards*. New York: William Sloane Associates, 1949.

Miller, Samuel. *Memoirs of the Rev. John Rodgers, D. D. Late Pastor of the Wall-Street and Brick Churches in the City of New-York*. New York: Whiting and Watson, 1813. http://www.forgottenbooks.com/readbook_text/Memoir_of_the_Rev_John_Rodgers_1000663639

Minkema, Kenneth P. "Jonathan Edwards—A Theological Life." In *The Princeton Companion to Jonathan Edwards*, edited by San Hyun Lee, 1–15. Princeton: Princeton University Press, 2005.

---. "Personal Writings." In *The Cambridge Companion to Jonathan Edwards*, edited by Stephen J. Stein, 39–60. Cambridge: Cambridge University Press, 2007.

Murray, Iain H. *Jonathan Edwards: A New Biography*. Edinburgh: The Banner of Truth Trust, 1987.

Pauw, Amy Plantinga. "Editor's Introduction." In *The "Miscellanies" (Entry Nos. 833–1152)*, edited by Amy Plantinga Pauw, The Works of Jonathan Edwards 20:1–39. New Haven: Yale University Press, 2002.

---. "Practical Ecclesiology in John Calvin and Jonathan Edwards." In *John Calvin's American Legacy*, edited by Thomas J. Davis, 91–110. Oxford. Oxford University Press. 2010.

Pomeroy, Ebenezer. "Northampton Church Committee on the Petition of the Minority, Mar. 5, 1752." In *Dismissal and Post-Dismissal Documents*, The Works of Jonathan Edwards Online 38. Jonathan Edwards Center at Yale University.

Prince, Thomas. "C91. Thomas Prince to Timothy Dwight and the Northampton Minority, c. April 1750." In *Correspondence by, to, and about Edwards and His Family*, The Works of Jonathan Edwards Online 32, edited by Jonathan Edwards Center at Yale University.

Schafer, Thomas A. "Jonathan Edwards' Conception of the Church." *Church History* 24/1 (1955) 51–66.

Stetina, Karin S. *Jonathan Edwards' Early Understanding of Religious Experience: His New York Sermons, 1720–1723*. Lewiston: Edwin Mellen, 2011.

Tracy, Patricia J. *Jonathan Edwards, Pastor: Religion and Society in Eighteenth-Century Northampton*. New York: Hill and Wang, 1979.

Williams, Ephraim. "C105. Ephraim Williams to Jonathan Ashley, May 2, 1751." In *Correspondence by, to, and about Edwards and His Family*, The Works of Jonathan Edwards Online 32. Jonathan Edwards Center at Yale University.

Winiarski, Douglas L. "Jonathan Edwards, Enthusiast? Radical Revivalism and the Great Awakening in the Connecticut Valley." *Church History* 74/4 (2005) 683–739.

———. "New Perspectives on the Northampton Communion Controversy I: David Hall's Diary & Letter to Edward Billing." *Jonathan Edwards Studies* 3/2 (2013) 282–94.

———. "New Perspectives on the Northampton Communion Controversy II: Relations, Confession & Experiences, 1748–1760." *Jonathan Edwards Studies* 4/1 (2014) 110–45.

———. "New Perspectives on the Northampton Communion Controversy III: Count Vavasor's Tirade & The Second Council, 1751." *Jonathan Edwards Studies* 4/3 (2014) 353–82.

Winslow, Ola Elizabeth. *Jonathan Edwards, 1703–1758: A Biography*. New York: Macmillan, 1940.

# 19

# Is God Really Angry at Sinners?
## *A Stylometric Study of Jonathan Edwards's Representations of God*

Michał Choiński and Jan Rybicki

## Introduction

There is no study of Edwards without the study of God. This sentence verges on blatant truism and can hardly be considered as affording any pioneering thought, as Edwards is universally deemed to be one of the most eminent theological minds to have ever been born in America—yet, the literary ramifications of this fact need to be explored. Since God is so ubiquitous in Edwards's writings, and since Edwards dedicated his life to the pursuit of divine truth, from the literary and linguistic perspective, in his writings, God functions as the most important motif, theme, and point of reference. Edwards's oeuvre is literally filled with textual representations of the Almighty that bear testimony to his evolving theological thought. At the same time, since Edwards was a prolific author who wrote texts of diverse genres and lengths, a detailed study of all the representations of God and references to God in the complete Edwardsean corpus poses considerable difficulties.

The goal of this article is to discuss Edwards's literary portrayal of God with the help of a computer-aided method of inquiry and to study the evolution of Edwards's representations of God by adopting a quantitative, rather than a qualitative approach. For this purpose, we have performed two experiments: in the first one we conducted a "sentiment" analysis of the lexemes associated with God and surveyed all of their collocations in the Edwardsean corpus as well as all the words associated with them; in the second one we applied stylometric software to show how the usage of the word "God" changed over time and how it differs in various groups of Edwards's texts. By combining these two quantitative methods, one focused on the relationships between words, and the other on the relationships between texts containing these words, we were able to draw conclusions about Edwards's literary portrayal of God over the entirety of his corpus.

## The Quantitative Study of Edwards

The observations included in the article are a part of a larger project of a quantitative study of American revival preaching tradition. The research is conducted under the auspices of a grant from the Polish Ministry of Higher Education being carried out in the Institute of English Studies at the Jagiellonian University.[1] It is aimed at determining the intertextual links between the preachers of various American "awakenings." The ultimate goal of the project is to arrive at a better understanding of the language of religion in the United States, and considering the enormous sizes of corpora to be compared and contrasted, no other method but stylometry seems to be feasible to yield the requested results.

The recent advancements in the quantitative study of literature offer a number of interpretative opportunities. First, with the growing numbers of accessible collections of texts and the steadily increasing power of software, stylometry can provide comparative results that a few years ago were computationally inaccessible; second, it can considerably augment other approaches such as rhetorical analysis. From a methodological point of view, it is an interesting question whether "traditional" readings of texts can be combined in any way with counting some features of these texts: and this usually means counting words or their combinations. It is still not a fully understood fact why patterns of similarity and difference between novels observed in a traditional qualitative close reading are very often echoed by observations made by non-traditional quantitative distant reading. While theoretical explanations are absent or unsatisfactory, there is mounting empirical evidence that signals of authorship, genre, chronology or (*horribile dictu!*) theme, are somehow concealed—and

---

1. This research was made as part of the K/PBO/000331 OPUS project funded by Poland's National Science Centre (NCN).

yet discoverable through statistics—in the numbers of words that are "meaningful" (God, love, sin, angry, to mention those most expected in Edwards) or "unmeaningful" (is, off, can, or).

Indeed, in our research so far, the stylometric study of Edwards's works has allowed us to establish the relationships between different elements of the corpus and to look into the connections Edwards's texts bear to the Bible, the works of Edwards's family members, as well as Locke's *Essay Concerning Human Understanding*. We have managed to distinguish between five clusters of Edwards's texts with distinct authorial "signals": private writings and letters, sermons, biblical comments, and two groups of philosophical and theological writings. The fact that one can draw clear borderlines between these five clusters means that, from the stylometric standpoint, Edwards's corpus is both diverse as well as multifaceted. Because of this diversity within the corpus, the employment of the word "God" also varies and undergoes a steady, chronological evolution.

Our stylometric research by no means constitutes the only research project that applies digital humanities for the study of Edwards's oeuvre. So far, two other scholars have turned to computer technology to arrive at a better understanding of the Northampton divine's thought. Boss's "Elemental Theology" project (2015) employs digital visualization models to demonstrate Edwards's views into the relationship between Scripture and Nature. The graphic modeling used there focuses primarily on the visual representation of Edwards's biblical typology. On the other hand, Michael Keller's doctoral project, which is being developed at Jonathan Edwards Center at Yale University under the supervision of Adriaan Neele, provides an insight into the functioning of different lexical units in Edwards, by means of the Dictionary of Affect in Language. The fact that different digital research projects have recently appeared almost simultaneously could signal that with the onset of new technologies there is potential for a new chapter in Edwards studies.

## God's Collocates in Edwards's Corpus

Most people with at least a rudimentary knowledge of American history and literature would promptly associate Jonathan Edwards with his *Sinners in the Hands of an Angry God*. Because of such an association, and the legendary impact the sermon had upon the Enfield congregation, Edwards is often viewed by the general public as a figure of rhetorical controversy. This certainly increases his recognizability, but, at the same time, such an association reduces him to a mere "fire and brimstone" preacher and harmfully simplifies both the Enfield sermon and the depth of its deliverer's thought. If asked about the prevalent image of God present in the Edwardsean corpus, most people, even those with a better knowledge of his texts or the colonial context, would construe that God in Edwards's texts is primarily angry and vengeful. When one leafs through the collection of his sermons, one can hardly avoid thinking in such a manner. The evocative imagery of such sermons as *The Future Punishment*, let alone the famous "spider image" from *Sinners* that inspired Robert Lowell, linger in the mind's eye much more strongly that the harmonious and benevolent images of *God Glorified in Man's Dependence*. Because of how salient, powerful, and evocative the fierce images of God are in some of Edwards's sermons, it becomes natural to assume that most often his literary representations of the Almighty constitute, to evoke Harriet Beecher Stowe's description, a "refined poetry of torture."

Our analysis aims to challenge this view since, by applying computational language processing and studying the "polarity" of the text, we can objectively determine the type of God's image present in Edwards's writings. The analysis presented in this section of the article has been conducted with the help of AntConc software 3.4.4, which allows users to seek out collocates, word clusters, and concordances within various corpora. As the corpus, we have used the collection of texts available on the Jonathan Edwards Yale Center website. In our study we omitted collocates which are used in the corpus in biblical quotations, as their frequent occurrence or high statistical relevance are not the results of Edwards's stylistic decisions but rather of intertextual influence. We were only interested in the texts and fragments of texts that Edwards created himself.

The lexeme "God" appears in the complete corpus of Edwards 33,015 times—it is a content word he used often, although not the most often. The density of its use differs greatly depending on the type of text. In Edwards's private writings there are relatively few usages of the word, while the collections of sermons and his biblical comments abound in references to the Almighty. From among Edwards's letters, it is definitely the correspondence addressed to his family members (especially to his daughters) where the word God is used not only most often, but also recurrently throughout the whole collection of texts. In the case of letters concerning his private, religious, and business affairs, Edwards uses the word "God" more unevenly, there are texts in which he employs it often (e.g., a letter to Lady Pepperrell, sent from Stockbridge on November 28, 1751 or a letter to Thomas Gillespie, Carnoc, also sent from Stockbridge on July 1, 1751), but also those in which God is not mentioned at all, like Edwards's fulsome correspondence concerning the affair with the boarding school for the Mohawks in Stockbridge.

Among the sermons, the frequency with which Edwards mentions God is very high. His earliest sermons (1720–23) have the fewest occurrences of this word, but the discourses published later, especially during the times of the revival, abound in references to God (e.g., in the rich collection of sermons published between 1734–38, Edwards mentions God almost 4,300 times). Other texts in which Edwards employs the studied lexeme most often include his narrative of the life of David Brainerd (more than 2,000 occurrences of the word God), *History of the Work of Redemption* (1446 occurrences), *Original Sin* (almost a 1,000 occurrences) and *Some Thoughts Concerning the Revival* (1,169 occurrences). The above preliminary statistics have obviously small interpretative value in themselves, but they are indispensable if one is to investigate the relevant collocates of the word God in the corpus and arrive at a quantitative study of Edwards's portrayal of the Almighty.

In our experiment, we first looked into the most relevant words Edwards associates with God. To study the collocates used by Edwards to describe him, we have focused on the lexical items that directly preceded those studied, set the minimal frequency to at least five occurrences in the whole corpus, and then sorted the results not only according to the number of occurrences, but also according to statistical relevance—in other words, we made AntConc not only count the collocations, but also arrange them in terms of the relative strength of the bond between the words in the corpus (taking frequency as the secondary factor).

The verbs most strongly associated with the lexeme God, and preceding it, include: glorify, bless, praise, fear, provoke, appease, serve, offend, exalt, love, and thank. At the same time, in terms of sheer frequency the three highest collocates are: glorify, praise, and serve. Thus, it would seem that, from the quantitative perspective, Edwards's God functions primarily as object of religious reverence and worship—and the actions most commonly associated with him involve glorification, adoration, and obedient servitude. In other words, in the entirety of Edwards's corpus, God is evidently not "angry," but inherently "sacred." This sense of sanctity and religious veneration includes also more negative emotions. Collocates such as fear, provoke, and offend may not be profuse, but their presence in the results cannot be omitted. They point to another important aspect of deity and testify to the fact that, apart from being an object of reverence, in Edwards's corpus God is at times viewed as an object of apprehension and awe, who grows angry at the sinfulness of natural men.

In terms of the verbs associated with God in which he is the subject, not an object, the Almighty is presented in an active, dynamic, and commandeering manner. In Edwards's corpus, out of all the actions associated with God, two are given definite prominence: "making" and "giving." The former is very recurrent (445 occurrences), although its statistical relevance is not very high, while the latter is the 50th most common collocation, with a very high frequency rate of 379 occurrences. Edwards's God is thus a giver and a maker—both these literary representations underline the paramount importance of God as an active creator and a perpetual upholder of the creation. Statistically, in Edwards's corpus God most often "makes" human beings (in the sense of "creates"), not uncommonly endowing people with "reason"—he also "makes" the visible world ("heavens," "creation") and its diverse elements. This active and grand role of God, expressed in the lexical items used by Edwards, is obviously not limited to mere construction and formation—in the words selected to describe God, it is visible that to Edwards, he permeates the creation, "making" covenants and manifestations, as well as "making [people] understand" truths about religion.

Also, a number of other verbs associated with Edwards's representation of the Almighty connote the sense of authority and power. God actively "deals" (5.56 statistical relevance,[2] 28 frequency; the usual collocates in this case include "with people" or "with men"), "bestows" (5.37 statistical relevance, frequency of 37—and here the most common complements include "mercy" and "blessing"), "commands" (4.63 statistical relevance and a very high frequency of 99), as well as "requires" (4.72 statistical relevance and the frequency of 48). The words Edwards uses in his corpus seem to testify to his idea of God as a sovereign ruler whose actions manifest the control he has over the creation. The collective implications of these lexical items are straightforward: the statistics prove that to Edwards, God is a source of sovereignty and reverence that is parallel to the aforementioned sense of sanctity. Edwards, in all his literary portrayals, consistently presents God as the authority incarnate who actively undertakes the sovereign actions he is eligible to undertake.

At the same, in sermons, one finds a few other verbs that are almost exclusive to Edwards's pulpit oratory and that modify the image of the Almighty as a ruler: God "threatens" (statistical relevance 4.94) the sinners who broke his laws. The usage of such words would be one of numerous differences distinguishing Edwards's sermons from the rest of the corpus.

---

2. The AntConc software tested the statistical relevance of each collocation using Student's t-test, and only included those with a strong statistical significance in the output; other than that, the significance values served for comparison only.

It would seem then that, from the quantitative perspective, the sense of authority and reverence of God that permeates all of Edwards's texts becomes more rigid and authoritarian in his sermons.

The "word" of God is the noun most commonly associated with the deity (with 215 occurrences and the 47th place in the ranking), right after "spirit" (212 occurrences), "glory" (199 occurrences), "love" (198 occurrences), and "wrath" (140 occurrences). In terms of statistics, these would be the most common attributes of God in Edwards's texts. Again, just as in the case of previously discussed lexemes, the Almighty is primarily characterized by words that connote the matters of religion—and of two words the positive "love" is given definite priority over the more pejorative "wrath." It is however hard not to notice that both these contrastive lexical items turn out to be intrinsically bound with God in Edwards's corpus—just as in the case of the verbs discussed in the previous paragraph, the Almighty is always presented in a positive way, with a negative "twist" in sermons.

The adjectives Edwards most often employs to describe God include: "omniscient" (statistical relevance 4.61), "almighty" (4.06), "jealous" (3.95), "merciful" (4.74), "living" (3.56), "invisible" (2.99), "sovereign" (2.84), and "true" (1.98). The two most common collocates illustrate Edwards's focus on the infinite power of the Almighty. Thus, if one takes into account the most common epithets employed by Edwards, the image of God found in his corpus is not that of an angry or vengeful deity, but that of a controlling and mighty godhead. Other epithets, referring to the attributes of God, stress those aspects of deity that also seemed central for Edwards—the Almighty being "invisible," as well as "true." Interestingly, these adjectives are not bound to a particular text, or a group of texts, nor are they accidental adornments that Edwards utilized for the sake of a local rhetorical strategy; rather, they may be viewed as a statistical representation of the most salient attributes of God in Edwards's theology.

Our quantitative investigation of the lexical items associated with God also focused on words whose semantics is dependent on the context. The three prepositions most commonly used in connection with the word "God" include: "towards," "against," and "before." The first of the three has a lower frequency rate (121), but the highest level of statistical relevance (3.14)—the other two, although more common in the corpus (the frequency of 203 and 301, respectively) form weaker bonds with the studied lexeme (2.62 and 2.51, respectively). These prepositions yield an insight into how God is presented metaphorically in Edwards's writings. It would seem that he is conceptualized as a central point of reference as well as a goal of activities described by the preacher in his texts. It is "towards" him that the actions described in Edwards's texts are directed. It is usually the sinful actions of people that are "against God," like "rising" against God, "sin" against God, live in "enmity" against God and "rebel" or "fight" against God. Statistically then, Edwards portrays the majority of human actions as opposed towards the Almighty. As to the phrase "before God" in Edwards's corpus, it is preceded by a great variety of words, like "humbled," "walk humbly," "turn heart out before," "rejoice." All these expressions metaphorically situate the Almighty at the core of all human activities—he is an omniscient onlooker and a witness to human endeavors; an all-knowing center of the figurative space towards whom the emotions, thoughts, and actions of men gravitate. One could argue that this figurative centrality of God, visible through the stylometric study of Edwards's corpus, might be symbolic of Edwards's theology.

## Edwards's Depictions of God from the Stylometric Perspective

The complexity of the image of God in Edwards's writings is determined by the diversity of the corpus, and to a larger extent reflects the division into five groups within the corpus we discuss in another article.[3] Within each of these clusters, Edwards uses a slightly different way of portraying God, and from the point of view of statistics, the manner in which he discusses God in his letters is markedly different from the manner of description found in sermons.

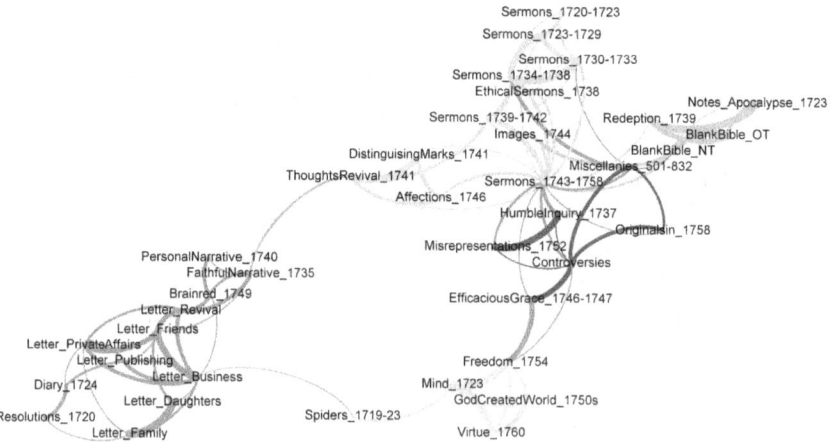

3. Choiński and Rybicki, *A Puritan Preacher in the Hands of Statisticians*.

The diagram above has been made with a combination of very simple arithmetic ("count instances of *God* in Edwards's texts") with relatively simple text retrieval ("find words that often co-occur with *God*") and some fairly complex statistics ("compare each Edwardsean text with each in terms of usage of those God-collocates"). In this last task, Cluster Analysis was used; its results were then visualized through network analysis, which applies a gravitational algorithm to bring together texts with the strongest similarity of God-collocate-usage (short thick lines on the diagrams) while allowing texts with little or no similarity to drift away from each other. Eventually, a balance is achieved between those linkages to produce such a "map" as in the Figure above. The first part of the analysis is performed with the stylometric package *stylo* for the R statistical programming environment;[4] network analysis alone is performed with Gephi.[5] The particular texts that constitute the network are labeled by salient words from the title (e.g., "Brainerd" standing for *Life and Diary of David Brainerd*), as well as the date of the publication (making it easier to study the chronological links).

As stated above, in most of his personal writings, Edwards does not mention God very often. Yet, the links between different groups of letters are well visible and they constitute a dense and congruent cluster of texts—from the statistical point of view, the epistles he addressed to his family and friends, as well as the letters in which he discusses his business and his private and publishing affairs, do not differ that much with regards their stylistic portrayal of God (bottom-left section of the Figure). At the same time, a few texts positioned themselves in the vicinity of letters: Edwards's *Resolutions, Diary, Faithful Narrative, Life and Diary of David Brainerd*, and *Personal Narrative*—with the last three texts gravitating most directly away from the letters. Not surprisingly, Edwards's account of the revival piloted by his grandfather, Solomon Stoddard, bears a resemblance to his epistles in which he talks about the Awakening, and to his account of the life of Brainerd.

The most interesting insight into the functioning of the lexeme God is offered by the stylometric analysis of his sermons. When one looks at the distribution of texts, one discovers that their alignment in terms of chronology is very easily distinguishable (top section of the Figure). The consecutive collections of sermons, starting with Edwards's earliest discourses, published 1720–23, positioned themselves on the net one after another, with the

---

4. Eder et al., *Stylometry with R*; R Core Team, *R: A Language and Environment for Statistical Computing*.

5. Bastian et al., "Gephi: an open source software for exploring and manipulating networks."

strongest individual resemblance link between the sermons of 1730–33 and 1734–38. Thus, in terms of the quantitative study of the collocates of God, one can observe a steady evolution of the sermonic representations of God in Edwards's sermons, leading from his earliest texts, towards more philosophical and theological treatises, like *Original Sin* or *Humble Inquiry*.

At the same time, as far as the collocates of the word God are concerned, there is a visible link between the sermons authored by Edwards during the Great Awakening and the texts connected with colonial revivalism. It would seem that Edwards's "rhetoric of the revival,"[6] a set of communicative strategies he employed to instigate the New Birth among his addressees as well as to defend the Great Awakening against the accusations of the Old Light ministers, indeed incorporates its own manner of portraying God. The semantic differences of collocates discussed in the previous section of the article, which can be observed on the micro-scale of one text, at the macro-scale of the corpus add up to a different manner of speaking about God that the preacher employed in the context of revivalism.

Our research revealed little difference between the "biblical" texts, like *Notes on the Apocalypse* or *The Blank Bible*. The stylometric network of the collocates of "God" shows that, as far as Edwards's biblical comments and the texts that are strongly bound to the Scripture are concerned, the preacher's language portrayal of God is extraordinarily similar to the one found in the New Testament and the Old Testament. It would suggest that there is not much evolution in Edwards's writing about God there—the texts offer a stable stylistic portrayal because they themselves remain in a stable intertextual relationship with the Bible.

## Conclusions

It is not the aim of the above paper to offer an ultimate insight into Edwards's representations of God; in order to undertake such a project and to publish the results, one would require a thick volume, if not a series of volumes, rather than a single article. We aim here to rectify the common misconception (common at least among the less theologically-oriented readers of Edwards in Europe) that the image of the Almighty found in the oeuvre of the Northampton divine is permeated with anger and resentment towards sinners, as well as to demonstrate the results the digital humanities approach may yield for Edwards studies. With the help of the quantitative methods applied we have been able to base our observations on statistics, instead of individual and unavoidably subjective hermeneutic experiences. The research

---

6. See Choiński, *Rhetoric of the Revival*.

proves that the image of God in Edwards's writings is both multifaceted and changeable. The complexity resides in the Almighty being portrayed simultaneously as an object of religious reverence and a dynamic sustainer of the visible world. Statistically, "an angry God" from *Sinners* or *Future Punishment* is but an addition to an otherwise deeply devotional and benevolent depiction. Also, central as Edwards's image of God remains for most texts within the oeuvre, one can hardly claim it to be perdurable. Looking at the rich corpus of the studied texts from a wider comparative perspective and with the help of stylometry, we have been able to discern a stable evolution of manner in which Edwards talks about God: a movement from the early sermons towards the style of the treatises and philosophical writings. This quantitative conclusion could be used to inspire a fresh qualitative study of Edwards's texts, looking into the evolution of the image of God on a microscale and explaining the insight offered on macro-scale.

## Bibliography

Boss, Robert L. *God-Haunted World: The Elemental Theology of Jonathan Edwards* Fort Worth, TX: self-published, 2015.

Choiński, Michał. *Rhetoric of the Revival: the Language of the Great Awakening Preachers.* Göttingen: Vandenhoeck & Ruprecht, 2016.

Bastian, Mathieu, et al. "Gephi: an open source software for exploring and manipulating networks." *International AAAI Conference on Weblogs and Social Media,* San Jose, 2009. https://gephi.org/publications/gephi-bastian-feb09.pdf.

Eder, M., et al. *Stylometry with R: a Suite of Tools, in Digital Humanities 2013.* Conference abstracts, 487–89. University of Nebraska-Lincoln, 2013.

R Core Team. *R: A Language and Environment for Statistical Computing.* Vienna: R Foundation for Statistical Computing, 2014. http://www.R-project.org/.

www.ingramcontent.com/pod-product-compliance
Lightning Source LLC
Chambersburg PA
CBHW071146300426
44113CB00009B/1105